A Nation in Crisis

A Nation in Crisis

Division, Conflict and Capitalism in the United Kingdom

Neville Kirk

BLOOMSBURY ACADEMIC
LONDON • NEW YORK • OXFORD • NEW DELHI • SYDNEY

BLOOMSBURY ACADEMIC
Bloomsbury Publishing Plc
50 Bedford Square, London, WC1B 3DP, UK
1385 Broadway, New York, NY 10018, USA
29 Earlsfort Terrace, Dublin 2, Ireland

BLOOMSBURY, BLOOMSBURY ACADEMIC and the Diana logo are trademarks of
Bloomsbury Publishing Plc

First published in Great Britain 2024

Bloomsbury Publishing Plc does not have any control over, or responsibility for,
any third-party websites referred to or in this book. All internet addresses given in
this book were correct at the time of going to press. The author and publisher regret
any inconvenience caused if addresses have changed or sites have ceased to exist,
but can accept no responsibility for any such changes.

A catalogue record for this book is available from the British Library.

A catalog record for this book is available from the Library of Congress.

ISBN: HB: 978-1-3503-7451-5
PB: 978-1-3503-7450-8
ePDF: 978-1-3503-7447-8
eBook: 978-1-3503-7449-2

Typeset by RefineCatch Limited, Bungay, Suffolk
Printed and bound in Great Britain

To find out more about our authors and books visit www.bloomsbury.com
and sign up for our newsletters.

Contents

Acknowledgements   vi

Introduction   1
1   A Political Earthquake: The 2017 General Election and Its Aftershocks   13
2   The Brexit Crisis, 2018–2019   49
3   The Triumphs, Trials and Troubles of Boris Johnson, 2019–2021   91
4   Scotland: Another Way is Possible?   131
5   To the Present   161

Notes   173
Bibliography   213
Index   223

Acknowledgements

The awards of a Harold White Fellowship at the National Library of Australia (NLA), taken up in 2013, and two Visiting Fellowships at the Humanities Research Centre (HRC), the Australian National University (ANU), in 2015 and 2019, played a major part in enabling me to think about and develop the ways in which I have conceptualised, approached and written about the subject of this book: the increasingly general or combined recent and continuing 'Present Crisis' in UK capitalist society.

As a result of some preliminary reading and many conversations with colleagues in Australia, the UK, north America and Europe, I soon came to the conclusion that, given the main focus of my book -the intensification of the crisis following the June 2016 United Kingdom (UK) European Union (EU) membership referendum and its after-effects- it would be necessary to write a critical chronological narrative primarily based upon a close and extensive reading of primary sources, for example newspaper and other media material. Quite simply, insufficient time had elapsed since the post-referendum period for many relevant and substantial secondary, book-length studies to appear and to provide a secure and extensive secondary basis for my study. The sheer magnitude, volatility and unpredictability of the relevant events and processes to be considered, also made the task of producing a comprehensive account of the crisis very challenging. Yet conversations with colleagues such as Professor Paul Pickering of the ANU, Bryan Palmer, Professor Emeritus, at Trent University, Canada, Professor Peter Gurney, of the University of Essex, and the fellows and other seminar participants at the NLA and the HRC, proved to be invaluable in persuading me to attempt both to negotiate these difficulties and to offer general as well as academic readers a new, original and wide-ranging study of the crisis.

I am, furthermore, heavily indebted to my partner, Kate, who read the entire manuscript and offered penetrating and constructive criticisms of it, especially in relation to the material on Scotland, and to a friend, Jonathan MacDonald, a retired medical consultant and canny observer of politics and the human condition, who read and made trenchant criticisms of chapter three.

Atifa Jiwa and Nayiri Kendir at Bloomsbury have been excellent editors. They have invariably been quick, efficient, fair-minded, helpful and friendly in their responses to my initial proposal and the subsequent development of the manuscript into a book. I owe them and their colleagues at Bloomsbury a special vote of thanks.

Neville Kirk,
Golspie, Sutherland, Scotland, 2023

Introduction

At the end of the twentieth century and the beginning of the new millennium there existed the widespread belief that the fall of communism and the seeming triumph of capitalist globalization would usher in a new era of largely uninterrupted economic growth, social stability, socio-cultural and ideological consensus and peace. For some, the 'end of history' had arrived.[1] Yet this has not proven to be the case.

To be sure, capitalist societies have continued to record impressive achievements in terms of aggregate growth, wealth and income and technological advancement, particularly in the field of communications. Yet they have also experienced often unexpected or underestimated serious economic and related problems. These have revolved, for example, around the effects of environmental degradation and climate change and the combined economic, social, political and ideological upheavals and conflicts of the global financial crash of 2007–2008 and the present and ongoing combined or society-wide crisis. Warfare and unnecessary human death and suffering still exist across the world. Glaring and increasing inequality and poverty also continue to disfigure many societies, including the leading capitalist societies of the Global North. Conflicts around class, race, gender, religion, ethnicity, nation and other forms of identity and belonging abound, as do political, cultural and ideological conflicts, often between the party-political and other forces and advocates of either the 'old' or the 'new'. The West, furthermore, faces formidable competition from China for global hegemony. In short, history has not come to an end, at least in the form of 'western' capitalism achieving total global domination, stability and peace. Capitalist societies, as predicted by Karl Marx in the middle of the nineteenth century, continue to be characterized by many contradictions and serious crises.[2]

My primary focus in this study rests upon one aspect of the very general picture sketched above: the combined and continuing 'present crisis' afflicting late capitalism in the United Kingdom (UK). I adopt the dictionary definition of crisis to refer to events and periods of intense tension, division, conflict, insecurity and instability. These dangerous happenings, situations and times, furthermore, may be mainly violent or non-violent in character. They involve conditions and processes of domination, subordination and accommodation. These may be achieved by varying degrees of physical force, persuasion, propaganda and consent. They are subject to change and continuity over time.

The present crisis is part of a long history of single, multiple and combined crises in the history of the UK and many other countries. For example, since the Thatcherite 'free-market revolution' of the 1970s and the 1980s, the UK has experienced a series of chronic and acute crises involving one or more aspects of the social system. From time to time, problems in the totality of the social system, in politics, society, ideology and culture, as well as in the economy, have interacted to produce periods of *systemic, combined* or *full-blown* crisis for UK capitalist society *as a whole*.

As the distinguished political scientist Andrew Gamble has maintained, episodes of systemic crisis are characterized by 'prolonged periods of political, economic and ideological impasse'. These affect the entire system rather than simply one or some of its parts. For example, while periodic economic downturns and recessions create problems, they have generally not, in themselves, threatened the system as a whole. Yet they may be part of wider economic, political, cultural and ideological conflicts which do constitute such a threat. Gamble, furthermore, has claimed that, while economic factors are present and influential in periods of systemic crisis, politics, in the forms of political beliefs, actions, relations and events, rather than economics, hold the key to outcomes. The present study supports Gamble's theses.

Gamble provided three examples of combined capitalist crisis to have taken place since the interwar years. These are, first, the international capitalist Slump of the 1930s. Second, the 1970s and 1980s, when the Keynesian post-war settlement, of managed capitalism and corporatism, was dismantled, with Prime Minister Margaret Thatcher and US President Ronald Reagan to the fore, in favour of a more free-market, deregulated or 'neoliberal' capitalist form of capitalism across the globe ('globalization'). Third, the years between 2007 and 2009, when the financial crash led to 'a wider crisis'. As Gamble has observed, the latter involved 'major global recession', continuing major international problems in the banking system, 'growing fears of a new protectionism in trade and finance' and 'increasing social and political unrest in many countries'.[3]

Gamble's excellent study, *The Spectre at the Feast: Capitalist Crisis and the Politics of Recession*, was published in 2009. Since then, historian Adam Tooze's outstanding book, *Crashed: How a Decade of Financial Crises Changed the World*, published in 2018, has substantially increased our knowledge and understanding of the financial crash and its global consequences during the following decade.[4] My book, mainly researched and written between 2014 and 2021, brings the story up to date in terms of the UK. It should be observed that, while aspects of the present crisis in the UK have been addressed, often in fascinating and enlightening ways, in the relevant literature, the crisis as a whole has not been covered in the integrated, systematic and comprehensive way that I attempt to bring to my subject matter.[5]

The present crisis in the UK certainly qualifies as another example of a combined or systematic crisis for UK capitalism. It is indeed probably the most serious in living memory. This is because of its deep, extensive, interlocking, long-lasting and continuing characteristics. Its emergence may be dated to the Cameron–Clegg coalition government's eager adoption of the assumptions, principles and policies of neo-classical political economy from 2010 onwards. In claiming, in the manner of Margaret Thatcher, that there was no realistic alternative to their philosophy, Cameron, Clegg and, above all, George Osborne, the then chancellor of the exchequer, applied their deflationary fiscal medicine, especially in the form of austerity or cuts to public expenditure and services, in a largely vain attempt to restore the economy and society to renewed growth and health in the wake of the financial crash and New Labour's alleged profligacy while in office between 1997 and 2010. In so doing, they simply ignored or denied the advice of many economists, both at home and abroad, that austerity did not work and that the most effective solution to the effects of the financial crash lay in expansionary Keynesianism.[6] Under the subsequent prime ministers, Theresa May (2016–2019) and Boris Johnson (2019–2022), the political economy of austerity was first questioned and then partly jettisoned, at least temporarily, in favour of a more pragmatic approach. But, as we will see in the course of this study, many of the economic and social problems intended to be addressed and resolved by austerity, remain.

Since the European Union (EU) referendum of June 2016 and its after-effects, the UK crisis, moreover, has become far more extensive, intensive, divisive and debilitating in character. It is upon this period of the intensification of the crisis – between the post-referendum period and 2021 – that my study concentrates its main focus. The final chapter, however, brings the narrative up to 'the present', namely the resignation of the prime minister, Boris Johnson, in July 2022. The brief period of Liz Truss as prime minister, from September to October, and the onset of Rishi Sunak's premiership, in October, are beyond the bounds of this study. Yet the crisis continues, and its outcome is indeterminate. In adopting this focus, I have tried to set myself a manageable and cohesive framework of reference and analysis. Otherwise, a detailed study of the entire crisis, from the onset of austerity to the present, would run to several hundred thousand words and two or more volumes.

Up to and including 2021, the crisis has comprised many individual, but linked, elements. These include the 2014 referendum on Scotland's future as well as that on continued EU membership, Brexit, the coronavirus pandemic, rapid party-political changes, fragmentation and turbulence, the poor state of the economy, declining and stagnating living standards and often bitter wider social, cultural and ideological divisions. In the course of the crisis, serious and largely unresolved contests and conflicts have arisen around questions of the power, control, leadership, domination, authority and the legitimacy of 'the establishment', or at least large parts of it, climate change and the environment and the material and other realities and identities of class, gender, race, ethnicity, nationalism, colonialism and imperialism. Towards the end of 2021, questions of government cronyism, 'partygate' – the alleged holding of parties in Downing Street and other government buildings in violation of the rules on social mixing during the pandemic – and Prime Minister Boris Johnson's denials over 'partygate' and his uncertain future, dominated the news. An unwarranted and brutal Russian invasion of Ukraine and a major cost-of-living crisis loomed. In 2023 the Scottish National Party (SNP) and the wider Scottish independence movement expect there to be a second referendum on Scotland's future (Indyref2). The following year will probably see a closely contested and extremely bitter general election. As matters stand, therefore, the crisis is ongoing and shows little or, more precisely, no sign of abating.

Systemic crisis has now been a chronic feature of many people's lives for a decade or more. While Boris Johnson seemed to exist on, indeed gain sustenance from, the chaos and conflict of crisis, there exists a widespread and profound public sense of bewilderment about the past, present and future in these very uncertain and insecure times. For many, crisis has become the 'new normal', something to be lived and hopefully coped with, but hardly enjoyed. In 2022 the *Collins English Dictionary* named 'permacrisis' as the word of the year. It signifies 'an extended period of instability and insecurity' and is an apt description of the present crisis.[7]

We have reached an impasse or interregnum in this crisis. As the communist Italian political philosopher, Antonio Gramsci (1891–1937), observed, in relation to the 'modern crisis', '[t]he crisis consists precisely in the fact that the old is dying and the new cannot be born; in this interregnum a great variety of morbid symptoms appear'.[8] We will examine these symptoms in detail during the course of the book. For the moment, it is sufficient to indicate that, as pioneeringly claimed by the writer and journalist, Fintan O'Toole, they are, for example, to be found in the 'sadomasochism' of the Brexit Right in England in its attitudes towards the EU. O'Toole characterizes this case of sadomasochism as consisting of a strange, punk-like 'psychic mash-up of revolt and pain, of bondage and freedom, of liberation and self-harm', of surrender and revolt, of a self-pitying combination of 'a deep sense of grievance and a high sense of superiority'. The powerful fantasy of a simple return to, and a future revolving around, the 'glories' of 'global Britain', is seen as the only effective cure for present ills, especially in England.[9]

As noted above, crises, including the present crisis, often centrally involve the key issues of hegemony, domination, subordination, conflict, consensus, contestation and legitimation. The crucial notion of hegemony was pioneeringly developed by Antonio Gramsci from his prison cell in interwar Fascist Italy. As noted by the eminent sociologist, Bob Jessop, 'Gramsci identified two main modes of class domination: *force* . . . and *hegemony*'. Force, observes Jessop, comprised, 'the use of a coercive apparatus to bring the mass of people into conformity and compliance with the requirements of a specific mode of production'. This was largely, but no means exclusively, identified with the state and, to use Gramsci's term, 'direct domination'. In contrast, hegemony was located by Gramsci mainly in the area of civil society and popular consent and accommodation to the rule of the dominant groups. Thus Jessop states that hegemony refers to 'the successful mobilization and reproduction of the "active consent" of dominated groups by the ruling class through its exercise of a political, intellectual, and moral leadership oriented to a "collective will" or "national-popular" consensus'.[10]

We may usefully add that consent and accommodation, and wider popular attitudes to hegemony, can take many forms and involve inconsistent and contradictory elements. As we will see in this study, these include points of conflict and opposition, as well as support and acceptance. We will, furthermore, observe that opposition to *particular* aspects of the rule of the dominant groups in the contemporary UK – around, for example, Brexit, austerity and scandal – has been combined with acceptance of the ruling groups' *overall* power and authority and the legitimacy of the capitalist system itself. The latter is generally seen as the only viable *system* on offer, as the best or only 'realistic' 'show in town' (Boris Johnson). Popular consciousness is rarely one-dimensional, consistent and totally logical. It can be, as is arguably currently the case in the UK, a chaotic and at times confused and confusing common-sensical mixture of consent and approval, opposition and disapproval, stoicism, world-weary cynicism, fatalism and even despair

In terms of capitalist hegemony and formal politics, the Labour Party and the labour movement in the UK have traditionally set out to achieve improvements and reforms largely within the shell of capitalism. At the same time, Labour's reformism has sometimes contained within it the hope that eventually and incrementally competitive capitalism and its elite rule will peacefully give way to cooperative socialism and the truly democratic ascendancy of 'the people'. This aspiration, however, has not been realized. Yet for a short period of time, between 2017 and 2019, Jeremy Corbyn's 'socialism for the twenty-first century' did offer a transforming and popular alternative to the 'broken' system of dominant neoliberalism and a peaceful means of its attainment. This alternative, however, effectively came to an end, at least in terms of formal politics, with Labour's massive defeat at the December 2019 general election. Since then, Labour under Keir Starmer has reverted to its far more cautious, centrist, accommodating and non-transformative form. Some, including the present author, maintain that left-of-centre 'radical Scottishness', in the form of the movement for Scottish independence and its desire to create of a fairer and more egalitarian society, now constitutes the main challenger and possible alternative to hegemonic Conservatism.

Gramsci saw the 'modern crisis' as resulting from a breakdown in 'authority'. This happens when ruling groups lose their ability to lead, or exercise hegemony, in the sphere of civil society by intellectual, moral and political means. They turn, instead, to coercive 'direct domination'. This is exercised through the state and 'juridical government'.[11] In contrast to many instances of interwar Fascism, rulers' moral and intellectual leadership during the present crisis in the UK has not so far given way to coercive domination in the Gramscian sense of the term. Despite its multiple problems, the contemporary UK still deals, 'from above', with its problems and crises, at least at home, in mainly non-violent ways. 'From below', there has equally been no recent and current evidence of a mass, popular turn to violent or revolutionary courses of action. Revolutionary socialist and communist movements in the UK enjoy very little support, while the traditional revolutionary spearhead for the revolutionary Left, the industrial working class, is conspicuous, at least in the UK, by its reformism, accommodation and, in some instances, quiescence and support for Conservatism and right-wing populism. When considered globally, however, including the UK, there is currently growing evidence of a spirit of revolt on the part of wide sections of 'the people' against neoliberalism and the destruction of the planet.[12]

While there has not so far been a full-blown crisis and total breakdown of hegemony and lack of trust and confidence in the ruling elite in the UK, the hegemony of the ruling groups has, as noted above, at times been *contested*, *contingent* and sometimes *crisis-ridden* and *fragile* rather than secure and stable in character. The present crisis has been characterized by a mixture of widespread popular mistrust, resentment, lack of respect and cynicism towards the thoughts and actions of important figures and groups within 'the establishment'. These include largely male politicians, especially leading Conservative ones, and often very rich and prominent figures from within the worlds of business, entertainment, the media, communications and even the royal household. They have been variously accused of cronyism, sleaze, extreme greed and selfishness, lack of regard for the public and the public interest, predatory sexual behaviour and racism. Boris Johnson's discredited role in 'partygate' and his longstanding practice of being 'economical with the truth' constitute the most obvious examples of some of these failings. As seen most prominently in the national and international Green, 'Me Too' and 'Black Lives Matter' movements, and, I would argue, in the phenomena of Corbynism and of left-of-centre civic nationalism in Scotland and, increasingly, Northern Ireland and Wales, some sections of the population are also attracted to radical and progressive 'alternative futures'.

Both before and during the present crisis, the ruling elite in the UK, moreover, has been *divided* rather than *united* on key issues and no single group commands overriding control and authority. This hard reality has placed serious obstacles in the way of attempts both to present a united front 'from above' to dominated, subaltern groups 'below' and the achievement of a 'collective will' or 'national-popular' consensus (see Jessop above). As we will see throughout this study, serious divisions and conflicts among the elite and the wider population, including the working class(es) and the labour movement, have revealed themselves in, for example, membership of the EU and Brexit, migration, particularly immigration from the EU, economic policy, the treatment of Covid-19, cultural and ideological differences, identities and 'wokeness' and the UK's past and present in relation to race, empire, gender and colonialism. As Ben Wray, the former editor of *Commonspace*, a radical Scottish-based digital media site, has observed, the elite has become so divided that it is 'unable to rule in the normal way'.[13]

Let us briefly consider the case of the divided nature of capital. As the leading historian David Edgerton, and the distinguished journalist and writer Will Hutton, have maintained, a marked process of *disconnect* between the traditionally close forces of British capital and the Conservative Party has arisen over Brexit. They convincingly argue that, in contrast to the situation existing for large parts of the twentieth century, much of the capital in Britain today is 'not British and not linked to the Conservative Party' (Edgerton), including that party's support for Brexit. The latter, in the words of Edgerton, is 'the political project of the hard right within the Conservative party, and not its capitalist backers'. For example, the dominant institutional representative of capital in the UK, the Confederation of British Industry (CBI) and many financial institutions in the City of London, prized their connections with the EU and unrestricted access to its massive single market. As a consequence, they overwhelmingly opposed a 'hard' Brexit and supported Remain or, as it became apparent that Brexit would take place, a 'soft' Brexit. Once hard Brexit became a reality under Boris Johnson, they attempted pragmatically to adapt to the new situation, however much they opposed it. It is, furthermore, hardly surprising that many of the foreign-owned businesses in the UK have also been opposed to Brexit.

Hutton and Edgerton correctly conclude that the hard Brexit Conservative Party no longer represents the 'business mainstream'. Rather, the capitalists who champion Brexit 'tend to be very loosely tied to the British economy'. They comprise 'very private, transnational finance-hedge funds, private equity, billionaires of whatever nationality' and right-wing donors and newspaper owners who are either foreign or tax-resident abroad' and who see 'a fabulous short-term profitable opportunity', power and public appeal in their 'Europhobia'.[14] Little wonder, then, that leading Brexiteer Boris Johnson could reportedly exclaim, 'Fuck Business', when alerted to corporate concerns about a hard Brexit in June 2018, just before Prime Minister Theresa May's crucial cabinet Brexit meeting at Chequers (see Chapter 2).[15]

Finally, as Gramsci concluded, hegemony is a developing and contingent process, rather than being simply given and fixed in ruling-class and popular consciousness and action. It is often, furthermore, based upon the complex interplay of a range of forces, both conflicting and harmonious, and the many and varied ways in which they interact and work themselves out over time. As a consequence, hegemony is often a messy, fraught and fragile process rather than one based upon easy consensus, stability, security and fixedness.[16]

Just as Gramsci's ideas can help us better define and understand the nature of crises and hegemony in the UK, so can the post-World War II thinking of the eminent German sociologist and philosopher Jürgen Habermas (1929–) aid our knowledge and understanding of the ways in which ruling elites win or do not win the consent, trust and respect of the mass of the population. In his book, *Legitimation Crisis*, published in 1973, Habermas examined the ways in which the developing and changing post-war capitalist system, moving from the 'liberal', free-market to the 'organized' or 'state-regulated' kind, managed to achieve legitimacy. How could this system be justified as normal and beneficial when it was based upon the collective production, but private and unequal appropriation, of wealth? For Habermas, the answer lay beyond economics, namely in culture. He saw the key to social integration and stability as residing in the widespread development of shared values and norms, freely entered into rather than simply imposed 'from above'.[17] In short, Habermas, like Gramsci, concerned himself with the important issues of hegemony, consent, the legitimacy of a social system and the possibility of its descent into conflict and crisis.

In my reconstruction of the present crisis, I have, in the manner of Gamble, focused in my text primarily upon politics, especially the politics of the main political players, the Conservative Party, the Labour Party and the Scottish National Party. Yet I have used politics as an entry point to examine important economic, social, cultural and ideological aspects of the crisis and, *ipso facto*, the wider context in which it must be properly set and understood. In this way, I have attempted to gain a more complete and satisfactory understanding of the crisis in its post-2016 period of intensification than is provided in the predominantly narrower focus adopted so far in the literature.

I have, furthermore, consulted, both in paper form and digitally, a much wider range and depth of sources, especially primary sources, than has generally been the case in other relevant studies. For example, book-length studies of the EU Referendum and Brexit rely very much, and sometimes somewhat uncritically, upon 'top-down' interviews with leading politicians and other 'establishment' figures and their oral testimonies. In contrast, my book is based upon the detailed investigation and balanced assessment of oral and written material contained in a wide range and depth of publications. These include newspapers and journals (the main sources), government and other official publications, those of political organizations and those of TV companies and polling organizations, as well as archival and secondary sources. These sources as a whole have enabled me to gain insights into relevant perspectives and actions 'from below' as well as 'from above'. Examples of the primary sources consulted include a wide range of mainstream newspapers and journals. These range from the

Guardian, *Observer* and the (pro-Scottish independence) *National* to the *Daily Telegraph*, *Daily Mail* and Scotsman, and from the *Spectator* to the *New Statesman*. I have also gained much from *BBC News, Channel Four, ITV* and *STV* publications and programmes, Conservative Party, Labour Party and Scottish National Party publications, those by *H.M. Treasury* and the *Scottish Government* and material on *YouTube* and *YouGov*. The *Scottish Independence Referendum Collection* at the National Library of Scotland is an invaluable archival source on the 2014 Scottish referendum.

I have undertaken this detailed, largely primary-based, research since 2014. I have constantly been aware of the fact that insufficient time has elapsed for the production and publication of a significant number of mainly primary-based books on the present crisis.[18] This, of course, has strengthened my reliance upon primary sources. A full list of my sources is to be found in my footnotes and the complete Bibliography.

Finally, a note of caution must be struck about my source base and its influence upon the nature of the book's arguments. The fact that many of my sources are mainstream, rather than 'alternative', especially of an explicitly anti-capitalist character, means that my picture of the development and reproduction of the full 'commonsense' of capitalist hegemony is necessarily limited. The presentation of a 'complete' picture of this commonsense (if that is possible), including more emphasis upon elements and points of conflict and contestation, would necessarily involve going beyond my primary framework of party-political politics to include the examination of more material on alternative cultures, ideologies and political economies. Yet my contention is that my study of politics, set as it is within its wider societal background, can and does make a useful contribution to our knowledge and understanding of capitalism, crisis and hegemony in the contemporary UK.

My book consists of five chapters. Chapter 1, entitled 'A Political Earthquake: The 2017 General Election and Its Aftershocks', explores the ways in which the crisis began to intensify from the build-up to the general election of June 2017. Following the EU referendum of June 2016 and the election of Theresa May to the Conservative leadership in the following month, the country had enjoyed a period of relative stability. May, the successor as prime minister to David Cameron, presented herself as being 'strong' and 'stable', and enjoyed something of a honeymoon with the post-EU-referendum public. The Conservatives' main competitor, Jeremy Corbyn's Labour Party, lagged way behind the Tories in the polls and Corbyn himself was widely disliked, demonized and dismissed as a hopelessly left-wing outsider and protester rather a genuine party leader and prime minister in waiting. In Scotland, the dominant SNP hoped to translate the country's majority vote, by 62 per cent to 38 per cent, to remain in the EU, into majority support for a second referendum on Scottish independence.

In April 2017, Prime Minister May unexpectedly decided to call an election in order to cement her power, pulverize Labour and successfully lead the country through the Brexit negotiations. Much against the odds, the election, however, proved to be an earthquake, complete with significant aftershocks. While May lost her majority in parliament, Corbyn greatly increased Labour's share of the vote, by almost 10 per cent, and claimed that, in real terms, the election amounted to a great success for his socialist alternative to 'broken' neoliberal capitalism. In Scotland, the SNP maintained its dominant position, even though it suffered a significant loss of twenty-one parliamentary seats as compared with its exceptional performance in winning fifty-six out of a total of fifty-nine seats at the 2015 general election. My chapter supports the view of journalist and academic, Gary Younge, that the election constituted an example of a revolt 'from below' against the adverse effects of globalization, neoliberalism, the financial crisis and the politics of austerity.[19]

The aftershocks saw May's popularity and confidence plummet, divisions and dissatisfaction in the Conservative party surge and Labour's confidence further increase. There also existed fears about the weaknesses of the economy and the potentially adverse effects of Brexit upon trade and continuing austerity upon living standards and social cohesion. In Scotland, in the face of disappointment at the election result and declining support for independence, the SNP became more cautious and introspective about pushing for Indyref2. Following the election, the SNP barely mentioned independence and highlighted the overriding importance of its fight against the politics of austerity. Chapter 1 ends by commenting on the remarkable ability of May, much in the subsequent manner of Boris Johnson, to bounce back in the face of adversity. By the beginning of 2018, the Prime Minister had recovered much of her confidence and authority.

This state of affairs, however, proved to be temporary. As shown in Chapter 2, 'The Brexit Crisis, 2018–2019', during the following two years the crisis considerably worsened, particularly at the political level. Brexit was the dominant issue. It involved the extremely complex, tortuous and unpredictable negotiations between the UK and the EU, Prime Minister May's many painful Brexit experiences, her failure to get her withdrawal deal with the EU through parliament on three occasions and her tearful resignation in May 2019. The travails of the Prime Minister were accompanied by sharp and ongoing wider divisions, conflict and fragmentation among the major political players and forces, most prominently the Conservative Party, the Labour Party, the SNP and Nigel Farage's Brexit Party. There were also intensified conflicts over the wider socio-economic, cultural and ideological effects of Brexit on immigration, race, the economy, the 'British way of life' and national identity. During these years, there developed a pervasive sense of continuing and, indeed, more profound and extensive, crisis. Based largely upon an extensive trawl of the primary sources, Chapter 2 offers a more substantial, original and extensive study of the Brexit crisis and related issues than is to be found in other studies.

Some left-wing commentators, most prominently journalist and writer, Owen Jones, maintained that 'out of May's calamity' and another general election, fairer, more tolerant and more progressive social ideas, actions and policies might emerge and even become dominant.[20] This, however, was very much a minority viewpoint, as well as being, as unfolding events demonstrated, inaccurate and far too optimistic, at least in the immediate and short terms. For most other political commentators, it was far more likely that it would be the unfortunate May's most likely successor, Boris Johnson, who would attempt to break the Brexit deadlock, move out of crisis and refashion UK society far more in old than new ways.

As I demonstrate in Chapter 3, 'The Triumphs, Trials and Troubles of Boris Johnson, 2019–2021', this second scenario proved to be accurate. In July 2019 Johnson was elected the new Conservative Party leader and became prime minister. I cover the eventful and turbulent period between his election and the successful campaign conducted by the Tories at the May 2021 local elections. Based once again upon a wide range of largely untapped primary sources, this chapter provides the first all-round published account of Johnson, his government and their wider societal influences and context during these times.

The chosen period, of almost two years, was one of acute and repeated crises, the most important being Brexit and the coronavirus pandemic. The Prime Minister, himself, as well as the whole of the UK, experienced numerous fluctuations in fortune. Johnson achieved his immediate and major goal of 'getting Brexit done', at least in terms of securing withdrawal from the EU and a future trade deal. He also trounced his opponents in the December 2019 election and triumphed in many of Labour's traditional, 'red-wall' strongholds by promising to end austerity, improve living standards and generally 'level up' regional and local inequalities. He purged, re-made and united the Conservative Party in his own right-wing, Brexit image, managed, albeit very controversially, to navigate the country through the worst period of the unprecedented Covid-19 pandemic and demonstrated considerable flexibility and pragmatism in his economic and social policies. By May 2021 he had regained much of his authority, control and popularity. He was winning the poll battles with Labour and the Liberal Democrats and was extremely upbeat about the future prospects for 'global Britain'.

At the same time, however, Johnson also experienced major difficulties, problems and criticisms. For example, in the eyes of his critics, he was inefficient, mendacious, chaotic and, as noted earlier, revelled in the seemingly permanent chaos and crises afflicting his government and the country as a whole. He made many enemies in the Conservative Party by the brutal, cold and calculating way in which he simply expelled 'No Deal' and Remain 'colleagues' over Brexit. His handling of the pandemic was and remains condemned by many as cavalier, ineffective, callous, inhuman, disastrous and deadly. The government and its friends were widely seen as being guilty of sleaze and cronyism, particularly during the pandemic. Johnson, moreover, not only disagreed with, but also came into fierce conflict with, many of those who were critical of the UK's past and present records on race and racism, nationalism and self-determination, class, gender, social mobility, patriotism, the monarchy, slavery, imperialism and colonialism.

Chapter 3 offers the reader two conclusions and raises a question. First, it maintains that Johnson's triumphs outweighed his trials and troubles from July 2019 to May 2021. Second, it suggests that, notwithstanding challenges, divisions and conflicts, Johnson's brand of 'One Nation' Conservatism remained the dominant form of political commonsense during this period of time, particularly in England. As a corollary, it offered the most likely way forward and out of the present crisis. The question, however, concerns the extent to which the crisis may be resolved in radical rather than conservative ways. For example, does the kind of left-of-centre progressivism and civic nationalism, represented by Nicola Sturgeon's SNP and the wider independence movement, offer a rallying point and a beacon for radical forces not only in Scotland, but also throughout the UK?

In Chapter 4, entitled, 'Scotland: Another Way Is Possible?', I further consider the question raised in the conclusion to Chapter 3. I do this by charting the recent and current history and fluctuating fortunes of the crucial issue of *self-determination* in Scotland. My focus rests mainly upon the key institutional expressions of the cause of self-determination for Scotland, the SNP and the independence movement, although the party rather than the movement constitutes my main object of study. In the manner of the other chapters in my study, this fourth chapter is largely based upon primary sources and offers the most up-to-date and comprehensive account of its subject matter. In so doing, it also makes the case for more attention to be paid to Scottish matters in studies claiming to be 'British' or 'UK-based' in character. In practice, these are, albeit to varying degrees, all too often Anglocentric in character and, as such, far from sufficiently attentive to relevant events 'north of the border', and in Wales and Northern Ireland.

The chapter sets the issue of self-determination within the context of the peaceful political revolution that has characterized modern Scotland. This has been seen in the recent sudden and spectacular rise and domination of the SNP, the precipitous fall, and perhaps even death, of the Labour Party and the continuing long-term decline of the Conservative Party. My chronological focus on self-determination largely covers the years from the referendum on Scottish independence in September 2014 to the SNP's most recent triumph in the May 2021 elections to the Scottish parliament at Holyrood.

My main arguments in this chapter may be summarized in the following ways. Following its failure in the referendum, the Yes argument in favour of Scottish independence and the fortunes of its main representatives, the SNP and the wider independence movement, showed a remarkable revival from late 2014 onwards. For example, as noted above, the SNP returned a truly outstanding fifty-six of the fifty-nine Scottish MPs at the May 2015 general election. Since 2014 the SNP has indeed been the dominant force in Scottish politics. This has been reflected in its continuous rule at Holyrood, and its wider hegemony within large parts of Scottish society and culture, especially among the working classes in large urban areas such as Glasgow and Dundee. The future, furthermore, looks bright for the SNP. It plans to hold a second independence referendum in 2023 and is confident of success.

Following the defeat of Yes in the 2014 referendum, the SNP, or at least its main leaders, saw its demand for greater democratic self-determination for Scotland as being more in favour of a 'stronger voice' for their nation within a more devolved UK than for complete independence. Between 2016 and the present, however, the SNP, claiming to be the foremost political representative of Scotland's 'voice', in the form of what may be termed 'radical Scottishness', has viewed self-determination and independence as largely synonymous. This change has resulted from the massive growth in support for independence and the independence movement in the wake of the referendum, the SNP's domination in the Scottish parliament and its strong representation at Westminster, its mounting self-confidence, its efficiency in government and the growing realization that the leading politicians at Westminster would not adequately fulfil their 2014 pledge (Gordon Brown's 'Vow') in favour of more devolution for Scotland. Meanwhile, both the movement and the SNP have combined a fundamental critique of 'Tory austerity' with plans to create a more dynamic, fairer, more just and egalitarian Scotland in the future. They, furthermore, anticipate that in the new society civic, or tolerant and inclusive, nationalism, will happily coexist with international co-operation, more immigration and a return to the EU. Scotland, unlike the Brexit-voting parts of the UK, will welcome immigrants.

While the polls showed that support for Scottish independence fluctuated between 2014 and 2019, and did not indicate any overall improvement, by the end of 2019 and throughout 2020 they did demonstrate a considerable and continuous rise. In 2020 a majority of people living in Scotland had indeed come to embrace independence. The main reason for this lay in Brexit, with 62 per cent of the Scottish vote in the 2016 EU referendum having been for Remain. Remain sentiment has widely been seen as the main, if somewhat delayed, trigger for increased opposition in Scotland to the Brexit government at Westminster, support for Scottish independence and a return to the EU fold. The continuing opposition, indeed increased hostility, of both the UK government and Labour under Keir Starmer, towards Scottish independence, its movement, particularly the SNP, and another independence referendum, have also had an important motivating effect. Within Scotland there was much greater confidence in the future of the Scottish economy under the SNP and independence than in 2014. The proven efficiency and competence of SNP governments and the first minister herself, stood in marked contrast to the blunders, chaos and incompetence of Boris Johnson and his government. In 2021, however, it appears that the pro- and anti-independence forces are evenly split. Still, and despite opposition from Westminster, the SNP, triumphant at the May 2021 elections, confidently expects to bring about and win a second referendum on Scottish independence.

The main conclusions to emerge from this chapter are that 'radical Scottishness' is alive and well in the country and that the Westminster government faces a stiff challenge from the formidable Sturgeon and forces of independence in the future. The rapid and often changing and unexpected nature of events, of course, mean that prediction is a perilous business. Despite this, I maintain that the balance of the available evidence suggests that the SNP and the independence movement do constitute a real and serious alternative to Conservatism. In sum, the further break-up of the UK could pave the way for the resolution of the crisis in radical ways.

Chapter 5, the concluding chapter, brings matters up to date, from the summer of 2021 to the summer of 2022. Entitled 'To the Present', it provides a brief overview of Johnson's mounting trials, blunders and tribulations and his eventual, reluctant resignation on 7 July 2022. The leadership contest to succeed Johnson took place in the context of major, escalating, and interlocking problems. These consisted of looming recession, spiralling inflation, a massive cost of living crisis and mounting strikes and other forms of industrial unrest. The chapter asks whether the Labour Party, the Liberal Democrats and Scottish Nationalists constitute a serious future alternative to the currently dominant Conservative Party. It ends by offering the thesis that at present the main threat to Conservative hegemony and a conservative outcome of the present crisis resides both in a resurgent centrist Labour Party in England and Wales and 'radical Scottishness' and its stimulus to the wider and deeper spread of radicalism and progressivism throughout the UK.

A Political Earthquake: The 2017 General Election and Its Aftershocks

Introduction

The general election was held on Thursday, 8 June 2017. It was widely expected that it would result in a landslide in favour of the self-confident and increasingly arrogant Tories against the seemingly hopeless Labour Party and its widely demonized, mocked and dismissed leader, Jeremy Corbyn. This was particularly the case following massive Tory gains and disastrous Labour losses during the local elections of early May.[1] As matters developed, however, the main foundation upon which Prime Minister Theresa May's electoral campaign and appeal had been built – that she was the 'strong' and 'stable' leader best equipped to lead the country into and successfully through the Brexit negotiations – began to crumble. In marked contrast, and to widespread disbelief in official political circles and the mainstream media, Corbyn, the so-called born loser, grew daily in self-confidence and popularity, especially among young voters using social media, marginalized groups and those who had not been inclined to register and vote in the past.

A small, but highly significant, example of the Labour leader's increasing confidence and appeal occurred on 20 May when Corbyn made the decision to throw caution to the wind and make a surprise appearance at a popular music festival held at Prenton Park, the home of Tranmere Rovers Football Club. Instead of catcalling the Labour leader for improperly importing a political message into a non-political leisure event, the 20,000-strong crowd enthusiastically serenaded him with the football-style chant of 'Ohhhh, Je-re-my Corrrbyn'. Corbyn's call to make music and sport available to all could barely be heard above the increasingly deafening chant. This 'absolutely amazing' reaction not only took Corbyn by surprise, but also went viral on social media. As writer Alex Nunns perceptively observed, it was one of those 'spontaneous moments that turns received wisdom on its head. The notion that young people are unreceptive to political ideas is wrong. The notion that Corbyn is universally derided is wrong. The notion that Labour is headed for a crushing defeat is-suddenly a little less certain'. As one of Corbyn's staff had been claiming for weeks, 'something subterranean is going on'.[2]

A few days after the Prenton Park festival, and in the immediate wake of May's panic-stricken U-turn on social care, there developed the increasingly widespread belief that May was 'not so strong and stable after all', but, as the *Guardian* observed, 'more weak and wobbly'. The gap between the Tories and Labour had considerably narrowed, from between 21 and 24 points at the outset of the campaign to around 5 points, while during the same period of time the 52-point personal popularity gap between May and Corbyn had plummeted to 4 points.[3] By the first week of June, on the eve of the election, poll predictions continued to differ widely, from a repeat of the resounding Conservative triumph of 1983 to a minority government. The predictions of Survation and YouGov came closest to the actual result of the election. The former put the Conservatives on 41 per cent and Labour on 40 per cent of the vote, while the latter correctly forecast a hung parliament. The transformation in polling intentions in the run-up to the election and the election result itself were truly unprecedented in modern British political history.[4]

This chapter will both analyse the shock election and its effects and chart the Prime Minister's desperate attempt to cling to power and authority into the autumn and early winter months. As a result of the election, May's honeymoon and 'magic moments' with the public well and truly gave way to a bitter battle for survival. In contrast, Corbyn and Labour enjoyed a post-election high and sought to convince the public of their fitness and right to govern. Meanwhile, the SNP sought to regain its authority and credibility in the wake of a disappointing election result.

Results of the election

Out of a total of 650 seats contested, the Conservatives won the largest number, 318. Although this constituted a loss of thirteen seats compared with their performance in the general election of 2015, the Conservatives increased their share of the UK vote by 5.5 per cent to 42.4 per cent. Voter turnout, at 68.7 per cent, represented a twenty-year high. The Conservatives lost seats in England and Wales to Labour and the Liberal Democrats, but performed extremely well (as in the previous month's local elections) under the leadership of Ruth Davidson in Scotland where they increased their number of seats from one to thirteen.[5] Ironically, the Conservatives remained the largest party at Westminster, but one now deprived of its previous majority of seventeen (twelve immediately after the general election of 2015). They failed to win the eight other seats necessary for an absolute majority of 326, albeit by only 1,688 votes. As a result of a post-election agreement, May's minority Conservative government became dependent upon a confidence and supply arrangement with the northern-Irish ultra-conservative, hard-line Democratic Unionist Party (DUP) in order to guarantee a government majority on specific pieces of legislation.

Labour came second with a total of 262 seats, a gain of thirty on 2015. Labour also increased its share of the vote by 9.5 per cent to a remarkable 40 per cent, and was naturally overjoyed. Widespread pre-election prophecies of doom and gloom gave way to euphoria. Labour received 3.6 million more votes than under Ed Miliband in 2015, and Corbyn went so far as to claim that his party had effectively won the election. The SNP was third, but the party's thirty-five seats constituted a loss of twenty-one on its albeit extremely high total of fifty-six in 2015. SNP heavyweights, Alex Salmond and Angus Robertson, were among its high-profile casualties. The fourth party, the Liberal

Democrats, increased their seats by four, to twelve, but experienced a mixed election night. Their vote share stood at 7.4 per cent, a loss of 0.5 per cent. While their former leader, Nick Clegg, lost his seat and the new leader, Tim Farron, survived a serious loss of votes, Vince Cable regained the seat he had lost in 2015. In truth the Liberal Democrats did recover somewhat from their disastrous 2015 election, but fell short of their anticipated electoral reward for being unambiguously in favour of Remain. In fifth place, the DUP increased its seats by two to a total of ten, a vote share increase of 0.3 per cent.

Among the other parties with seats, Sinn Fein increased its number from four to seven and its share of the vote by 0.2 per cent, Plaid Cymru went from three to four seats, a 0.1 vote share loss and the Green Party remained on one, with 1.6 per cent of the vote, a 2.1 per cent vote share loss. Somewhat surprisingly, the United Kingdom Independence Party (UKIP), however, ended up with no seats, a loss of one, and 1.8 per cent of the vote share. So prominent during the period of the EU referendum, UKIP's spectacular rise had proven to be short-lived. It had lost 10.8 per cent of its vote share since 2015, more than 3 million votes, with most of its erstwhile voters moving to support the Tories. UKIP's leader, Paul Nuttall, resigned after 'a disastrous night'.[6]

Press reactions

Public opinion responded to the election with an overwhelming mixture of surprise and shock. This was mainly because Labour performed well above, and the Conservatives so far below, expectations. Just as Jeremy Corbyn and his supporters were overjoyed, May and her party were devastated. By way of qualification, in Scotland the Conservatives surged, Labour recovered reasonably well, and the SNP was the disappointed party. Throughout the UK adverse public criticism was primarily directed at the Prime Minister. It was the secretive and authoritarian May and her unloved close advisors, Nick Timothy and Fiona Hill, who had been largely responsible for calling the unexpected election, and it was May who was seen to have miserably failed to realize her core objectives on 8 June. These were to increase her majority in parliament, enhance her seemingly strong public standing, pulverize Labour at the polls and further hasten its seemingly terminal decline, and convince Britons and Europeans alike that she was easily the best person to fight Britain's corner in the upcoming Brexit negotiations. May, her party, and most of the media, furthermore, had assumed that she would achieve her goals with ease. After all, there had been no pressure upon her to call an election, the Labour Party was weak and bitterly divided and Article 50, signalling the formal start of the UK's two-year withdrawal period from the EU, had been successfully triggered in March 2017.

Widespread public criticism of May's judgement and actions was reflected in press reports immediately after the election. Criticism, often intemperate and aggressive in character, moreover, was expressed not only by centre- and left news organs, but also by those on the right. The latter dominated the press in Britain. On 10 June the staunchly Tory *Scottish Daily Mail* concentrated its fire directly on the Prime Minister under the front-page headline, 'TORIES TURN ON THERESA'. According to the *Mail* and its columnists, 'furious' Tory MPs were already intent upon ousting the Prime Minister 'after her disastrous election campaign'. The party had been 'plunged into civil war after the Prime Minister lost her Commons majority, with MPs aghast at her campaign tactics that resulted in the Tories blowing a comfortable 20-point lead over Labour', according to the *Mail*. MPs demanded the 'resignation of Mrs May's closest aides' (Timothy and Hill did immediately stand down), while 'some ministers said she would be forced from office in months'. The *Mail* further reported the Tory MP, Dr Sarah Wollaston, as expressing the prevailing sentiment that 'the precipitous fall from predicted "landslide" to minority government was wholly avoidable – the result of hubris and a failure to listen'. The *Mail's* Paul Sinclair advised May to take a leaf out of Ruth Davidson's book. 'Ruth Davidson is a rarity who can both communicate and win. Theresa May can do neither', argued Sinclair. At the election, Davidson had been the architect of the great 'Tory Revival' in Scotland, with the party enjoying its best general election result since 1983 with 28.6 per cent of the vote, up from 15 per cent in 2015. In contrast, and to the *Mail's* obvious delight, the 'anti-independence backlash' was deemed responsible for the 'massive slump in support for the SNP' at the election. For the *Mail*, the Davidson-inspired Tory 'surge' in Scotland had 'killed off the prospect of a second referendum'.[7]

Another Tory newspaper, the London-based *Sun*, and its Scottish edition, ran the front-page headlines, 'Theresa's Own Goal after Election Kicking', and 'Scots Voters Saved Day for Crocked PM'. They were joined by the centre-left *Guardian*, a very late convert to Corbyn's cause. The *Guardian*, albeit in more academic language than the *Sun*, similarly highlighted the 'wounded' May's fall from 'Hubris to Humiliation' and argued that her fixed, preconceived ideas and her 'brittle insecurities' meant that her future as prime minister was very insecure. In Scotland the Labour-supporting *Daily Record* maintained that the election result signalled, 'The End of May', and the non-partisan, devolutionist *Herald* reported that 'Wounded May is told to abandon her Hard Brexit'. For Rupert Murdoch's conservative *Times*, May was staring 'Into the Abyss', while for the *Daily Telegraph*, the champion of a complete break with the EU, it was it highly questionable 'whether May can stay in Downing Street'. For the Labour-supporting *Daily Mirror*, Brexit meant 'Exit' for the Prime Minister who had formed a 'coalition of crackpots' with the reactionary DUP.[8]

In marked contrast, Corbyn received widespread and often totally unexpected praise in the press. For example, the *Scottish Daily Mail* declared that, 'love him or hate him', the election undoubtedly was a personal triumph and a 'considerable achievement' for Jeremy Corbyn, with Labour being 'brought back to life', and securing 'more than 40 per cent of the popular vote – more than any Labour leader since Tony Blair in 2001'. 'Blairite critics' would now be forced to 'eat their words after his spectacular election result'. According to the *Mail*, even Scottish Labour's leader, Kezia Dugdale, a critic of Corbyn, was forced to admit that the latter's 'positive vision' had helped transform Labour's performance. Labour had not only gained an impressive thirty seats at Westminster, but also increased its number of MPs in Scotland from one to seven and its vote share by 2.8 per cent on 2015.[9]

The consolations for the right-wing press were that Corbyn had been denied office and that the SNP had suffered a serious reverse. For example, the *Daily Mail* not only ran thirteen pages on Corbyn, Diane Abbott and John McDonnell just before election day under the headline, 'Apologists for Terror', but once the election result had become clear 'thanked God' that the country would not endure 'the nightmare of terrorist-sympathising, economically illiterate Marxists in Downing Street'. In a similar vein, Scotland had been 'saved' from the 'red-carded' SNP, according to the *Sun*. For the equally Tory *Scottish Daily Express* ('Voice of the New Scotland'), Nicola Sturgeon and her party were now 'On the Retreat'. According to the more cautious 'non-party, unionist' *Scotsman*, the SNP had admitted 'Independence lost them Election Seats'. It was predictably left to the defiant pro-independence voice of the *National* to declare that 'Setbacks will only make our YES Movement Stronger'.[10]

Explaining the election

In the 'Long Read' feature in the *Guardian* for 17 June, 2017, columnist Gary Younge observed that, 'Everyone thought the Election was a foregone conclusion', but that 'they had no idea what was really going on'. For Younge, 'the solid political ground we had been standing on was shaken by tectonic shifts below' and 'the whole rulebook had been shredded'. Younge attributed this unforeseen 'shock to the system' to mounting popular perceptions and anger at 'inequality in the economy', unfairness in society and power 'where it had not previously been held to account'. Younge observed that the widespread adverse effects of globalization, neo-liberalism, the financial crisis and the politics of austerity, had been responsible for a revolt 'from below' across the world. The latter had taken a variety of forms, ranging from right-wing populism to left-wing populist and class-based social movements. Yet before commentators began seriously to reflect upon the EU referendum result in the UK in June 2016 and Donald Trump's presidential victory in the United States in November 2016, this revolt from below had been largely neglected or even completely ignored by the predominantly top-down and metropolitan mainstream media and elites in the UK and many other countries. As Younge noted, this mainstream neglect continued to manifest itself in Britain up to the election of June 2017 and beyond.[11]

This chapter endorses Younge's model of analysis and conclusions. It maintains that the June election can be satisfactorily understood and explained only by bringing together Younge's 'tectonic shifts below'. These comprised both the neglected or hidden forces and structures of capitalist crisis, its effects and the responses it evoked, and what Younge termed the 'contingent' factors of 'context, place and many other factors'. In terms of contingent factors, we have to take into consideration material conditions and influences, political institutions and their leaders and wider ideas, values and cultures, the anticipated and unanticipated courses of events and the intended and unintended consequences of thought and action. The influences of structures, conditions, cultures and patterns of consciousness are thus brought to bear upon political behaviour. My core focus rests upon the three most important mainstream parties: the Conservatives, Labour and the SNP. I will also bring other political parties and actors into the picture at relevant points.

The Tories

There emerged a general consensus both during and after the election period that Theresa May's election campaign had been disastrously planned, managed and costed. During the campaign May herself came across as wooden, robotic – fully conforming to the *Guardian*'s sketch-writer, John Crace's unflattering description of her as 'The Maybot' – arrogant, secretive, controlling, hectoring, awkward and nervous. In keeping with her post-EU referendum practice, decision making during the election period was highly centralized and largely secretive. May and her advisers were far better at telling people what to do than arriving at decisions made collectively and democratically. May, Timothy and Hill made most of the key decisions, although Hill strongly disagreed with the policy on social care. The Australian Lynton Crosby, Cameron's closest advisor in 2015, was less involved in May's inner circle in 2017. Very few Tory MPs, or even cabinet ministers, were fully consulted or involved in working out electoral policy, strategy and tactics. While sometimes performing competently at pre-planned and highly stage-managed events, the Prime Minister was seemingly unable to think and act on her feet. She lacked the natural ease, wit and charm of David Cameron, was prone to moments of panic in public, and failed to relate easily and informally to people.

In contrast to Corbyn, May did not give the impression that she was interested in what ordinary members of the public had to say. Listening to people and affording their views adequate respect and consideration did not come easily to her. In her first televised programme of the campaign, on 29 May, the Prime Minister was savaged by her predictably aggressive interviewer, Jeremy Paxman. Paxman asked whether May's U-turns, on national insurance, social care and the election would 'lead EU negotiators to conclude that she was a "blowhard who collapses at the first sign of gunfire"'. During the same programme, sections of the audience heckled May when she miserably failed to convince them that her party's manifesto had been properly costed. Subsequent TV appearances, combined with her refusal to take part in a TV debate with other party leaders and pulling out of media interviews, were equally embarrassing and damaging for the manifestly nervous and unsure prime minister. The strong feeling emerged that May was losing her composure and confidence, and that she was hardly the strong and decisive leader portrayed in Tory propaganda.[12]

The Prime Minister's newly exposed and widely criticized personality and leadership failures were accompanied by disastrous policy and campaigning errors. As observed by May's Tory *bete noire*, George Osborne, who became editor of the *Evening Standard* in May 2017, the Tories' campaign meandered 'from an abortive attempt to launch a personality cult around Mrs May to the self-inflicted wound of the most disastrous manifesto in recent history'.[13] Against the background of a failing economy, rising inflation, a falling pound, stagnant and declining real wages and massive pay increases for the rich, May did little, if anything, during the election campaign to translate her post-EU referendum and manifesto rhetoric of improving and even transforming the lives of the 'barely managing' into concrete practice. Although May and Philip Hammond continued to stand by their pledge to modify Osborne's totally unrealistic austerity timetable and extend the plan to erase the deficit (by 2025), they remained extremely reluctant to ease the general purse strings. School teachers were to receive a 1 per cent pay rise, but this was set in the context of a massive flight from and deteriorating conditions in the profession. Despite more encouraging words about 'proper protection' for workers in the 'gig economy', and the promises of an increase in the national living wage by 2020 and real-terms health and education spending by 2022–2023 , there would be no legislation against zero-hours contracts and other forms of exploitation and insecurity in the workplace. In-work benefits were to be frozen for almost 7 million people. May and Hammond refused to lift the public sector pay cap, despite protests from leading Tories such as Boris Johnson and Jeremy Hunt. They also remained firmly opposed to a return to 'overbearing legislation' and the 'reckless' tax and spending policies traditionally associated by Tories with the Labour Party. May and Hammond repeated their long-established, if increasingly discredited, attachment to the crucial principle of 'living within our means' and, in the manner of Osborne, cited Greece as the most awful modern example of a failure to do so. As so often in the past, the Tories continued to see themselves as the party of responsibility, restraint and caution. In practice, the politics of austerity and cuts were to remain firmly in place until such a time as accelerated economic growth would provide the main source of increased wages and spending.[14]

The 'Key Message' of the Conservative manifesto, published on 18 May, was to provide 'strong and stable leadership through Brexit and beyond' and a 'declaration of intent' to tackle the five 'giant challenges', of modern Britain. These challenges comprised building a strong economy, carrying out Brexit, healing social divisions and successfully meeting the challenges of an ageing society and technological change.[15] Yet any detailed reference to the nature of the Brexit message delivered by May in her landmark Lancaster House speech of January 2017 – to unambiguously leave the EU's single market and customs union and be free from the jurisdiction of its Court of Justice (CJEU) – was conspicuous by its absence.[16] This message had served the Prime Minister well in her post-EU referendum honeymoon with the public. Instead, as observed above, the flawed judgement of May herself became *the* message of the election.[17]

The manifesto, with Timothy and May as the main influences, was un-costed, very light on detail and 'cobbled together'. It soon proved to be an unmitigated disaster. Its centrepiece was social care. The manifesto raised the social-care cost threshold or floor for individuals from £23,200 to £100,000, but also included the value of their home in their assets for the payment of both care at home and residential care. Assets had previously included the value of homes for those in residential care, but not for those receiving domiciliary care.

The manifesto was an attempt to face up to the mounting general crisis of social care in Britain in the face of an ageing population and the political economy of austerity. In July 2011 the Dilnot Report had recommended that the cost of social care should be shared by the state and private individuals, and that individuals' contributions should be capped at £35,000 over their lives. When the Tories won in May 2015, they accepted the principles of both a cap and a floor, but decided that these would not come into force until 2020. Wanting to be seen as both tough and fair, May decided in the manifesto to raise the floor and not introduce a cap. The Prime Minister and Timothy regarded the latter as unfair and regressive because they saw it as asking taxpayers, many of them young or in early middle age on modest incomes, and struggling to get on the property ladder, to subsidize many older and wealthier people 'who had got lucky on the back of rising house prices', especially in the South of England. The cap was thus a symbol to the Prime Minister of unfair differences and divisions based on chance, income, age, generation and geography. As such, a cap most definitely would not be included in the manifesto. As outlined in the manifesto, long-term care for older people would partly be funded by scrapping the winter fuel allowance for wealthier pensioners and replacing it with a means test. The manifesto also included what came to be seen as a third attack on pensioners by ending the triple lock. This guaranteed that the state pension would rise each year in line with earnings, prices or 2.5 per cent, whichever was higher. May defended her measures by noting that while pensioners' incomes had been protected since the financial crash, those of many working people had stagnated or been squeezed. Finally, the manifesto abolished free school lunches for infants in England, but, in partial compensation, the poorest pupils would receive a free breakfast. May saw this measure as fairly benefitting the children most in need rather than those from more affluent families.[18]

Within three days of its publication, the manifesto had encountered a massive backlash. This was totally unanticipated by May and most of her closest advisors, although Hill strongly disliked the measure on social care and Crosby was alarmed that the 'the detail and the framing of the manifesto "came from nowhere"' and had been sprung upon an unsuspecting public by the Prime Minister. In truth, neither May nor Timothy had tested their arguments and proposals against public opinion and prepared voters to expect and accept such important changes to government policy. This slapdash approach went completely against the established and highly successful political wisdom and practice of Lynton Crosby and, at least in the 2015 general election, David Cameron. The latter simply couldn't believe the fact that May had not played it boring and safe while well ahead in the polling stakes. Rather she had taken totally unnecessary risks and broken 'every rule'. Significantly, Cameron's views were not sought out and taken on board in any meaningful way by May.[19]

The backlash came in part from indignant middle-class and other families who resented the loss of free school meals for their children. There were echoes here of 'Thatcher the milk snatcher'. It was, however, far more pronounced among very large numbers of extremely angry pensioners, many of whom were 'natural' Tories. Pensioners were horrified by the prospects of having to pay massive, uncapped and incalculable bills for their social care and being stripped down to their last £100,000 by the Prime Minister's action. This, many declared to their MPs and the media, would prevent them from passing on the full value of their homes to their children. For while the manifesto would allow them to keep hold of their home and defer payment while alive, the state would deduct the cost of their care from their estate upon death. They claimed, moreover, that they would be unfairly hammered financially for the bad luck to suffer from dementia as opposed to other illnesses, such as cancer, which would be treated freely under the National Health Service (NHS).

May's political opponents, most prominently Corbyn and Farron, seized the opportunity. They joined and intensified the outcry against the 'dementia tax'.

Pensioners were further outraged by the fact that not only would they be unfairly punished by the changes to social care, but also by those to the winter fuel allowance and the 'triple lock'. As Shipman observed, 'On the doorstep the policy was toxic, and the widespread goodwill towards May had evaporated almost overnight'. The *Mail on Sunday* ran the front-page headline, '*DEMENTIA TAX BACKLASH*'. The Tories had lost five points in the week following the publication of the manifesto, according to a Survation poll.[20]

It was in this febrile atmosphere that May became 'the first major party leader to tear up the centrepiece of her general election manifesto in the middle of a campaign' and effect 'the most dramatic manifesto U-turn in history'.[21] Three 'torrid days' after announcing her care policy, May declared that further consultation would take place; that the government would eventually publish a green paper on social care and that henceforth there would be an unspecified 'absolute limit' on the amount people would have to pay for their care. In response to questions from journalists and the combative Andrew Neil on TV, May denied that a shift in position had been brought about by the public backlash, blamed Jeremy Corbyn for 'playing on the fears of older and vulnerable people' and, indeed, denied that a U-turn on principle had taken place. 'Nothing has changed,' insisted an increasingly angry, unconvincing and defensive prime minister, only the 'extra detail' provided had. No-one believed her: a U-turn was a U-turn. Indeed, another one was now following the U-turns on national insurance payments for the self-employed and on the calling of a general election itself. It was not only journalists from across the political spectrum who maintained that May was taking them for fools. Her general credibility and competence were blown apart. 'Not so strong and stable' anymore, concluded a *Guardian* editorial of 23 May, 'more weak and wobbly'. In the midst of the chaos, the policy on free school meals also unravelled.[22]

The three days of manifesto chaos constituted an unmitigated disaster for May and the Tories. They had displayed a combination of arrogance, complacency, laziness, incompetence and panic. They had made the dreadful mistakes of taking the electorate for granted, and of doing far too little proactively to persuade people of the soundness of their policies. Many falsely assumed that Corbyn's unpopularity would be mainly sufficient to drive the voters into their arms. Instead, Labour's standing had risen by five points and May's standing had plummeted.[23] Thereafter, it was too late fully to repair the damage. To be sure, the Tories did continue to attract many erstwhile UKIP voters, to make inroads into the Brexit sections of working-class electorates in 'predominantly white, former manufacturing communities', particularly in the Midlands and the North East, and even to command by mid-May an impressive national lead among skilled (C20), working-class voters. The latter held the key to many Midlands and North-West marginal seats that had 'not seen a Conservative MP since Margaret Thatcher's landslide victories of the 1980s', according to the *Guardian*'s Alan Travis.[24] Yet the 'entire Red Tory mission for the working North' simply failed to develop the expected momentum and success. Many of the 'left behind' and disillusioned workers in the North who had voted Leave in the EU referendum failed to embrace 'en masse' either UKIP or the Tories in the 2017 general election. Rather, they returned or stayed with their 'natural' party, the Labour Party, in their traditional Labour heartlands.[25]

Labour

In marked contrast to Theresa May and the Conservative Party, Jeremy Corbyn and the Labour Party fought an extremely impressive campaign and enjoyed a totally unexpected degree of success at the election. At the start of the campaign the polls suggested that Labour would experience its worst general election result since 1935. A *Guardian/ICM* poll recorded a 22-point lead for the Tories during the second week of May. Labour, at 27 per cent, stood three points short of Ed Miliband's 2015 performance. The Labour Party, moreover, was polled as having lost its lead among its traditional supporters, with the Tories enjoying a 55 per cent to 29 per cent advantage among skilled workers and even a 40 per cent to 36 per cent lead among the semi-skilled, unskilled and unemployed.[26] Yet, as outlined above, Labour's election result was very good. May lost her majority, while Labour gained seats for the first time since the 1997 electoral triumph of Blair and 'its greatest surge in vote share since 1945'.[27] Labour's 40 per cent share of the vote was its highest since Blair won in 2001 and higher than that achieved by the latter in 2005. In June 2017, Labour recorded notable gains in Kensington, Canterbury and High Peak in Derbyshire, and, contrary to widespread expectations, held onto many of its traditional seats in 'forgotten' Brexit-supporting working-class places in the North of England, South Wales and other run-down parts of England and Wales. In Scotland, Labour recovered reasonably well from its worst ever performance in 2015 to increase its number of seats from one to seven. Labour also won 'significantly more support' from the lower paid than in 2015, and increased its support from among the 'new working classes', especially those under thirty-five years of age, in precarious jobs and the service industries. As observed by Nunns, Labour's coalition of voters comprised 'the young, the well educated, and a still significant base in the "old" working class'.[28]

In successfully appealing to a 'progressive alliance' of manual workers, middle-class professionals and, in some instances, sections of the rich, Labour evoked memories of its successful coalition-building strategy of 1945. Even fierce anti-Corbyn Labour supporters and members, such as the Blairites Jack Straw, Peter Mandelson and Alastair Campbell, together with Hilary Benn and Owen Smith, were forced to eat their words and praise Corbyn's remarkable achievement. There was now no 'going back'. 'Despair' had given way to 'hope'. Having 'pulled off the most stunning surge in British political history', Labour now confidently expected to build upon its election success and 'achieve power in the not-too-distant future'.[29]

This constituted a remarkable turnaround in the experiences of Corbyn and his refashioned party. Between his election as leader, in September 2015 and May 2017, Corbyn, to say the least, had experienced very mixed political fortunes. His two successful leadership elections, in September 2016 as well as in 2015, initially owed much to good luck. In the first election, his name appeared on the ballot paper only at the last minute when he received the requisite thirty-five nominations from MPs. In 2016 Corbyn was also in grave danger of not receiving sufficient nominations, but he was rescued by the decision of Labour's National Executive in a secret ballot that, as the incumbent leader, he would automatically be placed on the ballot. In the September 2015 contest, the majority of those MPs who nominated Corbyn did so only because they believed that it was important for Labour to have, and to be seen to have, the widest possible debate and choice in relation to the election. They, and the overwhelming majority of their colleagues, gave Corbyn very little, if any, chance of winning. A rank outsider who had rebelled against the Labour leadership on hundreds of occasions, Corbyn enjoyed precious little support among his Labour parliamentary colleagues and other leading Labour figures. They saw him as a protestor who was ill-equipped, by experience and qualifications, to be a competent and popular party leader or prime minister. He was, moreover, subjected to widespread and enduring demonization and ridicule in the media and across mainstream politics, including prominent past and present Labour leaders, as unpatriotic, a terrorist sympathizer, a 'peacenik' and a 'loony Lefty' with hopelessly outdated socialist views.[30]

Yet in September 2015 Corbyn, quite remarkably, won almost 59.5 per cent of the votes cast in an emphatic first-round victory. Labour 'heavyweights', Andy Burnham and Yvette Cooper, came a distant second and third with only a respective 19 per cent and 17 per cent of the vote. While the parliamentary Labour Party voted overwhelmingly in favour of his opponents, by 220 to 20 votes, the extended Labour Party membership, including the votes of registered supporters as well as members, heavily supported Corbyn. He also received impressive support from members of the UK's largest trade unions, Unite, with 1.4 million members, and Unison, with 1.3 million. Many within these sections of the labour movement welcomed Corbyn's stated intentions to move on from the New Labour era of Blair and Brown and to provide a clear and thorough socialist critique and alternative to the politics of austerity and the 'broken' system of neoliberal capitalism. Seemingly a relic of the past, socialism had become of immediate relevance.[31]

A similar pattern clearly manifested itself in the September 2016 leadership contest. Corbyn won with an increased 61.8 per cent of the vote against the 38.2 per cent of his nearest challenger, Owen Smith.[32] This contest had arisen because a massive 81 per cent of Labour MPs, the vast majority of whom were pro-EU, had called on Corbyn to step down following his lukewarm support for Remain during the EU referendum campaign. There were also sixty-five Labour frontbench resignations. In the manner of a long line of Labour left-wingers, Corbyn had been a longstanding critic of UK membership of the EU. This was primarily because he saw the EU as a capitalist club with the potential power to thwart the socialist transformation of the UK. Yet he had also come to the conclusion that the EU also offered vast market opportunities and guaranteed protections for workers, the environment and equal rights. At the June 2016 EU referendum, Labour officially supported the principle of 'remain and reform'. At the same time, the party and its potential constituents were deeply divided over EU membership. While 65 per cent of Labour voters had opted for Remain, 70 per cent of Labour constituencies had voted to leave. Corbyn wanted to appeal to both Yes and No Labour constituents and the wider divided electorate. Henceforth, Labour would officially both recognize and abide by the democratic wish of the majority Leave voters and support withdrawal from the EU and try to go some way towards meeting the concerns of No voters by advocating a 'soft' rather than May's 'hard' Brexit. In February 2017 Corbyn instructed his MPs to vote for Article 50, triggering withdrawal. Yet almost a quarter of his MPs defied him and voted against, but did not suffer reprisals. Labour's highly controversial policy, increasingly known as one of 'constructive ambiguity', would evolve into support for remaining in the customs union and close alignment with the single market while leaving the EU. As we will see in due course, it would ultimately prove to be very unsuccessful.[33]

For the year between the leadership elections, Corbyn and his army of some 40,000 enthusiastic and predominantly young volunteers had redoubled their efforts to increase the Labour Party's membership and appeal. Momentum, formed in October 2015 by Corbyn's fellow political activist, Jon Lansman, stood at the centre of these efforts. A grassroots campaigning organization, Momentum helped to recruit new members, promote left-wing politics and encourage people to vote. It was extremely successful in transforming the Labour Party from being primarily an electoral machine into a left-wing, inclusive and crusading social movement. In numerical terms, the results were spectacular. By the time of the annual conference, in September 2016, the Labour Party's membership had surged to around 550,000, up from 388,407 in January. Labour had become the largest political party in Europe and, as declared by Corbyn at the conference, there were 'more fellow citizens in our party than all the others (in Britain) put together'. As shown by the detailed research of academics Monica Poletti, Tim Bale and Paul Webb, most of Labour's membership consisted of the same kinds of people as in the past, even though new members tended to be slightly less well off and included more women.[34]

Very popular among the rank-and-file, Corbyn and Corbynism, however, remained extremely unpopular among Labour MPs and performed very badly at the polls and in elections. Between the EU referendum and the June 2017 general election, the Conservatives remained a long way ahead of Labour in the polls. This was particularly so in terms of the crucial criterion of competence – of being perceived by those polled to be able successfully to run the country in general, and the economy in particular. For example, at the end of September 2016 the Conservatives were 17 points ahead of Labour in terms of economic competence, while May led Corbyn in the best prime minister stakes by a massive 58 points.[35] In late February 2017 Labour managed to hold on to its traditional stronghold of Stoke-on-Trent Central in a by-election, but also failed miserably in the by-election held in the supposedly safe seat of Copeland in Cumbria. Copeland was the home of the Sellafield nuclear plant and many voters disliked Corbyn's anti-nuclear stance. The constituency had also registered a 60 per cent-plus vote for Leave in the EU referendum. Large numbers of Labour MPs continued to argue that Corbyn was too weak and divisive a figure to be a strong and decisive leader and that he should step down. Even some of his previously strong left-wing supporters, such as journalist Owen Jones, reluctantly came to the same conclusion in the wake of Labour's defeat in Copeland.[36] Finally, the May 2017 local elections proved to be a disaster for Labour. It lost a catastrophic 382 seats and seven councils in England, Wales and Scotland in the face of massive gains for the Tories.[37]

It was no surprise, therefore, that by Easter 2017 May decided that the time was right to grind Labour into the dust in the course of a general election. Yet, as noted earlier, Corbyn remained upbeat and welcomed the challenge of an election.

Corbyn's relaxed and quietly confident manner and performance, combined with the popular, inclusive and enthusiastic social-movement character of his transforming campaign, contrasted strongly with that mounted by the secretive, wooden, awkward, flaky and error-stricken May. Contrary to the image cultivated by the Tory-dominated media, Corbyn once again revealed himself to be a person who was at ease with and interested in the concerns of 'the people', who liked to get out on the campaign trail, who was prepared to listen rather than simply lecture, and who was relatively open and flexible rather than closed and dogmatic. Unlike May, Corbyn performed calmly and convincingly on television and even got much the better of fierce exchanges with the aggressively hostile Jeremy Paxman and Andrew Neil. The Labour leader's last-minute decision to be part of a political party debate on television at the end of May stood in contrast to May's decision not to be involved.[38] As the *Guardian* commented in early June, Corbyn's refreshing honesty, decency and 'straight talking' contrasted sharply with May's joyless, negative, arrogant and hectoring manner. Corbyn was showing that there was a new honest and open way of doing politics. Yet a month earlier the same *Guardian* and most of its columnists had continued to criticize the Labour leader as being weak and unconvincing in contrast to the strong and credible Prime Minister.[39]

Throughout the campaign Corbyn simply defied the media demonization of himself as the unwelcome and threatening 'Other', a supporter of terrorism and an 'alien', unbending Marxist who was intent upon destroying all things cherished by 'respectable' and 'patriotic' Britons. He condemned violence and terrorism, whether carried out by the Irish Republican Army (IRA), Ulster Loyalists or Islamic fundamentalists, sought to pursue peace and reconciliation and persisted in his lifelong anti-racism. He unreservedly condemned the appalling terrorist attacks in Manchester and London, and showed genuine concern and sympathy with the victims and their families. Total condemnation of terrorism was combined with a measured and balanced approach to foreign policy. Corbyn argued that the 'war on terror' had failed to close down spaces for terrorists at home and abroad, and that as such there was a pressing need to re-think and formulate a new and effective foreign policy and counter-terrorism strategy. The latter would necessarily include the restoration of cuts to policing made by Theresa May while serving as the home secretary. Corbyn clearly and skilfully demonstrated that he was not 'soft' on security; attempts by May, Johnson and other leading Tories to claim otherwise fell flat.[40]

As in his successful campaigns for the Labour leadership, Corbyn, his immediate team and the extremely efficient and well-organized Momentum organization and its many supporters once again adopted a broad social movement, as opposed to a purely narrow, institutional, approach to politics and campaigning. In marked contrast to the dominant media image, team Corbyn, especially with the formidable 'street fighter' Karie Murphy to the fore, clearly proved itself to be united, well organized and highly competent. Corbyn and his supporters made excellent use of social media. They received impressive backing from prominent writers, particularly Ken Loach, and other well-known media personalities. They also rooted themselves and their politics in aspects of popular culture, for example music and sport, which enjoyed widespread appeal throughout the population, but particularly among young people. As in the past, Corbyn received encouragement and support from the prominent US social democrat, and Vermont senator, Bernie Sanders and his team.

Corbyn's campaign excited and energized people to become proactive politically in ways that May's elitist and laboured campaign never did. Corbyn's message found a very positive response among the young and others who, as noted by Gary Younge, had become alienated from, and sought to change the blatant injustices and inequalities of, post-crash neo-liberal capitalism. As Nunns observed, there was a 'big jump' in youth turnout and these young voters 'recorded a giant swing to Labour'. Labour won 'more than 60 per cent of the vote among the under-30s – a staggering number – compared to 36 per cent two years earlier'. In addition, Labour's strong encouragement to people to register to vote, and so expand the electorate, brought a rich reward: 38 per cent of the voters Labour gained in the election –around 2 million people – had not voted in 2015, either because they had chosen not to vote (about 1.5 million) or because they were not eligible.[41] There certainly was something 'subterranean' and 'tectonic' going on in the 2017 campaign, a fact belittled or entirely missed by most of the mainstream media until after the election.

Corbyn's personality, mode of operation and the nature of campaign in themselves, of course, did not constitute sufficient reason for Labour's newfound confidence and widespread appeal. Of crucial importance was the nature of the policies presented. Consistent with his fundamental guiding principles and recent practice, Corbyn offered the electorate both a 'genuine attempt to address a failing social and economic model' (the *Guardian*) and the clear alternative of a transforming, anti-austerity programme and the vision of a more equal, fairer, dynamic and co-operative society. Collectivism and universalism would replace the post-1980s hegemony of individualism and selectivity.[42]

Labour's policies, launched from Easter onwards and incorporated into its manifesto, 'For the Many, Not the Few', of 16 May (leaked to the *Telegraph* on 10 May), offered the electorate an attractive portfolio of 'well-packaged, eye-catching' and well-costed policies. As Nunns observed, these policies constituted 'an evolution of the platforms set out in his 2015 and 2016 leadership campaigns'. They formed the core of Corbyn's September 2016 annual conference speech. They consisted of '10 pledges' around 'full employment, a homes guarantee, security at work, a strong public NHS and social care, a national Education Service for all, action on climate change, public control and ownership of our services, a cut in inequality of income and wealth, action to secure an equal society and peace and justice at the heart of foreign policy'.[43] As such, they had the strength of continuity. This situation constituted a marked contrast to the untested and unexpected policies suddenly foisted upon the electorate in the Tories' manifesto.

Labour's policies included raising the minimum wage to 'at least £10 per hour by 2020', introducing free lunches for primary school children, to be paid for by charging VAT on private school fees, providing more free childcare and renationalizing the railways (with a cap on rail fares), the Royal Mail and the energy industry. Labour, furthermore, would end zero hours contracts and unpaid internships, introduce a maximum 20:1 pay ratio between the highest and lowest earners in the public sector and in companies bidding for contracts in that sector and require equal pay audits from big companies to reduce the pay gap affecting women and Black and Asian workers. It would abolish the widely hated work-capability assessments for those with disabilities, increase income tax for the richest 5 per cent, lower the threshold at which people paid the 45p rate of income tax, increase the main rate of corporation tax and clamp down on tax avoidance. Labour would increase spending on the NHS and education, reduce waiting lists, end university tuition fees and bring back the Educational Maintenance Allowance. The pay cap for public sector workers would be lifted, and the triple lock and the universal winter fuel allowance for pensioners protected.

The pledge to keep these popular protections, of course, strongly contrasted with the unpopularity of May's new policies. Labour, moreover, committed itself to using the revenue from increased taxation and borrowing, at historically low rates of interest, to repair the country's failing infrastructure and upgrade the economy as a whole. The proposed construction of over 1 million more homes (with at least half for social rent), rail electrification, the delivery of universal superfast broadband by 2022, the creation of a National Transformation Fund, a National Investment Bank and a Scottish Investment Bank, constituted some of the key means of realizing Labour's modernizing agenda. The popularity of the party's strategy for growth, and widespread dissatisfaction with a decade of austerity, cuts and talk of deficit reduction, meant that the Tories' attempt to discredit Labour's plans as a profligate tax and borrowing 'bombshell', failed to resonate as a major election issue.[44]

Corbyn and his strategists attached top priority to Labour's anti-austerity programme in the belief that voters were more interested in solutions to their concrete daily concerns than what Labour considered to be a continuing excess of party-political attention to Brexit. The latter, however, was not ignored, with Labour standing by its declared policy of abiding by the majority Leave vote, but at the same time opposing the 'hard' Brexit policy of the government in favour of a 'soft' Brexit. Under the latter, Labour would attach the highest priority to protecting jobs, promoting growth, and protecting and strengthening the public sector against the forces of privatization. Labour's election manifesto thus declared that it would place 'strong emphasis on retaining the benefits of the single market and the customs union', and put 'jobs and the economy first'. As Heather Stewart would later declare in the *Guardian*, the manifesto also left 'plenty of space for the policy to develop as the negotiations went on'.[45]

Against the background of net immigration falling to its lowest level, 248,000, for nearly three years, but still well above May's manifesto target of 100,000, Corbyn expressed his commitment to a 'fair', post-Brexit system of 'managed migration'. He praised immigrants' positive contribution to British society, and at the same time declared his determination to deal with the adverse effects of cheap competition in the labour market and population pressure upon public services.[46] As in the past, the Labour leader condemned racism, the scapegoating of migrants and xenophobia. Labour adopted a far more conciliatory and pragmatic approach to the EU, its leaders and Brexit than did May and her team. While the Tories undoubtedly became the main representatives of Leavers, in the process crushing UKIP, and Labour fared best among Remainers, Labour also increased its support among leave voters. We may endorse Nunn's conclusion that Labour was largely successful in neutralizing Brexit as a key election issue. Instead Corbyn's party could highlight its impressive domestic programme, which proved to be 'wildly popular'.[47]

In conclusion to this section, we have observed that the personalities and practices of Corbyn and May, combined with their policies and manifestos, provided the voters with a clear choice. They could either opt for the self-styled 'strong and stable' Prime

Minister, who in practice had shown herself to be 'weak and wobbly', or her Labour challenger, who had successfully defied his dreadful media image and reached totally unexpected levels of popularity and support for his anti-austerity policies. We know, of course, that May emerged as the winner in terms of aggregate votes in June, but at the same time both lost her parliamentary majority and failed to achieve most of her other key objectives. Corbyn, the official loser, had undoubtedly won the battle for hearts and minds. Would euphoric Labour now go on to consolidate its unexpected gains, or would the dogged May and the Tories be able to regain their seeming invincibility of the period up to May 2017? Before considering these matters, however, we must first attend to the electoral fortunes of our third mainstream political force, the SNP.

The SNP

Between the opening of the Scottish parliament at Holyrood, Edinburgh, in 1999 and the EU referendum, the SNP enjoyed a meteoric rise. Under the devolved settlement, the party won three consecutive elections to the Scottish parliament, in 2007, 2011 and 2016. Although it had experienced the great disappointment of the failed referendum on Scottish independence in September 2014 – lost by 55.3 per cent to 44.7 per cent – its membership, and that of the wider independence movement, surged in the wake of the referendum. In the May 2015 general election, the SNP captured an astonishing total of fifty-six of the fifty-nine MPs in Scotland. Although it would lose twenty-one seats in the June 2017 election, it still remained the dominant political party. By 2022 It had been in power at Holyrood for an unbroken fifteen years. There are, furthermore, no signs that its time in government is about to end in the immediate future. The recent and current triumphs of the SNP are all the more remarkable for the fact that, since its formation in 1934, the SNP had enjoyed very few successes during the twentieth century. Apart from the notable triumphs of Winifred Ewing in Hamilton, Margo MacDonald in Govan and the, albeit limited and patchy, successes of the party more generally, in Glasgow, Dundee and the Western Isles during the 1960s and 1970s, the SNP largely remained on the margins of Scottish politics. It was only from the 1980s onwards, moreover, that it firmly cast off its 'Tartan Tory' and predominantly Presbyterian reputation as, under the influence of Margo MacDonald, Jim Sillars, Alex Salmond and likeminded spirits, it moved to adopt social-democracy.[48]

As argued in more detail in Chapter 4, I maintain that the left-of-centre nationalism and progressivism of the SNP and the independence movement under devolution have become the leading or hegemonic force across much of Scotland, especially among the working classes in Glasgow, Dundee and other urban areas. They have come to represent the 'hope of the future', the radical voice of their country and a beacon for the further spread and re-awakening of radicalism throughout the UK. The SNP's demand for greater self-determination for the Scottish nation, either within or increasingly outside the Union, has been accompanied by the desires to oppose 'Tory austerity', Labour's 'light austerity' and build a more equal, fairer, just and dynamic society. The party's inclusive civic nationalism, moreover, has been combined with a strong sense of internationalism and a warm welcome to immigrants.

The SNP's meteoric rise and triumph have been part of what may be termed a peaceful political revolution in modern Scotland. The other parts of this story reside in the continued long decline of Conservatism and the sudden and precipitous fall, perhaps even death, of the Labour Party. The dominant political party during the interwar and immediate post-war years, the staunchly Unionist, protestant, patriotic and imperialist Scottish Unionist Party – it only became the Conservative Party in Scotland in 1965 – has experienced virtually continuous decline since the 1960s. From this decade until the time of New Labour, political hegemony in Scotland passed decisively from the Conservatives to Labour. Labour's hegemony was rooted in its very strong base in the mass labour movement, especially among trade unionists, and in the rise of public-sector housing and employment. The Labour Party in Scotland easily won all the general elections between 1964 and 1979 and continued to rule the roost during the period of Conservative supremacy in England during the 1980s and 1990s. During much of the period of New Labour ascendancy, Labour retained a strong presence in Scotland. For example, from 1999 and 2003, the new devolved parliament at Holyrood was dominated by Labour and its junior partner, the Liberal Democrats. Although it lost seats in Scotland between the general elections of 2001 and 2005, Labour still completely outstripped the Tories in Scotland, by fifty-six seats to one in the 2001 contest and forty to one in 2005. As late as the 2010 general election, Labour won forty-one seats in Scotland out of a total of fifty-nine. Yet when viewed in the context of the first two decades of devolution, Labour's fortunes have plummeted. Between 2007 and 2016 Labour representation at Holyrood fell by almost half, from forty-six to twenty-four MSPs. As a result of the most recent election, in May 2021, it stands at twenty-two. There has also been a truly spectacular fall in its performance at general elections, from fifty-six seats in 2001, forty-one in 2010 and to a truly miserable one seat in the 2015 and 2019 elections. As highlighted above, the SNP has benefitted most from Labour's collapse. Above all, perhaps, the SNP has managed to appeal to the 'old Labour' outlook of much of the working class in Scotland, while the Labour Party has often continued to fail them in their fights against austerity and the adverse effects of de-industrialization and globalization.[49]

Following the EU referendum, the SNP leadership believed that its main task lay in persuading many of the country's 62 per cent who had voted in favour of Remain to support and vote Yes in a second referendum on Scottish independence. As matters transpired, this development, however, was neither automatic nor straightforward.[50]

For a start, it became obvious during both the pre-election and election periods in 2016 and 2017 that the SNP's overall popularity and its clarion call for a second Scottish independence referendum had lost some of their former gloss. Research conducted at Herriot-Watt University, and involving Robin McAlpine, director of the radical thinktank, *Commonweal*, concluded that many electors in Scotland had become 'poll-weary'. Even some resolute SNP voters echoed the views of one committed SNP-voting family in Glasgow's Easterhouse that they didn't want another independence referendum 'for now', and that the party should 'leave that for five or ten years'.[51]

Skilfully playing to the popular mood, and branding the SNP's call as both divisive and unwanted, the Scottish Tories, moreover, 'surged'. They once again become a serious political force in the country after their long decades in the political wilderness.

Following their striking successes in the previous month's local elections, Ruth Davidson's Tories gained an impressive twelve seats and advanced from 15 per cent to 28.6 per cent of all the votes cast in Scotland at the June 2017 general election. In so doing, they pushed Scottish Labour into third place for the second time in just over a month. Significantly, in a sustained and precisely focussed, if largely single-issue and negative campaign, Davidson and her colleagues, alongside the equally pro-Union, but less influential, Scottish Labour and Scottish Liberal Democrats, had been highly successful in their attempt to make the general election in Scotland revolve almost entirely around the referendum issue and their unqualified and strident 'No' stance towards it. They had effectively defeated the SNP's attempt to make austerity, its anti-austerity stance and the 'disaster' of Brexit the cornerstones of the election.[52]

The Scottish Tories had also avoided May's grave error of attacking pensioners. Davidson and her colleagues continued to defend both the universal winter fuel allowance in Scotland, on the grounds that the weather was colder north of the border, and the triple lock on pensions. They also made the crucial decision to abide by the existing policy in Scotland of funding social care for older people from general taxation revenue rather than following May's disastrous social-care changes and U-turn. All these policy decisions brought the resurgent Scottish Tories a rich electoral reward. As we noted earlier, the increasingly exuberant Davidson was tipped by some media outlets and political commentators to become a future leader of the UK Conservative Party and prime minister. Most significantly, in terms of the immediate and foreseeable political scene, Indyref2 was now 'dead' in the eyes of Davidson, Labour's leader, Kezia Dugdale and Willie Rennie, leader of the Liberal Democrats.[53]

Faced with the Tory advance and the retreating prospect of Indyref2, Nicola Sturgeon and the SNP became more defensive and, at times, somewhat nervy and irritable. As the election approached, it also appeared to be the case that Corbyn's personal popularity and clear alternative to austerity, rather than Kezia Dugdale's uncompromising defence of the Union, was responsible for growing support for Labour in Scotland. (Corbyn's manifesto was seen by Alex Salmond and other SNP leaders as 'a snub for Kezia' and her proposal for a new 'Act of Union'.[54]) This was the context in which, to widespread surprise, Sturgeon changed direction, to argue that the SNP and Labour should combine to defeat the Conservatives. This was despite Labour's official opposition to a second Scottish independence referendum, its support for the triggering of Article 50 and the renewal of Trident, and the SNP view, expressed most eloquently by Salmond, that Labour under Corbyn had become a 'magpie party' that had 'pinched many policies of the SNP's in government'. Corbyn unsurprisingly did not accept Sturgeon's argument: Labour was intent upon increasing its influence and power in Scotland and elsewhere without the aid of any other party.[55]

To be sure, following the election the SNP remained by far the largest party with thirty-five seats out of a total of fifty-nine and 36.9 per cent of the vote in Scotland. Many people still saw Sturgeon's party as the best bet for a better future and 'the best hope for our economy'.[56] Yet the election saw a major loss of twenty-one seats, over a third, and over 13 per cent of the vote as compared with the SNP's, albeit exceptional, performance at the 2015 general election. The party also suffered a major blow with the defeat at the polls of some of its most prominent figures. These included the party's former leader, Alex Salmond, its former deputy leader and leading spokesperson at Westminster, Angus Robertson, and the influential and the well-respected economist and journalist, George Kerevan.

Nicola Sturgeon both regarded the result of the election as 'disappointing' and set about trying to restore the SNP's fortunes. In so doing, the SNP leader reaffirmed her belief in the soundness of the SNP's election manifesto and her determination to put as much of it into practice as was possible under a devolved system of government with many powers still being held by ('reserved') at Westminster. The manifesto, entitled 'Stronger for Scotland', reflected the SNP's proven progressive credentials and its desire to achieve increased levels of fairness, justice and equality in the future. Its main 'pledge' was to continue the fight against austerity. The SNP accordingly would oppose the freeze on working-age benefits and the two-child cap on tax credit with its associated non-eligibility rape clause of 'non-consensual conception', provide extra money for education, health and childcare, protect the triple lock on pensions, support women who had lost out as a result of the rise in pensionable age for their gender, end the public sector pay freeze and increase the minimum wage to the level of the living wage. The manifesto also proposed an increase in the rate of income tax, from 45p to 50p, on top incomes over £150,000, a continuation of the freeze on the basic rate of income tax and no increase in either VAT or national insurance. There was also total opposition to tuition fees, the bedroom tax and May's plan to create more grammar schools. Commitments to 'Strong Public Finances and an End to Tory Austerity', 'A Living Wage and Dignity in Work' and 'Support for Working Families' also figured prominently in the material put out by the SNP at constituency level. The clear intentions of both the SNP's manifesto and its constituency publicity were to afford top priority to socio-economic matters and to outflank Corbyn's progressivism.[57]

In marked contrast, the SNP's commitment to Scottish independence was barely mentioned. There was some condemnation of Brexit, especially its threat to '80,000 jobs' in Scotland, but this very much played second fiddle to the fight against austerity. Most significantly, the SNP manifesto listed its commitment to a second referendum on independence as only the tenth of its ten key pledges. Mainly in response to the large Remain vote in Scotland, and under pressure from Alex Salmond, Sturgeon had previously promised a second referendum on Scottish independence sometime between the autumn of 2018 and the early spring of 2019. This was a six-month period when the negotiated terms of Brexit were expected to become much clearer, but, crucially, before Britain's formal exit from the EU on 29 March 2019. Yet the manifesto now stated that a second vote on independence would come '*at the end of the Brexit process*' (my italics). In practice this could possibly mean a referendum vote in late 2019, but, more likely, 2020. Theresa May had also declared in May 2017 that if her party won the upcoming election a Conservative government would 'reject a second Scottish independence referendum for the entirety of the next parliament until 2022', according to the *Herald*.[58]

Two questions arise. First, what prompted the SNP to put back its timetable for a vote on Scottish independence by at least almost a year and probably more? Second, was it a sensible, pragmatic response to changing circumstances, or did it signify a failure of nerve and undue caution and procrastination on the part of the SNP leadership?

The answer to the first question is to be located in a combination of factors, many of which have been noted above. These comprised Scottish voter tiredness towards referenda, after ten years in government, the SNP's possible loss of dynamism and initiative, and its failure to more extensively translate into practice its anti-austerity and progressive rhetoric and the growing popularity of the SNP's opponents resounding 'No' to a second referendum in the period leading up to the June election.

During the election campaign, Sturgeon and her team had repeatedly criticized Davidson and the Scottish Tories for 'banging on so much' about independence to the almost total exclusion of any other issue.[59] Whereas the SNP's candidates chose to foreground both their achievements in government and socio-economic issues, their Liberal Democrat, Labour and especially Tory opponents highlighted 'The SNP and their Independence Obsession', and Alex Salmond's reported claim that a 'General Election Is a Vote on Indyref2'. 'Scotland', according to the SNP's opponents, had 'lost out' because the SNP, 'distracted by independence', had 'taken their eye off the ball' and neglected voters' daily concerns and interests. As a consequence, vital areas such as health, education, people's living standards and the economy had allegedly been neglected. Leading SNPer, George Kerevan, would argue in October 2018 that 500,000 voters had deserted the SNP between the 2015 and 2017 general elections 'because they lost faith in the our ability to oppose Tory austerity and deliver a better life in concrete terms'.[60] As the *Guardian* maintained, after ten years of 'remarkable success' and largely having things its own way, the SNP had also 'miscalculated the impact of the Brexit vote on Scottish opinion'. About one third of SNP voters had opted for Brexit, and the 62 per cent of Remainers in Scotland had not flocked to the cause of Scottish independence.[61]

The answer to the second question would suggest that a mixture of both pragmatic common-sense and exaggerated caution and delay was evident, but with the second element probably being more important than the first. We may argue that, in its response to the increasingly unfavourable political climate, the SNP made the right choice during the election campaign in deciding to downgrade the immediate importance of the referendum issue, and to await the arrival of more propitious circumstances. Yet whether the party was justified in going so far as to place independence last on its list of pledges may be seriously questioned. We may also argue that the SNP overreacted, both in acting so quickly, some would maintain impetuously, in making this decision and in delaying the proposed date of a second referendum by such a long period of time. It may well have made more sense to declare that the party would await the outcomes of May's Brexit plans, Brexit negotiations and their impact upon public opinion, especially in Scotland, in 2018, and then come to a swift and decisive decision about the preferred timing of a second referendum. This would certainly have been a less impulsive reaction to the setbacks of the first half of 2017. It may also have been the course most favoured by SNP members and the many others involved in the wider Yes movement.[62]

To extend a partial olive branch to the SNP, it must, however, be noted that the disappointing result of the election was at least partly responsible for the commendable decision of the party's leadership to be prepared to use the next twelve months to 'listen' to the voices of the public and make a special effort to win back the trust and support of 'disillusioned' independence supporters. In effect, this meant that a highly centralized, bureaucratic and disciplined party would, at least in theory, henceforth pay more attention and take lessons from political sentiments expressed at the grass-roots level.[63] The SNP also took encouragement from a YouGov poll for *The Times*, held just before election day, suggesting that about 31 per cent of voters in Scotland would be more in favour of backing independence in the event of Mrs May leading a re-elected Tory government. This included 15 per cent of NO voters from the 2014 referendum. The change of heart, furthermore, was most pronounced among Labour voters. Some of the latter may well have been influenced by Kezia Dugdale's 'revelation', at least as reported in parts of the media, immediately before election day, that she 'wanted Labour to change its approach to independence and back a fresh referendum'. Nicola Sturgeon revealed on television that Dugdale 'had told her privately that the Brexit vote had made her consider her approach to independence', and that the Labour leader was now 'close to switching sides'.[64]

The aftershocks

The Tories

The aftermath of the electoral earthquake of June 2017 followed a predictable course. For example, the disaster of the election was followed by several more severe shocks to the Tories' system. Early in July, *The Times* reported that the most recent poll gave Labour a commanding 6-point lead over the Tories and a 30-point lead among those aged eighteen to thirty. Tory support among young voters had 'slumped disastrously'. Both *The Times* and the *Guardian* agreed that, were an election to be held tomorrow, Corbyn would win it and the youth vote would be 'decisive'.[65] Equally predictably, while voicing her disappointment, May maintained that she had no regrets in calling the election and refused to be defeatist. The Prime Minister declared her intention to continue to 'get on with the job' by working out her deal with the DUP, proceeding with Brexit and making Britain a fairer place to live and work. Yet the tired and sometimes tearful Prime Minister could not conceal the fact that she had been badly shaken by the shock election result.

May's inept and totally inadequate response to the dreadful Grenfell Tower fire in London on 14 June added to the growing perception that she was fast 'losing the plot' and, as Shipman observed, 'cruelly exposed again her personal shortcomings'. The fire was an 'avoidable tragedy' in which seventy-two people died and seventy were injured. Well over 200 were forced to flee a building engulfed by thick smoke, toxic fumes and flames. Situated in Kensington, London's richest borough, Grenfell was the council home of many poor immigrants. For months residents, organized in the Grenfell Action Group, had repeatedly complained, without effect, of poor health and safety provision in the tower block. Following the fire, the worst in Britain's history, the new cladding and insulation in the building were shown to be highly flammable. There was a massive public outcry. The immediate responses of both the landlord, Kensington Council, and the government, were seen to be edgy, defensive, and in many ways inhuman. May visited the scene of devastation and met police and firefighters, but not residents. The Prime Minister had been told by the police, apparently for security reasons, not to meet the locals. Yet, in total contrast, Jeremy Corbyn, accompanied by cameras, did visit the scene of the disaster and 'hugged people affected at a makeshift refuge centre set up in a church'. May was widely and variously criticized, once again, as being wooden, lacking social communication skills and heartless. The 'Maybot was back at the worst possible moment', declared Shipman, and 'had the general election been held a week later, there seems little doubt that Corbyn would have won it'.[66]

Increasingly marked divisions in the Conservative Party added to the woes of the Prime Minister. Rumours immediately followed the election that May would be replaced by either Boris Johnson, David Davis, Amber Rudd or, more speculatively, Ruth Davidson. There also developed a 'concerted plot', according to Shipman, on the part of a group of former cabinet ministers, led by Grant Shapps, David Cameron's party chairman, to 'sound out MPs about whether they were prepared to sign a joint letter calling on the prime minister to quit'. The 'plot' lasted over a month before fizzling out because MPs were still prepared to give May one last chance to redeem herself.[67] Some Tories, including Davidson, with the former prime ministers John Major and David Cameron in the background, also argued that May should abandon her Lancaster House 'hard' Brexit position in favour of a 'softer' or more 'open' stance. In contrast, Boris Johnson and other 'hard' Brexiters strongly argued that the Prime Minister must not retreat from the unequivocally Leave position made public by May at Lancaster House.

This meant for Johnson, as indeed for May, that the United Kingdom would not adopt the middle-way 'Norway option' favoured by some Remainers both inside and outside the Conservative Party. Under this option, membership of the European Economic Area (EEA) would give non-EU Britain, in the manner of non-EU Norway, full access to the European single market, the opportunity to strike independent trade deals outside the EU and to make its views known to the EU, albeit in an advisory capacity. In return, Britain, like Norway, would be obliged to accept the free mobility rules of the EU concerning goods, services, people and capital, to accept rather than have a vote on EU rules – to be a rule taker as opposed to a rule maker – and would still pay into the EU's budget. None of these obligations or 'shackles' was acceptable to either the Prime Minister and her supporters or Johnson and his likeminded colleagues and supporters. They wanted to regain control from the EU. Having cleared off its EU debts at a reasonable price, a liberated Britain, according to Johnson, would also be in a good position to redeem the pledge made during the referendum campaign to divert a considerable part, if not all, of the £350m per week given to the EU to the needy NHS.[68]

For the time being, however, the grimly tenacious May survived these internal party divisions. In the month following the election the Prime Minister appealed for cross-party consensus, rather than continuing conflict, over Brexit and even went so far as to appeal to the Labour Party for 'policy ideas'.[69] Although talks on Britain's 'divorce' from the EU stalled over the summer months, May's speech in Florence on 22 September helped to restart them, albeit not enough to enable any substantive discussion of the likely shape of the future trading relationship.

May confirmed in her speech that there would be a formal transition period or an 'implementation phase' of 'around two years', between the United Kingdom leaving the EU on 29 March 2019 and the start of the permanent new trading relationship. The transition period would be conditional upon a legally binding withdrawal treaty being agreed and ratified before 29 March. The transition, designed as the EU's chief negotiator, Michel Barnier, would put it, to pave the way for an 'orderly withdrawal', would hopefully give sufficient time for the trading relationship to be fully worked out and prepared for implementation. It was also intended to give business and the other parties involved adequate time to adjust to the new situation and fully plan and prepare themselves for the future. The problem was that the nature of this future UK–EU trading relationship had still to be agreed upon. In line with EU protocol, it would be formally addressed and negotiated by Britain and the EU only after issues concerning citizens' rights, Britain's financial contribution to the EU, security and, most problematically as matters transpired, the preservation of an open or 'soft' border on the island of Ireland, had been successfully negotiated and incorporated into the withdrawal agreement.

May announced in Florence that positive advances had been made in the Brexit negotiations. For example, trade would continue on the same terms during the transition period and Britain would remain a member of the single market and customs union, be subject to the jurisdiction of the CJEU, and continue to honour its payment commitments to the EU. There would, furthermore, be continued legal protection for EU citizens in the UK and co-operation on security matters.

At the same time, however, 'hard' Brexiters were quick to identify actual and potential negative features, difficulties and dangers. For example, during the transition period Britain would not continue to enjoy voting rights in Brussels, and there was also a possibility that it might have to accept new EU laws and directives without having any control over or input into them.[70] The 'hard' Brexiters also believed the United Kingdom was being denied its due respect and importance by the EU. Rather, to use the terminology of Boris Johnson and likeminded Tories, Britain was being treated as a 'vassal' by an overbearing EU lord. This charge of vassalage would greatly increase in volume as Brexit negotiations further unfolded during 2017 and 2018.[71] Finally, in terms of the crucial Irish border question, the Prime Minister produced nothing of substance to advance negotiations.[72]

It may indeed be argued that May's most significant achievement during the summer months was to secure the agreement with the DUP on a 'confidence and supply basis'. This was important because it could guarantee the minority government a majority vote in parliament on the key issues of Brexit, budgets, confidence votes and terrorism. It, however, literally came at a high price. The British government agreed to give £1 billion of taxpayers' money to Northern Ireland in exchange for the votes of ten DUP MPs.[73]

The Conservative Party conference, held in Manchester between 29 September and 2 October, proved to be the nadir of May's post-election fortunes. Things began well enough with promises to cap energy prices (a measure denounced by many Tories as 'Marxist' when previously proposed by Ed Miliband), spend billions on new council houses, freeze university tuition fees and provide financial help for first-time buyers.

These were aspects of May's continuing mission to actively promote the 'British dream' of a 'great meritocracy' in which people would rise on the basis of merit, effort and character rather than inherited wealth, connections and privilege. (The satirical nature of sociologist Michael Young's pioneering *The Rise of the Meritocracy* (1958) – of meritocracy failing to end inequality and promoting a new entrenched elite of the 'well educated' and 'connected' – predictably failed to register in the Prime Minister's mind.) Tory policies were designed to appeal particularly to those young voters who had flocked to Corbyn at the election. But when set against Labour's promises to scrap tuition fees altogether and provide massive investment for housing and infrastructure in general, the government's policies appeared, at best, to be modest. In addition, Boris Johnson's continuing crusade against the threat of a soft Brexit and a 'simmering cabinet row' over Johnson's divisive presence, ensured that the mood at the conference was hardly harmonious and optimistic.[74]

To make matters much worse, on the last day of the conference May delivered what even the diehard Tory newspaper, the *Daily Telegraph*, described as a 'disastrous conference speech'. Suffering from a heavy cold and repeated coughing fits during her speech, which reduced her voice to 'a hoarse whisper, and then to a stop', despite taking drinking several glasses of water, May began by apologizing for her excessively 'presidential' role in the Tories' election campaign. After two minutes she was interrupted by a 'serial prankster', the comedian, Simon Brodkin, who had somehow managed to gain entrance to the conference hall, sit near the front and then make his way to the stage. As the Prime Minister stood at the lectern, Brodkin handed her a fake P45 (an official form for employees leaving work, colloquially the 'sack' or dismissal from employment) and declared, 'Prime Minister, I'm sorry, Boris asked me to give you this'. Brodkin then turned to Johnson, tried to shake his hand, 'gave a thumbs-up and said: "Boris, job done"'. In response Johnson 'barked, "Get lost, go away"'. A stunned conference looked on as May tried to 'soldier on', despite the continued 'faltering and, stumbling and lurching' of her voice. Brodkin was eventually led away by security guards. Despite May's pluck and determination in actually getting through her conference speech, ovations and cheers from her audience, a cough sweet from Philip Hammond and even a joke about wanting to give Jeremy Corbyn a P45, the whole experience amounted to a 'tragic farce' and left the Prime Minister 'distraught'. At the end of the speech her husband, Philip, 'rushed on stage' to hug and comfort her. The speech ended symbolically with letters falling from the slogan behind the stage. 'Building A Country that Works for Everyone' became the nonsensical 'Bui.ding A C..ntry th. .orks .or . . .ryon'. Hopes of rebuilding the Tories' post-election fortunes were dashed. Its policies were overshadowed by the disastrous speech and the actions of Brodkin. Theresa May's political future was left 'hanging in the balance'. Within hours there was once again talk among 'shell-shocked' Conservative MPs of asking May to resign.[75]

Declaring that she 'didn't come into politics for an easy life', the extremely resilient Prime Minister nevertheless survived the conference fiasco and the plotting of disgruntled Tory MPs. Yet May's post-conference successes were few and limited in number. At the October EU summit, the Prime Minister agreed that she would attempt to 'go further' than at Florence in relation to Britain's exit payment to the EU, but that there would be strong opposition at home to meeting the EU's full financial demand.

The summit ended with no specific figure being agreed. Despite the 'constructive' nature of the talks, the EU decided that insufficient progress had been made to start the second phase of negotiations on Brexit.[76] In the opinion of the *Guardian*, the public was 'losing confidence' in May's Brexit vision, while the 'economic skies are darkening'. Inflation and debt were rising and real wages and the pound falling. The effect of Brexit on the economy was proving to be 'much more severe and much more fundamental' than May had hoped, according to the newspaper.[77]

At the December meeting with EU representatives in Brussels, May 'surrendered to reality' and logically accepted 'a soft Brexit', although continuing politically to reiterate her 'hard' Brexit position, according to the *Guardian*.[78] The fifteen-page agreement struck between the EU and Britain did mark a breakthrough in the Brexit negotiations. For example, further progress was made on citizens' rights and the cost of the 'divorce' bill, and both sides had no wish to recreate a hard border on the island of Ireland. In overall terms sufficient progress was made to enable the negotiations to move on to the next stage of trade talks and further discuss outstanding immediate issues.[79]

At the same time, however, very important areas remained unresolved. For example, the future role of the CJEU, in relation to citizens' rights, remained vague, while no specific figure for the Brexit bill was agreed upon. Most significantly, the crucial Irish border issue remained highly problematic and a final solution was deferred. In the early stages of the Brussels meeting May agreed with the EU in a joint written report that in the 'absence of agreed solutions', the United Kingdom would 'maintain full alignment' with those rules of the internal market and the customs union which supported co-operation between Northern Ireland and the Irish Republic, the frictionless border and protection of the 1998 Belfast or Good Friday Agreement. This meant, in effect, that the Prime Minister and her advisors had accepted the EU's 'backstop' position. This stated that Northern Ireland, uniquely in the UK, would stay in the customs union and remain subject to many single market rules in order to ensure that there would continue to be no hard border between itself and the Republic. The backstop constituted an insurance policy against the failure to reach a trade agreement during the transition period. Both the UK and the EU, however, were reasonably optimistic that they could and would arrive at a mutually satisfactory free-trade agreement and thus avert the implementation of the backstop. It should be noted that the backstop would apply only to Northern Ireland. Scotland, with its 62 per cent vote for Remain, was not to be given the opportunity to remain in the EU.

At the eleventh hour in Brussels, May, however, backtracked on the backstop agreement. This was because an outraged DUP, which had not been consulted by May about the agreement and was not shown the final text, demanded that Northern Ireland should not be treated differently from the rest of the United Kingdom. With its key to a Tory majority vote in parliament, the DUP won the power play. The Prime Minister, disingenuously, suddenly declared that her overriding priority and guiding principle in the Brexit negotiations was to defend the Union. She would not accept in any circumstances both Ireland being treated differently and the creation of 'regulatory barriers' between Northern Ireland and the rest of the United Kingdom in the Irish sea.

This created an impasse. Despite being party to the written agreement, May, in effect, declared her government's unwillingness to accept the EU's backstop solution to the Irish border. As Lisa O'Carroll, Brexit correspondent of the *Guardian*, would later observe, 'This immediately sowed the seeds for an insoluble problem unless the UK struck a deal which involved remaining in the single market and the customs union, both red lines for the prime minister'.[80] As we will see in Chapter 2, the truth of O'Carroll's observation would become fully evident during the protracted, painful and ultimately unsuccessful negotiations between May and the EU over the Irish border issue during 2018 and 2019.[81]

A further cause of potential conflict lay in the fact that, although the DUP was the ruling party in Northern Ireland, it was no longer the largest party there, nor, given its resolutely Leave position, did it reflect the 56 per cent Remain majority in that part of the UK. These contradictions were highlighted by the DUP's main political rival, Sinn Fein. The latter was in favour of Remain, held 30 per cent of the Northern Ireland vote and had seven Westminster MPs. These did not sit in the London parliament because of their party's abstentionist policy. Along with many others throughout Ireland, Sinn Fein convincingly maintained that the wishes and interests of the Irish were largely marginal and peripheral to the dominant Anglocentric concerns of Brexiters. As *The Irish Times* and the *Guardian* columnist, Fintan O'Toole, astutely observed, Brexit at root was 'an English national rebellion wrapped in the union flag'.[82] Sinn Fein advocated a United Ireland and self-determination for the people of Northern Ireland. In the event of no deal on Brexit and the erection of a hard border in the island of Ireland, the party might well demand a referendum on the future of Northern Ireland in the hope that this would eventually lead to the unification of the North and the South. Seen through the eyes of the DUP, Theresa May and the strongly unionist Conservative Party in England, Wales and Scotland, this was a nightmare scenario. They could envisage, with horror, the voters in Northern Ireland and Scotland (despite the EU's insistence that its backstop policy applied to Northern Ireland alone) demanding continued membership of the EU and the further 'break up' of the United Kingdom.[83]

During December the Prime Minister suffered from disloyalty in her own ranks. Just as she prepared for the Brussels summit, her authority was openly challenged by eleven Tory Remain MPs who sided with Labour, the SNP and the Liberal Democrats successfully to vote in favour of a measure giving MPs a veto on the final Brexit deal. The *Daily Mail* ran the pictures of the eleven dissidents on its front page and labelled them 'self-consumed malcontents' who had 'betrayed their leader, party and 17.4m Brexit voters' and, 'most damning of all', increased 'the possibility of a Marxist in No. 10'. As the *Mail* observed, this was the Prime Minister's 'first significant Commons defeat'. It occurred just as the Tories had secured a lead over Labour in the polls for the first time since the June election and May doubling her lead over Jeremy Corbyn. A 'furious' May responded by sacking one of the most prominent rebels, former minister, Stephen Hammond, as Tory vice-chair. A further embarrassment lay in the fact that Alan Milburn, a Labour MP from 1992–2010 and chair of the government's Social Mobility Commission since 2011, resigned alongside all the other commissioners in protest at the government's failure to do more to translate into concrete practice its oft-repeated promise to increase social mobility.[84]

Yet by the end of the month, May, one of the most determined and resilient of politicians, was remarkably recapturing much of her early confidence and vitality. The

Prime Minister had survived the disaster of the election, the fiasco of the conference, internal Tory Party opposition and two enforced resignations and one sacking since early November of three cabinet ministers. These were respectively Michael Fallon, the defence secretary, over issues of sexual harassment and inappropriate behaviour towards women in Westminster, Priti Patel, the UK international development secretary, following her unofficial meetings with Israeli leaders, and first secretary of state, Damian Green, May's longstanding friend and close ally, over pornography allegations.[85] As the *Daily Mail* declared at the end of December in its editorial, '2018: Year of Destiny for a Resurgent May', 'What a difference six months can make in the capricious, febrile world of UK politics.' Following the election, May had been 'written off by almost every pundit … in October the knives were out again'. Following her disastrous conference speech, 'Mrs May was a dead woman walking'. But, 'as 2017 comes to its close', the prime minister has 'weathered all storms'. As a result of 'hard work and strength of character, the Middle England vicar's daughter is not only still in Downing Street, but showing signs of a remarkable resurgence'. The Prime Minister 'has the wind in her sails' and 'Brussels finally seems ready to negotiate a free-trade agreement'. In marked contrast, opined the *Mail*, Labour, 'with its risible flip-flopping over Brexit and bitter internal strife', had 'descended into a fractious, incoherent rabble'.[86] It is to a more balanced assessment of Labour's post-election performance that I will now turn.

Labour

The mood of optimism and euphoria generated by the election result continued to enthuse Jeremy Corbyn and his supporters during the summer and autumn months of 2017. Much in the manner of his 'rock star' reception at the music festival at Tranmere Rover's Prenton Park stadium in May, Corbyn's post-election appearance on stage and speech at the famous Glastonbury festival in June received 'deafening roars' of welcome and applause. To the now familiar chant of 'Oh, Jeremy Corbyn', the Labour leader enraptured Glastonbury's young, middle-aged and old festival goers alike with his message of hope, unity, peace and justice and his condemnation of the divisive and hate-filled politics of Trump and his ilk.[87]

In truth, in the post-election months there developed a 'cult of personality' around Corbyn, this most self-effacing and modest of people. This was evident not only at Glastonbury and at other public venues at which Corbyn appeared, but also at the Labour Party conference in Brighton at the end of September.

The conference adopted the slogan of Labour's manifesto, 'For the Many Not the Few'. In total contrast to the disasters about to befall May at her own conference, Corbyn was afforded a hero's welcome with delegates chanting his name and some waving red scarves above their heads. His keynote address on the last day of the conference was rapturously received. In his speech Corbyn addressed mainly familiar themes: the 'broken' nature of the neoliberal model; Labour's socialism as the 'new mainstream' of British politics and the only force capable of transforming Britain in modern, progressive and more democratic ways; the need for more state intervention in the market effectively to counteract the power of vested corporate interests; the promotion, in the public interest, of rent controls, the public ownership of utilities and the reversal of cuts to corporation tax. Labour now stood 'on the threshold of power', according to Corbyn. While delegates voted to exclude Brexit from formal debate, and so avoid a very public airing for serious intra-party differences of opinion, the conference did endorse the party's ongoing Brexit policy of 'constructive ambiguity'. Corbyn himself criticized the Tories' divided, self-interested and 'bungling' approach to Brexit. He also reiterated his pledge to put the economy first in dealings with the EU and to gain 'unimpeded access' to the single market. In turn, Keir Starmer wanted a 'new progressive relationship with the EU' that mirrored single-market benefits and declared that remaining in a customs union was 'a possible end destination' for Labour.[88]

On balance, both Corbyn's speech and the conference were judged by the media to be highly successful. Even Paul Dacre's vehemently anti-Corbyn *Daily Mail* declared that this had been Corbyn's 'most successful conference as leader' and that it had 'consolidated' his position.[89] At the same time, however, significant, if often predictable, differences of opinion remained. For example, while the centre-left *Guardian* regarded Corbyn's speech as his 'best yet' as Labour leader, and the former Labour leader, Ed Miliband, described it as 'excellent', the Tory-supporting *Sun* warned that Corbyn's 'hard-left' policies would take the country back to the conflicts and crises of the 1970s. Some Conservative politicians, furthermore, declared that Labour was 'unfit to govern' and that its excessive tax and spend policies would result in economic disaster.[90] Finally, the *Observer's* columnist, Nick Cohen, deplored the 'cultism' and 'idolatry' that surrounded Corbyn and that were 'everywhere at the Labour conference'. These had transformed Labour into 'a childish, sycophantic and unthinking party' and were preventing it from giving necessary attention to the key issues of the day, according to Cohen.[91]

Notwithstanding Cohen's negative comments, Labour did continue clearly and forcefully to criticize the government and to present its alternative policies to the public. This was reflected, for example, in its ongoing condemnation of the Tories' austerity policies and in its ability constructively to develop its position on Brexit. By the time of Philip Hammond's Autumn budget, in November 2017, there was widespread agreement on the centre and left that ten years of the politics of austerity, of cuts and a smaller state, had miserably failed to halt or reverse Britain's failing economy. The country was still characterized by low economic growth, poor productivity levels, a massive deficit, deficient public services, stagnant and falling wages and savage cuts to people's welfare. George Osborne's neo-classical promise to restore growth and wellbeing by means of cuts had simply failed to materialize.[92]

Theresa May had made a key pledge from the EU referendum onwards to improve the lives of the 'barely managing', largely by increased state intervention. Towards this end May and her chancellor, Philip Hammond, had abandoned Osborne's totally unrealistic targets for deficit reduction and erasure. Yet throughout 2016, and up to and beyond June 2017, May's rhetoric had not been translated into any significant ameliorative action. This continued to be the case up to the end of 2018. It was seen most clearly in Hammond's Autumn budget of November 2017.[93]

As the *Guardian* observed, instead of providing the 'big economic stimulus' or 'bazooka' of public spending required by the country to boost demand and the economy as a whole, the habitually cautious Hammond merely produced a 'pea shooter'.[94] The chancellor presented his budget within the context of a 'terrible outlook' for the economy. This comprised a continuing fall in real wages, slower than expected growth, low productivity, rising debt levels and inflation, sharply increased borrowing and the instability and uncertainty surrounding Brexit, albeit alongside the highest levels of employment for many decades. The lugubrious chancellor once more placed 'ideology above evidence', and continued to propose a modified form of Tory austerity. To be sure, what he characteristically described as his 'balanced' budget abolished stamp duty for first-time buyers up to £300,000, and announced extra cash for the NHS, a cut in business rate, a reduction in waiting times for recipients of universal credit and more investment in industrial strategy, hi-tech research and infrastructure. In truth, these, however, were very modest expansionary measures. While Hammond allocated a £2.8 billion to the NHS, he set aside £3 billion to prepare for Brexit. His budget fell way short of his stated 'bold' goals to build a Britain 'fit for the future' and 'revive the homeowning dream'.[95]

As most commentators, including leading Labour figures, were quick to point out, Hammond had failed to honour the Tory leadership's pledge, under the national living wage scheme, to increase the wages and living standards of the low paid. In effect, and despite May's promise, the situations of the 'just managing' and the neglected working class were barely improved, if at all, by the budget. The longest period of stagnation in living standards since records began in the 1950s was not about to be reversed. In practice there would be no ending of the pay cap for most public-sector workers in the short term. No additional money had yet been allocated for this purpose and the Treasury was committed to providing extra cash only for nurses. The independent Resolution Foundation (RF) and Paul Johnson, the director of Britain's leading financial thinktank, the Institute for Fiscal Studies (IFS), calculated that wages and living standards would not reach their pre-2007 crash levels and the budget deficit entirely cleared until the mid-2020s. The Resolution Foundation further estimated that the average family's income would suffer a cut of £1,000 per year. There were also £12 billion more cuts in welfare to come.[96]

While leading Tory papers, the *Sun*, the *Daily Mail* and the *Daily Telegraph*, expressed their 'delight' at Hammond's 'shrewd', 'well judged' and 'optimistic' budget, the Labour-supporting *Daily Mirror* and the *Guardian* agreed that it was a 'no hope' affair, a 'missed opportunity' to do some good.[97] Aditya Chakrabortty of the *Guardian* convincingly argued that, despite all his bold promises, Hammond had shown himself to be firmly attached to austerity, a practitioner of 'more of the same' and, perhaps most damningly, 'a real nowhere man, making all his nowhere plans for nobody'.[98] John McDonnell and Jeremy Corbyn eagerly joined the chorus of disapproval. They roundly condemned the 'empty promises' of May and Hammond and their cynical 'let down' of the people. In their opinion 'nothing has changed' in what had been billed as a 'bold', 'make-or-break' and even 'revolutionary' budget. The government quite simply was 'not fit for office'.[99] Their comments hit the mark and helped to put the post-election Tories once again on the defensive.

Despite its internal confusion and divisions over its Brexit policy in June and July, Labour developed a more coherent approach during the months from August 2017 to

January 2018. With Keir Starmer very much to the fore, the party's policy of 'constructive ambiguity' towards the EU and Brexit evolved from late August onwards into a new official policy in support of membership of the single market and the customs union during the transition period after March 29, 2019. Starmer also raised the possibility of permanent membership of both. Labour's new policy would necessarily embrace both membership of a form of customs union, in order to keep open the Irish border and protect supply chains for industry, and flexibility as to whether the benefits of the single market would be 'best retained by negotiating a new single market relationship or by working up from a bespoke trade deal'. In contrast to May's 'hard' Tory party, complete with its total rejection of extended membership of the customs union and the single market, Labour by late August had become the party of 'soft Brexit', according to the *Guardian*.[100]

To be sure, Corbyn, McDonnell and many others in the party continued to express reservations about membership of the single market. As noted previously, they saw membership as being incompatible with the wishes of the majority Leave voters in the EU referendum and as being problematic for state aid to industry, for tackling the problem of cheap competition in the labour market and for transforming the economy. They hoped that both the EU and the UK would display flexibility around these problematic but evolving issues. For example, there were already signs that the pressures of immigration, highlighted by many Leave voters, were easing. Immigration had fallen by over 80,000 between the EU referendum and the summer of 2017. This figure included many returning skilled EU migrants worried about the future in post-Brexit Britain.[101]

The Labour leadership also remained consistent in its belief that a Norway-style arrangement was unacceptable because it meant that Britain would not exercise democratic control over its dealings with the EU and would have to accept what was anathema to many of Labour's Leave supporters, the free mobility of labour. Yet there was general agreement within Labour's ranks that flexibility and pragmatism in the UK's negotiations with the EU were highly preferable to the 'high-handed' approach of the government. Labour continued to insist that it could not support a May Brexit withdrawal deal unless it met Labour's 'six tests', as outlined by Starmer in March 2017. These centrally revolved around a 'collaborative' future relationship with the EU, the continued protection throughout the UK of the rights and 'exact same benefits' currently enjoyed under EU membership, 'fair managed migration' and the avoidance of a 'race to the bottom'. Labour also declared that that the European Charter of Fundamental Rights should be incorporated into UK law and that full parliamentary scrutiny should be brought to bear upon plans to alter legislation relating to Brexit.[102]

By December 2017 there was growing evidence of a significant increase in the number of Labour members and intending Labour voters calling for the party permanently to remain in the customs union and the single market. Their case was argued in the parliamentary party by Chuka Umunna, Chris Leslie and likeminded MPs.[103] The leadership successfully resisted these calls. At the same time, however, Corbyn and his allies were under mounting pressure from Starmer and his supporters to commit Britain to membership of some form of customs union, to be negotiated with the EU, not only during but also following the transition period. This would ensure both a frictionless border in Ireland and no blockages in supply chains for business. At the same time, Starmer problematically wanted Britain to have the right to strike independent trade deals while being a member of the customs union. (The latter could limit such independent action.) Corbyn remained, to say the least, sceptical about Starmer's customs union plan. Yet, following fraught exchanges and apparently a threat by Starmer to resign, Corbyn and his close allies accepted Starmer's plan while continuing to criticize aspects of the single market.

By the end of January 2018 peace and unity had broken out in a party which had suffered from chronic divisions, conflicts and resignations ever since Corbyn's accession to the leadership. Labour henceforth was officially committed to membership of a customs union beyond 2020 and, while not a member of the EU, negotiating to remain as close as possible to the EU's single market. The leadership believed that the latter situation would hopefully enable Britain to enjoy the benefits of full access to the single market without suffering from the adverse effects of unlimited migration and limits upon state aid and intervention in industry and regional development. They maintained that they had successfully brought about a 'synthesis' between Labour members and voters wishing to remain or leave. In sum there now existed an even clearer divide between Labour and the Tories on Brexit. Labour had seemingly manoeuvred itself into a strong and mainly united position to face the challenges of Brexit during what proved to be the crunch year of 2018 without suffering from internal splits and resignations. In contrast, the Tories continued to be seriously divided.[104]

The months between the June election and the dawning of 2018 had thus proven to be highly successful ones for the Labour party. Yet two dark clouds remained. First, despite Corbyn's outstanding successes and May's abject failures, the polls continued to put the latter ahead of the former as the person best equipped to be prime minister. The difference stood at 5 points, according to the *Observer*'s Opinium poll of January 2018. The same poll had Labour and the Conservatives level on 40 per cent. Labour should have been well ahead by then.[105]

Second, despite Labour's revival in Scotland at the 2017 general election, from one to seven seats, the radical 'Corbynista effect' had far less impact in Scotland than in England. To be sure, on the eve of Corbyn's five-day visit to Scotland in mid-August, Scottish Labour was optimistic that it could successfully target eighteen marginal seats. Kezia Dugdale declared that a 'revival' was under way and that 'the party with the greatest potential to grow is the Labour party'.[106] In truth, however, it was the SNP that continued by far to exert the most important radical appeal in Scotland. The Scottish Labour Party vociferously preached anti-austerity and criticized the anti-austerity claims of the SNP. Scottish Labour, however, severely limited its appeal by sticking so inflexibly both to the defence of the Union and to opposition to Scottish independence. These causes, of course, were the 'natural' preserves of Ruth Davidson's Tories, and Labour had little to gain by remaining so unequivocally wedded to them. UK Labour's perceived lack of knowledge, moreover, of important aspects of Scotland's history, such as its separate legal system, its treatment of Scottish Labour as the 'branch office' and its seeming treatment of Scotland and its concerns as at best secondary to those of England, and especially those of London and the Westminster parliament, did not go down well among voters in Scotland.[107]

Scottish Labour also suffered from yet another debilitating leadership crisis. In August, Kezia Dugdale unexpectedly resigned. Dugdale, a strong critic of Corbyn, had succeeded the hapless Blairite, Jim Murphy, following Scottish Labour's disastrous 2015 general election result when it lost forty of its forty-one seats in Scotland. Dugdale gave, as the reason for her resignation, the need for 'fresh energy, drive and a new mandate'.[108] In truth it is hard to see how she could have carried on against the background of Corbyn's successes. Dugdale was succeeded as the leader of Scottish Labour by Richard Leonard, a privately educated Yorkshireman, a former industrial organizer and a socialist largely in tune with Corbyn. Scottish Labour now hoped for a period of stability and growth, but the odds were against it. It had elected nine leaders in the past eighteen years.[109] Yet, in the UK as a whole, Corbyn's Labour party could greet the New Year as a confident and reasonably united body.

The SNP

In contrast to Labour's upturn in its fortunes, the SNP, as noted earlier, was suffering from the serious setbacks of losing twenty-one Westminster seats at the June 2017 election and declining support for another Scottish independence referendum, at least in the short term. Sturgeon's immediate post-election response was to announce that the party would concentrate during the next twelve months on listening to the voters, pushing the case harder for Scottish independence, mainly at the grass-roots level, and winning back disillusioned independence supporters.[110]

Throughout the summer and autumn months, the SNP took measures to realize these goals. At the level of ideas, the SNP continued to highlight its core belief in the overriding importance of independence and self-determination to Scotland's wellbeing and prosperity. The key argument was that, far from being dependent upon and subsided by the rest of the UK, Scotland had the capacity, drive and talent to become, much like the Scandinavian countries, another highly successful independent small nation. Scotland, moreover, had often been prevented from reaching its full potential due to a mixture of the patronizing arrogance, indifference and neglect displayed towards it by the British state and its governing parties. As Mhairi Black, the impressive young SNP MP for Paisley and Renfrewshire, expressed the matter in September 2017:

> For too long Scotland has been treated as an afterthought by too many politicians in Westminster. Even those meant to be representing Scotland – such as David Mundell (the Secretary of State for Scotland) – seem to think that Scotland was extinguished as a nation after the 1707 Act of Union . . . changing the branch office manager will have little long-term effect on Scottish politics when you consider Labour's attitude to Scotland.[111]

The only solution for Black and independence advocates in general was for even more voters to trust in the SNP as the 'true' champion of Scotland's interest. Above all, the SNP would redouble its efforts to ensure that people living in Scotland would be treated by England and other countries as respected equals rather than as peripheral subordinates. Only self-determination, in the form of Scottish independence, would resolve this matter once and for all in Scotland's favour and bring to an end a long history of, to employ Michael Fry's apt description, 'metropolitan disdain'.[112]

In terms of policy, the SNP sought to further enhance its appeal by announcing major new initiatives to tackle poverty and inequality and further grow the economy. What were widely described as 'fresh', 'bold' and 'imaginative' policies, proposals and areas of discussion were incorporated into the SNP's Programme for Government, entitled 'Delivering for Today, Investing for Tomorrow'.

Published early in September, this document detailed the government's plans for 2017–2018. In introducing the document, Nicola Sturgeon described Scotland under the SNP as an 'ambitious nation'. With its list of considerable achievements – 'developing the economy', 'protecting jobs and businesses', abolishing prescription charges, safeguarding free university tuition fees, expanding free learning and childcare, investing in public services and so on – the ruling SNP had 'fashioned Scotland as a modern and outward-looking place', according to the first minister. It was now time to 'refocus our efforts and refresh our agenda'. This would involve £45m of extra funding for Scotland's high-tech firms to promote technological innovation and social change, support for graduate entrepreneurs and financial and other incentives to attract companies to invest in Scotland. The government would also end the 1 per cent pay cap, create a Scottish National Investment Bank to improve infrastructure, skills and productivity, further protect the environment by phasing out petrol and diesel cars over the next fifteen years, extend free personal care to terminally ill people under sixty-five and explore the possibility of the introduction of a universal basic income. Radical changes would be introduced to improve educational standards in schools, while two new £50m funds would help to eradicate child poverty, rough sleeping and homelessness. Holyrood's new tax-raising powers could be put to 'responsible' and 'progressive' ends, while further measures would be put in place in an attempt to strengthen the claim that Scotland's social security system had 'dignity and respect at its heart'. An extra £20m would also be invested in alcohol and drug services and moves taken to axe prison sentences of twelve months or less. This wide range of measures and proposals would further enable the country to realize its vast economic and social potential and become 'the kind of Scotland we all seek – an inclusive, fair prosperous, innovative country'.[113]

The SNP also kept up its strong criticisms of May's government. For example, the EU Withdrawal Bill was seen as a smokescreen for the Westminster government to attempt to take back powers which Scotland had won under the devolution settlement. These potential '111 power grabs' included the key areas of farming and fishing. According to the SNP's MSP and its Brexit Minister, Michael Russell, 'the founding principles' of the settlement, 'which people voted for so overwhelmingly in 1997', were 'endangered as never before'. In September the Scottish government advised the Holyrood parliament not to give its consent to the Withdrawal Bill in its present form, and worked jointly with its Welsh counterpart to draw up a series of amendments to it. These, however, proved to be unsuccessful.[114] Undaunted, the SNP continued its attacks on 'Tory Brexit'. In the first week of September Sturgeon denounced a leaked Home Office paper calling for the end of the free movement of labour 'immediately after Brexit'. The proposals in the paper were 'morally bankrupt', according to the first minister. They coldly ignored both the human dimension of migration, including the possible break up of families and the 'devastating' effect that reduced immigration would have on the Scottish economy.[115]

In all probability, the SNP's initiatives contributed to a partial improvement in its fortunes. By mid-September the polls indicated that support for Scottish independence had increased by 3 points since June, to reach 46 per cent. By the beginning of December support stood at 47 per cent. This led Kevin McKenna to declare that 'in Scotland the shambles of Brexit' had 'played out beautifully for the cause of independence', and that, very optimistically, 'without a single day of campaigning', independence was now 'ours for the taking'.[116] By the time of its annual conference in Glasgow in October, the SNP's membership had also risen to 120,000. By any standard this was a most impressive achievement. The party now stood third in terms of national membership, behind Labour, way ahead in first place, and the ailing Tories in second. The year 2018, moreover, would see the SNP's membership outstrip that of the Tories. As McKenna reminded the party's critics, the SNP had enjoyed spectacular growth and success since 2007 and was still comfortably in control at Holyrood.[117]

At the same time, however, a number of concerns and weaknesses were clearly evident. For example, the mood of the conference was far more downbeat than at previous triumphalist gatherings. Some observers pointed to signs of 'burn out', while delegates identified a need for more organizational initiatives at the regional and local level. According to Martin Kettle of the *Guardian*, Scottish opinion, furthermore, was 'currently 58% to 42% against a second referendum at any time in the next five years' and 56 per cent to 44 per cent against independence.[118] Derek Mackay, the financial secretary, announced at the conference that the expected pay increase for public sector workers in Scotland would depend upon Philip Hammond increasing public spending. Sturgeon, herself, played a less prominent role than at past conferences and, with her ratings down, was 'invincible no more', according to Kettle. Yet the first minister's performance, as usual, was polished and well received. The highlights of her conference speech comprised pledges to set up a state-owned energy company, a £6m rural tourism fund and a rebuke to the EU for failing to condemn police brutality against pro-independence Catalonians. Sturgeon also reiterated the party's policy that there would be a second referendum on Scottish independence soon after Brexit.[119]

Scotland's low rate of economic growth continued to be a matter of considerable concern. In August, Keith Brown, the economy secretary, proudly announced both that Scotland's rate of employment was 'at its highest recorded level' and that the country's rate of growth, at 0.8 per cent, was 'four times faster than that of the UK over the last quarter'. This bald announcement, however, concealed more than it revealed. The record rate of employment also applied to the UK as a whole, while the rate of growth for Scotland referred to by Brown had been preceded by a quarterly decline of 0.2 per cent. Most significantly, Scotland's rate of growth continued to be significantly lower than that of the UK. For example, the rates were 0.7 per cent for Scotland and 2 per cent for the UK for 2016–2017 and 1.2 per cent and 4.5 per cent during the past two-and-a-half years. Since 2010 Scottish economic growth had averaged only 1.1 per cent per annum, about half that of the UK as a whole. Both Scotland and the wider UK, moreover, continued to suffer from the longer-term problems of low productivity, low investment and low wages. Their growth rates increasingly lagged behind those of other EU countries, while real wages across the UK were also still below their pre-crash levels. As Sturgeon and her colleagues, however, realized, Scotland's continuing ability to ensure that the quality of its public-service provision was better than that south of the border was dependent not only upon increased funding from Westminster, but also the adoption of measures in Scotland itself significantly to improve infrastructure, productivity, skills and education and to reduce the high fiscal deficit. Herein lay major challenges for the SNP. Only time would tell whether the measures adopted in the Programme for Government and other government socio-economic initiatives would bear fruit.[120]

Despite its undoubted policy successes, the SNP also continued to face criticisms from the left. These revolved around the party's centralized decision making, its unduly cautious and managerialist approach and its alleged failure to be more radical and reach out more to those sections of the working class most likely to vote for independence, rather than mainly trying to attract past No and disillusioned Yes voters, including conservative sections of the middle class. McKenna and McAlpine were particularly vociferous in the call to the SNP to do more effectively to tackle inequality in all its forms and offer a popular radical alternative for the future.[121]

The SNP leadership was largely successful in fending off these criticisms. Yet at the same time there were signs within the party and the wider Yes movement of growing unease about the leadership's decision to delay a second referendum on Scottish independence until after Brexit. Some, albeit probably a minority, began to feel that the issue of independence would now become secondary to, and delayed even more by, the increasingly all consuming, complex and protracted Brexit negotiations. Other SNPers counselled caution and patience and, for the time being at least, held their more frustrated and radical colleagues in check.[122]

The main reason that the more cautious voices prevailed lay in the fact that the opinion polls, despite their short-term fluctuations, provided little or no overall encouragement for all those arguing in favour of a referendum on Scottish independence immediately or in the short term. Experts agreed that the polls, with almost ninety taken between 2014 and 2018, showed little significant change in support for independence over those four years. The message was clear: it would be foolhardy of the SNP and the Yes movement to rush into another referendum at a time when the polls showed that they had little chance of success. For Henry McLeish, McAlpine and others, resort to a successful referendum campaign required 'a much greater degree of consensus and an understanding of the likely consequences', and 'a much wider, more mature, informed and inclusive ongoing debate than just another binary vote'. A more intensive and extended period of education and discussion would help to ensure that 'a greater proportion of Scots are convinced that they are clear about what is best for Scotland'. McAlpine also maintained that the SNP and the Yes movement needed to be more proactive in setting the agenda, outlining the options and clearly explaining the benefits of independence.[123]

By the beginning of 2018, the SNP's fortunes were still mixed. On the positive side, those in Scotland in favour of Remain had risen from 62 per cent (at the time of the EU referendum) to 68 per cent, while a record number of 54 per cent now believed that

Scotland would be economically better off, or remain the same, if it became independent. A Scottish government study, furthermore, calculated that all the Brexit options would have a detrimental effect upon the Scottish economy, including living standards. The SNP continued strongly to oppose both May's plan and Labour's 'cheerleader' role for a 'Tory Hard Brexit'. Richard Leonard was seen as being particularly 'feeble' in slavishly following the Corbyn line on Brexit and much else. On the negative side, however, the polls stubbornly refused significantly to move in favour of Scottish independence, while critics continued to remind the Scottish government that despite some real-term funding improvements, austerity was still abroad and many local public services 'still in crisis'. The Scottish Trades Union Congress (STUC), for example, urged the SNP to restore cuts to pay and local services.[124]

Conclusion

This chapter has addressed some of the important political aspects of the present crisis. I have concentrated in particular upon the major shock of the result of the June 2017 general election and its turbulent and conflict-ridden aftermath. We have seen that Theresa May and the Tories experienced serious unexpected setbacks and fluctuations in their political fortunes between June 2017 and the beginning of 2018. In marked contrast, from a seemingly hopeless position in the period leading up to the general election, Jeremy Corbyn and his supporters in the Labour Party performed, against the odds, very well in the election and reasonably well thereafter. The SNP experienced mixed results. While remaining the dominant political player in Scotland, the party was disappointed by its performance at the election and the failure of Scotland's majority vote for Remain to translate itself into consistently increased support for Scottish independence. The years 2018 and 2019 would be dominated by the Brexit negotiations, complete with their countless twists and turns, ongoing major political divisions, conflicts and fragmentation, the downfall of May and her Brexit plans and continuing deep socio-economic divisions. In short, there developed throughout the UK a strong sense of continuing and, indeed, more profound and extensive, crisis. It is to a consideration of this intensifying crisis, with special reference to Brexit, that I turn in Chapter 2.

The Brexit Crisis, 2018–2019

Introduction

On Friday 24 May 2019, a visibly drawn Theresa May announced in front of 10 Downing Street that she would step down as Conservative Party leader on 7 June and remain as prime minister until a successor was chosen. Faced with her cabinet and her party in mutiny over her latest compromise on Brexit – a last-ditch and duplicitous attempt to woo Labour and its supporters by offering a temporary customs union and a public vote on her deal – the Prime Minister had effectively reached the end of the road. As the *Australian*'s Jacquelin Magnay declaimed, May had entered the 'death spiral'. The Prime Minister had been informed by Sir Graham Brady, the chair of the Tories' 1922 Committee, that most Conservative MPs had lost faith in her as leader and wanted her to go immediately. In effect May could either tender her resignation or wait for a rule change and the ensuing certain defeat in a vote of confidence by Conservative MPs.[1]

Defiant to the end, the Prime Minister offered a brave, if futile, defence of her government's record in front of the cameras outside Downing Street. She claimed to have made progress in a number of areas ranging across the economy, the environment, housing, mental health, fairness, equality, justice and security. She had, moreover, flatly refused to countenance the further breakup of the United Kingdom. In familiar fashion, May maintained that she had worked 'not just for a privileged few, but for everyone', to have tackled 'the burning injustices that still scar our society' and to have attempted to 'honour the result of the EU referendum'. Yet the Prime Minister was forced to conclude that her three efforts to command a parliamentary majority for her Brexit deal, negotiated with the EU in November 2018, had failed. It was now almost three years since the EU referendum and well past the UK's official leaving date of 29 March 2019. May declared that it was, and 'will always remain, a matter of deep regret', that she had 'not been able to deliver Brexit'. In this situation, it had become clear to her that it was now 'in the best interests of the country' for a new prime minister to lead the Brexit process and, by means of 'compromise' on 'all sides of the debate', to arrive at the successful consensus that had eluded her. At the end of her speech May's confidence went, her voice faltered and the tears began. She would 'leave the job that it has been the honour of my life to hold – the second female prime minister but certainly not the last' – 'with no ill will, but with enormous and enduring gratitude to have had the opportunity to serve the country I love'.[2]

On the day before May's resignation speech, the European Parliament elections had been held. In Britain Nigel Farage's insurgent new Brexit Party easily topped the polls. Whereas the latter won twenty-nine seats, the Conservatives won only four and finished in fifth place. This was a catastrophic result for the Tories and an outstanding one for Farage. For the Tories it was mitigated only by the fact that Labour also suffered badly, finishing with ten seats and in third place behind the second-placed resurgent Liberal Democrats.[3] Would Theresa May's successor as Conservative leader and prime minister be able, as desired by the leading contender, Boris Johnson, to put Farage 'back in his box'? Or would the Brexit Party continue to steal the Conservative's thunder, hasten the latter's decline and possibly fall and even lead to the 'nightmare' scenario of victory for Labour in a general election and the instalment of 'a Marxist', Jeremy Corbyn, in Number 10 as prime minister?[4] Would the crisis be resolved in the passing of the 'old' conservative UK and the ascendancy of Labour's vision of socialist transformation?

The story of the continuing fluctuations of Brexit and developments in UK politics and society following the fall of Theresa May, however, properly belong to the next chapter. The main purpose of the current chapter is to describe and explain how and why the Prime Minister and her party ended up in the divided, chaotic and sorry mess they did. This necessitates central attention to the crisis-ridden and tortuous Brexit negotiations that dominated UK politics, almost to the total exclusion of other issues, from early in 2018 to May's resignation. As the distinguished sociologist Bob Jessop has written, 'The Brexit vote was a singular event that is one symptom of a continuing organic crisis of the British state and society and a stimulus for further struggles over the future of the United Kingdom and its place in Europe and the wider world.'[5]

The chapter outlines and explains the many twists and turns, ups and downs (mainly the latter) and conflicts and tumult surrounding Brexit. This is done with particular reference to events and developments among the parties at Westminster, although the wider public picture is not ignored. My focus is necessarily selective because it is impossible, in a single chapter, to provide a comprehensive account of Brexit for the period in question. I have accordingly attempted to highlight what I consider to be the key events and developments. In keeping with the format adopted in Chapter 1, this is achieved by looking at chronological developments largely, but not exclusively, through the eyes of the main political parties, the Conservative Party, the Labour Party and the Scottish National Party. The Conservative Party and Prime Minister May constitute my initial point of departure and indeed my main point of focus throughout the chapter. This, of course, is because they stood at the very centre of the unfolding Brexit drama.

The UK and Europe: the historical context

Before starting to look at this drama, it, however, is important to set the EU referendum and Brexit within the context of the UK's developing historical relationship with the EU and its predecessor, the European Economic Community (EEC). This will enable us to increase and deepen our understanding of the predominantly tense and conflict-ridden nature of the post-2016 UK–EU relationship. This is because *divisions* and *conflicts* between the UK and European powers and their institutions have extensive and deep roots in the pre-2016 past.

In the nineteenth century, for example, Britain, as the dominant *global* power, was keen to ensure that it was not seriously challenged by European nations such as France (the traditional Catholic enemy) and what was increasingly seen in Britain as authoritarian and overmighty Prussia, the unifier of the German states in 1871. By the turn of the century, Britain, however, was increasingly outstripped, especially in terms of manufacturing, by the United States and Germany. By the time of the post-World War II period, talk of 'decline' and outdated 'British traditionalism' was in the air. 'Traditionalism', often by implication, was extended from Britain to include Northern Ireland as part of the United Kingdom. (The independent Republic of Ireland, Eire, had been created in 1937.) Traditionalism, above all, signified increasingly entrenched resistance to change at most levels of society. This was also the period of accelerated de-colonization and the marked decline of the British Empire. As David Edgerton has written, 'declinism' became 'a central feature of intellectual discourse from the 1950s into the 1990s'. Yet, as Edgerton concludes, the picture of decline was greatly overdrawn. While 'at most . . . any index of strength showed . . . that British capitalism was behind US capital and perhaps German capitalism', it remained 'by most indicators one of the top three capitalisms in the world'.[6]

The widespread perception that the UK was in decline, however exaggerated and relative in character, strongly influenced cross-party and wider political thinking about Europe. From the 1960s onwards, the idea gained ground that closer ties with the EEC, founded in 1957 under the Treaty of Rome, would help counter the UK's relative decline by opening up new markets in Europe and achieving closer economic integration with European countries. This 'turn to Europe' was resented by major Commonwealth countries such as Australia and New Zealand.[7] Yet it undoubtedly took place, alongside the wish for the UK to be less dependant upon the United States. In 1963, and again in 1967, the EEC, most prominently its French member, rebuffed the attempts of respectively Conservative Prime Minister Harold Macmillan and Labour Prime Minister Harold Wilson, to join the EEC. President De Gaulle's famous 'Non' was based on the beliefs that the UK, by tradition and instincts, was both far too insular and global to be genuinely committed to the pan-European project. The French also did not welcome more direct competition and rivalry with the UK inside the EEC.[8]

The Conservative prime minister, Edward 'Ted' Heath, nevertheless, successfully took the UK into the EEC in 1973. Two years later, in a referendum initiated by the Labour prime minister, Harold Wilson, on the UK's continued membership of the EEC, 67 per cent of those taking part in the UK as a whole and 58 per cent in Scotland voted to remain. Under Margaret Thatcher, her successor, John Major – who signed the Maastricht Treaty in 1991, which paved the way for the EEC to become the EU in 1993 – Tony Blair, Gordon Brown and David Cameron, the UK remained in the EU, but not a member of the eurozone, until the referendum of 2016.

Continuity of membership between 1973 and 2016 must not, however, be allowed to hide deep and persistent divisions within the UK over the European Community. For example, the Conservative Party has been repeatedly, profoundly and acrimoniously divided since the 1980s.[9] Margaret Thatcher welcomed EEC membership as providing a good opportunity to extend trade and her free-market views. As prime minister, Thatcher helped to bring about the Single European Act in 1986. At the same time, however, the Prime Minister fought hard against what she considered to be the country's excessive financial contribution to the EEC and won a rebate in 1984. More crucially, Thatcher was vehemently opposed to further EEC political integration and what she saw as the probable creation of a European super state dominated by Germany and France. These sentiments were expressed most forcefully and famously by the Prime Minister in her Bruges speech of 1988. In this speech, Thatcher presciently placed a premium upon UK sovereignty, an emphasis which has recently become central to the Brexit campaign and Boris Johnson's battle against UK 'vassalage' to the EU. Following the Bruges speech, Euroscepticism 'became mainstream', according to historian Nicholas Crowson. Conflicts and fierce rows over Europe, furthermore, between Thatcher and pro-EEC members of her cabinet, most prominently Geoffrey Howe, Michael Heseltine and Nigel Lawson, significantly contributed to the 'iron lady's' resignation in 1990.

John Major strongly believed in the European project, even though he kept the pound sterling and opted out of the 'Social Chapter'. The latter offered protection around, for example, workers' rights and working conditions. Major's period in office (1990–1997), however, was repeatedly troubled by serious internal Conservative Party conflicts over Europe, especially between Major himself and those he labelled Eurosceptic 'bastards', reportedly Michael Portillo, Peter Lilley and Michael Howard. In 1992 Major's government was humiliatingly forced, by the weakness of the pound sterling, to withdraw from the European Exchange Rate Mechanism (EERM). A year year later the Prime Minister survived serious attempts by Conservative rebels to derail his pro-European policies, most notably over the implementation of the Maastricht Treaty. Crowson observed that, following Major's defeat at the 1997 general election, Euroscepticism 'took control of the Conservatives'. This was reflected in the views of Major's successors as Conservative Party leader, respectively William Hague, Iain Duncan Smith and Michael Howard.[10]

Euroscepticism was also both evident and growing beyond the divided ranks of the Conservative Party. For example, the DUP, which would become the largest political party in Northern Ireland by 2004, was identified with Euroscepticism, Ulster Protestantism, Loyalism, the Union, 'Britishness' and social conservatism and opposition to Irish nationalism, Catholicism, socialism and what it perceived to be the threat of 'ever closer union' at the European level. Although Northern Ireland would vote Remain in the 2016 EU referendum, the DUP was overwhelmingly in favour of Leave.[11]

The years between 1994 and 1997 saw the short-lived existence of Sir James Goldsmith's Referendum Party (RP). Goldsmith wanted people to be given the right to vote on continued membership of the EU. In 1991, historian Alan Sked formed the Anti-Federalist League. This was renamed the United Kingdom Independence Party (UKIP) two years later. Sked resigned as leader in 1997. Thereafter, under the right-wing populist leadership of Nigel Farage, UKIP became vociferously anti-EC, the free mobility of labour and, increasingly, racist in its negative portrayal of the nature and supposedly adverse effects of EU, and other, kinds of immigration to the UK. UKIP became increasingly popular. It came first in the elections to the European parliament in 2014 and received almost 13 per cent of the vote in the 2015 general election. UKIP would achieve much publicity, success and appeal as an outspoken advocate of Leave and as a defender of UK sovereignty against EU 'dictatorship', during the EU referendum campaign of 2016.[12]

In succeeding Michael Howard as Tory leader in 2005, David Cameron wanted his party to stop 'banging on about Europe' and adopt a more conciliatory and balanced approach. This, however, proved to be impossible. After Cameron's coalition government (2010–2015) experienced several backbench rebellions on Europe, and in the context of UKIP's surge, it became almost inevitable that a referendum on continued EU membership would take place. While Cameron criticized the EU for its 'excessive' regulations, controls and immigration to the UK and desire for further political integration, he wanted to 'renegotiate and reform' rather than to leave. Yet, very much against the odds, the Leave side won by 52 per cent to 48 per cent in the June 2016 EU referendum. Cameron felt betrayed by those whom he considered to be his allies, most prominently the Conservatives Boris Johnson and Michael Gove, who became leading figures in the Leave campaign. Upon unexpectedly losing the vote, Cameron immediately resigned.[13] May, as Cameron's successor, swallowed her referendum vote for Remain and pledged her unqualified support for the majority 'will of the people' to leave the EU. Henceforth, as we will see below, for May, 'Brexit meant Brexit'.

The Labour Party also has a long history of divisions and conflicts over Europe. In the 1960s the party opposed entry to the Common Market. Hugh Gaitskell, Labour's leader, declared in his famous speech in 1962 that in the event of 'the mother country' becoming a 'province of Europe', 'a thousand years' of his country as an 'independent state' would come to an end.[14] In 1974, Prime Minister Harold Wilson was faced with a party mainly opposed to the UK's membership of the EEC and a cabinet and a country deeply divided on the issue. Yet in the 1975 referendum Wilson's government as a whole successfully campaigned in favour of continued membership. They maintained that, on balance, membership was good for the economy in an increasingly unsettled domestic and international economic and political climate. On the other hand, as noted in Chapter 1, the Labour Left was profoundly opposed to the EEC. Both Tony Benn and Michael Foot saw it as being undemocratic and a capitalist club that would place obstacles in the way of the implementation of socialism in the UK. Jeremy Corbyn became part of the Left opposition. It also included the Communist Party of Great Britain (CPGB).[15]

Neil Kinnock, the Labour Party's leader between 1983 and 1992, reversed his initial opposition to the EEC. While he continued to see it as too centralized, Kinnock came to believe that continued membership was economically beneficial, especially in developing depressed parts of the UK, and that it strengthened the UK's stability and security in an increasingly supranational and insecure world.[16] These positive beliefs were endorsed and added to by Kinnock's successors, John Smith, Tony Blair, Gordon Brown and Ed Miliband. They all continued to see Labour's and the country's places as being firmly within Europe, although not within the Eurozone.

Only with the accession of Jeremy Corbyn to the Labour leadership in 2015, did a far more ambivalent attitude towards the UK's membership of the EU return to a central position in the party. As seen in Chapter 1, Corbyn and Labour supported Remain in the 2016 referendum, but in a lukewarm and qualified way. At the same time, Corbyn wanted to appeal to Labour members and supporters who voted Leave and accordingly supported May's invocation of Article 50 in March 2017. As we will see in more detail later in this chapter and in the next, the policy of 'constructive ambiguity' would further develop both as a compromise and an attempted solution to the Labour Party's, the labour movement's and the wider working class's and radical people's divided loyalties over membership of the EU.

In terms of the two other main parties, the Liberal Democrats have been the most consistent and wholehearted advocates of EU membership. From its reinvention as a social-democratic party of the left from the late1980s onwards, and greatly influenced by the socialist Jim Sillars, the SNP adopted its 'Independence in Europe' policy. Under its first ministers Alex Salmond (2007–2014) and Nicola Sturgeon (2014 to the present), the party has been particularly keen to present itself as strongly pro-EU, strongly pro-immigrant and strongly 'civic nationalist' and internationalist (see Chapter 1).[17]

The UK and Europe: the EU referendum

The predominantly party-political differences and divisions outlined above were reflective of wider societal fractures. These were both triggered and highlighted by the EU referendum campaign, won by Leave, in 2016. They revolved around differences and conflicts between Leavers and Remainers in terms of age, geographical place, social class, occupation, income, living standards, gender, ethnicity, race, life experiences and cultural and ideological traditions, values, norms and identities. This section provides a summary of them.

I will first profile Leave voters. The core Leave vote was concentrated among older and relatively affluent white, middle-class people, mainly Tories, in the villages and smaller towns of southern England. In the UK as a whole, a total of 59 per cent of voters over sixty-five chose to leave, while only 34 per cent in the same age bracket opted to stay. In aggregate terms, voters aged 25 and over displayed a clear and increasingly marked pattern, as they aged, to vote Leave. The process of ageing beyond 25 and the fact of old age won the vote for Brexit.[18] Every region in the country, except Scotland, Northern Ireland and London, voted to leave. Leave was the rule 'right across' East Anglia, Wales and Midlands. In the Midlands, the north of England and in Wales many traditional working-class Labour supporters and constituencies turned to leave.[19]

Many commentators at the time, especially those writing in the 'Brexit press', exaggerated the extent to which Labour and non-Labour voting, working-class 'traditionalists' dominated the Leave vote. As journalist Owen Jones wrote in April 2017, this was, misleadingly, to accept a 'simplistic narrative' in place of what was in reality a 'complicated reality'. The latter resulted from the fact that 'many low-paid white workers opted for remain', while 'millions of relatively comfortably-off Britons . . . voted to leave'. Yet, when considered as a whole, and taking on board variations and complexities, it is true that 'a decisive majority of working-class people' voted to leave. They were, moreover, often non-unionized, lacking skills, training and post-16 education. And, even though two-thirds of Labour Party supporters followed their party's preference for Remain, 149 out of 232 Labour constituencies voted Leave.[20]

Many of these working-class 'traditionalists' lived in increasingly run- down towns and smaller communities outside the big cities. These were the 'barely managing' and 'neglected' people whom Theresa May sought to appeal to (see Chapter 1). They had often suffered from de-industrialization and the adverse effects of globalization. They saw the EU as part of these 'outside' and largely 'alien' forces that, they believed, had adversely affected their living standards, their quality of life and their communities. They also resented being lectured, 'talked down' to, and sometimes being branded as stupid, by members of the establishment, especially distant members of the elite, whether in London or Brussels, who saw Remain as the only rational and sensible choice to make. The key slogan of the Leave campaign, coined by its leader, Dominic Cummings, of 'Taking Back Control', made perfectly rational sense to them.[21]

A large number of them, moreover, believed that the EU's policy of the free mobility of labour had damaging consequences, in terms of competition in the labour market, lowered wages and living standards and increased pressure upon public services around health, education and accommodation. From early in the campaign, charges of 'excessive' EU and other kinds of immigration to the UK, and its allegedly deleterious consequences upon living standards and the 'traditional British way of life', became central to the thoughts of leavers and the Leave leadership, especially right-wing populist demagogues such as Farage and many others in UKIP. The actual fact that academic research proved that immigration had an overwhelmingly beneficial effect on UK society did not matter to these right-wing populists and their many followers: myth became reality.[22]

Many old and older voters across the classes were strongly attracted to the radical-reactionary populist Leave message, whether expressed by UKIP, members of the Conservative Party or the overwhelmingly right-wing press, that a return to the past would ensure a bright future. According to this largely false, but extremely powerful, right-wing populist propaganda, the pre-EU and EEC UK had enjoyed stability, harmony, security, greatness on the world stage, unquestioning and widespread patriotism and national sovereignty. It also centrally involved the barely spoken but highly persuasive assumptions that Britain and the UK as a whole had been mainly white, with little immigration. In the eyes of Boris Johnson, Farage and others Brexit would involve the UK casting off the necessary 'chains', 'vassalage' and 'red tape' of a 'dictatorial' EU. The post-Brexit UK, furthermore, would become an autonomous, *sovereign* nation and a confident and outward-looking *global* power. In the manner of Trump's vision for the United States, the UK would become 'great again'.[23]

Remain voters were heavily concentrated in the young and younger age brackets. Polling showed that 78 per cent of the 64 per cent or so of voters aged between 18 and 24 chose Remain, while only 19 per cent wanted to leave. Many Remain voters lived in large, ethnically and racially mixed urban areas such as the major cities of London, Manchester and Glasgow. They tended to be at ease with the issues of multiculturalism, immigration and cosmopolitanism associated with EU membership. The latter also provided good opportunities for travel, new contacts and new job opportunities. Many young and younger Remainers were well educated and saw themselves as part of the modern and potentially more progressive and tolerant world. Unlike the Leavers profiled, they did not seek to turn the clock back to a largely mythical homogeneous, conformist and somewhat boring past. They were joined, furthermore, by millions of 'ordinary' people who also appreciated the important economic, social and cultural benefits and opportunities provided in the EU. Some of these belonged to the organized labour movement. As seen above, their Labour Party officially supported the 'remain and reform' position. The trade-union movement was mostly in agreement, although some trade union leaders, such as Len McCluskey, then the General Secretary of Unite, with some 1.4 million members, and rank-and-file members were worried about the possible cheapening effects of EU immigration in the UK.[24]

As noted above, London, Scotland and Northern Ireland constituted the three regions in which remain sentiments were in a majority. Despite wide internal variations, London as a whole voted decisively in favour of Remain, by almost 60 per cent to 40 per cent. The fact that London is a well-educated, multicultural, relatively well off and cosmopolitan city, worked in favour of Remain. It is also the home of many financial services in the City of London. Their unrestricted access, or 'passporting' rights, to the EU and the vast benefits offered by the single market, meant that most City institutions were heavily in favour of Remain. The member institutions of the Confederation of British Industry (CBI) likewise appreciated the extensive market opportunities of the EU and strongly opted to stay.[25] As noted in the Introduction to this study, as a consequence, the predominantly Brexit-supporting and increasingly hard-right Conservative Party lost its traditional role as being the main political representative of the 'business mainstream'. The capitalists who keenly supported Brexit, including billionaire venture capitalists and right-wing newspaper owners who were either foreign or tax-resident abroad, increasingly tended to be only loosely connected to the UK economy. As we will see in Chapter 3, Brexit would mean that finance and business operate in future in a far less favourable and far more uncertain and unwilled European context.

Most of the 56 per cent who voted Remain in Northern Ireland were concerned about Brexit's adverse effect upon continued free trade and open borders, both within the EU as a whole and in the island of Ireland. They did not wish to see a return to the borders and conflicts of Ireland in the period preceding the Belfast or Good Friday Agreement of 1998. In Scotland, an even more impressive 62 per cent voted Remain. Every council in Scotland, moreover, returned Remain majorities. As seen in Chapter 1, the SNP believed that the size of the Remain majority augured extremely well for the holding of a second referendum on Scottish independence. Nevertheless, beyond the large urban centres, complete with their generally radical working classes and mainly pro-EU middle classes, a more varied picture emerged. In this context, it is important to remember the frequently neglected or overlooked fact by victorious Remainers that 38 per cent of the referendum voters in Scotland, or just over 1 million of the 2,679,513 total number of voters, chose Leave. This, of course, was a minority vote, but potentially not an insignificant one in terms of Scotland's future in terms of the Union and independence.[26]

In conclusion, this section has established the context in which Theresa May would conduct her Brexit negotiations with the EU in 2018 and 2019. The reader's attention has been drawn to the serious differences, divisions and conflicts in UK society surrounding Europe and membership of the EU. They suggest that, irrespective of her abilities and, above all, her determination, the Prime Minister would have great difficulty in satisfying both Leavers and Remainers and in achieving a satisfactory Brexit outcome.

Theresa May: from resurgence to humiliation, January–September 2018

We saw in the last chapter that by the end of 2017 Theresa May was enjoying a remarkable resurgence in her political fortunes. Above all, the Prime Minister had demonstrated to her considerable number of critics that she possessed formidable staying power and determination. In relation to both Brexit and her domestic agenda, May reiterated for the umpteenth time her commitment to 'get the job done'.[27] Yet by the end of March 2018 her fortunes had become far more mixed. Four months later, and following the tumultuous aftermath of the 6 July Chequers cabinet agreement in which David Davies, the Brexit secretary, Boris Johnson, the foreign secretary, Steve Baker, Brexit minister and seven other leading Tories resigned, matters had seriously deteriorated. Even worse was to follow. In September at its Salzburg summit the EU humiliated May by bluntly declaring that her Brexit proposals agreed at Chequers would not work. In which direction would the embattled Prime Minister now turn?

January–March

Between January and March, May's position was adversely affected by four discrete but increasingly linked developments. First, in an early manifestation of the dominant trend to emerge in 2018 and 2019, conflicts and divisions around Brexit became far more pronounced. For example, within the Conservative Party leading hard-Brexiters, most prominently Boris Johnson, David Davis and Steve Baker, Jacob Rees-Mogg and their colleagues in the European Research Group (ERG), stepped up their case against what they saw as the intransigent and high-handed stance of the EU and its negotiators. They mistakenly worked on the assumption that the EU needed the UK and its markets for German cars, Italian prosecco and other continental European goods far more than the UK needed the EU. The conclusion they drew from their false assumption was that a hard, personalized, presidential-style stance towards the EU, including the threat of a no-deal outcome, would bring rich dividends with the latter soon giving in to the UK's demands. Often shared by Theresa May and further embraced by her successor, Boris Johnson, in 2019, this conclusion ignored the fact that the EU was not only a strong economic bloc in an increasingly insecure and uncertain globalized world, but also that it was seen by its member states, especially its dominant power, Germany, as a wider political project deliberately designed to prevent the continent of Europe descending into the war, conflict and poverty which had so disfigured its past. It was not the weak and wobbly institution portrayed by the hard Brexiters and would not be allowed to fall apart. For example, the EU would not give the impression to the UK that it could leave on a no-deal basis and not incur serious economic and other costs. The exit door must not be opened to other dissatisfied members of the European club. As a corollary, and while keen to strike a deal with May, the EU took the firm and *united* position that it could not and would not do a special deal with the UK. The established procedures and rules of negotiation were to be strictly observed and adhered to by both sides. These structural and cultural characteristics of the EU were either never fully understood or consciously and selectively ignored by the hard Brexiters in the Conservative Party including, for much of the period from 2017–2019, Theresa May herself. This breakdown in communication and understanding constituted a major obstacle to the successful realization of May's, and subsequently, Johnson's Brexit plans.[28]

The hard Tory Brexiters also became increasingly loud in their warnings that the Prime Minister must not compromise and certainly not renege on her unequivocal Lancaster House commitments to quit the single market and the customs union and escape from the jurisdiction of the CJEU. They were already suspicious of the Chancellor, Philip Hammond, and other 'soft' Brexiters within the Tory cabinet who reportedly were not in favour of leaving the customs union.

They now warned that they would not accept May's rumoured support for a two-year transition period after March 2019 in which the UK would continue to pay the country's full financial contribution to the EU and obey EU rules without having a say in them. UK 'vassalage' to the EU simply was not acceptable to Johnson, Rees-Mogg et al. 'Insurgency' on the Tory backbenches was turning into 'open warfare' in February and there reportedly was a plot to 'install Boris Johnson as prime minister, Michael Gove as his deputy and Jacob Rees-Mogg as chancellor', according to the *Guardian*.[29] From the other side of the Brexit debate, Tony Blair, Nick Clegg and other prominent Remainers became more active in their public campaign for a second vote, while Andrew Rawnsley, the *Observer*'s chief political commentator, declared that, according to the most recent polls, 78 per cent of Labour Party members were now in favour of a second referendum and 46 per cent against; 42 per cent of the members of the public polled believed that Brexit was the wrong choice.[30]

Second, many commentators from across the political spectrum maintained that May had repeatedly shown herself to be a very limited, inflexible and wooden political leader in general, bereft of charisma and vision and lacking clarity and precision in the Brexit negotiations. They argued that the Prime Minister had failed, since her accession to the leadership and premiership in 2016, to 'build a consensus for change'.[31] For example, in the eyes of the *Guardian* and *Observer*, May had insisted upon setting her own narrow and rigid right-wing ideological 'red lines' and had sought to curry favour with the Tory right, rather than searching for cross-party alliances and solutions and attempting to build bridges in the country between Leavers and Remainers. In turn, there was more general agreement that she had failed to maintain authority and control in her own party and successfully manage and resolve its internal divisions over Brexit and domestic affairs. May's early-January 2018 cabinet re-shuffle, involving the disgraced Damian Green, Michael Fallon and Priti Patel, was also widely seen to have been a chaotic mess. Some claimed, furthermore, that May had been told in no uncertain terms to 'raise her game or face revolt' and that, somewhat speculatively, 'dozens' of Tory MPs had written to Graham Brady to express their dissatisfaction with the PM (forty-eight letters, written by 15 per cent of Tory MPs to the chair of the 1922 committee, were required to trigger a vote of no confidence in May and a leadership contest). In the opinion of Matthew d'Ancona of the *Guardian*, the argument that May's resilience 'is somehow noble' was now being made 'much less frequently'. In the midst of 'political mayhem', it looked 'increasingly like stubborn political delusion'.[32] For Polly Toynbee, the endlessly warring Brexit factions in the Conservative Party, meant that May 'can't win'.[33]

Third, EU negotiators, most prominently its chief negotiator, Michel Barnier, grew increasingly frustrated with the UK's 'constantly changing and contradictory' Brexit demands, its lack of clear purpose, consistency and direction and its seeming inability to obey the mutually agreed and enforceable rules of negotiation. According to Barnier, the UK was attempting the impossible: to 'cherry pick' those aspects of the customs union and the single market favourable to it and rejecting those it disliked even as it sought to leave the EU altogether. The UK could not 'have cake and eat it', declared Barnier. The single market was indivisible and leaving the customs union and the single market would lead to 'unavoidable' barriers to trade. Contrary to the view of the May government, a seamless and bespoke free-trade deal for the UK was simply not an option for the EU, according to Barnier. Britain, furthermore, could not seriously negotiate with the vast bureaucratic organization, the EU, with its clearly established rules and procedures on the basis of the 'relaxed' approach seemingly favoured by David Davis, the Brexit secretary. The days of informal contacts among leaders, nods and winks and, at least on the UK side, assumptions of 'natural' British rule and command in international affairs, were quite simply no longer relevant or acceptable. UK procrastination and prevarication, furthermore, were proving to be counterproductive. This was seen above all in the thorny issue of the Irish backstop. As Jonathan Freedland of the *Guardian* presciently maintained in February 2018, the continuing failure of the UK seriously to address and attempt to resolve the backstop issue in Ireland, was 'putting the transition deal in doubt'.[34]

Fourth, these unfavourable political developments for the government took place against worsening economic news and forecasts. The authoritative Office for National Statistics reported in May 2018 that economic growth in the UK had slumped to 0.1 per cent in the first quarter of the year, the worst quarterly figure for five years. This amounted to a virtual economic standstill.[35] Economists and an official government document for the most part agreed, despite denials from within the government that Brexit would make matters much worse. They estimated that in the event of a no deal outcome, the economy would shrink over the next fifteen years by 8 per cent, by 2 per cent if the UK retained its current access to the single market as a member, like Norway, of the European Economic Area (EEA), and by 5 per cent with a comprehensive free-trade agreement with the EU. A no-deal Brexit, furthermore, would hit many of the Leave-voting areas, such as north-east England, hardest.[36]

While the dramatic quarterly downturn of early 2018 could partly be attributed to the adverse effects of the very bad weather caused by the snowy 'beast from the east' in early March, not all of it could. Productivity levels were still poor, output was generally down, hiring on hold and pessimism certainly on the increase. To be sure, employment was very high, but many new jobs were insecure, poorly paid and lacked trade-union defences and government protection. Despite May's oft-repeated pledge to improve the lot of the 'just' or 'barely managing' and Chancellor Philp Hammond's declaration in his Spring statement that a modest improvement in the public finances would permit a judicious increase in public spending, the government could not hide its continued practical adherence to the politics of austerity and their widespread adverse effects. Average earnings were flatlining, while working conditions, job security and satisfaction, benefits and living standards for the majority, much-needed infrastructural investment and public services all continued to suffer. There was a steep fall in manufacturing output and the thriving parts of the economy, most prominently services and finance, were failing, on balance, to take up the slack.[37] To be sure, from June onwards economic prospects did improve, but these came too late to fully compensate for the earlier gloom.[38]

This negative picture, however, was partly offset by two favourable developments. First, despite May's own problems and her party being in 'disarray', the polls continued to show that the Conservative Party was not falling behind Labour. Most polls put the two parties 'neck and neck' or slightly apart. While there was little chance, furthermore, of 18–24-year-olds voting Tory, the party was retaining its popularity among those older voters who supported a 'clean' Brexit, strong censorship, 'traditional' morality, harsh penal policy, low taxes and public spending and were opposed to the 'spendthrift' and nationalization plans of Labour.[39]

Second, there were significant developments in the Brexit negotiations. At the end of February, the European Commission (EC) published the EU's draft withdrawal agreement, based on the EU–UK Brussels meeting in December 2017, in which particular attention was drawn to the importance of avoiding a hard border in Ireland. The EU was now beginning the process of turning the December agreement into a binding legal document in draft form. The latter was published in the absence of concrete written proposals from the UK side, although the Prime Minister promised a 'robust rejection' of any EU proposal which she believed threatened 'the constitutional integrity of the UK'. This led the *Guardian* to conclude that May was displaying an 'abdication of leadership' in that she lacked concrete proposals of her own and could only resort to the language of strong leadership and 'aspirational and magical thinking'.[40]

The Mansion House speech and beyond

On 2 March, however, the Prime Minister did set out her 'vision' for 'the future economic partnership between the UK and the EU' in her important Mansion House speech. The latter was wide-ranging in scope and content. May claimed that 'real progress' was being made in negotiations with the EU. She reaffirmed the UK's commitment to the Joint EU–UK Report of December which contained 'the key elements of our withdrawal' and declared that the UK, too, was turning that agreement into a draft legal text. The Prime Minister also maintained that the two sides were close to an agreement concerning the terms of the implementation period. The latter had been a 'key element' of the December deal, according to May. It was true that some differences remained, but the Prime Minister was 'confident that these can be resolved in the days ahead'.

Building upon her landmark Lancaster House speech of January 2017 and her important speech in September of the same year in Florence, May declared that the future agreement with the EU must respect the referendum result by means of the UK taking control of 'our borders, laws and money', protecting jobs and security and strengthening 'our union of nations and our union of people'. The Prime Minister once again registered her opposition to the Canada and Norway options on the grounds that they variously involved rule-taking, free movement, customs and regulatory checks and reduced market access to the EU. May declared that five 'foundations' should underpin the future agreement. They were rigorous, fair and open competition and no 'unfair' subsidies by national governments to their national industries, trade to be as frictionless as possible, no hard border in Ireland, common regulatory standards and an end to the Common Fisheries Policy and the Common Agricultural Policy. The latter would allow the UK to regain control over its agriculture and waters. Financial services would be part of the 'deep and comprehensive partnership' between the UK and EU, but this would be different from the passporting system intrinsic to the single market. (Under the system a business applied to the EU regulator for a passport in order to undertake financial services in countries throughout the EU.) The UK also wanted to have the right to negotiate trade agreements with other countries around the world as a continuing member of the EU customs union during the implementation phase. Although the decisions of the CJEU would continue to affect the UK, the latter would leave the jurisdiction of the former, just as it would leave the single market and the customs union. There would also be no 'race to the bottom' around workers' rights and environmental protection.

In short, the Prime Minister was seeking to honour the referendum result and carry out the democratic wish of the Leave majority, while simultaneously aiming to gain as much as was economically, socially and politically possible for the UK from the EU. May declared that she was confident that 'we can reach agreement' even though 'neither of us can have exactly what we want'. In carving out a 'bold new positive role' in the world, May would create a post-Brexit Britain that 'works not for a privileged few, but for every one of us': 'no community in Britain would ever be left behind again'. This 'pledge', made, as we have seen, repeatedly by May during her term as prime minister, constituted her 'guiding' principle in her negotiations with the EU.[41]

While staking claim to a bold vision, the Mansion House speech, nevertheless, left unanswered many *practical* questions. For example, how would the Irish backstop issue be resolved? How could the Prime Minister reconcile a written commitment to the agreement in Brussels of December 2017, including the Irish backstop, with equally strong promises to the DUP and other hard Brexiters to preserve the 'precious union' and have no customs and regulatory border down the Irish sea? In leaving the EU's single market and the customs union, could the UK realistically expect trade to continue to be largely 'frictionless'? How could extra bureaucratic costs and restrictions on UK exports to the EU be avoided? Could the EU realistically be expected to accept Britain's right to strike independent trade deals while it remained in the customs union during the implementation period? How would Leavers respond to May's announcement that the CJEU would continue, post Brexit, to have a 'significant role' in the UK? Finally, was there really the slightest chance that the EU would accept the unprecedented bespoke, 'have cake and eat it', selective free-trading arrangement desired by May and her advisors? Wouldn't the latter be totally at odds with the fundamental principle, as frequently expressed by Barnier, of the indivisibility of the single market?

In responding to these questions, the *Observer* correctly considered the speech to be contradictory and offering no real and lasting solutions for the country as a whole. In adopting a 'pick-and mix' approach and asking for special treatment, May was demanding far too much of the EU. Donald Tusk, the European Council president, declared, in the same vein as Barnier, that there could be no 'cherry picking' on the UK's part. For Tusk the only realistic option open to the UK outside the single market was a Canada-style free-trade agreement. At the same time, however, the *Observer* correctly noted that the speech did go some considerable way towards bringing about a truce within the ranks of the divided Conservative Party. For Conservative Brexiters, it continued to offer, albeit with some exceptions, a clean break from the EU in line with the Prime Minister's stated positions at Lancaster House and in Florence. For Conservative Remainers, the Prime Minister had at least shown that she was prepared to genuinely negotiate with, rather than lay down the law to, the EU and that she was open to compromise. As such, the speech brought about a 'blurry reconciliation', albeit probably temporary, between the party's 'schismatic factions'. Yet it also constituted a 'sobering defeat' for the UK, declared the *Observer*.[42]

On a more positive Brexit note, two and a half weeks after the Mansion House speech, the EU and the UK formally agreed the terms of the transition period. As observed by journalists Alex Barker and Martin Arnold, this 'long-awaited' agreement marked a 'milestone in the Brexit negotiations'.[43] Under the deal, the transition period would begin when the UK formally left the EU on 29 March 2019, and last until 31 December 2020. This was almost the two-year period desired by the UK. Under the agreement, the UK, contrary to May's stated intentions, accepted both the substance, but not the exact wording, of the backstop deal struck in December 2017 and the EU's demand that EU citizens arriving in the UK during the period of transition would not be afforded fewer rights and guarantees than those arriving before Brexit. The UK would also remain in and continue to enjoy the advantages of the single market and the customs union and be able to make independent trade deals during the transition period. At the same time, however, it would lose its voting rights and be obliged both to continue to pay its financial contribution to the EU and accept the free movement of labour. The UK, furthermore, and contrary to the promise made by several Tory politicians in Scotland and south of the border, would leave the Common Fisheries Policy, and so regain full control of its fish stocks and vessel access, *only* at the end rather than the beginning of the transition period. This aspect of the agreement caused uproar in Scotland, especially among fishing communities on the east and north-east coasts, which were strongly pro-Brexit. They claimed that they had been 'betrayed' and 'sold out again' by politicians and the government of the day.[44]

It will be evident that the negotiations over the transition period necessarily involved a process of compromise, of give-and-take. On the unequivocally plus side, they confirmed that transition was 'the preferred outcome for both sides' and that it would definitely take place on agreed terms. As such, the agreement conferred much-needed certainty and stability on the Brexit proceedings in order to promote what

Michel Barnier termed an orderly British withdrawal. Yet we must highlight the fact that the future agreement would come into effect only in the event of a full withdrawal treaty being agreed and ratified before 29 March 2019. Hence the transition agreement was conditional rather than absolute and ran the risk that political failures and breakdowns might derail a smooth withdrawal. As Barker and Arnold presciently observed, the question of avoiding a hard border in Ireland still constituted 'by far the most important risk'. Despite the UK's commitment to the substance of the December 2017 agreement, the chief negotiators, Barnier and Davis, continued in March 2018 to 'largely set aside the vexed issue of how to avoid a hard north-south border'. In addition, Theresa May had 'rejected outright' the EU's fallback plan to create a border down the Irish Sea, In short, there was still much work to do to resolve the backstop issue to the mutual satisfaction of the UK and the EU.[45]

Responses, problems and initiatives: the Tories, Labour and the SNP

The main question arising out of the transition agreement for the British press, the public and politicians was whether May had conceded too much in the short term in order both to secure the immediate agreement and further to pursue her longer-term and overriding objective of leaving the EU with a satisfactory deal. May and her inner circle didn't think that the negotiations had resulted in too many compromises. They were joined by most Tory Brexiter backbenchers who, despite some misgivings, were largely prepared at this stage to give the Prime Minister the overall benefit of the doubt. Some reservations and outright opposition, however, were expressed. The former UKIP leader, Nigel Farage, predictably opined that May should be removed from office for her 'appeasement' of the EU. Equally predictably, Rees-Mogg was concerned that May had made too many concessions, especially on fishing and free movement, to an overweening EU. At the same time, however, Rees- Mogg agreed with the majority of Conservative MPs that progress had been made and that the new situation was 'tolerable if the end state is a clean Brexit'.[46] Yet, as the respected *Guardian* political columnists, Daniel Boffey, Anushka Asthana and Lisa O'Carroll declared, May's deal on transitional arrangements was met by a 'storm of protest' on the part of some senior Tories, such as Iain Duncan Smith, and sections of the public, including many fishing communities not only in Scotland, but also across the UK.[47]

The responses of Labour and the SNP to the Brexit developments of March were entirely predictable. Labour reiterated its commitment to an alternative Brexit which met its six tests of March 2017 and maintained that May's 'chaotic' and 'vague' approach and her narrow and inflexible 'red lines', manifestly failed these tests. Labour continued to prioritize the protection of jobs, the promotion of growth, the freedom to transform the economy and society in a socialist direction without being hampered by EU rules on competition and state subsidies, the continued membership of a permanent customs union (to avoid a hard border in Ireland and to keep open vital supply chains for industry), close alignment with the single market and managed migration which both met the needs of the British economy and avoided racism and xenophobia.[48]

Yet questions were raised in the press and elsewhere about whether Labour's own Brexit policy, especially its ongoing attempt to satisfy *both* its majority Remain and minority Leave members and voters, was still viable. Did it amount, as suggested by a growing number of critics in the press and within the party itself, to 'fence sitting' and a 'fudge' rather than a constructive and viable alternative to May's hard Brexit?[49] Labour's failure to make the expected big gains at the local government elections in May, against a background of Brexit uncertainty and 'chaos' and the worrying state of the economy, constituted a further area of concern for its leaders, members and supporters.[50]

During the spring and summer months, the growing publicity, furore and the lack of swift and decisive leadership action in relation to the issue of antisemitism within the Labour Party, created further divisions and conflicts. A party which prided itself, albeit exaggeratedly, upon its historical opposition to racism, including antisemitism, was criticized by Margaret Hodge and other prominent Labour opponents of Corbyn and antisemitism for its actual and growing antisemitism. The Labour Party also began to lose the trust and support of influential sections of the Jewish community and the wider public. It appeared to be the case that justified criticisms within the party and on social media of the Israel government's policies of denying equality and justice to Palestinian Arabs in Israel and in occupied Palestine, had spilled over, in totally unacceptable and racist ways, into condemnations of Jewish people themselves and the very right of the state of Israel to exist.[51] As we will see below, the row over Labour and antisemitism would refuse to go away. It would, indeed, erupt again with even more force and divisive consequences during 2019.

It was little compensation to Labour that the Tories were also guilty of acts of racism. These were seen mainly in relation to the Windrush Scandal, but also around the issue of Islamophobia within the Conservative Party. As home secretary in Cameron's coalition government, Theresa May had deliberately set out to create a 'hostile environment' for illegal immigrants to the UK. In the spring and summer months of 2018, it was discovered that some of the Windrush generation of immigrants from the Caribbean had been wrongly caught up in the government's illegal net. The ship, empire SS Empire Windrush, carried the first pioneers from Jamaica in May 1948. They had been encouraged by the UK authorities to migrate to Britain in order to help to fill the country's post-World War II labour shortage. They and their children had lived in the UK for decades, only to be told by May's government that they were in Britain illegally because of a failure to produce the official papers concerning their arrival, rights and citizenship status. Many of them, of course, had been born British subjects. Yet thousands had been wrongly detained and denied their legal rights, while more than eighty had already been deported. Many had lost their jobs, benefits and homes. The scandal saw a belated apology from May and the resignation of home secretary Amber Rudd. The fallout from the scandal would continue into 2019.[52]

The scandal and public outcry around Windrush, however, did not prevent Boris Johnson from further inflaming debates about racism by comparing women who wore the burka in public to letterboxes or bank robbers. Johnson's appalling comments 'led to a surge in anti-Muslim attacks', according to the authoritative monitoring group, Tell Mama. In addition, there was strong evidence that a majority of Tory Party members regarded Islam as 'un-British', as a 'threat to the British way of life'.[53] Tory Islamophobia pointed to the wider problem of racism within politics and UK society. This problem had intensified after the EU referendum, but, at least in terms of public attitudes towards immigrants and multiculturalism, had generally eased off somewhat by the summer of 2018 in the face of reduced immigration.[54]

In contrast to many Leave-voting Conservatives and Labourites, the majority of SNP members and supporters adopted a positive stance towards immigration. In the context of Scotland's ageing population, a shortage of skilled labour and the ruling SNP's unqualified opposition to racism and its equally unequivocal support for the free mobility of labour, immigrants from the EU and elsewhere were warmly welcomed by the Scottish government. The SNP resolutely condemned Islamophobia and xenophobic and predominantly white English nationalism within the Conservative Party.

Sturgeon, however, was wrong in her claim that Jeremy Corbyn's opposition to cheap immigrant labour carried 'echoes' of the racism of Nigel Farage.[55] Corbyn was a lifelong anti-racist. He welcomed immigrants and the contribution they had made and were continuing to make to UK society. At the same time, however, Corbyn, along with the labour movement, condemned cheap competition everywhere in the labour market, including cheap immigrant labour, because it constituted a threat to working-class working conditions and living standards. The crucial point, conveniently by-passed by Sturgeon and the SNP, was that Corbyn viewed cheapness as an economic, class-based phenomenon rather than a racialized one. As such, cheapness and labour-market competition were to be found among all manner of workers, both immigrant and non-immigrant, men and women, Christian, Muslim, agnostic and atheist, British and non-British and so on. Labour would accordingly take measures, such as opposition to exploitative employers and agencies seeking to employ cheap labour and support for increased wages and living standards for all, effectively to tackle the problem of cheapness.[56]

In terms of Brexit, the Remain SNP continued to attack the weaknesses and failures of May, the 'chaos' of her divided party and government and Labour's equivocation and lack of clear direction. The SNP was operating on the assumptions that as the 'shambles' of Brexit unfolded, so would support for the separate but increasingly closely linked causes of the party itself, Remain and Scottish independence, increase.

In this context, the SNP was buoyed by the improved performance of the Scottish economy during the first quarter of 2018, when, in contrast to its historic problem of low growth, it grew at twice the rate of the UK. A poll also showed that for the first time a majority of voters in Scotland believed that they would be better off or have the same level of prosperity under independence.[57]

In January 2018 it was estimated that 68 per cent of people in Scotland were now in favour of Remain, while journalist Nan Spowart reported Sturgeon as declaring that 'Indy must be an option' amid the Brexit 'horror show'.[58] By February the 2017 Tory surge under Davidson was faltering and the SNP had taken a 17-point lead in the polls, according to *Commonspace*. In the same month finance secretary, Derek Mackay, produced a budget committed to a more progressive system of income tax in Scotland. It was designed to make seven out of ten tax payers better off, while increasing the rate for top earners. The government also announced plans to invest more in the NHS and protect public services against continuing Westminster-imposed cuts.[59] These measures and plans were billed by SNPers as highlighting the difference between progressive Scotland under their rule and reactionary, austerity-driven England under the Tories.

The landmark report of the Sustainable Growth Commission, published in May, also sought to persuade voters and the wider public in Scotland, especially the majority who had either voted No or abstained in the 2014 independence referendum, that they had nothing to fear and much to gain in an independent Scotland. The 354-page report, authored by Andrew Wilson, economist, business person, SNPer and former SNP MSP, had been commissioned by the first minister in September 2016 and financed by the SNP. The report declared that only when the Scottish economy had met six stringent tests concerning its overall strength, stability and soundness, would a new currency be adopted. In the meantime, probably for a decade after independence, Scotland would continue to use the pound sterling as its currency, reduce the predicted deficit of around 7 per cent of GDP in a 'sensible' manner to below 3 per cent (in 2017–2018 it had reached the very high figure of 8.1 per cent), 'responsibly' keep public spending at least 1 per cent below the rate of growth and prudently not allow new debt to accumulate above the value of 50 per cent of GDP. At the same time, measures would be taken to improve productivity and growth and provide tax incentives for immigrants. In the brave new independent Scotland, people's incomes, pensions and mortgages would be safeguarded. The fears and anxieties of No voters in 2014 would be put to rest and Scotland's economy would no longer be characterized by its historic problems of low growth and a high deficit.

Widely criticized, particularly by political economists and the left as being far too cautious, orthodox and conservative, Wilson's report, nevertheless, was strongly defended by the SNP leadership and academics such as Michael Fry and Tom Devine. Its critics maintained that it ceded, at least in the initial stages of independence, control to London bankers over Scotland's currency, money supply and interest rates. Lacking its own currency, newly 'independent' Scotland would not be able to issue debt to finance growth. It would also continue to suffer heavily from the negative effects of the economic policies of the Westminster government, particularly around austerity, low growth and Brexit. As political economist and tax expert Richard Murphy concluded, Scotland would remain 'enslaved by the pound and tied to the apron strings of London'. In contrast, its defenders saw Wilson's report as realistic, responsible, pragmatic and intellectually convincing. They argued that if the independence issue was on a knife edge, the report would help to tip 'persuadable' but 'uncertain', 'middle-ground voters' to plump for the 'safe and prudent' option of Yes.[60] At the same time, however, they paid little heed to the views of those predominantly working-class voters in Glasgow, Dundee and other urban areas who had proved so vital to the radical Yes vote in 2014. Around half a million of these voters, however, had lost faith in the radical potential of the SNP by the time of the 2017 general election. As economist, journalist and former SNP MP George Kerevan would observe, these working-class voters wanted an end to austerity, decent, secure jobs and an improved NHS.[61]

The SNP leadership believed, furthermore, that their principled opposition to Westminster's attempted 'power grab', in relation to a number of key issues around the devolution settlement, especially farming and fishing, would further increase support for the party and Scottish independence. Matters came to a spectacular head in the

Westminster parliament in June when no Scottish MP was given time to speak on the withdrawal bill and devolution. (The Scottish parliament had already refused to give its consent to the withdrawal bill.) Only fifteen minutes of the debate at Westminster was devoted to the issue of devolution. To make matters even worse, Tory David Lidington spoke for all fifteen. The SNP's leader in the House, Ian Blackford, declared that it was a 'democratic outrage' that no SNP MPs had been given time to speak on a matter of such direct importance to Scotland and warned that, 'we will not simply sit by while Scotland's voice is scandalously silenced'. There was particular concern in the SNP that Westminster was planning to reserve key powers over issues currently held by the EU to itself, rather than returning them to the devolved parliament at Holyrood. This was an 'unprecedented power grab', an attempt to 'dismantle the . . . devolution settlement', with the Tories arrogantly thinking that they 'can do anything to Scotland and get away with it', according to Blackford and his colleagues. There followed bedlam in the House. After a fierce exchange with the speaker, John Bercow, Blackford was forced to leave the chamber. He was followed, en masse, by his equally outraged and loyal SNP colleagues.[62]

The effects of the 'power grab' incident were significant. According to the Scottish Greens leader Patrick Harvie, it demonstrated that the ruling Tories had torn up the principle of 'devolved consent', while for historian Tom Devine it showed 'contempt' for Scotland and its democratic wishes. Support for Scottish independence, already boosted by Andrew Wilson's report and a highly successful mass Yes march in Glasgow in early May, reached a high point of 48 per cent. For some commentators, a majority in favour of independence was now within 'touching distance'.[63] Membership of the SNP also surged. By June the party had a membership of around 118,000, members, just 6,000 below the membership of the Conservative Party, but well below Labour's total of 552,009.[64]

The key area of debate within the SNP and the wider independence movement now revolved more around the timing rather than the level of support for another independence referendum. The major difference lay between radicals and gradualists. For journalist and former Scottish Socialist Party (SSP) MSP, Carolyn Leckie, and many other activists, the time was now 'perfect' to call Indyref2. Confidence and support were at an all-time high. The longer the delay, the more 'negativity', 'factionalism' and 'fragmentation' would set in.[65] For others, including the majority of party leaders, more patience and persuasion were in order. For example, for Andrew Wilson, 'mainstream Scots' still had to be convinced of the superior virtues of an independent Scotland. Most leaders, including Sturgeon, continued to argue that only when the Brexit fiasco and its disastrous consequences had fully manifested themselves and the fog had cleared, would it be time for another independence vote.[66] Even prominent left-wing supporters of independence from outside the SNP tended towards gradualism. Robin McAlpine, of Commonweal, believed that there was still much preparatory work to be done to make independence a truly hegemonic force among the people of Scotland. McAlpine also pointed out that although support for independence had ranged from 43 per cent to 48 per cent over the past three years, there had been no sign of 'consistent improvement'.[67] Kevin McKenna advised against going too soon in the spring of 2019 or before. McKenna declared that it would be better to wait two years, 'when the full extent of the Brexit apocalypse will be apparent to all' – and life outside the EU would be unthinkable.[68]

The Chequers agreement and its aftermath

Meanwhile, just as the political temperature rose in Scotland, it soared in the UK as a whole around the Chequers agreement reached by May and her cabinet on 6 July. The main purpose of the cabinet meeting, held at the Prime Minister's country residence of Chequers, was to make progress on May's Mansion House speech. The Prime Minister intended to do this by hammering out cabinet agreement on her plans for the shape of the UK's trading relationship with the EU after December 2020.

The omens before the Chequers meeting were not good. Most ominously, there arose divisions in the cabinet over May's reported plan for a post-Brexit customs arrangement under which the UK would levy tariffs on behalf of the EU in order both to avoid the need for a hard border in Ireland and a resort to the Irish backstop. Boris Johnson and other hard Brexiters declared that this plan continued to tie the UK too closely to the EU, that May needed to show more 'guts' on Brexit and that there did exist a preferred technological solution to the Irish border question.[69] In the immediate run-up to the meeting at Chequers there was anger among many cabinet ministers that they were allowed to see the government's 100-page plus document only one day before the marathon Friday meeting. Upon arrival at Chequers, furthermore, all members of the cabinet were required to hand in their mobile phones and were informed that ministerial cars would not be available to transport anyone who resigned the forty plus miles back to London. Rather, the details of local taxi firms were placed in the foyer. May also reminded them of their 'duty' to parliament and the nation to reach agreement. In short, the secrecy, control freakery and high-handedness characteristic of May's period as prime minister surfaced acutely at the Chequers meeting.

At first May's tactics and strategy seemed to have worked. The Prime Minister announced that collective cabinet agreement had been reached on her plan for the future trading relationship. May, furthermore, saw her plan as being 'consistent with the mandate of the referendum' and her general election policy. Her objectives, as in the past, were to negotiate in good faith and accept the necessary compromises of negotiation. The process would involve maintaining the 'deep and special' partnership with the EU, but also gaining the maximum negotiated benefits for the UK.[70]

Under the Chequers agreement, the UK sought to negotiate a comprehensive free-trade and customs agreement with the EU. This involved the maintenance of 'a common rule book' for all goods with the EU, including agricultural products and the continued harmonization with EU rules. The aim was to achieve frictionless trade, although there would be a different arrangement for services. Cases would still be referred to the CJEU concerning the interpretation of EU rules, but the CJEU would no longer be able to resolve disputes between an independent UK and the EU. This would be done in the UK by UK courts and in the EU by EU courts, although decisions by UK courts would involve 'due regard' to EU case law where the UK continued to apply a common rule book. This policy was consistent with May's oft-repeated desire to end the role of the CJEU in the UK and return legal sovereignty to the latter.

The Chequers agreement also sought to agree a 'facilitated customs arrangement' with the EU whereby the UK and the EU would be treated as a 'combined customs territory'. Under this arrangement, the UK would operate a complex 'dual tariff' scheme, applying domestic tariffs and trade policies for goods intended for the UK and charging EU tariffs and their equivalents for goods which would end up in the EU. The idea was that this would avoid the need for a visible border in Ireland and remove the need both for extra border checks and the troublesome backstop. It would also prevent Northern Ireland from being treated differently from the rest of the UK. The latter, of course, was of crucial importance to the DUP.

The agreement, furthermore, declared that once the transitional period had ended, the UK would be free to make independent trade deals and to bring to an end its annual payments to the EU and the free movement of labour. A 'mobility framework', however, would be set up to allow UK citizens to travel, work and study in the EU and vice versa in selected mutually agreed instances. The details of the Chequers agreement were set out in a White Paper published on 12 July. It is important to remind ourselves that the agreement was a statement of intent on the part of the cabinet rather than the product of a negotiated agreement with the EU. The potentially painful business of negotiation still awaited the Prime Minister.[71]

As matters transpired, it also awaited cabinet unity. For, contrary to the Prime Minister's view that unity had been reached, it took only a matter of days for serious differences and divisions to emerge. Most dramatically, David Davis, the Brexit secretary, followed by Boris Johnson, the foreign secretary, backtracked upon their initial support and resigned on 8 and 9 July respectively. They were joined by Steve Baker, Davis's number two, who resigned on the same day as Johnson. Seven more leading Tories left their posts in July in opposition to the Chequers agreement. Davis declared that May was 'giving away too much and too easily' and that the EU would demand even more concessions. For Davis, the agreement signalled that it was now 'less and less likely' that the UK would leave the customs union and the single market, that the common rule book would hand 'large swathes of our economy' to the EU and that parliamentary sovereignty and control over our laws would become illusory. May disagreed with Davis's analysis. The latter, while admitting the 'possibility' to the Prime Minister that 'you are right and I am wrong', nevertheless decided that under the circumstances it made sense to step down and allow someone else, who was wholly committed to the Chequers agreement, to take over as Brexit secretary.[72]

Johnson, Rees-Mogg, Iain Duncan-Smith and the ERG were more outspoken and unforgiving in their rhetoric and claims. In their eyes, the Chequers agreement, quite simply, was a betrayal of May's Lancaster House speech. Adopting a long-term perspective, they saw the agreement as a feeble abandonment of what Johnson defined as Britain's centuries-old 'first-mover' role in terms of the development of industrialization, parliamentary democracy, freedom, progress and national self-determination. May had gone into Chequers 'waving the white flag', according to Johnson and her actions amounted to 'treachery', 'collapse', 'humiliation' and 'surrender'. The agreement reached at Chequers was not Brexit. It was not the 'clean break' the majority of voters in 2016 had demanded. The 'free-born' British 'people' had been denied their birthright, declared Johnson. Under the terms of May's proposed transitional and trading deals, they would become 'vassals', 'abject' rule-takers rather than proactive rule-makers, 'shackled' to the EU and its plans for a federalist European 'superstate'. Under its 'colony' status, the UK, as an 'abject supplicant' (Rees-Mogg), would be denied both the moment of 'national liberation' and 'real democratic control' voted for in 2016 and many of the 'global opportunities' that Brexit was 'intended to release'. As in wartime, declared the hard Brexiters, it would be necessary to rally the freedom-loving British people once again to oppose the 'tyranny' of some European powers, particularly what were seen as the arrogant, overmighty Germans and the untrustworthy French, in order to 'truly take back control of our laws and our lives' (Johnson). May's 'half-in-half-out' Chequers plan constituted the very antithesis of the overriding Leave desire for 'national self-determination', according to Johnson.[73]

As noted earlier, while this right-wing view of Brexit and the UK's past owed far more to myth and fantasy than fact, it, nevertheless, was extremely powerful as a political and social mobilizing force. As former Conservative MP and cabinet minister, Michael Portillo, would later observe in his 2019 TV programme on the Tories and Europe, it owed much to the rhetoric of Margaret Thatcher in her later 1980s turn against the European behemoth and its alleged denial of British sovereignty.[74] To be sure, this view did not command total support in the Conservative Party. After all, the majority of the cabinet stuck with the Chequers agreement despite continuing divisions between and within the Tory Remain and Tory Leave parliamentary and extra-parliamentary camps. 'Soft' Brexiters, such as David Lidington and, at that point in time, Michael Gove, saw the agreement as the best possible option in the circumstances. Like May, they believed that it would bring about Britain's exit from the EU in a 'smooth' and 'orderly' way.[75]

Yet the *overriding* fact was that the Chequers agreement was proving to be an extremely explosive and divisive issue for the Conservative Party. Some Tories even argued that it was better to stay in and enjoy the advantages of continued EU membership than be in the 'fudge' situation created by the Chequers plan. Others agreed with the 'Blue Collar' Conservative MP, Ben Bradley, that the Chequers agreement marked 'the beginning of the end'. Like Boris Johnson, Bradley concluded that the agreement 'bore no resemblance' to May's Leave rhetoric 'of the previous months'. This conclusion led Bradley to resign his position as the Conservative Party's vice chair for youth in July.[76] The Chequers agreement thus constituted a veritable watershed for the Conservative Party and its Brexit policy. Henceforth, May's Brexit problems would only get worse.

Beyond the Conservative Party, the reaction to the Chequers agreement was also mainly critical. For example, Peter Mandelson, one of Tony Blair's closest allies and Britain's former trade commissioner in Brussels, attacked May's 'humiliation'. Like Johnson and many others, Mandelson believed that the 'half-in and half-out' Chequers plan offered only 'the worst of both worlds'. In his opinion, it amounted to loss of sovereignty and control and 'moral and intellectual humiliation' for the UK.[77] In terms of the press reaction, the right-wing *Daily Telegraph* and the *Daily Express* predictably echoed Johnson's and Rees-Mogg's cry of surrender, while, equally predictably, from the centre-left the *Guardian* and *Observer* saw 'inevitable' Tory divisions over Brexit as threatening to constitute a disaster for Britain.[78]

The Labour Party reiterated its position that it would only back the Chequers plan if May was willing to keep Britain in a permanent customs union, protect workers' rights and safeguard supply chains for industry. Corbyn and his colleagues also continued to argue that May was unsuccessfully attempting to manage and resolve probably irreparable divisions within the Conservative Party rather than speak for the nation as a whole. In attempting to appeal to both Remain and Leave voters around its policy of constructive ambiguity and a soft Brexit, Labour claimed to be the only party attempting to bring people together and achieve a national consensus. It is very difficult to evaluate the public response to this claim, mainly because Corbyn and other party leaders failed to get their message across clearly and loudly enough. Many members of the public were, to say the least, not fully aware of the nature of Labour's Brexit policy. Yet there is no doubt that the Chequers agreement and its aftermath did provoke a polling backlash against the Tories and in favour of Labour. In the months prior to the Chequers agreement every poll but one had given the Tories a clear lead over Labour. Following the chaos and divisions around the Chequers plan, Labour forged ahead, while May's 12-point personal lead over Corbyn was halved.[79]

For their part, Nicola Sturgeon and the SNP warned that Tory 'disarray' and 'chaos' threatened to push the UK over the 'cliff edge' of No Deal and in so doing inflict serious economic self-harm. For some, the fall of the pound to a new low against the US dollar and the euro in early August appeared to presage this.[80]

From the other side of the Atlantic, Donald Trump pitched into the Brexit debate in his own inimitable way. Within the space of two days he shifted from seemingly criticizing May's Chequers plan as sounding the death-knell for a successful future trade deal between the UK and the United States, to denying that he had criticized the PM. The latter was 'fake news', according to the mercurial US president.[81]

As we will see in the following pages, in the months following the Chequers agreement, the Prime Minister was far more inclined to side with and attempt either to retain or regain the support of the hard Brexiters in her party rather than to win over Tory Remainers and Tory waverers for her Brexit plan. This was seen as early as mid-July when May accepted hard-line Brexiters' amendments to the customs bill to the effect that Her Majesty's Revenue and Customs (HMRC) could not collect duties or value-added tax (VAT) on goods on behalf of the EU unless there existed a reciprocal obligation on the part of the EU. This was highly unlikely to meet with the agreement of the EU, even if, in the equally unlikely event, the latter accepted in the first place May's Chequers plan for a facilitated customs arrangement. The very next day, the government defeated, by just six votes, a Tory Remainers' proposal that the UK would join a customs union with the EU in the event of there being no agreement on frictionless trade. May was helped by the fact that four Brexit-supporting Labour MPs – Kate Hoey, John Mann, Frank Field and Graham Stringer – and one former Labour MP turned Independent – Kelvin Hopkins – voted with the government.[82]

The success of the Chequers plan, of course, was dependent upon support not only from parliament, but also from the EU. Once again, however, the outcome for May was very disappointing. For example, Michel Barnier responded to the plan by once again declaring that the UK could not 'cherry pick' the single market. It could not enjoy the benefits of the single market on goods and agriculture alone and exclude capital, people and services. May's proposals challenged the EU's sacrosanct principle of the indivisibility of the single market and, as such, the very existence of the EU itself, declared Barnier. He also warned that frictionless trade between the EU and the UK would 'come to an end' after Brexit because they would be separate markets and legal entities. This new situation, furthermore, would impact badly upon British car makers' crucial reliance on interrupted supply chains and 'just-in-time' production methods.

May's proposed facilitated customs proposal was also deemed by Barnier to be unworkable and probably illegal. The EU could not have an outside country collecting customs on its behalf. All sorts of other third countries could insist that the EU offer them the same benefits as the UK, while there would be insufficient controls over fraud, unfair competition and the movement of dangerous goods. In opposition to the view expressed by Boris Johnson, Barnier was adamant that the technology to prevent a hard border simply did not exist at the present time. Contrary to May's wish at Chequers, the backstop, furthermore. would have to stay as the indispensable guarantee that the border in Ireland would continue to be open and the Belfast Agreement on peace in Northern Ireland maintained. Finally, Barnier agreed with May that the UK would be able to make independent trade deals once the transitional period had ended. But this, of course, would be conditional upon the EU and the UK agreeing to a withdrawal agreement. In overall terms, therefore, the response of the EU to the Chequers plan, as expressed by its chief negotiator, Barnier, was overwhelmingly negative.[83]

Matters came to a head at the EU's informal summit in Salzburg, Austria, on 20 September. Fully endorsing Barnier's criticisms, the summit totally rejected the Chequers proposals and afforded May only ten minutes to address the twenty-seven EU leaders. Particular attention was drawn by Angela Merkel, the chancellor of Germany, and other EU leaders to the absolute indivisibility of the single market and the threat posed to it by May's plan. Donald Tusk bluntly declared that May's plan 'does not work' and insisted that unless the UK made progress on the backstop issue before October, the Brexit talks as a whole would collapse. Other leaders took turns to 'rubbish her plan'. So unexpectedly and undiplomatically rebuffed and humiliated, an understandably angry May both demanded more respect from her hosts and retorted that Chequers was the only viable plan on the table and that a Chequers-based deal was still possible. This, however, plainly was not the case.[84]

Meanwhile, further domestic challenges arose for the Prime Minister. At the end of September Boris Johnson wrote an important article in the *Telegraph* setting out 'his vision for an alternative' to what he termed May's ill-fated Chequers plan. Seeking 'the same freedoms and opportunities in its relations with the EU as any other independent and democratic country', the UK should opt for a 'Super Canada' free-trade deal, declared Johnson. This deal had already been 'adumbrated' by the Prime Minister 'in her earlier speeches', including the landmark Lancaster House speech, according to Johnson. What the latter forgot to mention was that, as we noted earlier, May had already ruled out the Canada option in her Mansion House speech. Johnson also underestimated the negative effects of this option upon the open border between Northern Ireland and Ireland. Yet he stuck by his conclusion that the Super Canada option offered the opportunity for 'Global Britain' to 'become more dynamic and more successful'. His argument was shared by David Davis, Rees-Mogg and likeminded colleagues in an open letter to May in the middle of October.[85]

May also faced a reinvigorated Labour Party and a confident SNP. At its conference in Liverpool from 23 to 26 September, and after five hours of debate, the Labour Party decided that it would oppose May's Chequers plan, or 'whatever is left of it', if it did not keep the UK in a customs union and protect workers' and consumers' rights after Brexit. If May's plan, furthermore, failed to get through parliament, Labour would call for a vote of no confidence in the government and a general election. If these actions were not successful, Labour would attempt to keep all options on the table apart from a no-deal Brexit. These options included a confirmatory public vote in a referendum on any proposed deal. In practice, this meant that the options of *both* Leave and Remain would be included in a referendum.

On the plus side, not only Labour Remainers and Leavers, but also the wider Remain and Leave public, would thus be given the opportunity in a public vote to express their views on Brexit. Labour would be seen, in line with its policy of constructive ambiguity, to be maximizing democratic choice, seeking alone among the parties to bring about much-needed national reconciliation over Brexit and, whatever the result, of putting the referendum result into practice. On the negative side, the policy could be seen as too complicated, lacking in conviction, abdicating responsibility and fence sitting. I will return to these issues in Chapter 3 in my discussion of the general election of December 2019. For the moment, however, it is sufficient to highlight the fact that this was a momentous decision. It constituted, along with the party's early 2018 commitment to a permanent customs union, a milestone in the evolution of Labour's Brexit policy. Some prominent Labour leaders, furthermore, including Keir Starmer, immediately voiced their preference for Remain in the event of a second referendum.

In their conference speeches, Corbyn and John McDonnell claimed both that Labour now represented the new political common sense, and that (in the manner of their speeches during the 2017 general election) its policies were the only credible alternative to a broken social system. Along with its Brexit policy, a Labour government would bring about a green revolution, maintain the triple lock on the state pension, invest in the economy and so overturn austerity and promote employee share ownership. A relaxed and confident Corbyn also promised to 'draw a line' under antisemitism after the party finally adopted the full definition of antisemitism as drawn up by the International Holocaust Remembrance Alliance (IHRA). The antisemitism issue had caused 'immense hurt and anxiety in the Jewish community and great dismay in the Labour Party', declared Corbyn. After some initial questioning, he also accepted that the Russian state was responsible for the poisoning of a former Russian military officer and double agent, Sergei Skripal, and his daughter, Yulia, in Salisbury in March 2018. Both Corbyn's and McDonnell's speeches were extremely well received by the delegates. There was also wider agreement that the conference had been very successful. 'United', 'purposeful', 'energized' and even 'Corbyn catches the zeitgeist at a crucial moment for his party', were some of the journalistic responses. The only potentially serious problem was that Chuka Umunna, Chris Leslie and allied Labour Remainers wanted the party to commit itself more strongly to a second referendum and Remain. Their views, however, could not detract from the general verdict that the conference had been a triumph for Corbyn.[86]

The SNP held its conference in Glasgow between 7 and 9 October. It took place against a favourable backcloth. Between 75,000 and 100,000 pro-independence supporters had marched in Edinburgh the day the conference began. This was the largest pro-independence event in Scottish history. It followed other impressive marches in Scotland held during the summer. The SNP's standing continued to be high. The party was 20 points ahead in the polls in Scotland, although support for independence had varied little since 2014 in overall terms. The SNP had also replaced Labour in its traditional stronghold of Glasgow, including Glasgow City Council. Nicola Sturgeon told the faithful at the conference that Indyref2 was 'on the way' and promised more support for health and education. As earlier in 2018, however, the matter of the timing of independence continued to divide opinion within the party. As in the past, the dominant leadership view was to await further clarification over Brexit.[87]

Theresa May: from success to failure, October 2018 to March 2019

How would the beleaguered May respond to the serious setbacks and challenges outlined above? In the immediate to medium term, the Prime Minister adopted an upbeat pose and registered significant successes. These were seen, for example, in the way May repelled the challenge from Boris Johnson during October and, most significantly, in the Withdrawal Agreement and Political Declaration drawn up by the Prime Minister and the EU in November 2018. Success, however, was short lived. By 29 March 2019, the official date of the UK's exit from the EU, an increasingly desperate May had unsuccessfully presented the Withdrawal bill to parliament three times.

October–November

At the Conservative Party conference, held in Birmingham in late September and early October, the Prime Minister once again demonstrated her formidable determination, staying power and her quite remarkable ability to bounce back from adversity. Showing no signs of her mauling at Salzburg, a beaming and seemingly rejuvenated May strode onto the stage to deliver her keynote speech and, swaying her hips, danced to the tune of Abba's 'Dancing Queen'. Her dancing skills, first revealed, at least on a public stage, on her August trip to South Africa and Kenya, met with a mixture of merriment and compliments from the assembled delegates.

In her speech the Prime Minister joked about her travails at the disastrous 2017 Tory conference. This time, a far more relaxed Prime Minister met with a very positive response. Appealing to moderate and decent patriots to pull together around the centre-ground of politics and promote the national interest, May promised to bring austerity to an end. After a decade of suffering, the 'hard work' of the British people had 'paid off' and 'the end is in sight', declared the Prime Minister. The improved state of the public finances would allow the government to lift the cap on local authority borrowing and so enable the latter to build much-needed new social housing. The government would also freeze fuel duty and improve early cancer detection. May's twin goals were to achieve Brexit and build an economy that 'works for everyone in our society'. Her message was directed not only at the Tory faithful, but also those 'moderate' and 'patriotic' Labour voters who had seen their 'once-great-party' go 'wrong' and brought into 'disrepute' by Corbyn, according to the Prime Minister.[88]

In the period immediately following the conference season, the Tories and Labour were level on 39 per cent. The Tories, however, had recovered well from their marked decline in fortunes during the Chequers and Salzburg crises when Labour had gained a 4-point advantage. May's confident performance at the conference had in all probability contributed to the Tory revival. The Prime Minister also remained well ahead of Corbyn in terms of the prime-ministerial popularity stakes and succeeded in seeing off the challenge of Boris Johnson. Twice as many voters at large thought that May, rather than Johnson, was the best person to lead the Conservative Party, while among Tory voters the figure was even higher, standing at 62 per cent for May to only 15 per cent for Johnson. In Scotland. Johnson was particularly unpopular among both the electorate as a whole and many Tory voters.[89]

To be sure, May's successes were by no means unqualified. Philip Hammond's autumn budget at the end of October eased rather than ended austerity. In practice, welfare cuts would continue and low earners gained little or nothing from the chancellor's £3bn income tax cuts. There also arose recurring fears that not only would Brexit be an economic disaster, but also that another global financial crash might soon be on the horizon.[90] Meanwhile, Johnson and likeminded Tory critics continued to voice their total opposition to May's Brexit plan. Johnson's younger brother, Joseph, resigned as transport minister on 9 November. A Remainer, Joseph Johnson claimed that May was offering MPs an awful choice between the 'vassalage' of her proposed deal with the EU and the 'chaos' of No Deal. Johnson resigned in order to campaign for a second referendum. He was supported in his claim that Brexit constituted a 'failure of British statecraft on a scale unseen since the Suez crisis' by none other than his Brexit brother. Boris reportedly called upon the cabinet to stage a 'mutiny' against May's Brexit plan.[91]

November as a whole constituted an extremely taxing month for the Prime Minister and a critical one in the history of Brexit. Despite continuing to insist that her Chequers blueprint remained a viable option, May had moved in the middle of October to address the EU's dismissal of her plan at Salzburg by proposing that in the event of a failure to reach a deal by the end of the transition period, all of the UK, and not solely Northern Ireland, would temporarily remain in the customs union. In effect this new backstop would involve Northern Ireland being much more deeply entwined in both the customs union and aspects of the single market than the rest of the UK. At the same time, however, the implementation of the backstop would both avoid a hard border on the island of Ireland and hopefully meet the DUP's demand that Northern Ireland must not be treated differently from the rest of the UK. The EU, furthermore, signalled a willingness to extend the transition period beyond December 2020, but the UK government replied that this would be unnecessary.[92]

Despite increasingly frantic negotiations, widespread pessimism about the UK meeting the late November EU summit deadline and even more unrest and poisonous exchanges and recriminations within the Conservative Party and beyond, a draft deal between the UK and the EU was unexpectedly agreed on 13 November. Following a six-hour deeply divided and cantankerous emergency cabinet meeting on 14 November – with eighteen members in favour of the deal and eleven opposed – May announced that a favourable 'collective decision' had been taken in the 'national interest'. The Prime Minister continued to believe 'with every fibre of her being that 'the course I have set out is the right one for our country and all our people'. The draft deal was signed off at a special EU summit in Brussels on 25 November. By the end of November, therefore, May, much against the odds, had gained a withdrawal agreement as well as a political declaration on the future trading relationship between the UK and the EU.[93]

In reality the deal, however, came at a very heavy price for the Prime Minister. First, the terms of the deal clearly demonstrated that the views and wishes of the EU had prevailed over those of the UK. Above all, the key aim of May's Chequers plan – to achieve a comprehensive free-trade and customs agreement with the EU – had not been realized. The centre-piece of the plan – a mutual UK–EU commitment to a frictionless future trading system in goods and agri-business through a 'common rule book' – had been successfully rejected by the EU in favour of a relationship based upon an 'easing' of restrictions, 'separate markets' and 'distinct legal orders'. The other key aspect of the Chequers plan – a 'facilitated customs arrangement' and 'dual tariff' system, criticized so roundly by the EU at Salzburg, was also dropped under the deal in favour of the new backstop. The latter, while initiated by May, met the demands of the EU in relation to both the continuation of the open border in Ireland and the integrity of the single market. Contrary to May's wish, the backstop would neither be time-limited nor able to be terminated unilaterally. It also signified that the insistence of Boris Johnson and likeminded Brexiters that a technological solution could be found for the border conundrum in Ireland was simply 'magical thinking'. While in the customs union and the single market during the transition period, the UK, furthermore, would keep up its payments to the EU, be a rule taker rather than a rule maker, not have the right to strike independent free-trade deals around the world and would be obliged to abide by EU rules on state aid, competition, the environment, tax and labour conditions.

The troubled question of fishing rights, including EU access to British waters, furthermore, had, much to the anger of fishing communities in Scotland and elsewhere in the UK, effectively been 'put out into the long grass'. The UK's demand for a bespoke deal on financial services had failed. After Brexit, the UK and its financial sector would be treated like any other country. Instead of 'passports' allowing the City of London to operate across the EU, financiers would rely upon a system of 'equivalence' which allowed Brussels to withdraw market access at thirty days' notice. Finally, the political declaration amounted only to brief and aspirational generalities.[94] In truth, the November deal marked the death of the Chequers agreement and a victory for the EU.

Second, to make matters even worse, there was an overwhelmingly negative reaction to May's deal by parliamentarians, the press and many members of the public at home. Above all, 'fury' among large sections of the Conservative party, and the Right more generally, reached even greater heights. While a few leading Tories such as Michael Gove, Nicky Morgan and other self-styled pragmatists in the party at Westminster were to be found voicing support for May's deal as the best possible way forward, they constituted a 'distinct minority' among their parliamentary colleagues and were vastly outnumbered by Conservatives in the country at large. The massed ranks of Tories echoed Johnson's charges of 'vassalage', 'surrender' and 'sell-out'. They were particularly outraged by the possibility of being indefinitely 'trapped' inside the customs union, accepting rules over which the UK had no say and yet being obliged to continue contributing financially to the EU. The days following the stormy cabinet meeting of 14 November saw the resignations over the deal of seven ministers and senior Conservative MPs. These included the high-profile and potentially very damaging resignations of the then Brexit secretary, Dominic Raab, and the secretary for work and pensions, Esther McVey. Both maintained that May's agreement tied the UK too closely to the EU and, as such, constituted a retreat from her original Brexit agenda. Jacob Rees-Mogg and Boris Johnson accused the Prime Minister of betraying her promises to Leavers, of making a 'historic mistake' (Johnson) and urged her to quit. Rees-Mogg signalled his intention to write to Sir Graham Brady expressing no confidence in May. Another right-wing Conservative, John Redwood, declared that the half-in-half out situation was 'even worse for us than staying in the EU'. Predictably the DUP was angered by the new backstop arrangement. Arlene Foster, Nigel Dodds and other DUP leaders continued to protest that Northern Ireland was effectively being treated differently from the rest of the UK. They sought another deal in which the backstop would be entirely abolished. They were joined by Boris Johnson, who wanted to 'junk the backstop'.[95]

Other political parties and most of the press maintained that May's deal was a 'failed fudge' that further inflamed rather than healed the serious divisions in parliament and the country. For example, from the right, the *Daily Telegraph* declared that May's deal did not satisfy competing domestic interests and seemed acutely to 'displease' most, and perhaps all, of them. May, furthermore, had failed to show 'visionary' leadership and had capitulated to EU demands.[96] From the centre-left, the *Guardian* saw it as a divisive 'economic and political disaster'. May had been more concerned to 'manage the warring factions of the Tory party', albeit unsuccessfully, than represent the interests of the country as a whole, according to the *Guardian*.[97]

The Liberal Democrats, Labour and the SNP all predictably opposed the deal. The Liberal Democrats and the SNP, of course, were firmly pro-Remain, as were the 700,000 people who marched in London on Saturday, 20 October. The marchers formally demanded a 'people's vote' on the final terms of any Brexit deal. Their march was the second largest protest in the UK this century behind the Stop the War demonstration of around 1 million in 2003 against the Blair government's proposed invasion of Iraq.[98] For Labour, Jeremy Corbyn dismissed May's deal as '26 pages of waffle' and the 'blindfold Brexit we all feared'. After two years of 'bungled negotiations', the government had produced a 'botched deal that breaches the prime minister's own red lines' and 'does not meet our six tests', declared Corbyn.[99]

For Nicola Sturgeon, it was a 'bad deal' characterized by 'chaos'. Rather than potentially suffering from competitive disadvantage in terms of access to the single market post-Brexit, Scotland should be afforded the same opportunity as Northern Ireland to stay in the single market, maintained the first minister. In a familiar complaint, Sturgeon and many other SNPers also deplored the fact that Scotland had barely been consulted by May. In their eyes the fact that Scotland was not mentioned once in the withdrawal document and the failure of May to contact Sturgeon before her crucial cabinet meeting typified the UK government's total lack of respect and 'contempt' (Ian Blackford) for the views of the SNP and Scotland's population. The ongoing lack of clarity concerning fishing rights also led to SNP calls for the Conservative secretary of state for Scotland, David Mundell, to resign. As the Tories 'imploded' and treated Scotland with what *National* columnist, Michael Fry, termed 'metropolitan disdain', so did calls for Indyref2 to happen sooner rather than later intensify.[100]

Prominent advocates of a second referendum also increased the volume of their protesting voices. For example, Tony Blair, writing in the *Daily Telegraph*, deplored the 'perpetual purgatory' of doing a 'half-in, half-out' deal – 'Brexit in name only' – and concluded, somewhat arrogantly and, as events proved, incorrectly, that, 'it's elementary, the only way out is a referendum'.[101]

Despite the depth and extent of opposition, May, nevertheless, continued to defend her deal and herself as the 'true' embodiment of 'the people's will'. The Prime Minister urged MPs both to listen to 'the mood of the country', as expressed in the majority Leave verdict of the EU referendum and respect the fact that the EU had signed off on the deal.[102] Yet events had moved on significantly since June 2016. Following the fractious cabinet meeting and Tory resignations of mid-November, Leave supporters appeared to be deserting the government 'in droves', while a mid-November *Opinium* poll for the *Observer* showed that public support for the Tories had dropped from 41 per cent to 36 per cent during the past month. Over the same period, Labour had increased its share from 36 per cent to 39 per cent and so moved into a 3-point lead.[103] According to reliable economic forecasts, moreover, all forms of Brexit, including, of course, May's deal, would make the country significantly worse off than if it remained in the EU.[104] The only consolation for the beleaguered Prime Minister was that she was still ahead of Corbyn, albeit by a reduced margin, as the person best equipped to lead the country.[105]

December 2018–March 2019

By December, it had become obvious that the Prime Minister had very little chance of persuading parliament to back her deal. On 5 December the *Guardian* reported that May 'staggered on' after three Brexit-related defeats in a single day.[106] On the same day the *Daily Telegraph* maintained that May's authority in parliament was 'draining away'. At the end of the week Michael Crick declared on ITV's *Channel Four News* that divisions in the Conservative Party over Brexit were as deep as ever and May's deal inevitably faced a 'big defeat'.[107] The government planned to have a vote on the deal on Tuesday, 11 December, but at the eleventh hour it pulled it in the realization that it had no hope of success. May then declared her intention to go back to the EU to secure 'legally binding assurances' that the backstop would be time limited and that the UK would be able to pull out of it unilaterally. These measures were designed to bring the DUP, the ERG and other hard right-wing Brexiters on board, but this was all outdated and, as matters predictably transpired, totally unrealistic. The EU had no intention of changing the withdrawal agreement and despite its promises that the backstop would be temporary, it simply reiterated its positions that there would be no legally binding assurances and no re-negotiation.

May failed to take note and, once again, carried on regardless. The shambles was widely condemned both inside and outside parliament. The Prime Minister did survive a vote of no confidence, by eighty-three votes, triggered by Tory MPs on 12 December and announced that a meaningful vote on her deal would take place in January.

The vote eventually took place on 15 January. It resulted in a loss to the government by the absolutely staggering margin of 230 votes. This constituted the largest government defeat in parliamentary history. May, nevertheless, survived another vote of no confidence – this time initiated by Labour – by nineteen votes and declared that she would consult with her MPs on other possible ways forward. Gaining heart, the Prime Minister explored plans 'b' and 'c' with Tory Remainers and Brexiters. In essence the new plan(s) was to find an alternative to, rather than modify, the backstop. Brussels, however, would not entertain this latest ploy and the U-turn fell flat.

As the official Brexit withdrawal month of March drew ever closer, the prospect of a successful deal remained as remote as ever. Under pressure from Remain ministers, May carried out another brazen U-turn, this time in agreeing to a vote on the extension of article 50, much to the outrage of Andrea Leadsom and other Brexiter members of her cabinet. Ominously for May, Nigel Farage announced his decision to head a new party, the Brexit Party, in opposition to May's 'surrender' and in support of a 'clean' Brexit. In January around 100,000 people joined Farage's party in its first week of existence. Meanwhile, in February three Tory 'modernizers', Heidi Allen, Anna Soubry and Sarah Wollaston, left the party in protest against it having been taken over by the hard right. By March May had more than confirmed her reputation for a contradictory mixture of steely determination, inflexibility, self-doubt, sudden changes of mind and direction and false, unrealistic thinking and expectations.[108]

From December to March both the Labour Party and the SNP kept up their criticisms of May's deal and her various manoeuvrings and shifts of position. Corbyn continued to argue that Brexit 'chaos' prevailed, that the Prime Minister was failing both to listen to the views of those outside the Right and to make the necessary compromises for a Brexit proposal to command a parliamentary majority. Labour, however, failed to maintain its mid-November lead in the polls and Corbyn's personal poll ratings continued to be dreadful. As Jonathan Freedland of the *Guardian* would declare in October 2019, 'The Labour leader has the lowest poll numbers of any leader of the opposition since records began. His net satisfaction is minus 60, outstripping the previous negative record held since 1982 by Michael Foot.' Even among 18–24-year-old voters, Corbyn continued to be less popular than the deeply unpopular May.[109] Consistently damning polling evidence, however, failed to trigger a leadership bid against Corbyn. Labour MPs doubtless were acutely aware of Corbyn's remarkable ability to 'bounce back', as demonstrated in his successful leadership contests and in the 2017 general election. As time moved on, however, several Labour MPs, members and voters must have been moved to ask, as Freedland did, whether the party under Corbyn would be able to emerge with success from a future general election.

Polling evidence, furthermore, showed that Remain had enjoyed an unbroken national lead over Leave since March 2018, even though, as the authoritative political scientist, John Curtice, concluded, this lead was 'modest'. In so far as it was possible to predict with precision, it stood, in reverse order to the 2016 EU referendum, at 52 per cent for Remain and 48 per cent for Leave. As seen, for example, in the 2018 poll conducted by Ann Coffey, the then Labour MP for Stockport, there was also local evidence that there had been a shift, sometimes significant, among voters from Leave to Remain positions.[110] Yet such evidence failed to convince Corbyn that the party's policy should change from one of constructive ambiguity to unequivocal support for Remain. Labour was obliged to support its Leave as well as Remain voters, according to its leader and Len McCluskey. The Labour Party thus remained consistent in its opposition both to May and to proposed changes in its official Brexit policy. The latter, however, met with growing criticism from Remainers both within and outside the party.[111]

The fragile state of the Labour Party, and the increasingly polarized and fragmented nature of English politics more generally, were reflected in the decision of eight Labour MPs to quit the party and form the Independent Group for Change (also known as Change UK) in February 2019. The members, Mike Gapes, Coffey, Chuka Umunna, Luciana Berger, Chris Leslie, Gavin Shuker, Angela Smith and Joan Ryan saw themselves as a centrist, pro-European, mixed economy and philo-semitic group who had had enough of Corbyn's Brexit, socialist and allegedly antisemitic Labour Party. They saw themselves as moderates and modernizers, much in the manner of their ex-Tory counterparts, Heidi Allen, Anna Soubry and Sarah Wollaston, referred to above, and with whom they would soon make common cause.[112]

A confident, determined and generally united SNP remained firm in its commitments to Remain and Scottish independence. In late 2018 the party urged Labour to trigger a vote of no confidence in the Prime Minister or for the latter simply to resign. Describing the government as a 'laughing stock', Ian Blackford declared that May had 'led the country into a national crisis' with 'not a single word renegotiated and not a single reassurance given' by the EU. It was time, concluded Blackford in December, 'to get on with the vote' and 'move to consider the realistic alternatives'.[113] There was also widespread agreement within the SNP and the wider independence movement that Scotland continued to be treated dismissively, and sometimes with contempt, by May's government.

Debate continued within the SNP about the best time to move towards another independence referendum. As in the past, the more cautious voices of Sturgeon and like-minded colleagues prevailed, although the first minister announced in January that her plan for a second referendum would be confirmed 'in a matter of weeks'.[114] Sturgeon also fully supported the initiative of Angus Robertson, the former SNP deputy leader, and Mark Diffley, who had served as the lead pollster for the UK government in the run-up to the 2014 Scotland referendum, to establish a new organization, Progress Scotland, to find out why older voters had opted for No in 2014 and what could realistically be done to recruit them to the Yes cause in 2019 and beyond.[115]

Towards the end of January, Alex Salmond, the SNP's former leader, appeared in court in Edinburgh on fourteen charges. These comprised nine of sexual assault, two of attempted rape, two of indecent assault and one of breach of the peace. Salmond denied any criminal wrongdoing, while the SNP leadership insisted that the Salmond case, however shocking, upsetting and embarrassing, would not delay the push for independence. Sturgeon defiantly declared that the independence movement was 'bigger than any one man'.[116]

May's fall, March to June 2019

By 29 March 2019 – the official date of the UK's withdrawal from the EU – parliament had still failed to give its majority support to the withdrawal agreement. During the first four weeks of March, parliament had taken three important steps in relation to Brexit. First, it had rejected May's purportedly revised deal with the EU. Second, it had adopted, in the face of government opposition and last-minute whipping, an albeit non-binding commitment to oppose No Deal in all circumstances. Third, and once again in opposition to the government's wishes, it had agreed to an extension of Article 50 concerning the date of the UK's withdrawal from the EU. On 12 March parliament rejected, for the second time, May's deal. This time the margin of defeat was 149 votes. While this did not compare to the staggering 230 votes margin of 15 January, it still constituted a massive defeat for the government. As the *Guardian* columnist Heather Stewart concluded, Mrs May had suffered 'two of the four biggest ever parliamentary defeats in the past 100 years'.[117]

The totally unexpected ruling on 18 March by the speaker of the House of Commons, John Bercow, to refuse May's second deal a third meaningful vote in parliament on the grounds that it offered nothing 'fundamentally different' and that, as such, it would 'break parliamentary conventions', stopped the Prime Minister in her tracks, at least for a few days. Downing Street was forced to concede, for the first time, that a Brexit *crisis* existed. The Prime Minister now had little option but to return to the EU and request both an extension to Article 50 – to create the necessary time to conclude a deal – and presumably, in the light of Bercow's action, the 'substantial changes' to her deal required to submit it to parliament for a third time.

As matters transpired, and in full keeping with the character of the long-running, tragi-comedy of Brexit, nothing, however, could logically be predicted but unpredictability itself. In a letter to the EU, May requested a short extension to the end of June in order, despite Bercow's ruling, to get her deal through parliament at the third attempt. May demanded that parliament make a 'final choice' and settle upon one of three options: her existing deal; no deal; or the revoking of Article 50 and the UK remaining in the EU. The EU, in the person of Donald Tusk, replied to May that the EU would accept an extension to 22 May, rather than the end of June, provided that May's deal was accepted by parliament. Otherwise, the UK would be given until 12 April to both 'indicate a way forward' and agree to hold European elections in May. This would still include the option of May's deal, no deal, a longer extension period and the revoking of Article 50. In sum, 12 April had become the new 29 March. The question of the length of a longer extension period remained 'open'.

A second march in support of a second 'people's vote' took place in London on 23 March. This one involved around 1 million people, the largest demonstration in Britain's history. In addition, there were growing rumours that a number of cabinet ministers wanted May to go immediately, while some 6 million people signed an online petition in favour of Remain. Yet the Prime Minister, who had also infuriated many MPs by blaming parliament for the failure of Brexit in a televised speech to the nation (May subsequently apologized for the tone of her speech) still seemed determined not to listen. She would press ahead with the vote if her deal was likely to command 'sufficient support' and make another attempt to win over the DUP and other hard Brexiters.

Yet, by the end of the last week in March, the Prime Minister once again had failed to realize her goals. Her proposed deal, modified to meet Bercow's requirement of 'substantial change', confined itself to the immediate issue of withdrawal and excluded the political declaration about the future UK–EU relationship. However, it was still defeated, at the third time of presentation, on 29 March, albeit by the substantially reduced margin of fifty-eight voters. This was despite the fact that May's declaration that she would resign after completing the first stage of Brexit had won her the support of her erstwhile enemies, Boris Johnson, Rees-Mogg and some of their likeminded colleagues. They now maintained that May's deal was the best possible option, with no deal possibly off the table. In contrast, the DUP remained steadfast in its opposition to May's deal. Between late March and early April, a range of indicative votes in parliament on a customs union, a second referendum and a common market failed to command majority support, although the motion in favour of a customs union lost by only three votes. Yet, on 3 April, a bill sponsored by Labour's Yvette Cooper and the Conservatives' Oliver Letwin passed parliament by one vote. It forced the government to seek a delay to Brexit with the intention of preventing a No Deal outcome.[118]

Fast running out of options, May desperately and belatedly turned to the Labour Party in early April in the hope of arriving at a cross-party solution to Brexit. This turn predictably outraged the vast majority of Tories. Corbyn accepted the Prime Minister's offer of talks. By early May 2019 discussions between May and Corbyn were still ongoing, although the prospects of success were very slim. May was extremely reluctant to modify or change her 'red lines', particularly her unbending opposition to Labour's key demands for a permanent customs union and a confirmatory public vote on a new deal. Commitment to a customs union ran the totally unacceptable risk, in the eyes of Tory Leavers, of completely tearing apart their party and condemning it to electoral meltdown. By the middle of the month of May, it had become obvious that these differences were simply too great for a successful deal to be struck. May and Corbyn blamed each other for their collapse. Meanwhile, in the course of another desperate trip to Europe in April, May had been offered a further extension – to 31 October 2019 – in the hope that Britain would finally get a deal through parliament. In accepting this offer, the Prime Minister went back on her previous insistence that she would not accept an extension beyond 30 June.[119]

The Prime Minister's fall was now imminent. During the week beginning Monday 20 May, the Prime Minister caused uproar among Conservatives, both inside and outside parliament, by announcing that she had come up with a ten-point, 'new deal' compromise, supposedly agreed at a cabinet meeting. This included a temporary customs union, a public vote on her new proposed deal and a pledge that existing EU workers' rights and environmental protection would not worsen as a result of her deal. The intention was to present the deal, in the form of a fourth withdrawal bill, to parliament during the first week of June. Labour hopefully would be brought on board as a result of May's concessions.

Yet her hopes were quickly dashed. Jeremy Corbyn dismissed the Prime Minister's new offer as 'not enough', all 'ifs and buts' and in essence 'a repackaged version of the same old deal'. The vast majority of Tories were appalled. In their eyes May had 'betrayed' Brexit by offering a totally unacceptable second referendum and a customs union. The cabinet was in revolt, with some members claiming that in fact they had not agreed to May's proposals. Andrea Leadsom resigned from the cabinet and declared that she would launch a leadership bid. The DUP saw May's proposal as a 'hodge podge'. In terms of parliament as a whole, May's deal was immediately rejected by a wide range of MPs. It failed to please most and obviously stood no chance of being put to a fourth vote in parliament.

Patience had finally snapped. As the *Daily Telegraph* reported, 'furious' Tories were demanding May's head, while the Prime Minister was 'besieged' inside No. 10. For the *Daily Mail* it was the 'end of the Road'. As noted in the Introduction to this chapter, following her meeting with Sir Graham Brady, and despite her continuing denials to the contrary, the Prime Minister had no alternative but to resign. This tearful denouement took place on Friday 24 May. The future would now lie in the hands of another Tory leader.[120]

May: an assessment

Despite her strong sense of public duty and her impressive determination and resilience, often in the face of great odds, the fallen Prime Minister does not readily command much sympathy, support or praise. Above all, as I have emphasized throughout, May had committed the fundamental mistake of intransigently laying down her narrow and inflexible 'red lines' on Brexit from the very start of her premiership. These greatly limited her options, especially her ability to build bridges between Leavers and Remainers, both inside and outside parliament, and to compromise in order to achieve a negotiated outcome broadly acceptable to people with different views on Brexit. This admittedly would have been a very difficult task to achieve. Some might argue that it was impossible, in view of the breadth and depth of divisions within and outside parliament around Brexit, the extreme reluctance of most interested parties to put aside their narrow sectional interests in favour of arriving at a broad consensus and the EU's insistence upon playing strictly by the rules. I, however, maintain that the largely uncompromising May could have put far more effort into trying to bring it about.

A prime minister representing the interests of the whole country rather than solely the sectional interests of the Leave part of it, might also have been reasonably expected to adopt a more understanding, inclusive, tolerant and comprehensive view of the matters under discussion and the perspectives of all the key players represented and directly involved in the Brexit negotiations. Instead, May's approach and practice for the most part were narrowly partisan of the party-political kind, stubborn, secretive, exclusive, inflexible and often resistant to and dismissive of attempts to modify or change 'her deal'. In practice, of course, faced with insurmountable opposition to her plans and an adverse balance of power, May was repeatedly forced to retreat from her initially hard-line bargaining stance. Contrary to her advice to her successor – to compromise in order to reach a consensus – May sought compromises with forces outside her own party only when other options were very limited or had been exhausted. In this context her late, desperate, appeal to Labour was more or less bound to fail. For the most part she wilfully sought to plough on in the same way and to present to parliament fundamentally the same deal time and again, even though it had been previously defeated and stood little or no chance of future success.

This revealed her unproductive stubbornness, lack of flexibility and very limited vision and tactical and strategic awareness. A staggering total of forty-nine resignations blighted her government – a sure sign of her failure to take people along with her. In truth, May lacked the ability skilfully to identify in advance and think and navigate her way around, admittedly very difficult, problems and obstacles in order successfully to achieve her desired objectives. On far too many occasions she was simply the prisoner of events, processes and structures. These were seemingly way beyond her control and influence or agency. Up to her resignation and the very end of her time as prime minister, May's lack of awareness and her false consciousness about her own weaknesses – for example, her own intransigence, 'absolutism' and pinning the blame for her Brexit failure upon parliament – were both striking and alarming. Days before her demise, May refused to resign, even though there was common agreement among politicians and across the press that her fall was inevitable. May was fatally short-sighted and self-interested. Despite her claims and protestations to the contrary, the overwhelming mass of evidence strongly lends itself to the conclusion that, as prime minister, she was far more interested in her own power, control and legacy than the national interest and was a prisoner of her own mainly unrealistic and false rhetoric.[121]

In short, May miserably failed Australian journalist Laura Tingle's leadership test of 'building a consensus for change, giving people a map to follow and bringing together different parties to achieve an outcome'. Rather than adhere to this liberal and consensual view of leadership, May had sought, much in the manner of other 'macho' political leaders across the globe, to be autocratic, intransigent, secretive and highly divisive.[122] As the *Guardian* maintained, in the process May had lost many actual and potential allies at home and abroad and moved from being 'a bad prime minister to a rogue one' who was in important respects 'in flagrant defiance of parliament'. By March 2019 her political capital was 'all spent'. Some 90 per cent of Britons saw Brexit as a national humiliation'.[123] There also developed the widespread perception overseas that the once mighty UK was falling apart and had completely lost its ability to lead and set an example. Rather it had become an embarrassment, a 'global laughing stock'.[124] The incontrovertible fact and sense of political and societal crisis had become both more widespread and acute.

The European elections, consequences and responses

Meanwhile, the European elections, dreaded by Conservatives, had taken place on Thursday, 23 May, the day before the Prime Minister's resignation. The results were known by Sunday in England, Wales and Scotland and on Monday in Northern Ireland. As in the local elections of early May, when the Tories had experienced their worst election results since 1995, losing 1,334 seats and 44 councils,[125] the European elections, as noted at the beginning of this chapter, constituted a catastrophe for the Conservative Party. Many regular Tory voters joined some Tory leaders, the most prominent being the grandee, Ann Widdecombe, a 'conviction' politician, in voicing their great disappointment at May's failure to leave the EU and voting for the Brexit Party on 23 May.[126] As expected, the Brexit Party won a resounding victory in the European elections, while there was a significant improvement in the fortunes of the Liberal Democrats, Greens and other pro-Remain parties. Labour, which had suffered at the local elections, losing eighty-two seats and six councils, also fared very badly on 23 May. In marked contrast, the SNP registered a historic victory in Scotland, while the non-sectarian, centrist and liberal pro-Remain Alliance Party of Northern Ireland, performed impressively.

The Brexit Party topped the European elections almost everywhere in England and Wales. In Britain as a whole it won twenty-nine seats and 31.6 per cent of the vote on a low overall turnout of 37 per cent. The unequivocally pro-Remain Liberal Democrats enjoyed a resurgence, coming second, with sixteen seats and 20.3 per cent of the vote. Labour came a very disappointing third, with ten seats and 14.1 per cent of the vote. The Greens were fourth, with seven seats and 12.1 per cent, and the Conservatives a miserable fifth on seven seats and 9.1 per cent. In Northern Ireland, with a higher turnout of 45 per cent, three MEPs, all women, were elected under the single transferable vote system, one each from the DUP, Sinn Fein and the Alliance Party. Most significantly, the Alliance Party, seeking to appeal to moderates across all parts of the community, surged and won a seat for the first time. In Wales Farage's party was dominant, with 32.5 per cent of the vote and two of the country's four MEPs. Plaid Cymru came second, with 19.6 per cent and one MEP. Labour had narrowly won, with UKIP surprisingly second, in the 2014 European elections in Wales. This time, however, Labour was beaten into a poor third place, recording only one seat and 15.3 per cent of the vote. Labour only narrowly beat the Liberal Democrats. The Conservatives finished fifth in Wales, with a miserly 6.5 per cent of the vote.

Scotland represented an unqualified triumph for the SNP and an unmitigated disaster for Labour. The SNP achieved its best ever European election result, with 37.7 per cent of the vote and three of the country's six MEPs. The Brexit Party came second, with almost 15 per cent of the vote and one MEP, while the Liberal Democrats finished third, with 13.9 per cent and also one MEP. The Tories were fourth, with only 11.6 per cent of the vote, but the remaining MEP. Labour in Scotland both lost its single MEP and finished fifth, with a catastrophic 9.3 per cent of the vote. The Greens, in sixth place, underperformed on 8.2 per cent. Finally, the polls now predicted a Brexit Party victory in the event of a general election.[127]

The Tories, Labour and the SNP responded to May's fall and the election results in their distinctive ways. The Tories started the process of holding a leadership election and attempted to revive their ailing fortunes by confronting the serious threat of Farage and the possibilities of a general election and Jeremy Corbyn's entry to Downing Street. Boris Johnson immediately emerged as the clear favourite and declared his intentions to leave the EU, with or without a deal by 31 October, promote balanced regional regeneration, cut taxes for the better off and bring the country together.[128]

Labour was forced by its poor election results to re-examine its 'soft Brexit' policy of support for a permanent customs union, close alignment with the single market and managed migration. Serious question marks had arisen, both during the elections and more generally, around the continued viability and wisdom of Labour's policy. For example, psephologists produced conclusive evidence to show that the public had definitely moved in a pro-EU direction since 2016, even though this movement had taken place largely among those who had not voted in the 2016 referendum, either because they abstained or because they were too young to vote. Conversely, among those who had voted, there was little or no evidence of a change of heart. Yet, as Polly Toynbee observed, between June 2018 and June 2019 there was 'an eight-point lead for remain among all polls'. Many argued that this lead would increase further as the full economic and social perils, indeed catastrophe, of Brexit, and especially a No Deal Brexit, more fully entered public consciousness. There also existed the fact, as demonstrated in the indicative vote in parliament, that Labour had not been able to win a parliamentary majority for its soft Brexit option. This would probably remain the case for the rest of the year because the new Tory leader's and government's attempt to leave the EU would dominate the political agenda up to 31 October, and probably beyond. As of June 2019, the prospects of a general election, a Labour victory and a Labour attempt to negotiate a soft Brexit deal with the EU were all highly speculative.

There was, moreover, absolutely no doubt that the vast majority of Labour's members and voters supported Remain. The most recent polls also showed that far more Labour Remainers than Leavers would be likely to desert the party in the event of its adoption of a soft Brexit policy at a general election. Labour was, furthermore, seriously alarmed by the flight of Labour supporters to the Liberal Democrats, the Brexit Party and less so the Greens in the May elections. During the latter, many voters had bemoaned Labour's lack of clarity and indecision on Brexit. Some also condemned the fact that a high-profile Labourite, journalist Alastair Campbell, Tony Blair's former spokesperson and campaign director, had been expelled from the party for admitting publicly that he had voted for the Liberal Democrats at the European elections. The parliamentary defeat on 12 June, by eleven votes, of the Labour-led cross-party attempt to prevent No Deal, furthermore, increased the likelihood of a no-deal outcome on 31 October especially if, as expected, Boris Johnson were to become the next Tory leader and prime minister. To cap it all, Farage's spectacular resurgence was further evidence that British politics and society were becoming even more polarized and that right-wing populism was once again on an upward trajectory.[129]

In the eyes of many Labour members, their party's policy of constructive ambiguity made little or no tactical or strategic sense in such a perilous and divided situation in which Labour potentially faced a further serious loss of support. This viewpoint was strongly expressed by Corbyn's deputy, Tom Watson, ably supported by Keir Starmer and Emily Thornberry. They argued that their party should move immediately to support a second referendum and Remain. Otherwise, by sitting on the fence, it would continue to lose support to both the unambiguously Remain and Leave parties, face almost certain defeat in a general election and see the country drift even further to the right.

Corbyn promised to consider their views. Yet he continued to argue in June that, while any proposed deal should be subject to a public vote, the party should not, as matters stood, commit itself unequivocally to Remain. A major concern for Corbyn and his likeminded Labour colleagues was the fact that the majority of Labour's target and defensive seats were in Leave constituencies in the Midlands and the North of England. Yet political scientist Robert Ford, and his colleagues at the University of Manchester, produced conclusive evidence to show that Remain voters had outnumbered Leave voters among the Labour vote in almost every one of these Leave constituencies at the general election of 2017.

Corbyn's critics warned that he was being too cautious, that party morale was very low, that it would soon be too late to revive Labour's flagging fortunes and that the electoral consequences would be dire. This warning was belatedly taken on board by the leader of Scottish Labour, Richard Leonard. In the wake of Labour's dreadful performance in Scotland at the European elections and grassroots anger that their party had once again become the 'branch office' of Labour south of the border, Leonard declared that henceforward he would openly back a second EU referendum and would vote Remain. How would Corbyn respond to these loud and popular calls for himself and his party to get off the fence? Following Labour's unexpected, if narrow, victory at the Peterborough byelection on 6 June, would he agree to change course? These key questions and related issues will be fully addressed in the next chapter.[130]

In marked contrast to Labour, the SNP was greatly encouraged by its recent experiences. For example, the party's conference of late April had been a success. To be sure, a majority of delegates voted for an amendment in favour of the introduction of a new Scottish currency 'as soon as practicable' after Scottish independence. This was in defiance of the leadership's desire, based on the recommendations of Wilson's Sustainable Growth Commission, for a more cautious approach and a longer period of change to the currency. Yet the vote was interpreted as a modification to, rather than a complete rejection of, the Commission's overall currency plan. The latter passed by fifty-two votes and Wilson himself welcomed, at least publicly, the modification. Sturgeon, as usual, made an effective and rousing conference speech in favour of social justice, fairness and urgent attention to the 'climate emergency'. Following the conference, a very impressive 'All Under One Banner' pro-independence march of around 100,000 people was held in Glasgow at the beginning of May. This was the first of several independence marches planned for the summer months. There was, furthermore, clear and indisputable evidence that support for independence was on the rise. At the time of the SNP's conference, it had risen to 49 per cent, according to the most recent YouGov poll. This was the highest percentage point reached during the past four years. As John Curtice remarked, 'the pursuit of Brexit might yet produce a majority for independence'. Scotland as a whole, moreover, had become even more Europhile since 2016.[131] Some commentators, most notably Kevin McKenna, continued to criticize the SNP's 'patchy record' on health care, education and the stated pursuit of equality. In general, however, most observers regarded the SNP's record and aims more favourably.[132]

Upon May's resignation, and faced with the 'utterly horrifying' prospect, to quote Ian Blackford, of Johnson succeeding May, Sturgeon immediately renewed calls for Indyref2 and set in place plans to fast-track the necessary preparatory legislation in order to hold a new vote in 2020. In the eyes of the SNP, May had 'completely ignored' the democratic wish of the majority of voters in Scotland by seeking to force her Brexit plan upon them. Her legacy would not be to protect and strengthen the Union, but to hasten the day of independence in Scotland. Johnson's even higher level of unpopularity in Scotland would not only accelerate the process of national liberation and social progress, but also probably destroy the Conservative Party north of the border, according to the SNP.[133]

Conclusion

This chapter has provided a detailed account of the Brexit crisis from 2018 up to the summer of 2019. It has highlighted the complex, tortuous and unpredictable nature of the negotiations between the UK and the EU and, above all, the disastrous failure of Theresa May to gain a parliamentary majority for her proposed deal with the EU. The Brexit crisis exposed, even more acutely, the Conservative Party's longstanding and profound divisions and conflicts over Europe. The fall of May suggested to many observers that the Conservative Party was on the verge of being as completely torn apart over Brexit as it had been long ago in 1846 over the Repeal of the Corn Laws. By the summer of 2019, it had also become apparent that right-wing populism, in the form of Nigel Farage's Brexit Party, was in the political ascendancy. It had won the European elections in May and many saw it as the favourite to win the next general election. The Labour Party was also deeply split over Brexit. While the party had managed to gain a poll lead over the hapless May by November 2018, it failed to maintain it and Corbyn was proving to be the most unpopular leader of the opposition since polls began. By the summer of 2019, moreover, Labour, like the Tories, had performed very badly at the European elections and there was a growing feeling that the former's policy of constructive ambiguity amounted to ineffectually sitting on the fence. The policy was increasingly perceived to be too complicated, too unclear and failing sufficiently to appeal to either committed Leavers or Remainers. In contrast, the SNP and the cause of independence had rediscovered much of their strength and promise.

Brexit, the fall of May and the outcome of the European elections further illustrated the highly fragmented and deeply polarized nature of politics and society in the UK as a whole. There appeared to be little chance that not only Brexit, but also the wider societal crisis, of which Brexit was a part, would be resolved in the immediate future. This combined, and ongoing, crisis of austerity, conflict, fragmentation and legitimacy, suggested that the UK had reached an impasse or an interregnum, to use the Gramscian term, in which 'a great variety of morbid symptoms', had indeed appeared. The key questions facing the UK as a result of May's resignation were twofold. First, what did the future hold? Second, how would the deadlock be broken, if at all? Some commentators on the left, most prominently journalist Owen Jones, maintained that, 'out of May's calamity' and another general election, a new fairer and more progressive society might well emerge and even become dominant.[134] Yet this was very much a minority view. For many other political commentators, it was far more likely that it would be May's most likely successor, Boris Johnson, who would attempt both to break the Brexit deadlock and refashion society and the crisis far more in old than new ways. It is to an examination of the fascinating, unpredictable and highly volatile manner in which the crisis unfolded between the summer of 2019 and 2021 that I turn in Chapter 3.

The Triumphs, Trials and Troubles of Boris Johnson, 2019–2021

Introduction

On 23 July 2019 Boris Johnson won the election to become the new Conservative Party leader. He had received almost twice as many votes from the party's membership, 92,153 to 46,656, as his nearest challenger, the secretary of state for foreign and commonwealth affairs, Jeremy Hunt. The following day Johnson became the new prime minister. Despite several setbacks and defeats, Johnson, closely advised by his senior aides and Leave colleagues, Dominic Cummings and Lee Cain, had come to enjoy spectacular triumphs by the end of his first six months in office. Above all, unlike his unfortunate predecessor, Theresa May, and true to his promises, he had ended the paralysis of Brexit and brought about the UK's withdrawal from the EU, on 31 January 2020. He had also heavily defeated Jeremy Corbyn and his other opponents at the December 2019 general election and put Nigel Farage 'back in his box'. He, furthermore, had purged the Conservative Party and transformed it from being a minority party at Westminster and one deeply divided over Brexit, to one both enjoying a massive eighty-seat majority as a result of the general election and wholly committed to a 'clean' Brexit. On a personal level, he had not only experienced in the short space of a few months many of the key stresses of modern life – divorce, engagement, the prospect of becoming the father of another child, moving house and a new job – but also seemed to thrive, like his hero Winston Churchill, on the challenges of everyday life. By February 2020 the future, indeed, looked rosy for the Prime Minister and his government. Johnson had gained a widespread reputation in much of England for being an upbeat, bold, resolute, decisive, ruthless and successful, if somewhat quirky, prime minister who, unlike the hapless May, knew how to win.[1]

Yet, unlike the first six months, the second stage of Johnson's premiership – from the end of February 2020 to January 2021 – proved, with only minor exceptions, to be one of growing trials, troubles and tribulations. The government, above all else, was charged with the formidable task of addressing major health and economic crises. For it was during these eleven months, and beyond, that the coronavirus pandemic took its dreadful grip and toll on the health and economy of the UK and many other countries across the world.

There is no doubt that, whatever its political persuasion, any government would have been hard pressed both to suppress the pandemic and its awful consequences in the UK and subsequently promote national recovery. This chapter argues, however, that the Prime Minister and his colleagues were not up to the task. It endorses the views that Johnson's spoken and policy responses to Covid-19 were mainly incompetent, indecisive, negligent, badly timed and unclear and that they resulted in many unnecessary deaths. By January 2021 the officially projected 'good' total of 20,000 Covid deaths had reached the totally unexpected and unacceptable figure of over 100,000. Just before Easter 2021, there were over 4 million cases of infection and in excess of 127,000 deaths from Covid in the UK. While the Prime Minister expressed regrets about the extremely high death toll, he did not accept that his government was in any way responsible for it.

As matters transpired, the overall situation for Johnson and his government, however, did improve. Despite the catastrophe of Covid-19, the government, albeit at the last minute, had managed to agree a free-trade, no tariffs and no quotas deal with the EU on Christmas Eve 2020. The government did expect some 'teething problems' in the early stages of the deal, but it failed to anticipate the size, extent and persistence of the problems concerning customs checks, controls and added costs to trade. At the same time, however, and notwithstanding the facts that the economic damage to the UK economy from the pandemic 'far outstripped' that done by the 2008 financial crisis and that it destroyed 'a decade and a half of growth', there was a growing view among economists that, if 'things go well, all the ground lost in 2020 will be made up by 2022'. By mid-February 2021, furthermore, the target of offering anti-Covid vaccines to all the people in the UK aged seventy and over had been successfully realized.

The government lauded the vaccination programme as a great success story for itself, even though it had largely been organized and carried out by the NHS. Johnson and his colleagues also loudly criticized the EU for its tardy roll-out of vaccines and its plan to hinder exports of the AstraZeneca vaccine to the UK. The successful vaccine roll-out in the UK resulted in Johnson moving into a commanding poll lead over his main rival, Keir Starmer. During March the Prime Minister offered further hope to the longsuffering population by producing a roadmap out of the pandemic. The expectation was that all adults would have been offered the vaccine and that life would be returning to something approaching normality by the summer of 2021.[2] The future once again looked rosy for this seemingly most resilient of prime ministers.

This chapter provides the reader with an account and analysis of the developments outlined above, with particular reference to Johnson's rollercoaster political fortunes. The chapter concludes by suggesting that by May 2021, the time at which I completed the writing, the Prime Minister's somewhat eclectic brand of Conservatism seemed to many to offer the most likely way out of the worst combined crisis of UK capitalism in living memory.

From July 2019 to March 2020

Assumptions

In his victory speech of July 2019, and at many points both before and since, Boris Johnson outlined the key personal and philosophical assumptions and guiding principles which fundamentally informed his political beliefs and actions. It is important briefly to convey to the reader a sense of these because they underpin many of his actions during the period under review. At the same time, however, they were qualified or even changed, at least temporarily, by the unexpected sequence and consequences of events. Three underpinnings may be highlighted as being of crucial importance.

First, in the conscious manner of the woman he saw as the greatest of post-war prime ministers, Margaret Thatcher, Johnson adopted a 'can do' approach which sought to 'turn the country around'. In Johnson's view, just as Thatcher had reversed the chronic and fundamental weaknesses and troubles of the UK during the 1970s – of, for example, debilitating industrial and class conflicts, economic decline and excessive state intervention – so would he, as the new upbeat and optimistic prime minister, cast aside the doom and gloom of recent years and bring Britain a bright new future as a recharged and dynamic global power. As in the 1980s, costs would be involved, but, in the Prime Minister's view, these would be greatly outweighed by benefits. In his victory speech, he declared that 'We are going to energise the country' and 'get Brexit done' by the set date of 31 October. 'Once again,' he declaimed, we are 'going to believe in ourselves, and like some slumbering giant we are going to rise and ping off the guy ropes of self-doubt and negativity.' The contrast with the doubts and pessimism of the May years was palpable.[3]

Second, like his greatest hero, Winston Churchill, during World War II, Johnson was adamant that he was prepared to have the courage, to 'stand alone', for what he believed to be the right and proper course for the UK as a whole. In so doing he would, in his opinion, be following in the footsteps of both Churchill, who had defied the doubters, appeasers and 'cowards' around him to fight Nazi tyranny head-on, and Thatcher, who had taken on and crushed militant trade unionism and other forms of collectivist 'dictatorship'. Above all, Johnson saw himself as the 'true' embodiment of the 'people's will' in the sense that he would carry out the democratic wish of the majority, as expressed in the 2016 referendum, to bring about Brexit and to regain sovereignty or 'control' for the UK.

There, of course, were parallels and continuities with May in these sentiments. Johnson's rhetoric, however, was far more high-blown and his determination seemingly greater. For example, he declared that the 'liberated' UK would no longer be a 'vassal' of the EU behemoth. And despite potential setbacks, doubters and opponents alike would be taken on and defeated. There would be no 'surrender'. Significantly, Johnson also bestowed the new title of Minister for the Union upon himself. This was to signify his unqualified commitment and leadership of the United Kingdom as a whole and his determination to make the Union even more 'mighty' in the face of the 'divisive' threat to it from within Scotland and to a much lesser extent Wales and Northern Ireland.[4]

Third, Johnson saw and justified his Brexit policy and his wider, Churchillian- and Thatcherite-inspired system of politics and philosophy as integral parts of the UK's long history of the advocacy and resolute defence of *liberty* against 'tyranny'. Whether in fighting the 'Norman Yoke', the Spanish Armada, the French Revolution or the 'tyrannical' global ambitions of the nineteenth-century Papacy and twentieth-century Nazi Germany, Soviet Communism and their allies and 'dupes' at home and abroad, the

United Kingdom had been in the forefront of the long and continuing struggles for *individual* freedom and liberty, according to Johnson. Socialism in Britain, while more democratic than many variants abroad, was also anathema to Johnson because of its alleged 'communistic' levelling-down agenda, its glorification of the state and its opposition to the wealth-creating private sector and individual enterprise, freedom and liberty.

To be sure, Johnson was critical of unrestrained capitalism in which rampant individualism and gross inequality prevailed. His stated commitment to One-Nation Conservatism, complete with an important place for community, philanthropy and a 'reasonable' level of taxation, however, was perfectly consistent with his fundamental and enduring beliefs that Marxism and socialism were 'dead' and that the 'free-market economy' was 'the only show in town'. For the Prime Minister, the course of events since the 2007–2008 financial crash had confirmed rather than negated or qualified these beliefs. In Johnson's eyes, it was the private sector, rather than the public sector, or even a mixture of the two, that was the true generator of wealth, economic growth and individual independence and freedom of choice.

As we will see below, Johnson's decisions massively to increase state intervention in the economy and to enforce lockdowns of normal life during the coronavirus pandemic, did not signify a fundamental philosophical conversion to either Keynesianism or collectivism. Rather they marked a pragmatic and temporary response to the immediate and formidable economic and public-health crises generated by the pandemic. Once Covid had been controlled and suppressed, the 'free market' and 'normal' individual liberties of 'free-born' English people and Britons – the 'inalienable' rights to 'go to the pub' and to resist excessive state interference in their lives – would be restored, according to Johnson.[5]

Setbacks, defeats and triumphs

In moving to a summary of the course of relevant events between July 2019 and January 2020, it is first of all important to register the fact that up to November 2019 Johnson's overriding goal – to 'Get Brexit Done' and so 'restore control' – was mainly characterized by setbacks and significant defeats. Only towards the end of the year and in January would he achieve his major triumphs.

When parliament reconvened in early September 2019, after its summer recess, Johnson quickly revealed his determination to succeed where May had failed. He filled his cabinet with ardent Brexiters and did not hesitate to have the whip withdrawn from twenty-one Conservative MPs who voted to have No Deal removed from the negotiating table with the EU. These MPS included the former cabinet ministers Philip Hammond and David Gauke, and the parliamentary veteran of forty-nine years and leading pro-EU figure of Kenneth Clarke. Despite pleas from the Prime Minister not to rebel against the government, these twenty-one high-profile Conservatives voted in favour of the 'Benn Bill'. Co-sponsored by the Labour MP, Hilary Benn, this bill sought to outlaw a No Deal Brexit, unless parliament consented to it, before the EU deadline withdrawal date of 31 October. On 4 September the Benn Bill passed the House of

Commons with a majority of twenty-nine and the government abandoned its plan to attempt to block it in the House of Lords. It became law five days later. This constituted a significant defeat for the government. Johnson's preference was to strike a new deal with the EU, but have a strong No Deal card in reserve. The Prime Minister and his advisors speculated that the EU might well make concessions when faced with the UK's threat to 'walk away'. The potentially crucial No Deal card, however, had now been removed from the high-stakes negotiating table.[6]

The effective sacking of the Tory rebels, furthermore, meant that the government was in a very weak voting and bargaining position in the Commons. On 3 September it had lost its working majority of one when Conservative Philip Lee crossed the floor to join the Liberal Democrats. The situation was made worse within a matter of days with two high-profile resignations. First, Jo Johnson, Boris's younger brother, resigned his recently accepted post as a business minister and announced his intention to stand down as an MP. The younger Johnson explained his actions in terms of the 'unresolvable tension' facing him between the 'national interest' and 'family loyalty'. He was critical of Boris's Brexit strategy and supported a second vote on the EU with Remain as an option on the ballot. Second, Amber Rudd resigned her position as work and pensions secretary and accused Boris Johnson and his advisors of an act of 'political vandalism' in purging 'loyal, moderate MPs'. There was speculation in some political circles that the government might 'implode'.[7]

These particular reverses, moreover, were part of a uniformly depressing month for the government. During September it suffered seven successive parliamentary defeats over Brexit matters and three parliamentary rejections of its call for a general election to settle Brexit once and for all. Johnson's most brazen and notorious act – his proroguing of parliament on 9 September for five weeks in order to by-pass its opposition to No Deal and ensure that the UK left the EU by 31 October – resulted in total failure. Johnson had received the Queen's agreement in late August to suspend parliament for five weeks in September and October. The Prime Minister, however, had typically been economical with the truth in maintaining that prorogation would allow the government space to carry out the standard practice of establishing and setting out its agenda for the new parliamentary session. In reality, however, there was general agreement that Johnson would use the allotted time to muzzle parliament and advance his Brexit plans, even as he continued to insist that the prorogation had nothing to do with Brexit. In any event the Supreme Court unanimously ruled on 24 September that Johnson's action was illegal. This brought to an end Johnson's ruse. The sorry episode did nothing to diminish his widespread and longstanding reputation for dishonesty, deviousness and effrontery.[8]

Yet the Prime Minister, much in the manner of the obstinate May, remained undeterred and unrepentant. On 5 September, the day when his brother resigned, Johnson famously declared in the course of politicizing a speech to police recruits in Yorkshire, that he would rather be 'dead in a ditch' than seek another delay to Brexit. To do so, in the eyes of the Prime Minister, would be to equivocate in the manner of May and run directly counter to his 'Churchillian' stance of 'no surrender'.[9] At the Conservative Party conference, in Manchester, at the end of September and beginning of October, Johnson reiterated his familiar mantra of 'let's get Brexit done on October 31' and his criticisms of all those who 'simply don't want Brexit delivered at all' and who were taking as 'fools' all those who had voted Leave.[10]

The withdrawal agreement with the EU

Faced with continued parliamentary opposition to both his Brexit plans and a general election, the Prime Minister, however, had to think and act quickly and imaginatively. Johnson's aim was to formulate and agree a deal with the EU and to secure parliamentary approval in time to meet the 31 October deadline. To his credit, and much against the odds, he successfully negotiated a deal.

On 17 October Johnson and the EU announced that they had reached a new withdrawal agreement and a (non-binding) political declaration. In practice, the principle of compromise, however much equated with surrender by Johnson, proved to be the only viable basis for an agreement. Despite its repeated insistence that the withdrawal agreement reached with Theresa May could not be revisited, the EU did precisely that. It agreed that the cornerstone and crucial sticking point of that agreement, the backstop, would now be jettisoned.

Under the terms of the new agreement, the UK would no longer remain in the customs union. In turn, Johnson gave up his prior insistence that the question of the border on the island of Ireland could be resolved by technological means. Instead, and while protecting the open border and the Good Friday Peace Agreement, he effectively agreed to the establishment of a border in the Irish Sea. Under the new agreement, Northern Ireland would still formally remain in the UK customs territory, but it would *de facto* align itself with the EU's rules and regulations concerning the passage of goods from third countries to those of the EU.

This meant that, in practice, Northern Ireland would continue to be part of the EU's single market for goods and apply EU customs rules at all its ports. A customs border would henceforth be established between Great Britain and the island of Ireland, with exported goods being checked at 'points of entry' into Northern Ireland. While taxes would be paid only on goods moved from Britain through Northern Ireland and then on to the Republic of Ireland, the new deal signified that there would be checks and controls and added costs to the movement of goods across the Irish Sea. In short, the new agreement protected the indivisibility of the single market, but at the cost of creating a new border in the Irish Sea.

In reality, the agreement flew in the face of Johnson's, like May's, often-repeated promises that the unity of the 'precious' and 'mighty' Union would not be compromised and, as declared by Johnson at the party conference in Manchester that, 'We will under no circumstances have checks at or near the border in Northern Ireland'. Johnson continued to insist upon the truth of his false declaration, but it would come back to haunt him in 2020 (and beyond) when his Internal Market Bill sought to override aspects of his withdrawal agreement relating to Northern Ireland and Ireland.

In most other essentials the new agreement was the same as that drawn up between the EU and May. Yet there was one important addition. The Northern Ireland Assembly at Stormont, suspended since January 2017, would henceforth be reconvened. It would, moreover, and have the power every four years from the time the agreement came into force to vote on its future.

Johnson's agreement predictably provoked outrage on the part of the DUP and alarm on the part of the SNP. The DUP, the Tories' erstwhile necessary ally and sometimes saviour in the House of Commons, accused their previously close defender and friend, Boris Johnson, of deviousness and betrayal. In the opinion of the DUP, the Prime Minister's deal had, at the very least, placed Northern Ireland in a very ambiguous position vis-à-vis the EU and the rest of the UK. Contrary to Johnson's denials, the agreement would both 'undermine the integrity of the union' and be injurious to 'the economic wellbeing of Northern Ireland', according to the DUP. Johnson's act of 'treachery' would not quickly or easily be forgotten and, even less so, forgiven. As we will see in more detail below, within fifteen months Arlene Foster, the DUP's leader and first minister, was declaring Johnson's Northern Ireland protocol to be 'unworkable'. 'Serious problems' had developed with post-Brexit trade between Northern Ireland and Great Britain, according to Foster. The DUP was calling for 'the entire deal affecting the region to be withdrawn'. For its part, the SNP declared that Northern Ireland had been placed by Johnson's agreement in a situation of potentially unfair competitive advantage by the fact that it would continue, for at least four years, to enjoy the free-trading benefits of being part of the single market. In contrast, the future trading relationship between other parts of the UK and the EU was far less certain.[11]

After the conclusion of the agreement, the Prime Minister still faced a race against time to get it through parliament before 31 October. This proved to be impossible. While the House of Commons agreed in principle on 22 October to accept Johnson's deal, by a majority of thirty, it would not accept, by 322 to 308 votes, the extremely tight three-day deadline demanded by the Prime Minister. Parliament agreed that this simply did not give it enough time properly to scrutinize the bill. Johnson threatened to pull it, and once again press for a general election to break the deadlock. Parliament, however, refused to give way.

In the days before these crucial votes, the Prime Minister had been forced, much against his will, to write a letter to the EU to request an extension. This was in compliance with the 'Benn Act' that, if parliament had not approved a deal by 19 October, then the Prime Minister would be obliged to ask for an extension. The EU duly agreed to extend Brexit to 31 January 2020. Despite his severe loss of face, Johnson survived to fight another day.[12]

The general election of December 2019

Having failed to 'Get Brexit Done' in parliament, Johnson henceforth put all his efforts into achieving it by means of a general election. A government source was quoted as saying that 'we will not allow MPs to continue holding this country hostage'.[13] Under the existing provisions of the Fixed-Term Parliaments Act, the Prime Minister required the support of two-thirds of MPs to call an election. After failing three times to secure this, Johnson successfully introduced the Early Parliamentary General Election Bill. This required a simple majority for its enactment. The bill became law on 31 October and made provision for a general election to take place on 12 December.

The failed opposition: outright Remainers

The two most implacable party-political opponents of Leave, the SNP and the Liberal Democrats, declared their willingness and readiness to accept Johnson's challenge and fight the election. The anti-Brexit, anti-'Tory austerity' and pro-independence SNP would contest the election in Scotland and easily win, with forty-eight out of a total of fifty-nine seats. Nicola Sturgeon, furthermore, offered to help to form a 'progressive alliance' in the event of a Conservative defeat. This would be conditional upon the other parties to the alliance being prepared to accept a vote on Scottish independence, the revocation or, failing that, a second referendum on Brexit with Remain on the ballot paper, an end to austerity, the removal of nuclear weapons from Scotland, making 'right' Scotland's 'cuts' and an increase in health spending.[14]

The Liberal Democrats were buoyed by their resurgence at the May 2019 European elections, when they had come second, and the election in July of a new, upbeat, and overly confident leader, Jo Swinson. Born in 1980, Swinson was the first woman and youngest person to become leader of the Liberal Democrats. She seriously believed that her party could win the election and that she could become the new prime minister. The key to success was perceived to be Swinson's and the party's decision to change its core policy, from the demand for another referendum and hopefully Remain, to revoking Article 50 at a stroke. The assumption was that all true Remainers would flock to the Liberal Democrats. As matters transpired, this, however, did not come to pass and exposed Swinson's political naivety and hubris. Swinson lost her own seat, East Dunbartonshire, and was immediately obliged to step down as leader. She now held the unenviable record of being the shortest leader on record of the Liberal Democrats. Swinson had thus experienced a truly meteoric rise and fall. In an extremely disappointing election, the Liberal Democrats lost one seat and their total parliamentary representation fell to eleven.[15]

The other mainstay of unqualified opposition to Brexit, the People's Vote (campaign) was a cross-party political organization. It was formed in April 2018 and held well-attended marches in favour of a second Brexit referendum. The most impressive was in March 2019 when an estimated 1 million plus people gathered in London. In October 2019, however, the organization was torn apart by internal conflicts and collapsed. It would be dissolved on 31 January 2020, but would rebrand itself, in a much-weakened form, to push for a 'fair deal' following the UK's formal exit from the EU. After its initial promise, it thus failed miserably in its opposition to Brexit.[16]

The same conclusion applied to the insurgent 'centrists' who had left, either willingly or unwillingly, the Tories and Labour. None who stood at the election was successful and the Independent Group for Change was disbanded. The centre ground and centrist forces thus collapsed in December 2019.[17]

The failed opposition: humiliated Labour

Corbyn's Labour also fared very badly. Labour had initially been opposed to a general election until a No Deal Brexit had been taken off the table and an extension agreed with the EU. Once these preconditions had been met, Corbyn declared his readiness, indeed eagerness, to take on Johnson in a battle over the fundamental future direction of the country.

As seen in their debates on TV and elsewhere, while Corbyn saw his chosen future as one of Scandinavian-style social democracy, Johnson saw his as continuing to revolve around free-market capitalism, albeit of a 'moderate and compassionate, One-Nation' kind.[18] Yet, after his initial scepticism, Corbyn was in danger of acting too hastily because his party was by no means unanimously in favour of an election. This was most clearly seen when more than 100 Labour MPs absented themselves or abstained from the vote on the Early Parliamentary General Election Bill and eleven voted against the holding of an election. Many of these MPs agreed with Tony Blair that Labour was falling into the trap, as set by Johnson and his advisors, of agreeing to a general election before the Brexit issue had been resolved. The danger was that the election would revolve around Brexit rather than the wider issues preferred by Labour.[19]

Yet Blair's advice, which proved to be prescient, was not heeded by Corbyn and the leadership. Instead Corbyn threw himself wholeheartedly into the contest and declared that, in a manner strongly reminiscent of the 2017 general election campaign, he and the party would fight on 'the most ambitious and radical' programmes for 'real social change' that 'our country has ever seen'.[20] They would do so without Tom Watson. Corbyn's deputy quit parliament and stepped down as Labour deputy leader early in November. Watson declared that his decision to step down was 'personal, not political', but many thought that the 'moderate' Watson was not in accord with Corbyn's brand of socialism and the direction in which the latter was taking the party.[21]

The Labour Party predictably adopted a transforming manifesto entitled, 'It's Time for Real Change'. This included a massive increase in public spending on health, education, the minimum wage, an environmental 'Green Deal', selective nationalisation, transport, communications technology, a national care system and the scrapping of universal credit and age rises for the state pension. As in 2017, the manifesto sought to address and transform the 'broken' system of neoliberal capitalism complete with its poverty, inequality and injustice.

In terms of Brexit, Labour continued its policy of constructive ambiguity. It declared that, in the event of winning the election, the incoming Labour government would seek to renegotiate a new Brexit deal with the EU within three months of achieving office. The deal would have at its core continued UK membership of the customs union, a liberal commitment and sympathetic attitude towards the virtues and value of EU migration, amounting to 'managed' rather than 'free' movement, and close EU-single-market alignment. Within six months the Labour government would put the deal to a legally binding referendum, alongside an option to Remain. The government would abide by the outcome of the referendum and the leader, Jeremy Corbyn himself, would remain neutral in the event of a second referendum. By means of this policy Labour sought to appeal to *both* Remain and Leave voters and 'unite the country'.[22]

Labour's strategy and campaign, however, proved to be disastrous. The election revolved around Johnson's endlessly repeated mantra of 'Get Brexit Done' and his promise to finally honour the pledges made to the Leave majority in 2016 to respect democracy and 'restore control'. Despite Corbyn's best efforts, the election did not amount to a re-run of the 2017 contest in which Labour's full-frontal challenge to the 'broken system' was a cardinal feature.

Even so, Johnson was fully prepared to 'take on' what he saw as the 'unpatriotic' and 'terrorist-sympathizing' 'Marxist' Corbyn to argue, as noted earlier, that socialism and Marxism were defunct and, despite its problems, free-market capitalism was alive, well and the only option available to the country. In turn, large swathes of the electorate internalized the negative portrayal of Corbyn offered by Johnson, the *Daily Telegraph* and most other right-wing and even more centrist media outlets.

While many voters were attracted by specific aspects of Labour's manifesto, they, furthermore, simply did not believe that it was affordable or viable as a total package. Labour's Brexit policy similarly was seen as confused and confusing. It lacked the simplicity, clarity and decisiveness of the 'Get Brexit Done' slogan. After three and a half years of interminable and unsuccessful wrangling between the UK government and the EU, most of the public were in no mood to countenance and endure the new negotiations, delays and possible reversal of policy proposed by the Labour Party. To put the matter simply, they wanted finality, closure and, at least in terms of Leavers, due government respect for the rational and democratic decision they had made in the 2016 EU referendum.

These were precisely the prizes that Johnson was offering, while Corbyn was perceived to be further procrastinating, prevaricating and dithering. As we saw in the last chapter, Labour and other critics of the constructive ambiguity policy feared that it would not work because those determined to leave the EU would vote for either the 'true Brexiters', the Brexit Party or the Conservative Party, rather than the equivocating Labour Party and that many Remainers would choose the Liberal Democrats and other unequivocally pro-Remain organizations rather than 'fence-sitting' Labour.

This fear was fully realized in the December election when the Labour Party endured its worst defeat since 1935. What appeared to Corbyn and his allies to be a rational, fair and considered attempt to bridge the gap between Leavers and Remainers, within both the Labour Party and beyond, and to bring the country together, had turned out to be an ill-considered political catastrophe.[23]

Triumphant Tories

In the weeks between the dissolution of parliament in the first week of November and the mid-December election, the polls had consistently suggested that Johnson would win. While there was evidence to suggest that Corbyn was doing very well among black and Asian voters, the Conservatives had taken a commanding lead of 19 points over Labour less than three weeks before election day. Five weekend polls, furthermore, put the Conservatives 11 points ahead. As the *Guardian*'s Dan Sabbagh wrote three days before the election, it was clear that 'unless something dramatic' occurred, Johnson was 'heading to Downing Street with an overall majority'.[24]

The actual result of the election exceeded Johnson's confident expectations and punctured Corbyn's inflated hopes. The Conservatives won a total of 365 seats. This was a net gain of 47 on 2017. They secured a landslide majority of 80 seats. The party's 43.6 per cent of the vote share was the highest won by any party since Margaret

Thatcher's 1979 landmark election. Labour's 'red-wall' seats, including many Leave-voting former mining communities which had seen Margaret Thatcher as the devil responsible for their decline, 'crumbled' to the Tories. Boris and Brexit became their new saviours. Johnson profusely thanked the new converts to Conservatism in these constituencies for 'lending' him their votes and reiterated his pledge, despite the modest amount actually committed by the government to extra public spending, to 'level up across the country' by putting more money into schools, hospitals, the police and infrastructure. In so doing, he was continuing, albeit more emphatically and vociferously, May's promise to improve the lot of the 'left behind' and creating clear blue water between himself and the politics of austerity.

In contrast, Labour suffered a disaster. It lost fifty-nine seats and its vote share declined from 40 per cent in 2017 to 32.2 per cent. As Lord Ashcroft discovered in his survey of 13,000 people on election day, the key issues were Brexit, management of the economy and the person best equipped to be prime minister. Johnson won easily. Corbyn was deeply mistrusted and disliked, even by many Labour voters. While Labour remained more popular than the Tories among young and younger voters, the reverse was the case among those in their mid-fifties and older. Significantly, the Conservatives had won among all socio-economic groups by margins of between 6 and 20 points.[25]

As noted above, the Tories, however, were easily defeated by the hegemonic SNP in Scotland. In Northern Ireland the non-Unionist parties did very well and in Wales Labour retained its traditional electoral dominance. It won twenty-two out of a total of forty seats, as opposed to the Conservatives' fourteen and Plaid Cymru's four. At the same time, however, Labour in Wales lost six seats in comparison with the election of 2017, the Tories gained six and Plaid Cymru's number of seats remained the same.

Despite these failures and disappointments for the Tories, in overall terms there is no doubt that Johnson had won a stunning victory, largely on the basis of his promises to 'Get Brexit Done' and restore Britain's control over its own affairs. The many failures, wrangling and despair of May's premiership had largely been overcome. To be sure, the Prime Minister had been greatly helped by the weaknesses and divisions of the opposing Remain forces and Labour's unsuccessful attempt to steer a middle course. He had also immensely benefitted from Nigel Farage's decision in the second week of November to withdraw his Brexit Party candidates from the 317 constituencies won by the Conservatives in 2017. Farage declared that he had carried out his U-turn so as not to split the Leave vote.

This, of course, meant both that he supported Johnson's Brexit deal and that the Conservatives would enjoy a clear run in these constituencies. In practice, Farage indeed had been 'put back in his box', although he continued to insist, with much justification, that pressure from both UKIP and the Brexit Party had played a key role in moving the Conservative Party to the right and the adoption of a hard Brexit position. Farage also declared he would continue to keep up a close eye on Johnson to ensure that the Prime Minister remained true to his principles in future trade negotiations with the EU.[26]

We should, furthermore, not underestimate the important contributions of Johnson himself and his advisors to his election and Brexit triumphs. To many on the centre and left of politics, Johnson embodies the narcissism, cynicism, self-interest, anti-social behaviour, sexism and buffoonery characteristic of some of the ex-public schoolboys who dominate politics and social life in many parts of the UK. There, of course, is much truth in this picture. By all accounts Johnson certainly has the capacity to display the inefficiency and incompetence, indecisiveness, selfishness, insecurity, narcissism, mendacity and cavalier attitude to sex, women and matters of fact depicted so well by John Crace in the *Guardian*.[27] Yet this is by no means the whole picture. In securing his withdrawal deal and winning the election so convincingly, Johnson and his advisors displayed clear, decisive and ruthless decision making and leadership.

Johnson also epitomized a certain style of Conservatism which has proven to be so popular in the UK, especially in England, among wide cross-sections of the public since the nineteenth century and which has stood in marked contrast to both Liberalism and Labourism. This style of Conservatism has manifested itself not only in routine political support for the established institutions of UK society and patriotism, but also in a daily culture based upon informality, bonhomie, eccentricity, not taking life too seriously and support for the robust 'pleasures and pastimes' of the 'free-born' British and especially English 'people' – of sport, betting, eating and drinking, shopping, consumerism in general and loyalism. The Prime Minister's belief in a 'home-grown', common-sensical, relaxed, good-natured, tolerant, pragmatic and emotional as well as rational approach to politics, people and life is part and parcel of this tradition.

As voters in the 'red-wall' constituencies of Hyndburn, Stoke and Darlington who voted Tory for the first time in December 2019, declared to author Deborah Mattinson, 'Boris' appealed on a personal level because of his 'warmth', 'positivity', his 'optimistic patriotism', his 'authenticity' and, despite his upper-class birth and upbringing, the fact that he was 'down-to-earth'. 'Boris' was seen, in the words of one women voter, to have 'de-snobbified the Tories'. These and other voters favourably contrasted Johnson's love of 'fun' and his somewhat clown-like chaotic and eccentric but endearing appearance and mannerisms, with what they saw as the wooden, straitlaced and excessive seriousness of Corbyn. Yet Johnson's bonhomie and 'clownish' behaviour is also part of a deliberate ploy to obtain power and control over people.[28]

As seen during the interwar period and since the 1980s, Labour socialism and Marxism, furthermore, have often been successfully branded by Conservative luminaries, including the prime ministers Stanley Baldwin, Winston Churchill and Johnson himself, as 'alien' to 'Britishness' and 'Englishness'. These 'outside' political forces have been heavily criticized for their 'continental' seriousness and, at times, for being too sanctimonious. They have been seen as too logical, rational and cold, as too elitist, authoritarian, critical and removed from the daily experiences and emotions of 'the people', as lacking knowledge and understanding of what life and 'human nature' are 'really like' with their warts and all. In the eyes of Johnson, the EU and Corbyn have, albeit in their distinctive ways, been part of this largely 'alien' tradition.[29]

Brexit

Having won the election, Johnson moved towards the first stage of closure on Brexit. His massive majority in parliament ensured an easy passage for his withdrawal deal. On 31 January 2020, the UK officially left the EU and Johnson looked forward to securing a post-transition free-trade deal and successfully selling his vision of a resurgent 'global Britain' to the rest of the world. In a speech at the Royal Naval College in Greenwich in early February he declared that the country was 'on the slipway' of 'global economic dominance' and indicated that he would rather walk away with no trade deal at the end of 2020 than meekly accept EU rules on competition, state aid and oversight by European courts.[30] His refashioned Tory party ruled supreme and looked forward to being in power until at least the next scheduled general election in 2024. The party included ten of the twenty-one rebel Tory MPs who had had the whip restored to them in late October in the officially stated interests of moving the party forward and restoring One-Nation Conservatism.[31]

In contrast, the start of the new year saw both Labour and the Liberal Democrats humiliated and in disarray. Both had to start the potentially painful process of finding a new leader and a much wider social base for their policies. Immediately following the hugely disappointing general election result, Corbyn, who retained his own seat of Islington North, announced that he would stand down as party leader after a 'period of reflection'. While 'very sad', Corbyn felt 'proud' of Labour's manifesto and the issues it raised. The party had had the misfortune to be defeated on the central election issue of Brexit, according to Corbyn. The failure of the leadership effectively to tackle and eradicate antisemitism within the Labour Party once again became of major importance, while internal divisions around Brexit and the future trade deal with the EU remained.[32]

From March 2020 to May 2021: trials, tribulations and recovery

As events unfolded, the Prime Minister's triumphs, however, proved to be far from untroubled or complete. Even in the immediate- and short-terms, a combination of familiar and new problems arose. For example, Johnson's threat not to comply with EU rules, combined with the EU's insistence that the Prime Minister honour his pledge made in the October 2020 political declaration that the UK would 'stay true to EU rules on subsidies and standards', meant that talks on the future trading relationship between the UK and the EU did not begin well. Over the next six months there were few, if any, signs of real progress in the negotiations and by early summer it was beginning to look as if no-deal would be the likeliest outcome by the cut-off date of 31 December.[33] Brexit, furthermore, was far from being a welcome and accepted fact throughout the UK. By the end of January 2020, the Scottish parliament, the Welsh Senedd and Northern Ireland's restored Stormont Assembly had voted overwhelmingly against Johnson's withdrawal agreement.[34]

Despite employment being at record levels, persistent economic weaknesses and problems also came to the fore and demanded action on the part of the government. Investment, productivity and economic growth continued to be very low. The year 2019 had seen UK economic growth of only 1 per cent and this constituted the weakest twelve months of growth outside recession since World War II.[35]

In response, Johnson's new chancellor, Rishi Sunak, began the task of attempting to stave off the threat of recession, boost growth and fulfil Johnson's election pledge to the 'red-wall' converts to Conservatism to 'level up', by presenting an expansionary budget on 11 March. Seen by some as a victory for Dominic Cummings and his opposition to George Osborne's austerity measures, Sunak's budget 'splashed the cash' to the tune of £30 billion. As the *Guardian's* Larry Elliott and Heather Stewart observed, Sunak 'ditched a decade of Conservative economic orthodoxy ... and claimed that the Tories were now "the party of public services"'. Sunak also committed extra temporary money to households and businesses to combat the growing threat of the spread of coronavirus. Johnson's Britain was now 'on course to have a bigger state than under Tony Blair's Labour governments'. This was an indication of much more extensive state intervention to come in the face of the worsening economic, social and health effects of the pandemic. The Bank of England also slashed the bank rate from 0.75 per cent to 0. 25 per cent, the UK's 'first emergency rate cut since 2008'. Rates now stood at their lowest level in the Bank's 300 plus years history. Yet the independent Office for Budget Responsibility predicted that 'the largest sustained easing of policy by the Treasury since ... 1992 would fail to prevent growth over the next five years being even slower than in the decade after the financial crisis'.[36]

By no means all leading Conservatives welcomed the government's newfound embrace of expansionary economics, more extensive state intervention and its seeming abandonment of their party's traditional financial restraint and caution. After all, it was Labour that was traditionally seen by the Conservatives as too interventionist and too profligate with taxpayers' money. The former chancellor, Sajid Javid, who had resigned a few weeks earlier rather than accept advisers selected by Cummings, warned the government against 'junking all spending rules'. He was joined by Theresa May who advised the government to stick to the time-honoured Conservative principle of 'sound management of the public finances'.

Yet the expansionary, 'Keynesian', nature of the budget further demonstrated that Johnson wanted to be rid of any damaging polling associations with the politics of austerity. The Prime Minister was entirely willing and committed to put aside traditional Conservative deflationary ideology in the interests of the pragmatism and flexibility demanded by the UK's changing circumstances. Whether the budget would be successful in meeting its goals, however, was an open question.[37]

There also developed a number of troubling political issues for the government. For example, nationalist sentiments within the UK were on the rise, especially in Scotland. As we will see in Chapter 4, Johnson's election victory, combined with his and Brexit's unpopularity north of the border and his point-blank refusal to countenance another Scottish referendum, had a major part to play in persuading a majority (52 per cent) of those polled in Scotland in February 2020 to support Scottish independence and the holding of another referendum.[38]

Meanwhile, at the December election, the non-Unionist parties in Northern Ireland won a majority of votes for the first time, with Sinn Fein gaining just one seat less than the DUP. The latter lost two MPs, including its leader at Westminster, Nigel Dodds. The electorally bruised DUP continued vociferously to claim that it and Northern Ireland had been betrayed by Johnson's withdrawal deal. The election result in Northern Ireland and the totally unexpected surge of Sinn Fein in the Irish Republic's general election in February suggested that during the 2020s the unification of Ireland might once again become a live political issue.[39]

The hostility to Brexit in Scotland and Northern Ireland developed alongside and in opposition to a marked rise in a narrow and backward-looking form of nationalism in England. The majority of members of the Conservative Party indeed prized Brexit and English sovereignty over Scotland's continued existence as part of the UK. This fact signalled that the further break-up the Union was now a distinct possibility. In Wales, too, Johnson's highly centralized and increasingly authoritarian form of Unionism triggered mounting opposition. By March 2021 the polls would show that support for independence in Wales remarkably stood at around 38 per cent.[40]

In March 2020 further important problems arose for the government. These included severe flood damage from climate change and the biggest hit to global stock markets since the financial crash in the face of the growing coronavirus pandemic and the oil price war between Saudi Arabia and Russia. Within Westminster and the Civil Service, there was continued fall-out from Javid's resignation and Cummings' alleged bullying and excessive power over the Prime Minister and policy matters. Further Civil Service staff complaints of lying and bullying followed. This time they were directed at the Home Secretary, Priti Patel. They were taken up by Patel's chief civil servant, Sir Philip Rutnam. The issues were not resolved and led to the dramatic resignation of Rutnam. He announced his intention to sue the government for constructive dismissal and an alleged 'vicious and orchestrated campaign' against him. Yet Johnson continued to defend Patel and her 'outstanding' work. This incident exemplified the growing war between, on the one hand, a government seemingly controlled by Cummings, the permanent-revolutionary who had little time for civil-service 'traditionalism', and, on the other hand, established civil servants and their staff.[41]

The coronavirus pandemic

All the issues and problems outlined above, however, were overshadowed from March onwards by the biggest crisis facing the UK since World War II. This was the coronavirus pandemic, complete with its profound and widespread adverse effects upon health, the economy and the social and cultural life of the UK and the world in general. It would constitute a major watershed in global history. What follows below is a brief outline of the pandemic's chronological development in the UK and an analysis of the strengths and weaknesses of the Johnson government's initiatives and responses to it during 2020 and up to Easter 2021. The fact that the pandemic has not yet run its course means that complete accounts of it are yet to be written.

On 11 March 2020, the day of Sunak's budget, the Word Health Organization (WHO) declared Covid-19 to be a world pandemic. The majority view, at least in the West, was that the virus had its origin in a wet market in the city of Wuhan in China. This view held sway, especially in Trump's United States but also in many western countries, for several months. It has now, however, been discarded, at least by the WHO, in favour of the a more general and somewhat vague hypothesis that the virus somehow managed to pass swiftly across vast geographical areas from animals, perhaps bats, to humans and that it manifested itself first, at least on a large scale, in Wuhan. We know that cases of the virus were reported in China in December 2019 and that by March 2020 it had increased thirteen-fold outside China and the number of affected countries had tripled. The WHO declared that the 'vast majority of cases- 90% of the 118,000' – were now in 'just four countries: Italy, Iran, South Korea and China'.

The WHO also maintained that, despite its rapid and alarming spread, the virus 'could be controlled'. The most effective way to achieve this was for governments, irrespective of their political and ideological complexions, to take fast, decisive, clear, comprehensive and tough action. Their citizens also had to accept that a strong collective approach and enforcement were absolutely necessary in order safely to protect themselves, their families and friends and their societies in general from the worst effects of the virus. In the process, individual freedom of choice would have to take a back seat to the wider issues of societal health and safety until the virus had been suppressed. According to the WHO, China and South Korea were showing the way by locking down affected geographical areas and introducing strict border controls, enforcing social distancing and putting in place effective systems of mass testing, treating, contact tracking and isolating. The WHO recognized that the resources necessary to fight the virus varied from country to country, but emphasized that it was crucial for all governments to send clear and unambiguous messages to their citizens to act responsibly. Unfortunately, concluded the WHO, there was a lack of 'capacity', 'resources' and 'resolve' in some countries.[42]

In the following months it became evident that those countries in the East that had experienced the horrors of the Sars coronavirus in the early years of the millennium were both more prepared for and more willing to undertake the drastic and at times authoritarian action necessitated by the Covid-19 pandemic. Other countries, for example, New Zealand and to a lesser extent Australia, characterized by high degrees of social integration in which the tradition of rugged individualism existed alongside that of 'mateship', of 'pulling together' and widespread acceptance of 'the rules', followed suit.

In contrast, lack of government resolve would manifest itself most strongly in many of those rich western countries, and their non-western admirers and imitators, in which the right of individuals to do largely as they chose was generally prized more highly, at least in 'normal', peacetime conditions, than those of social and collective responsibility, mutuality, reciprocity and discipline. For example, adopting the rhetoric of bellicose nationalism with his reference to the 'China virus', and prizing US 'freedom' over Chinese 'authoritarianism', president Trump irresponsibly and erroneously spread the word that China was responsible for the virus and that Americans had little to fear from a flu-like illness that would soon disappear of its own accord. The similarly free-market, authoritarian, bullying and purveyor of 'fake news', Bolsonaro in Brazil, followed Trump's lead. These leaders set themselves up as 'libertarians' versus 'authoritarians', even though they could and did act in very authoritarian and intolerant ways themselves. In both the United States and Brazil the virus would spin wildly out of control.[43]

Boris Johnson also continued throughout the pandemic to highlight the importance of his cherished individual 'British freedoms', especially the rights to socialize, visit the pub and move around freely, and his fundamental opposition to what he saw as excessive, dictatorial and socialistic state intervention and controls over individuals' lives. At the same time, however, there were important complexities and even contradictions at work. In this context it is important to point out to the reader that, alongside its longstanding and important tradition of individualism, the UK also possesses a strongly collectivist tradition of community-mindedness, of people acting together and behaving responsibly and making sacrifices in the public interest. The period of the coronavirus would see examples of both individualism and community togetherness and social responsibility. The latter, indeed, would generally overshadow the former. While some people would strongly defend their right to individual freedom of choice and action, the vast majority of the public would display a greatly enhanced sense of connection and community spirit. Millions would undertake a range of volunteering activities in their communities and would provide very impressive moral and financial support to frontline workers fighting the virus in the NHS, the care services and elsewhere.[44] Significantly, as we will see below, Johnson attempted to draw upon both these traditions, of individualism and community, of laissez-faire and collectivism, in his fight against the virus.

The UK government's responses to the pandemic between March 2020 and January 2021 may be described and evaluated in the following way. In February and March 2020, when the WHO expressed 'deep concern about "alarming levels of inaction" in the fight against the spread of the disease' and made a plea for governments to do 'what is necessary', the UK was among those lacking any real sense of urgency.[45] On one level this was understandable. While the first confirmed case of coronavirus in the UK was on 31 January, there were no deaths and fewer than 100 confirmed cases by the end of February. Thereafter, however, complacency, casualness, 'over-promising and under-delivering', incompetence, unclear messaging, indecision, U-turns and, it must be said, many acts of gross negligence, combined with a staggering absence of regret and apology for its own serial failures and wrongs, became the dominant characteristics of the Westminster government's health policy throughout 2020. This was despite incontrovertible evidence at the time that the virus posed a grave and increasingly widespread threat to people's health and wellbeing.

As we will see below, the overwhelming weight of this and other evidence flatly contradicts Johnson's claim, made in January 2021 when the UK death toll from Covid reached the appalling figure of 100,000 – the worst in Europe and one of the worst per capita in the world – that his government had 'truly' done 'everything we could' to fight the virus and minimize loss of life. As the *Guardian* editorialized,

> Mr Johnson expresses sadness without taking responsibility. He is sorry that so many died, but not for his failure to prevent their deaths. He says lessons will be learned but 'now is not the time to reflect'. He will never learn. Lessons were available from the first wave that he ignored in the second one ... There will one day be a reckoning ... the story of Britain's pandemic will long serve as a monument to bad government.[46]

Between February and the middle of March 2020 the UK government, like that of Trump, seemed to think of coronavirus as being on a par with seasonal flu. Notwithstanding the warnings and pleas of the WHO and other international bodies, Johnson continued to maintain that life should continue as normally as possible and that 'we can turn the tide within the next twelve weeks'.

The government stopped its community-based testing and tracing programme in mid-March and seemed to favour the notion of 'herd immunity', whereby it was erroneously assumed that as a result of letting the virus take its course sufficient mass immunity to it would be built up in the population over time. This hypothesis of herd immunity, however, lacked a sound evidential base, underestimated the amount of probable suffering and death involved, especially among old and older members of the population, and did not adequately take into account the fact that some among the younger age groups would inevitably transmit the disease to their elders. The Prime Minister, himself, continued to attend meetings, boasted about shaking hands with all and sundry, including people he met in a hospital, and did not observe social distancing or wear a face covering. Sporting events, including mass events such as the four-day March Cheltenham Racing Festival and Liverpool Football Club's home Champion's League game against Atletico Madrid on 11 March, were, despite public misgivings, allowed to go ahead. Travel from continental Europe into the UK, including that by football fans, was allowed to continue, even though the virus was ravaging parts of Italy and had spread to other European countries. Unlike New Zealand and Australia, which both took the unprecedented step in March of closing down their borders to foreigners, the UK refused, in the interests of freedom of movement and trade, to do the same. Yet the evidence showed that international travellers were important carriers of the virus. As Devi Sridhar, the professor of global public health at the University of Edinburgh, noted, the UK at that time 'had no border policies in place'. It would take months to put them in place and even then they were 'lax and unmonitored'. As a result of personal laxness, the Prime Minister, himself, moreover, contracted the virus and in April spent three nights in hospital in intensive care. He fortunately recovered.[47]

By the end of the third week in March, the government had abandoned its previously cavalier attitudes and policy in favour of a national lockdown. This was officially introduced by Johnson on 23 March, although a week earlier Matt Hancock, the secretary of state for health and social care, had announced that the virus was spreading quickly and that all 'unnecessary social contact' should cease. From 23 March, until further notice, everyone, except in exceptional circumstances, would have to stay at home in order to protect the NHS from the heavy pressure the virus would necessarily place on it and 'save lives'. The public welcomed decisive action, although, in the eyes of a growing number of critics, the government had provided 'too little, too late'. For example, according to Professor Neil Ferguson of Imperial College, London, who sat on the government's Scientific, Advisory Group for Emergencies (SAGE) during the early stage of the virus, the introduction of the lockdown a week earlier than it had taken place could have saved 'thousands of lives'. The Prime Minister, however, insisted that he had taken the measures 'that we thought were right for this country' on the basis of scientific advice.[48]

The government's claim to be acting on the advice of 'the science', would become a familiar refrain in the months that followed. Yet 'the science', of course, was made up of different and sometimes competing claims and interpretations rather than a single absolute truth. Prominent scientists also argued that instead of 'pitting the economy against public health' – a 'false dichotomy' (Neil Ferguson) – and adopting a piecemeal approach, the government should have followed the maxim that 'a healthy economy depends upon a healthy population'. As a corollary, the government should have acted quickly and decisively to suppress the virus and so promote a quicker and more sustainable form of economic recovery. This was the path being followed by more successful countries, such as South Korea and China. As matters stood, the UK's 'partial lockdown to get partial recovery' ended up 'failing both'. The UK economy would experience the worst economic crisis of any major industrial economy, while cases and deaths from the virus were growing at an alarming rate.[49]

To be sure, the government did build upon Sunak's initiatives in the budget to offer an increasingly wide range of support and rescue measures for those organizations, industries and people hit hardest by the pandemic. In March the most important of these was the Coronavirus Job Retention Scheme (CJRS), commonly known as the furlough scheme. Designed to prevent mass unemployment and a further catastrophic fall in demand, the furlough programme ensured that the state would provide 80 per cent of the salaries and wages of those employees placed on leave by their employers, up to £2,500 per month. (Subsequent modifications meant that furloughed workers would be able to undertake some work for their employers and also continue to receive the 80 per cent.) Employers were required to provide the insurance and pensions contributions of those furloughed. This scheme provided an essential lifeline for millions of the employed. Intended to end in October, it would be extended throughout 2020 and well into 2021. Other ameliorative measures adopted during these two years embraced both the private and public sectors. They included grants, loans, start-up schemes, apprenticeships, tax breaks and deferrals, cuts to business rates, other job-support schemes, self-isolation payments and an increase in universal credit.[50]

In acting in these ways, Johnson and Sunak fully demonstrated their ability and willingness to place pragmatism above ideology. An unprecedented peace-time level of state intervention and support was resorted to in the fight against the deep and extensive adverse economic effects of the pandemic. The Prime Minister maintained in June 2020 that he was providing the UK with a 1930s US New Deal-style recovery programme.[51] Three months later, the left-wing economist, Larry Elliott, declared that the government had 'gone even further' than the socialist Tony Benn 'on state aid'.[52]

At the same time, however, while declaring that he did not want a return to the past of austerity, the 'left behind' and gross regional inequalities, Johnson looked forward to a post-pandemic 'normal' economic future in which the private sector and the free market, rather than the state, would play the leading role. The Prime Minister claimed that they would be the key players in building what he exaggeratedly billed as a 'New Jerusalem' by 2030.[53] As would be revealed, furthermore, in Sunak's budget of March 2021, plans for significant cuts to public spending and for tax rises also suggested that the Tories would seek to reclaim their traditional reputation for 'sound finance' once the exceptional circumstances of the virus had become less severe.

Therein lay an important source of possible future tension in terms of the government achieving a judicious balance between saving and spending. Sunak, more so than Johnson, was committed to the ideas of monetary caution and restraint. This had the potential to threaten Johnson's expansionary economic plans for regional regeneration and 'levelling-up' as key parts of his 'One Nation' agenda.[54]

Apart from the months from July to September, Johnson's government experienced a series of acute problems and abject failures of policy between March and October.

Many of these issued from its own incompetence and ideological blinkers. For example, against its commendable provision of new emergency field, or Nightingale, hospitals to treat Covid sufferers, the government woefully failed to 'shield' those most at risk from the virus. These were the elderly reliant upon professional residential care. Even though Matt Hancock claimed in May that the testing of symptomatic care-home residents had been 'a top priority right from the start' for the government, its care-home policy as a whole in fact proved to be both extremely distressing and calamitous. The moving of more than 25,000 elderly and Covid-untested hospital patients into care homes in order to free up hospital beds saw the number of Covid transmission cases and deaths among those in care homes escalate. The hard-working, but poorly paid staff in care homes, moreover, widely complained about not having access to the necessary personal protective equipment (PPE), while some of the private care-home owners brought in 'outside' staff who had not been tested. The upshot was untold suffering, misery, death, sadness and no little anger on the part of patients, staff, relatives, friends and local communities. As the year progressed, it became evident that around one third of all Covid deaths had taken place among care-home residents. Many of their distressed families demanded that the government take its full share of the blame.[55]

Johnson's promised 'world-beating' test, trace and isolate system also proved to be ineffective and shambolic. Shelved in March, the system was resurrected in May. Test, trace and isolate was an essential feature of the successful anti-Covid strategy developed by South Korea and other countries in the East. Yet, instead of relying upon the proven experience and expertise provided by public health institutions, Hancock decided, in his free-market wisdom, largely to by-pass the public system in favour of outsourcing most of the responsibility to the private sector. This was mainly concentrated in the hands of the huge outsourcing company, Serco, with its questionable record in the fields of security and immigration. Baroness 'Dido' Harding, the Conservative life peer, was appointed the head of NHS Test and Trace.

Yet neither Serco nor Harding possessed the relevant expertise and experience of the public-health system's professionals and workers. The privatized Test and Trace system not only paid private consultants over £1,000 per day on average, but also had a dreadful record of managerial inefficiency and very poor results. Untrained or barely trained staff were appointed, with some of these declaring that they were 'sitting around doing nothing' and being 'paid to watch Netflix'. Some people seeking tests were instructed to travel a ludicrous number of miles to receive them, including, in one case, a return car journey from Lincoln to Inverness of 654 miles! As claimed by Dido and Hancock, their system did test millions, but many who tested positive were either not traced or did not give details of their contacts. As such, it failed both to be comprehensive and to provide sufficient types of data necessary to assess its overall effectiveness on levels of infection and transmission over time.

There were, furthermore, expensive computer glitches and other errors. The government jettisoned its own app, 'after spending millions of pounds on technology that experts had warned would not work', according to journalist Lucy Campbell. Johnson's 'Operation Moonshot', an ambitious plan for the government to spend £100 billion on a mass expansion of testing to cover 10 million people a day by early 2021, was shelved, in October 2020, a month after being launched with great fanfare by Matt

Hancock but to disbelief and jeers among MPs. By the end of the year and, indeed, well into 2021, England was still searching for the promised 'world-beating' system. In March 2021 parliament's spending watchdog, the Public Accounts Committee, damningly reported that, despite receiving some £37 billion in public funding since May 2020, the Test and Trace system had failed to meet its objectives of preventing further lockdowns and had not made a 'measurable difference to the progress of the pandemic'. In the same month, the government offered NHS staff, whom it rightly lauded as 'heroes' during the pandemic, a miserly 1 per cent pay award. This was a cut in terms of real income. Meanwhile, Wales and Scotland had put public health authorities and staff in charge of their systems and were rewarded by the considerable amount of public respect and trust gained.[56]

The manifest failure and financial scandal of the privatized Test and Trace system were one aspect of a much wider and deeper problem of what critics rightly termed 'government cronyism'. The latter manifested itself in the granting of Covid-related contracts to private organizations without sufficiently going through, or at times seemingly entirely neglecting, the usual tendering and advertising processes and making public the full details of those contracts within the thirty-day time period, as required in law. Critics maintained that contracts were handed out on the basis of contacts, friendships and handshakes, with Tory friends and acquaintances who were generally ill-equipped to undertake the required work. For example, a contract to provide Covid test vials for the NHS was given to the former local pub landlord and friend of Matt Hancock, while Michael Gove's Cabinet Office allegedly awarded a contract, without competition, to a public relations and opinion research company with links to Dominic Cummings.

This 'cronyism racket', reminiscent of the way in which eighteenth-century British governments handed out lucrative contracts to private organizations, involved billions of pounds. In February 2021 the High Court ruled that, by not publishing the details of procurement contracts within thirty days, Matt Hancock's department had acted unlawfully. Hancock defended the government's action by declaring that the exigencies of Covid meant that rapid action was required to provide the necessary expertise, equipment and 'save lives' and that on average the contracts were published just over a fortnight later than they should have been.[57]

In late March, Cummings, Johnson's chief adviser, flagrantly ignoring the government's rule to 'stay at home' during the first national lockdown, drove 260 plus miles from London to Durham to take up the offer of childcare for his four-year-old son from family members. The journey took place when Cummings's wife, the journalist, Mary Wakefield, had developed coronavirus symptoms and Cummings feared that he had also become infected while they were still in London. Following the Cummings's return journey, trust in the government plummeted. It appeared to many that there was a complete and unforgivable contrast between the very flexible travel arrangements afforded to the powerful Cummings and the compulsory, 'stay-at-home' rule for Joe Public. Boris Johnson's argument, that Cummings was simply following his natural fatherly 'instincts' in seeking care for his child from family members in Durham, met with widespread incredulity. Cummings's televised attempt to defend his behaviour fell flat. A petition calling for Cummings's dismissal gathered over a million signatures, while an *Opinium* survey for the *Observer* at the end of May showed that 81 per cent thought that Cummings 'broke the rules' and some 68 per cent that he should resign.[58]

During the later part of May, and throughout June, the government's attempts to ease the lockdown by means of opening up schools and shops, and encouraging people once again to travel to work, appeared to many to be premature – 'too much, too soon' – and all too often mismanaged and characterized by dithering, 'U-turns', 'missteps' and confused and unclear messaging. The clear 'stay at home' message of the ten-week lockdown had been replaced with the far more vague one of 'stay alert'.[59]

Despite the Prime Minister's boasts that he was 'very proud' of the government's record on coronavirus and that 'we have turned the tide', the reality was very different.[60] For example, the 'good outcome' of 20,000 deaths from coronavirus predicted by Sir Patrick Vallance, the government's chief scientific adviser, in April, had already been greatly exceeded. Despite the methodological difficulties involved in reaching accurate UK and comparable international statistical aggregates, the UK had probably seen over 26,000 of its population die from Covid-19 during the particularly bad month of April. A total of over 52,000 deaths by June meant that the UK had overtaken Italy as having the highest death toll from the virus in the whole of Europe.[61]

The government also failed to convince large numbers of people that it was safe to travel to work and return to school. The economy, furthermore, was suffering more than most of its industrial counterparts. The popularity of footballer Marcus Rashford's campaign to extend free school meals over the summer also forced Johnson into an embarrassing U-turn. Only twenty-four hours after initially rejecting Rashford's plea, Johnson completely changed his mind. Rashford was subsequently awarded an MBE, in October 2020, in recognition of his services on behalf of vulnerable children. By the middle of June, the government's handling of the coronavirus crisis had reached a 'new low', with only three in ten offering approval.[62]

Brexit problems and a reinvigorated Labour Party

The political outlook for the government, in terms of Brexit and the state of the Labour Party, also became increasingly gloomy. The Brexit trade negotiations were going nowhere. The two sides remained at loggerheads around the key issues of state aid to industry, access to fishing grounds and fish quotas and the alignment of standards and protections. The EU was determined that the talks would not result in giving the UK an unfair competitive advantage, while the latter was equally insistent that the EU fully respect its newfound position as an 'equal sovereign state'.[63]

The Labour Party, crushed in December 2019, was making a decent comeback. In the wake of the Cummings affair, the Conservatives' lead over Labour fell by 8 points in a single week. By the end of May it stood at just 4 points, the lowest of Johnson's premiership to date. Two months earlier it had been 26 points. By mid-June it had fallen to between 2 and 3 points, and by the end of that month Starmer had overtaken Johnson as the preferred prime minister.[64]

This sudden reversal in party-political fortunes largely resulted from two factors. These were the government's catalogue of errors around Covid-19 and Starmer's impressive performance as the new Labour leader. Elected by a commanding 56.2 per cent of party members in the first round of voting, Starmer had succeeded Corbyn as Labour's leader in early April 2020. Starmer was determined to restore the party's internal unity and common purpose and transform Labour into a strong body, both as a credible opposition and a future government. He prided himself on his decency and patriotism and declared that the unfairness and deep inequalities revealed by Covid-19 must be ended and the 'broken' system 'mended' and made fairer in the post-pandemic recovery years.[65]

Starmer regularly outperformed and embarrassed Johnson in the House of Commons, especially during Prime Minister's Questions. The Prime Minister's sloppiness, lack of attention to detail, unconvincing blather and 'pie in the sky' rhetoric, contrasted most unfavourably with the ex-lawyer Starmer's forensic mind and formidable command of his brief. Starmer employed his skills rationally to analyse key issues and offer realistic solutions. For example, he made telling criticisms of the government's initial 'too little, too late' coronavirus policy and its late-spring and early-summer botched attempts to ease the lockdown. Starmer also made it plain, in relation to Brexit, that the Leave versus Remain argument was over and urged the Prime Minister to 'get it done'. In the spirit of patriotism and the national interest, he offered to work 'constructively' with the government to find effective solutions to the health and economic crises, but was effectively ignored by Johnson.

By late September Starmer remained more popular than Johnson and Labour led the Tories by 3 points, 42 per cent to 39 per cent. This was the first time Labour had been ahead in the polls since Johnson became prime minister. By October Starmer was claiming, in the face of rising infection rates and hospital admissions and 'the looming threat of a second national lockdown', that the Prime Minister had 'lost control' and that he didn't have 'a plan and a strategy in place'. Rather the 'serially incompetent' government was staggering from one crisis to another and blaming everyone else for its disastrous mistakes, according to Starmer. By the end of October Labour's lead stretched to 5 points.[66] Labour's joy, however, was not unqualified. Most importantly, the party still had a long way to go to convince the electorate that it could manage the economy better than the Conservatives. This was a key area in most elections and one on which Labour traditionally polled badly.[67]

Starmer also had to persuade the public that he and his party would resolve the thorny problem of antisemitism in Labour's ranks. Towards this end, he acted quickly and decisively on two fronts. First, at the end of October he fully accepted the damning report of the Equality and Human Rights Commission (EHRC) into antisemitism in the Labour Party. Starmer apologized profusely for Labour's proven past antisemitic transgressions and pledged to take the necessary measures to ensure that in future there would be 'zero-tolerance of antisemitism'. (Labour had eventually, after considerable internal tensions and conflicts, accepted in full the International Holocaust Remembrance Alliance's (IHRA) definition of antisemitism in September 2018.) Second, while taking 'no pleasure' in it, he fully supported the decision of Labour's general secretary, David Evans, and chief whip, Nick Brown, to suspend Jeremy Corbyn for his failure to fully accept the findings of the EHRC report. While declaring his total opposition to antisemitism, Corbyn had also claimed, in response to the report's findings, that the scale of antisemitism had been 'dramatically overstated' by Labour's opponents and parts of the media while he was leader. Starmer firmly declared that those who 'pretend' that antisemitism is exaggerated or factional, 'were part of the problem'.[68]

The government remains upbeat

Despite the increasing number and frequency of their trials and tribulations from March onwards, Johnson and his government ministers remained true to form in continuing to be upbeat about the present and future and not apologizing for any mistakes and failures in relation to their Covid-19 policies and actions. As in the past, what the *Guardian*'s Martin Kettle termed the tactics of 'diversion and scapegoating' were employed by the government to cover its power-driven tracks. In the eyes of the government, the 'guilty' 'others' variously included 'disloyal' civil servants and MPs, pro-Europeans or Remainers, infected foreigners coming into the country, the 'untrustworthy' and the 'authoritarian' Chinese government, which had allegedly 'exported' the virus to the rest of the world in the first place. A minority of those at home, who were portrayed as 'letting the side down', even in frontline organizations such as care homes and in Public Health England, by their 'lax' and 'anti-social behaviour', were also targeted.

Johnson even went so far as to brazenly attempt to deflect public criticism from his government's failure to provide care-home workers with adequate PPE and the extremely high number of Covid-related deaths in care homes, by claiming that 'Too many care homes didn't really follow the procedures in the way they could have'. Predictable and justifiable widespread outrage ensued.[69] Armed with a massive parliamentary majority of eighty, a mostly supportive press, a largely accommodating and often supine wider media, extensive popular support for himself and his 'wartime' emergency policies and the legal impossibility of mass protest under Covid-19 rules, the Prime Minister, however, continued to be in a very strong position successfully to deal with the health, economic and political problems outlined above.

Johnson was also fortunate in that the reduction in the severity of the pandemic between later June and early September paved the way for the restoration of his precious freedoms. The Office for National Statistics (ONS) reported that while the total number of deaths in England and Wales (involving both Covid and non-Covid factors) had been more than twice their normal levels between 10 and 24 April, and were highest among black males and those aged sixty-five and over, especially in care homes, the rate of increase had significantly fallen by the summer months. The same trend prevailed in Scotland and Northern Ireland.[70] In addition, new infections 'reached a low point in June', which 'levelled off in August', according to the ONS.[71]

Taking its cue from the improving Covid situation, the government re-opened England's pubs, restaurants, hotels, travel, including foreign holidays, schools, playgrounds and tourist attractions and reduced the two-metre social distancing rule. Johnson also encouraged people to travel to work again. The rest of the UK followed suit, albeit more cautiously and unevenly.

In an attempt to boost demand, consumer spending and public confidence, Sunak's mini-budget of early July made a short-term VAT cut for hospitality and tourism, abandoned stamp duty for nine months, provided government support for job creation for young people and for the month of August an 'eat out to help out' discount of £10 per person on restaurant meals. In mid-July the Prime Minister offered the prospect of a 'significant return to normality' by Christmas, even as he boosted NHS funding to plan for the prospect of a second wave of Covid-19 during the winter. In September, Johnson and Sunak ruled out a further extension of the furlough scheme beyond 31 October. The continuing economic crisis and the frightening prospect of immediate mass unemployment, however, effected a change of heart. Sunak later made extensions to furlough, first for a month until the end of November, then until the end of March, and eventually September 2021.[72]

The move out of lockdown provided a much-needed boost to the Prime Minister's and his party's popularity, at least in the short term. Coming shortly after the very damaging Dominic Cummings affair, Johnson, as noted above, promised the UK a 'New Deal', on the lines of President Roosevelt's New Deal for the United States in the 1930s, successfully to fight the effects of Covid-19.[73] By the middle of July the Tories' lead over Labour was back to 8 points.

The Prime Minister's habitual supporters in the media rallied behind him. For example, his home base, the *Daily Telegraph*, congratulated Johnson on having 'dealt with so much' in a 'remarkable' first year in office as prime minister. He had 'in large part' confounded 'the doubters, the doomsters, the gloomsters' by getting Brexit done, winning the election, 'finishing off Corbynism for good' and even capturing much of Labour's erstwhile 'Red Wall in the North'. He had, furthermore, survived divorce and hospitalization from Covid-19 and celebrated engagement and fatherhood. His mission was to complete Brexit and defeat the virus, concluded the *Telegraph*.[74] Martyn Brown of the *Daily Express* was very effusive in his praise. 'Mr. Johnson', with his 'bulldog spirit and irrepressible good humour', declared Brown, had 'epitomised the country's collective efforts against the spread of the epidemic.' Brown maintained that since leaving hospital in April, Johnson had 'carefully guided Britain through and out of the lockdown' and was 'preparing the country for the economic, public health and diplomatic battles ahead'.[75]

As was to be expected, those on the centre and left had a very different view. For Martin Fletcher of the *New Statesman*, the Prime Minister's actions during his first year had been characterized by 'incompetence and maliciousness' and a 'lamentable' response to the virus.[76] For the *Mirror*, Johnson's record was 'worse than we could have possibly imagined': it was a 'nightmare', one of lies, incompetence, confusing advice, laziness and scandal.[77]

The government's trials and tribulations return

The Prime Minister's popularity in the polls during the summer was short-lived. By the end of August 2020 Labour was neck and neck with the Tories for the first time since Johnson took over in July 2019.[78] As noted earlier, Labour gained and extended a lead, as did Starmer personally over Johnson, throughout September and October. These marked poll setbacks for the Prime Minister were the result of a catalogue of serious government mistakes.

Most significantly, and in contrast to the far more cautious Nicola Sturgeon in Scotland, the cavalier Johnson had opened up the economy and society of England far too soon and too quickly. Sunak's eating out scheme in August had unintentionally accelerated the transmission of the virus, as in all probability had large social gatherings and increased travel. During the same month the government had effected a U-turn in response to the mass protests and outrage against the downgrading of A-level and GCSE grades. Johnson and his hapless education secretary, Gavin Williamson, became laughing stocks and the objects of widespread anger. These mistakes were followed in September by the opening up of universities throughout the UK to around 1 million students. This deeply misguided policy most definitely increased transmission and led many distressed and angry students, confined to their small rooms in halls of residence, to complain that they were being effectively locked in by the educational and political authorities. From September onwards, rates of infection, sadly but entirely predictably, started once again to rise alarmingly in England, especially in the south-east of the country.[79]

There followed a period of widespread government chaos, confusion and mixed messaging. Many Conservative, as well as Labour, MPs observed that Johnson seemed to be 'ill-prepared and at sea' and had 'lost his grip' in the eyes of themselves and many of their constituents. Early in October, the Prime Minister's standing among Tory MPs 'plunged to a record low' and even the usually loyal *Telegraph* declared that there was 'a general sense of Government that is not fully in control'.[80]

A few weeks earlier the chief medical officer for England, Chris Whitty, and his SAGE colleagues, observed that a 'critical point' had been reached in the pandemic and strongly advised the government to respond to the alarming rise in the number of infections by imposing a two-week long 'circuit-breaker'. This would involve, for example, a return to working from home, a ban on household mixing in homes, the closure of bars, cafes and restaurants and restricting universities and colleges to online teaching and learning. Fearful of the potentially adverse effects on the economy and freedoms of a second full lockdown, Johnson did not act on SAGE's advice and did not follow the Scottish government's policy of a two-week closure of all pubs and restaurants in the most highly infected geographical areas.[81]

During the second week of October, the Prime Minister, however, did increase, albeit unevenly, restrictions in England under his new three-tier system for local authorities. Under this system, local authorities would be ranked medium, high or very high and an appropriate level of controls and restrictions imposed by central government. SAGE members' reservations about the effectiveness of the new scheme of things, however, proved to be accurate. Infections continued to escalate, and local dissatisfaction spread. For example, Labour's Andy Burnham in Manchester vociferously argued that the new system was badly conceived, unfairly executed and that central government was failing adequately to consult with those responsible for its operation at the local level.[82]

The Prime Minister, however, once again responded to mounting criticism by remaining upbeat. In typical fashion he, indeed, upped the ante. At the virtual Conservative Party conference during the first week of October, Johnson held out the wildly inflated promise of creating a 'New Jerusalem' by 2030. In his assumed

Churchillian mode, he declared that 'just as this country has seen off every alien invader for the last 1,000 years', so would 'British pluck' 'repel' the pandemic. It would not be appropriate 'just to go back to before', to 'normal', to the 'status quo', for we had 'lost too much' and 'mourned too many' for that. At the same time, however, there would 'come a moment' when 'the state must stand back' and allow the most dynamic, innovative and productive force in the economy, the 'private sector', to 'get on with it'. The task, Johnson continued, would be to green the economy, promote 'entrepreneurialism', transform social care, create more skilled jobs, encourage more home ownership and affordable accommodation in general, improve education and infrastructure and 'level up' to meet the interests and needs of those people 'who felt ignored and left out'. This was an exposition of Johnson's One-Nation Conservatism and a pledge to make the UK, 'once again', the 'greatest place on Earth'. In the process of building this 'New Jerusalem', the Prime Minister clearly set his face against 'lefty human rights lawyers and other do-gooders' – all those who want to 'pull statues down, to rewrite the history of our country (and) to edit our national CV to make it look more politically correct'.[83] Johnson thus adopted, in characteristic fashion, counter-attack and overblown optimism as the best means of defence.

Even so, high-blown rhetoric was no substitute for effective government action in relation to the pandemic. What was perhaps most significant about Johnson's speech and his policies during this period was that they met with a mixed response among habitual Tory supporters. For example, the *Telegraph*, the *Mail* and the *Sun*, along with prominent Tory 'libertarians', such as the Brexiter MP, Steve Baker, questioned whether the Prime Minister's turn to more restrictions in the autumn of 2020 was justified by the available evidence. To give one example, the *Telegraph* doubted that there was sufficient incontrovertible evidence to substantiate the claim that pubs and restaurants were hotbeds of Covid-19 transmission and that, *ipso facto*, should be closed. These 'freedom lovers' counselled Johnson to abandon restrictive 'excess' and return to 'normality' as a matter of urgency.[84] At the same time, however, other organs of the right-wing press remained fully supportive. For example, in October 2020 the *Daily Express* declared that Johnson's conference speech was a 'comeback moment' and urged its readers to 'back Boris and his vision for Brexit Britain'.[85]

The second and third national lockdowns

The UK government's responses to Covid from late October 2020 to January 2021 were characterized by further indecision, inconsistencies and sudden switches in policy. On 31 October the Prime Minister finally jettisoned his favoured tier system and adopted a more uniformly draconian one for England. This would take the form of a second lockdown. It would last from 5 November to 2 December. During this period, people would be strongly advised to stay at home, pubs, restaurants, gyms and non-essential shops would close and there would be severe restrictions upon mixing, meetings and travel. Schools, colleges and universities, however, could stay open. North of the border the Scottish government introduced a more restrictive five-level system. People in Scotland were also advised not to travel to and from England except for essential purposes. In Wales Mark Drakeford's seventeen-day firebreak was in place.

Johnson's change of heart, away from the partial and variable freedoms of the tier system to the compulsion of the lockdown, did not come easily. We have seen that the Prime Minister had previously defied the strong advice of SAGE members and other professionals to introduce a circuit breaker. Yet by the end of October there existed even more convincing evidence that the Covid situation was in danger of spinning out of control. As Chris Whitty declared, the virus was spreading 'extremely rapidly'. Unless more rigorous restrictions were introduced, there was a very real danger that deaths would reach 'several thousand a day' and that mortality would outstrip its peak of April. In turn, the NHS and the hospitals would be placed under intolerable pressure by December. Even the freedom-loving Johnson was forced to concede that a lockdown was necessary in order to prevent this 'medical and moral disaster'. Yet, at the same time, he was keen to offer some light at the end of the tunnel. For example, the loss of freedom would be tempered by the fact that it would be temporary. The English lockdown would end in early December and be replaced by the tiered system. In turn, although Christmas would be 'different', it would at least enable families to 'get together'. A doubtless exasperated Keir Starmer observed that in implementing the lockdown, the government had 'finally taken the decision it should have taken weeks ago'.[86]

Johnson's projected light at the end of the tunnel, however, failed to materialize. During the second half of November, a new and highly infectious variant of Covid was discovered in Kent. As Neil Ferguson pointed out, while this new variant could not have been predicted, it proved to be far more infectious and therefore had a much higher rate of transmission than the original virus. Writing in March 2021, Ferguson maintained that the new variant had been responsible for 'around half' of the UK's Covid deaths to date.[87]

The 50,000 plus deaths from Covid in the UK by November increased sharply to reach just over 67,000 by mid-December and 73,512 by the end of the year. The small amount of mixing that did take place at Christmas was very short-lived. For example, in Scotland it was limited to only Christmas Day. On Boxing Day all of Northern Ireland moved into lockdown and all of mainland Scotland moved to level four, the most restrictive tier. At the beginning of January, Nicola Sturgeon announced a new lockdown for Scotland for the rest of the month, while in Wales Mark Drakeford had introduced a national lockdown on 20 December. By the beginning of January, new cases of the virus in the UK exceeded 60,000 daily for the first time and the number of Covid patients in hospital was 40 per cent higher than during the peak of the first lockdown. During the second week of January the UK recorded a new peak of 101,060 deaths from Covid. Between late December and early January more than 1 million people in England were suffering from the virus. Many of the new cases were heavily concentrated in London and the south-east of England, with more than one in thirty of them concentrated in private households in the capital.[88]

This was the rapidly deteriorating situation in which Boris Johnson announced on 4 January that he had 'no choice' but to give up on his tier system and impose England's third national lockdown. This effectively came into being two days later. Wales, Northern Ireland and most of Scotland were also in lockdown. Regulations allowed the lockdown to remain in force until the end of March 2021. As in the first lockdown, people were obliged to stay at home and go outside only for essential purposes. Schools and colleges were to be closed to most pupils (although in practice there were U-turns and confusion around school closures) and universities were required to teach by on-line means where at all possible. The total of 28,000 plus UK deaths during January set a new monthly record. By Easter, 2021, the UK, with a population of 67.61 million inhabitants, had recorded over 4 million cases of Covid and over 127,000 deaths.[89]

The UK government and the pandemic: an assessment

The overall effects of the UK government's failure to tackle the virus more effectively from March 2020 to the end of March 2021 are reflected in national and international comparisons. In terms of national comparisons during this period of time, the UK occupied a depressing fifth position in the world with respect to deaths from the virus. The United States, with 550,000 Covid deaths in a population of over 331 million, topped the global mortality table, followed by Brazil (314,000 out of 212 million plus), Mexico (202,000 out of *c.* 130 million), India (162,000 out of 1.393 billion) and the UK. The UK also held the dreadful records of possessing the highest death toll in Europe and, as Ferguson has noted, 'the worst per capita mortality for Covid-19 in the developed world'.[90]

A number of countries of various and contrasting political complexions in the East, moreover, experienced much lower rates of infection and mortality from Covid than the UK. These included China, Japan, South Korea, Taiwan, New Zealand and Australia. By March 2021 Taiwan, with a population of 23.8 million people, remarkably had a record of only ten deaths and 1,022 cases. Out of a population of 4.8 million, New Zealand had only twenty-six deaths and 2,493 cases, while the 23.855 million people of Australia had endured 909 deaths and 29,228 cases. South Korea's population of 51.3 million had 1,726 deaths and 102,000 cases. Mainland China, with its massive population of over 1.4 billion, had staged a truly outstanding recovery from Covid in 2019–2020, to have only 4,636 deaths and 90,159 cases. Japan's 126 million plus inhabitants had 9,079 deaths and 470,000 cases.

These examples put the UK's record to shame. Despite their many differences, all these countries in the East had learned the central importance of locking down and closing borders sooner rather than later, and of having effective test, trace and isolate systems, clear, decisive and effective messaging and leadership and populations willing to abide by the rules. The government at Westminster not only failed to learn from the experiences of these countries, but all too often assumed that Britain, and especially England, was exceptional and superior to the rest of the world. This arrogance and complacency had truly dreadful consequences.[91]

A key conclusion to emerge from the UK's Covid catastrophe, especially at its height between December 2020 and March 2021, is that, in line with the advice given by many experts at the time, the government at Westminster should have locked down much earlier and more forcefully than it did. This would have clearly signalled to the public that Johnson and his colleagues were determined to suppress the virus in the manner of the far more successful countries outlined above. As a corollary, the government should not have returned to the tier system in early December and, even in the pursuit of freedom and 'togetherness', should not have opened up over Christmas.[92] The limited social mixing at Christmas, nevertheless, further increased the rapid transmission of the virus. The governments of Northern Ireland, Scotland and Wales were right to be more cautious and restrictive than their Westminster counterpart. Johnson should have prolonged the second lockdown rather than reverting to tiers in early December and introducing the third lockdown just over a month later. In all probability, this alternative course of action would also have significantly reduced what turned out to be the record surge in Covid cases and deaths between January and February 2021. As on many other occasions during the pandemic, Johnson and his colleagues had dithered, changed tack and acted too late effectively to tackle Covid.

By any reasonable measure of assessment, the government's Covid policy, therefore, was very unsuccessful. We indeed may go further to endorse the damning verdict of Gabriel Scally, a member of SAGE, that it amounted to a 'phenomenal failure'.[93] By March 2021, the anniversary of the first lockdown, demands for an independent inquiry into the government's handling of Covid were gathering force.[94] This has yet to take place.

Economic and social shocks

To compound matters, the economy and society suffered very badly in the first year of Covid. Between March 2020 and March 2021, the UK experienced the deepest domestic recession in 300 years and the effects of the worst global recession since the 1930s. The overall shock to the system was much greater than that felt during the financial crisis of 2007–2008. The country's economic crisis and performance turned out to be worse than those of any other major industrial economy. While the UK narrowly avoided a double-dip recession, it experienced a decline of 9.8 per cent in GDP over the twelve-month period. This was the largest fall since 1709. Government borrowing also hit a record figure, outside of wartime, of £303 billion.[95]

To be sure, there were some mitigating factors. Sunak's rescue packages were the most successful. His extended furlough scheme managed to cover almost 5 million people, and both staved off mass unemployment and limited financial hardship. Some business people, retirees and some of those working from home, furthermore, managed to save money and improve their living standards. Retail sales remained resilient due to the boom in online spending, even as many high street shops suffered, some terminally. The independent Office for Budget Responsibility (OBR) also predicted that the economy would 'bounce back rapidly' and 'pencilled in growth of 7.3%' in 2022, 'the fastest rate of expansion since the second world war'. As early as March 2021, the economy was showing signs of recovery after contracting by 2.9 per cent in January. By the following month the projected growth rate for 2021 was 6.8 per cent.[96]

On balance, however, negative factors greatly outweighed positive ones. For example, the OBR estimated that the economy would be 3 per cent smaller by 2026. The furlough scheme is expected to have cost the Treasury around £65 billion by September 2021. Unemployment, standing at 6 per cent in March 2021, is predicted to rise to between 6.5 per cent and 7 per cent later in the year. At the same time unemployment and other benefits paid to UK workers compare badly with those paid out in other major industrial countries. The pandemic has so far depleted the savings of around 40 per cent of the population and exerted a particularly adverse effect upon the health and wellbeing of the lower paid and less skilled. It has had its worst effect upon the health and living standards of black and Asian people, particularly those living in overcrowded urban conditions and often forced to travel to work irrespective of the health risks involved. The fact that a decade of austerity had hollowed out much of the public sector has also greatly reduced the capacity of that sector adequately to cope with the economic and health crises. In March 2021, furthermore, millions of NHS and other public sector workers, lionized during the worst of the pandemic, were informed by the government that it would recommend a miserly pay increase of 1 per cent or less. For many of them this meant a cut in terms of real pay. This stood in marked contrast to the 4 per cent later promised by the government in Scotland. In comparative terms, Sunak's boost to demand was dwarfed by President Biden's $1.9 trillion Covid recovery stimulus, plus a $2.3 trillion package for the economy.

Finally, in his March 2021 budget, Sunak declared that the massive hole in the economy would have to be financed in the post-Covid recovery period by significant tax increases and massive cuts in public spending. He thus signalled, and would emphatically do so again at his party's annual conference in October, that the Tories would return, as wished by May, Hammond and many others, to their traditional principles of financial 'discipline' and 'sound' saving and spending. As observed earlier, this raised the possibility that future financial limitations could be placed upon Johnson's pledges not to return to the pre-Covid past of austerity and to 'level up' class-based and regional imbalances, especially in the 'red-wall' constituencies.[97]

A remarkable government recovery

The situation did not, however, amount to unqualified doom and gloom for the Prime Minister and his government. As noted in the Introduction to this chapter, from February 2021 onwards, the government's fortunes indeed markedly improved and Johnson, once again, proved himself to be the most resilient and fortunate of politicians. The government's remarkable recovery manifested itself in four main areas: Brexit; Covid policy; the economy; the polls. I will address these in turn.

Brexit

Against the increasing expectation of a 'No Deal' outcome, the government had achieved a post-Brexit trade deal with the EU just a week before the 31 December 2020 deadline. For most of 2020, the UK and the EU had failed to reach agreement around the key issues of state aid to industry and fair competition; alignment on rules and standards concerning labour, the environment and social matters such as health and safety; and mutual agreement on access, quotas and a tariff-free fisheries deal.

The EU was particularly keen to ensure that the post-Brexit UK did not enjoy an unfair competitive advantage by means of state subsidies in its trade with Europe, while the issue of sovereignty – of not being told what to do by an overmighty EU – was of central importance to Johnson and his key negotiator, David Frost. Yet in December the UK government decided to withdraw the controversial sections in its Internal Market Bill which would break the terms of the Withdrawal Agreement of January 2020 in relation to the Northern Ireland protocol and so threaten an 'open' border on the island of Ireland and, *ipso facto*, the safeguarding of the Good Friday Peace Treaty. This decision greatly eased the way towards the successful completion of a trade and security deal.[98]

The deal guaranteed that there would be no tariffs or quotas on the movement of goods between the UK and the EU. This represented something of a success for the UK in that it went beyond the EU's more limited deals with Japan and Canada.

In the spirit of compromise, the UK would leave the common fisheries policy and there would be a transition period of five years in which EU vessels would continue to be able to fish six to twelve nautical miles from the British coastline, but the EU's share from fishing in British waters would be reduced by 25 per cent over five-and-a-half years. One quarter of the financial value of the EU's catch would be 'repatriated' to UK-flagged vessels by the end of those years. Thereafter the UK and the EU would hold annual negotiations around fishing arrangements. Some fishing communities in Scotland and elsewhere, claimed that they had been 'sold out' by the government.

In a 'major concession', the UK would set up its own body to determine whether state aid had distorted trade. At the same time, however, the UK would have to make sure that its subsidy respected 'key principles set out in the treaty'. To ensure that a level playing field continued to operate, both sides agreed to abide by 'a minimum level of environmental, social and labour standards'. This arrangement would be reviewed after four years. If it were found to be working in an unsatisfactory way, tariffs could be introduced subject to the agreement of an independent arbitration panel.

In short, after months of often bad-tempered negotiations, involving much posturing and finger-pointing, a free-trade compromise was reached. Both sides would be obliged, at least in the first few years, to respect mutually agreed trading rules and standards. As the *Guardian's* Lisa O'Carroll and Daniel Boffey concluded, provided that the agreement worked in practice, the UK would not become a source of cheap competition to the EU, a 'Singapore on Thames'.[99]

The press responded in predictable ways. The *Observer* joined its sister newspaper, the *Guardian*, in declaring the deal to be a disaster. The *Guardian's* view was that Brexit was a 'tragic national error', while the *Observer* declared that, far from being a 'political triumph', the deal would cost the UK dearly, 'deepen rifts within the union' and 'one day surely be regarded as one of the greatest-ever deceits inflicted on the British electorate'.[100] In complete contrast, the *Scottish Daily Mail* claimed that the deal would help to trigger an economic 'bounce back in 2021' and a 'business boom'. The *Scottish Daily Express* was in full agreement. 'Victory; in the Brexit trade deal would "help the UK emerge as (a) leading economic powerhouse"' and, as maintained by 'Boris', herald a new 'Golden Age'. Writing in the *Daily Telegraph*, Charles Moore, the veteran journalist and former editor of the newspaper, opined that the public had to acknowledge that Johnson was a winner and that he had succeeded by accepting 'the logic of Brexit'.[101]

Yet the trade deal was by no means an unqualified success. First, it was not scheduled to, and did not in practice, include financial services. The latter were to be dealt with in a separate process from 2021 onwards. As noted earlier in this book, financial services had highly prized their automatic access, or 'passporting rights', to the EU. These now came to an end and the UK's financial institutions henceforth would be required, under the equivalence system, to apply to the EU for the right to access its markets by complying with individual member states' requirements. By its very nature, the equivalence system would be more limited, conditional, uncertain and lengthy for UK financial institutions than its passporting predecessor. As such, it was not welcomed in the City. Financial institutions, however, would pragmatically adapt to the new situation by increasingly moving part of their operations and staff to EU countries. The City remains a global financial powerhouse, but over time the balance of financial power, in terms of the UK and Europe, will shift to Frankfurt, Paris and Dublin. This will probably be a process of 'slow bleed'. In any event, Johnson's promised future 'certainty' for finance, most certainly did not take place. Theresa May would express disappointment at Johnson's failure to strike a deal on financial services.[102]

Second, between January and Easter 2021, the 'teething problems' expected by the UK government immediately to follow the new deal quickly became something far more serious. Of central concern was the fact that, contrary to Johnson's prediction, important parts of the trade between the UK and the EU, including exports to Northern Ireland, did not become frictionless. Many UK businesses, and especially small ones in food and drink, found that they faced many new obstacles in attempting to continue their exports to the EU. These hurdles included added paperwork, new checks and controls, and problems and delays in shipping and access.

All these added to costs, sometimes large ones that businesses were unable to afford. In January alone, total UK exports to the EU fell by 41 per cent and those in food and drink by 75.5 per cent. Scottish exporters of seafood to the EU, for example, found that their produce now had to pass new health tests and could not easily and quickly be shipped. Given the perishable nature of their product, this situation quickly turned into a 'nightmare'. Many in fishing communities who had wholeheartedly supported Brexit in the belief that it would increase their control and quotas, now felt betrayed by the Tories.

In terms of the UK's relationship with Northern Ireland, the deal was found, in reality, to involve added checks and controls on goods crossing the Irish Sea. As noted earlier in this chapter, these checks and controls had been mutually agreed as an integral part of the Withdrawal Agreement. Yet the Prime Minister who, of course, had willingly signed up to the 'oven ready' agreement, still refused to acknowledge this fact. As a result, there was much ill-feeling in Northern Ireland among the DUP and other loyalist groups. They felt that Johnson had misled them and undermined the unity of the Union. They claimed that the Prime Minister had acted in these ways in order to achieve what they saw as a shoddy deal, by keeping Northern Ireland in the EU single market for goods. They were also concerned that the Northern Ireland protocol could lead to more widespread demands for a united Ireland and called for it to be abandoned as unviable. Some supermarkets in Northern Ireland also experienced shortages on their shelves and there were reports of verbal and even physical abuse directed at border staff. Albeit small, but highly disaffected, loyalist groups, protesting partly against the terms of Brexit, attacked the police in Belfast and Londonderry during late March and April. Meanwhile, Michael Gove, the cabinet office minister, was charged with contacting the European Commission and demanding that the three-months grace period on checks and controls in the Irish Sea be extended. None of this augured well for either the UK's future trading relationship with the EU, or peace in Northern Ireland and the security of the Union.[103]

Covid policy

Despite experiencing these post-Brexit trade difficulties, and even when announcing the third lockdown in early January, Johnson declared that he remained 'full of optimism and fundamental hope' that things would be different by spring. This hope was largely realized. The government's anti-Covid vaccine policy was crucial to the government's recovery.

The roll-out of the vaccines by Pfizer, the American multinational pharmaceuticals company, and the British-Swedish company, AstraZeneca, from December 2020 and early in 2021 onwards, proved to be a great success. The government was particularly proud of the fact that the 'English' AstraZeneca jab was to the fore and that most EU countries were lagging well behind the UK in their vaccination programmes. The target of giving the first dose of a coronavirus vaccine to over 13 million people over seventy, the most clinically vulnerable age group, and front-line health and social care workers by mid-February, was successfully realized. By the beginning of April, furthermore, more than 32 million people in the UK had received at least one dose of the vaccine in what had become the biggest inoculation programme the country had ever undertaken. The UK was on track to offer the vaccine to all adults by July and the public was duly very relieved and grateful.[104] Although Johnson succeeded in taking much of the credit, the success of the vaccine roll-out in reality owed far more to the excellence and efficiency of the NHS and its staff than that of the government.

The economy and the polls

The highly successful vaccination programme was accompanied by renewed growth in the economy and an upsurge in public support for the government. Despite the continuing economic problems outlined above, there were signs of renewed growth from February onwards. In April experts predicted that the economy, having shrunk by almost 10 per cent in the previous year, would grow by 6. 8 per cent in 2021. This would be the 'fastest rate since 1941'.[105]

Labour's closing of the polling gap between itself and the Tories between April and December 2020, furthermore, was quickly reversed. Between January and April 2021 the Tory lead over Labour in the polls increased, from 3 to 7 percentage points. By April the Conservatives stood on 43 per cent, while Labour was on 36 per cent. Although Keir Starmer attempted to present a 'bold' vision of a new Britain – united, secure and offering prosperity and opportunity for all – in place of Johnson's tired, 'broken' and unequal system, he appeared to be fighting a losing battle, at least in the short term. It was highly likely that the Tories would do very well in the local elections in England in May, while Labour seemed to have little chance of recapturing its erstwhile support in the 'red wall' constituencies and well beyond.[106]

As the *Guardian's* Martin Kettle wrote at the beginning of April, the 'palpable success of the vaccination rollout and the readiness of most voters to want the government to succeed in the emergency', were key factors in the recovery.[107] Kettle and other commentators correctly observed that many people compared the Covid crisis to a wartime emergency and accordingly set out stoically to 'do their bit' for their country and its leaders. Above all, they wanted to be healthy, safe and to survive rather than appear to be negative and defeatist.

It also helped that the media in general, and the BBC in particular, gave Johnson a relatively easy ride, especially during the tempestuous year of 2020. We have seen throughout this chapter that the centre-left *Guardian* and the *Observer* were highly critical of many of the government's coronavirus policies. The same may be said for the Labour-supporting *Mirror* and, albeit far less so, the somewhat strangely muted liberal *Channel Four News*. Yet these organs were far from representative of the mainstream media as a whole. For example, while the Conservative-supporting *Telegraph, Express* and *Mail* did criticize certain aspects of government policy, they generally felt that the government was doing its best in extremely difficult circumstances, that the trajectory of the pandemic had been pretty much the same in most other countries and that some blame lay with the irresponsible and anti-social behaviour of individuals. The *Daily Mail* declared that there was a link between obesity and Covid and, that 'regrettably' but bluntly, Britain was 'the fat man of Europe'.[108] The right-wing newspapers would undoubtedly have been much harsher and impatient if Jeremy Corbyn had won the December 2019 general election.

The government also played a part in improving its own ratings. Following the departures of Cummings and Cain from Downing Street in November, confrontation, chaos and permanent revolution certainly appeared to give way to a far more emollient, cautious and civilized approach on the part of Johnson and his team towards parliament, the civil service, the public and the pandemic. The arrival in Downing Street of Allegra Stratton, the former journalist, as press secretary, along with other government advisers, may well have had something to do with this change. To her credit, Stratton counselled 'civility' and good public relations. Johnson seemed to agree. He certainly gave the appearance of at least listening far more attentively than at many points in the past to his SAGE and other likeminded advisers not to take any undue risks in relation to Covid. As a probable consequence, the lockdown of January–April 2021 was enforced for longer and far more efficiently and uniformly than the flawed ones of 2020. Gung-ho prime ministerial rhetoric, particularly around the notion of British freedoms, gave way to a far more circumspect, sober and realistic approach. As a result, Johnson was able to offer a cautious, staged and seemingly viable roadmap out of lockdown.

Finally, the Prime Minister's popularity and strength were aided by the divisions and conflicts suddenly afflicting the independence movement in Scotland. These mainly revolved around the Alex Salmond affair, involving allegations of sexual misconduct on the part of the former first minister, and Salmond's potentially very damaging claim that Nicola Sturgeon had knowingly misled the Scottish parliament over the timing and details of meetings with him (see Chapter 4). By Easter 2021, in early April, the Prime Minister once again appeared to be firmly in the national driving seat.[109]

More twists and turns

A few weeks before the May elections, there took place three more unexpected and extraordinary twists in our tale of the fluctuating fortunes of Johnson. First, in April 2021 a 'chatty rat' or 'rats' leaked new and very serious allegations to the press about Tory cronyism, clientelism, sleaze, mendacity, hypocrisy and unfitness for public office. A key allegation was that Johnson had improperly used money donated to the Conservative Party as a contribution to the total funding needed to refurbish his apartment in Downing Street. Johnson and Carrie Symonds wished the apartment to be furnished to luxury standards and not, as under Theresa May, those of 'John Lewis'. Johnson did respond to questioning by Keir Starmer and many others by angrily declaring that he had used his own money to pay for the refurbishment. It was widely reported, however, that the total sum required was around £200,000 and that part of it had come from a donation made to Conservative Party funds by a Tory peer, Lord Brownlow.

A marked lack of transparency characterized this issue. In the opinion of Dominic Cummings, who strongly maintained that he had been unfairly suspected by the government of being the 'rat', Johnson's original plans to get donors to pay for the renovations were 'unethical, foolish, possibly illegal and almost certainly broke the rules on proper disclosure of political donations'.[110] The announcement that the Electoral Commission would open a formal investigation lasting months into whether the Conservative Party had broken electoral law by making a financial contributions to the refurbishment ensured that the 'cash for curtains' row would not quickly disappear.[111]

Second, there was widespread condemnation of text messages Johnson had exchanged with the Brexit billionaire Sir James Dyson, who had moved his head office to Singapore in 2019. In March 2020, Johnson had texted Dyson to the effect that he would 'fix it', so that Dyson's employees making ventilators in the UK to aid the fight against Covid-19 would not have to pay extra taxation. The outraged and vengeful Cummings once again insisted that he had not been responsible for the leak of the texts.[112]

Third, it was leaked that, following a meeting on 30 October 2020 about a possible second lockdown, Johnson had 'ranted' that he would rather see bodies 'pile high in their thousands' than order a third lockdown. This story was first printed in the *Daily Mail* on 26 April 2021. Johnson again angrily denied this charge and challenged the media, Starmer and other accusers to provide evidence for their claim. Yet the highly respected journalist and presenter Robert Peston declared on television that two eyewitnesses had 'corroborated the *Daily Mail*'s account to me'. The *Guardian* and the *BBC* also revealed that they had corroborating witness accounts.[113]

Johnson had set up an inquiry in an attempt to find out the identity of the October 2020 leaker. Yet, according to Cummings, the Prime Minister had attempted to close down the inquiry because it would lead to the identification of a close friend of Carrie Symonds as the 'rat'. Cheekily, if not outrageously, presenting himself as a paragon of public responsibility and virtue, Cummings further declared that he would be prepared to give full evidence to a parliamentary select committee in May into the government's policy concerning the pandemic in general, including its failure to close the UK's borders in time to limit the spread of the virus and prevent deaths.[114]

The Prime Minister also turned down another request from the Covid-19 Bereaved Families for Justice group for an urgent inquiry into the government's handling of the pandemic. Johnson maintained that such an inquiry was 'not appropriate' at the present time and that 'the very people who would need to give evidence' were too busy, 'working round the clock' delivering vaccines and preparing for 'the effects' of a possible third wave of the virus. The pain and grief of members of the group would thus continue. They, along with many others, saw Johnson's alleged rant as being totally insensitive and unacceptable.[115]

To add to this sorry and disturbing picture, the leaks also cast a very damaging light upon the political and business practices of the former Tory prime minister, David Cameron. The latter, who prided himself upon his high-minded sense of public duty and service, was accused of improperly having mixed politics and business and the pursuit of the public with his own private interest. As Kalyeena Makortoff, the *Guardian*'s banking correspondent, observed in April, Cameron was now 'at the centre of the UK's largest lobbying scandal in a decade'.[116]

Cameron had allowed Greensill Capital, a supply-chain finance firm founded by an Australian, Alex Greensill, security access and desk space in his prime-ministerial offices in Downing Street. In 2018 Cameron, furthermore, became a 'part-time' special adviser to Greensill and was partly paid in share options. The former prime minister expected to gain £200 m in the event of Greensill being floated on the stock market, according to the *Guardian*.[117] During 2020, however, the company was obviously experiencing serious financial problems. Taking advantage of his many contacts in the establishment, Cameron lobbied Rishi Sunak and high-ranking figures in the Bank of England and the Treasury in several attempts to gain government financial support for Greensill during the pandemic. These efforts, however, proved to be unsuccessful and Greensill filed for insolvency in March 2021.

Cameron, ironically, had expressed the views in February 2010, just months before becoming prime minister, that he disapproved of the excessively cosy relationship between big business, the government of the day and the state and that lobbying was the country's 'next big scandal waiting to happen'. In April 2021 Boris Johnson set up a formal, independent investigation into the Greensill affair, including Cameron's lobbying activities on behalf of the company. Yet Cameron continues to insist that while he 'should have gone through more formal channels', he has 'broken no rules at any point'.[118]

It is difficult to know if these various allegations of cronyism and sleaze will adversely affect public support for the government. In the immediate term this would not appear to be the case. While polls carried out during the second half of April showed, on balance, that the Conservative lead over Labour had fallen, as had Johnson's popularity, they also agreed that the Tories were still in the lead.[119]

This positive message for the Tories was endorsed, indeed greatly strengthened, by the results of the May elections. Notwithstanding the fact that a majority of the MSPs elected to the Scottish parliament were pro-independence and that Labour retained its dominance in Wales, the Tories easily performed best in the local elections in England.

In addition, they spectacularly won the by-election in the north-east constituency of Hartlepool, one of the 'red-wall' seats, by almost 7,000 votes and a swing of 16 per cent. This was the first time since its creation in 1974 that the constituency had not returned a Labour MP. The Conservatives owed much of their striking success to the popularity of Brexit in Hartlepool (70% had voted Leave), the vaccine roll-out, the promise of the government's 'levelling-up' agenda to ease extremely high unemployment in the area and the optimism for the future offered by Johnson and Jill Mortimer, the successful Conservative candidate. [120] They were also greatly helped by Labour's years of neglect, inaction and complacency in the face of deleterious socio-economic change in Hartlepool and elsewhere in the north-east of England.

The Tory cause, both locally and nationally, was further boosted by the fact that the Bank of England revised upward its annual growth forecast for 2021 from 5 per cent in February to 7.25 per cent at the beginning of May.[121]

Conclusion

This chapter has charted the triumphs, trials and troubles of Boris Johnson during his eventful and turbulent period as prime minister from July 2019 to May 2021. We have seen that this period was one of acute crises, ranging from Brexit to Covid-19, in which the government's trust and legitimacy were often questioned. We have also observed that the Prime Minister experienced numerous fluctuations in his personal and political fortunes. Yet the main conclusion to be drawn from the evidence is that Johnson's triumphs outweighed his considerable trials and tribulations and the long 'charge sheet' levelled against him. Thus, there was no complete breakdown in Johnson's and the government's authority, control and standing, no full-blown 'legitimation crisis' in the sense employed by Habermas.[122]

These triumphs were particularly marked from the beginning of his rule to the onset of the pandemic in the UK in late February and March 2020. Thereafter, as primarily reflected in the error-strewn and tragic Covid policy in 2020, Johnson's government made serious and, doubtless for many grieving families and other members of the public, unforgivable major mistakes. Yet the Prime Minister tried to make amends by adopting a more cautious and considered approach to Covid in 2021.

In addition, and despite his ruthlessness towards his 'colleagues' in the Conservative Party and elsewhere who opposed him, and his betrayal of the DUP over a border in the Irish Sea, he did succeed, unlike Theresa May, and against the odds, in 'getting Brexit done'. Whether Brexit will mark the beginning of a bright new dawn for 'Global Britain' and whether ongoing disputes over the Northern Ireland protocol and 'frictionless' trade with the EU as a whole will be resolved, of course, are issues that only future observers will be able fully to address.

Johnson, furthermore, achieved a stunning triumph over the Labour Party and his other political opponents in the December 2019 general election. The result of that election killed off the idea that Corbyn's left-wing socialism might constitute a viable alternative future national path to that of Toryism. Johnson's and Sunak's interventionist economic rescue measures, particularly the furlough scheme, furthermore, both signalled that the government was prepared to put aside, at least temporarily, its fundamental 'free-market' principles in order to offer immediate economic relief to millions of people and avert mass unemployment. At the same time, however, the sheer scale and depth of both the economic and health crises affecting the UK and the expansionary relief measures adopted by the government, made it very likely that at some point in the not-too-distant future Johnson and Sunak would have to make very difficult choices around the issues of saving and spending and state intervention versus free-market neoliberalism.

On a personal level, Johnson displayed carefully, and long-cultivated, clown-like behaviour, eccentricity, buffoonery, bonhomie and charlatanry. His character is a mixture of joviality, charm, luck, mendacity, duplicity, calculated ruthlessness, determination, self-interest and narcissism. He craves to be liked, especially by women. He showed that while fundamentally committed to capitalism and the primacy of the private sector, he could also be very pragmatic and flexible about economic policy. Above all perhaps, he attached the utmost importance to self-aggrandisement, power and control. In order to achieve domination, he has often opportunistically changed direction and ditched former colleagues, allies and policies previously held to be immutable and sacrosanct. He is nobody's fool and should not be underestimated.[123]

By May 2021 Johnson had regained much of his former authority, control and popularity. His eclectic combination of the post-Brexit mixed economy, One-Nation Conservatism, Unionism, 'Little Englandism' and general positivity and bonhomie constituted, in Gramscian terms, the hegemonic force or dominant common-sense in England. As such, Johnson's practice and vision constituted the most obvious and popular way out of UK capitalism's ongoing and most challenging combined crisis of modern times.

Yet an outstanding question remained. To what extent did the left-of-centre, independence programme of radical Scottishness, offered by the ruling SNP and the wider independence movement in Scotland, offer a realistic alternative future pathway, for both Scotland and, as a beacon, for other parts of the UK, to that offered by Johnson? It is to a consideration of this difficult but crucial question that I turn in Chapter 4.

Scotland: Another Way is Possible?

Introduction

I have drawn the reader's attention at various points in this book to the peaceful political revolution which has taken place and continues to evolve in modern Scotland. This revolution has resided in the recent meteoric rise and domination of the SNP, the precipitous fall of Labour and the continuing long-term decline of the Conservative Party. In this chapter I bring together and further develop my observations up to the outcome of the May 2021 elections to the Scottish parliament. The main objective is to present an integrated and up-to-date picture of the main player in this revolution, the SNP, and its key aim of creating an independent Scotland.

Organized chronologically, the chapter largely concentrates on the successful SNP and the more variable fortunes of the wider movement for radical Scottish self-determination between the failed Scottish independence referendum of September 2014 and the May 2021 elections. In the run up to these elections the SNP re-affirmed its pledge, made on several occasions during the previous five years, to hold another referendum on Scottish independence – Indyref2 – as soon as practicably possible.

Three key questions emerge from the material presented in this chapter. First, to what extent do the SNP and the independence movement offer a serious and viable left-of-centre, alternative future to the Conservatism proffered by Boris Johnson and his government? Second, if they do so, will the future consist not of more extensive devolution, but the further break-up of the United Kingdom and the creation of a new, more economically dynamic and fairer Scottish nation? Third, will an independent, radical Scotland constitute a positive role model, a beacon of democratic and progressive hope, to the other subordinate nations within the UK?

2014: the Scottish independence referendum

The result: the success of No

The failed Scottish referendum of 18 September 2014 constitutes my point of departure. The referendum campaign constituted a widespread and vibrant exercise or 'festival' in grass-roots debate and democracy. On an extremely high turn-out of 84.59 per cent, victory went to the No side by 55 per cent to 45 per cent. In January 2012 only about

35 per cent of the eligible population in Scotland said that they would vote in favour of Scottish independence. This number of Yes voters, moreover, declined to less than 25 per cent a year later. The No side remained well in the lead until the end of August 2014, but thereafter the gap began to narrow. On the eve of the referendum, a remarkable turnaround for Alex Salmond's SNP and the wider pro-independence movement had indeed taken place. Those in favour of independence now constituted 51 per cent, as opposed to the 49 per cent against, according to the polls.[1]

As recorded by David Cameron in his book *For the Record*, this dramatic turnaround in the polls, just two weeks before the date of the referendum, sparked off a surge of frantic activity on the part of defenders of the Union. The cross-party 'Better Together' campaign which was launched in May 2013 by the Scottish Labour Party leader, Johann Lamont, and chaired by Alistair Darling, the former Labour chancellor of the exchequer and close ally and friend of Gordon Brown, intensified its propaganda and other activities. In a highly contrived move, the three pro-Union leaders of the main parties, David Cameron, Nick Clegg and Ed Miliband, along with sixty Westminster-based Labour MPs, rushed to pay an albeit fleeting visit to Scotland more directly and urgently to plead their case and 'save the union'. Gordon Brown, seen by many No voters as the true 'saviour of the Union', made important, heartfelt and effective speeches in favour of Scottishness *and* Britishness. As Cameron observed, Brown placed particular emphasis on his view that 'voting No was a patriotically Scottish act'. Just two days before the vote, Cameron, Clegg and Miliband, very strongly influenced by Brown, made a pledge, popularly known as the 'Vow', to give 'extensive new powers' to the Scottish parliament and to make it clear that 'healthcare spending was a decision for the Scottish government', according to Cameron. This clarification was intended unreservedly to reassure the public in Scotland that the UK did not plan, contrary to the view expressed by some on the pro-independence side, to run down and privatize the NHS.[2] Alarm and panic were not confined to Unionist politicians. There were market forecasts that in the event of a Yes victory there would be a run on the pound, while major banks and companies threatened to move their headquarters out of Scotland.[3]

As matters transpired, these forecasts were rendered redundant. The No side won with a very comfortable majority of 10 per cent. Campaigners for No were highly successful among the voters in contrasting the perceived *benefits* of the Union – the 'greatest family of nations for 300 years' – with the purportedly huge *risks* of an independent Scotland. In their eyes, the devolved Union constituted, to employ Darling's phrase, the 'best of both worlds', with Scotland 'making its own decisions, keeping the pound and backed by the strength and security of the UK'. The Union symbolized hallowed tradition, proven stability, the preservation of longstanding ties of kith and kin across open borders, the effective pooling of resources and sharing of risks and more or less guaranteed material and mental comforts and security. The rest of the UK constituted by far Scotland's biggest export market for its goods and services with almost four times as much going there as to the rest of the EU. In marked contrast, independence signified the considerable fears, risks and dangers of the great unknown. For the No side, an independent Scotland would be a small country, lacking the security and other protections offered by membership of the Union and the EU and struggling to achieve strength and status in an increasingly competitive and troubled world. No campaigners claimed that on the domestic front an independent Scotland would be faced with dwindling oil reserves, an unacceptably high budget deficit and the prospects of increased taxation, low growth, reduced public spending and declining living standards and pensions. As observed by the pro-Union civil servant and professor of government, Jim Gallagher, strong economic growth and productivity gains following independence would not in themselves be remotely sufficient, at least in the short- to medium-terms, to offset these major economic disadvantages.[4]

It was also the case that, as things stood in 2014, an independent Scotland would face a 'leap in the dark' financially. In the eyes of the chancellor, George Osborne, 'if Scotland walks away from the UK, it walks away from the pound'. The pound, furthermore, was one of the most valued, oldest and stable currencies in the world. David Cameron joined Osborne in declaring that the UK government would not countenance Alex Salmond's post-independence plan for a currency union with the UK. In that event, declared Darling in a damning comment during his first TV debate with Salmond, the SNP leader and his party simply lacked a plan B.[5] As highlighted by many on the No side, including Professor Gallagher, while an independent Scotland in fact could use sterling, it would, at least in the form of Salmond's sketchy and unconvincing plan, lack an 'effective central bank', a 'sophisticated financial system' and 'very restricted capacity for government borrowing'.[6]

These adverse economic and financial comments and judgements proved to be especially damaging to the Yes cause. This was particularly the case among older voters aged sixty-five years or over, 73 per cent of whom were the most ardent supporters of No. In a poll of just over 2,000 voters taken immediately after the referendum, Lord Ashcroft found that keeping the pound constituted the main reason for opposing independence among 57 per cent of No voters. Fears about the future of their pensions, funding of the NHS and tax and public spending were also 'mentioned by at least one third of No voters'.

These issues were also seen to be more important than 'a strong attachment to the UK', even though 'more than three-quarters of Scots' saw themselves as 'wholly or partly British', according to Gallagher.[7] As Ashcroft concluded, the 'biggest overarching reason' for voting No was 'the risks of being independent looked too great when it came to things like the currency, EU membership, the economy, jobs and prices', and access to free healthcare and schooling. This was the case even in the prevailing climate of austerity.[8] The Union, furthermore, was believed to afford preferential treatment to the people of Scotland, vis-à-vis other UK subjects, in terms of comparatively lower levels of taxation, higher levels of public spending per head of population and the running, without any immediate costs, of a high budget deficit.[9]

Economic and financial concerns thus lay at the heart of both the No campaign and its successful appeal to the Scottish electorate. Many doubtless endorsed the sentiments of the proud and famous Scot and extremely successful manager of Manchester United Football Club, Sir Alex Ferguson, that the protection of the economy, the NHS, schools, hospitals and family and kinship ties across the UK demanded that it was better for the Union to be 'together' rather than divided. 'Let's stay united', Ferguson urged, and keep Scotland 'united with our team mates from the rest of the UK'.[10] The sobering message for the SNP and other advocates of independence was that unless they paid more careful and detailed attention to the economics of independence, then a future Scottish referendum would surely go the way of the first.

The result: the failure of Yes

In turning to the case made by the Yes side and its appeal, the principle of *self-determination*, in the form of Scotland's democratic right more extensively to control and shape its own affairs, was of fundamental importance. After all, the ruling Tories had not enjoyed a majority in Scotland since 1955. As Ashcroft observed, albeit in an exaggerated way, 'the principle that all decisions about Scotland should be taken in Scotland' was 'the most powerful overarching reason for a Yes vote'.[11] The demand for greater Scottish sovereignty was closely related to the widespread and growing perception that for the most part Scotland had not been and was not being treated by Westminster fairly and as a proud and equal partner nation within the Union. Rather it was variously being neglected, treated as an inferior and even with contempt by successive UK governments. Ashcroft concluded, 'by far the biggest driver' for the Yes vote and Scottish sovereignty was 'disaffection with Westminster politics'.[12]

This disaffection had developed with particular force under the authoritarian and 'alien' rule of the hated Margaret Thatcher. John Major had been less highhanded and New Labour, of course, had delivered devolution. Devolution, however, far from resulting in Labour's goal of 'killing nationalism stone dead', had helped to fuel its impressive rise in Scotland, particularly in the form of the rapidly ascendant SNP.[13] In turn, Blair and Brown, Brian Wilson and other prominent English and Scottish Labour MPs were unremitting in their opposition and disparagement of the SNP and, as Wilson put it, 'the politics of grievance'. With Brown and Wilson to the fore, these Labour leaders conveniently overlooked the inclusive, tolerant and forward-looking civic-nationalism, multi-culturalism, anti-racism and internationalism of the SNP and the Yes movement. They misleadingly depicted them – the 'Nationalists' – as absolutist, divisive, backward-looking, intolerant, mean-spirited, anti-English, anti-British and anti-Enlightenment. They would continue to do so in the future.[14] By their very involvement in Better Together, Brown, Darling and Ed Miliband, furthermore, were perceived by Yes campaigners to have 'got into bed' with the 'noxious' Tories.[15]

The Tories had opposed devolution in Scotland and Wales in the 1990s and, on David Cameron's own admission, 'had struggled ever since to find a constructive stance'. Cameron, himself, while supporting devolution as a means of 'giving people a real stake in their nation's affairs' and so continuing to 'justify the Union and retain support for it', was contemptuous of the SNP and other nationalists. They wanted to 'stoke up national grievances and shout at Westminster, "Give us more money"', according to Cameron. He saw the SNP, led by the 'slippery Salmond', as 'angry' without sufficient cause, 'grudging' and 'bad at governing'. Much in the manner of Brian Wilson, Cameron saw the SNP as the main expression of a 'never-ending grievance culture' in which 'no matter what the issue, Westminster took the blame'.[16]

Disaffection with Westminster has constituted a key factor in the impressive rise of a radical form of Scottish identity – radical Scottishness – from the later twentieth century onwards. Despite Gallagher's claim that most of the people in contemporary

Scotland see themselves as 'British', a claim repeated on many occasions by Gordon Brown,[17] there is no doubt that pride in either being Scottish or living in Scotland or both, has become far more extensive in Scotland in the recent past and continues, perhaps even more strongly, into the present. This form of Scottishness has sometimes existed within the shell of Britishness, or alongside it, rather than the two invariably being mutually exclusive. Yet, as convincingly argued by Tom Devine, radical Scottishness, especially upon the part of the native-born and bred, has, despite its hybridity and complexity, become a very impressive, dynamic and arguably hegemonic force in its own right, particularly since the period immediately preceding Scottish devolution of the late 1990s.[18]

We have also seen in this study that radical Scottishness has been reflected in the independence movement's demands for a fairer, more autonomous Scotland and left-of-centre, arguably social-democratic, opposition to Toryism, New Labour's 'light Toryism', the politics of austerity and the 'arrogance' and 'authoritarianism' of Theresa May and Boris Johnson. I have, moreover, claimed that, although the object of increasing criticism from parts of the broad independence movement for its alleged and mounting conservatism, caution, centralization and managerialism, the SNP, on balance, has been a radical, progressive force and the main, but by no means, sole institutional expression of radical Scottishness. For example, from the very start of her leadership in November 2014, Nicola Sturgeon championed 'social justice and equality, not just the need to leave the UK'. During the independence referendum campaign, Alex Salmond, furthermore, had invoked the 'Spirit of Arbroath' – the famous letter written in 1320 by Scottish earls and barons to the pope in favour of Scottish independence – to commit himself to a 'Declaration of Opportunity' for a fairer, more open and independent Scotland.[19] In its referendum campaign literature, the SNP-dominated government highlighted the fact that Scotland was already a rich country which, despite the No side's claim to the contrary, could 'afford to become independent'. A future independent Scotland would resourcefully make the most of its extensive 'strengths' and 'potential' to guarantee its more empowered and self-confident citizenry many newfound opportunities and entitlements. These would reside, for example, in greater democracy and 'stronger' public finances than in the UK, a guaranteed and generously funded minimum wage, a 'safe, triple-locked pension', a 'fairer' welfare system as seen in 'a halt to the rollout of Universal Credit' and the abolition of the 'Bedroom Tax', a more comprehensive system of childcare and more affordable homes. These benefits, argued the Scottish government, would come on top of the SNP's proven commitments to the three-year freeze of the council tax, the phasing out of prescription charges, free personal, non-residential care for the elderly and free bus travel for older citizens. As a result, 'everyone' in an independent Scotland would 'get a fair deal'.[20]

The other pro-independence organizations also put 'Fairness, Equality, Democracy' and an end to 'Tory austerity', at the centre of their campaigns. Two examples may serve to demonstrate this point. First, the organization Women for Independence, founded in 2012, sought to achieve not only independence, but also gender equality and women's liberation. This group campaigned for the better representation of women in public and political life, improved 'healthcare and education for all', more jobs and free childcare, the living wage, empowered communities and a 'more prosperous' and 'caring' Scotland in which women no longer bore the brunt of economic adversity and austerity. The organization counted among its founder members Jeane Freeman, former Communist and Labour Party member and from 2016 onwards an SNP MSP, and the former Scottish Socialist Party (SSP) MSPs, Carolyn Leckie and Rosie Kane. It prided itself upon being a grass-roots 'open and diverse network of women', a 'broad-based campaigning group' committed to ensuring that 'there will be a space for women's voices and interests in the campaign'. Women for Independence was a social and cultural as well as a political organization. It organized meetings devoted to art, poetry, comedy and music and was skilful in its use of political iconography. Its 'Spirit of Scotland' postcards, designed by Edinburgh artist Stewart Bremner, featuring a woman holding a thistle and wearing a tammy with tartan trimming and a feather clasp on it, a tartan shawl, and set against the saltire, were particularly striking. By September 2014 Women for Independence had forty local groups. It has since become a strong and popular national organization.[21]

Second, Labour for Independence was an organization of Scottish Labour Party members, voters and supporters who disagreed both with their party's official commitment to the Union and its involvement in the Better Together campaign. These Labour dissidents believed that Scottish independence was 'the best way to create a fairer, more equal and just Scotland' and 'free' their country from 'incompetent London rule'. Basing itself upon 'the founding principles of the Labour Movement', rather than those of New Labour, Labour for Independence defended the NHS, demanded improved living standards and economic growth, more equality, fairness and social housing and strongly opposed austerity, nuclear weapons and privatization. Like the other Yes organizations, it saw itself as a standard bearer of 'hope' and 'change'. The No movement was roundly and widely condemned as 'Project Fear'.[22]

The Yes movement was characterized by optimism, hope and what Devine termed a 'quasi-evangelical mission of liberation'.[23] Apart from the activities of the more centralized and professional SNP, the movement often relied upon impressive examples of 'bottom-up' initiatives and organization. As observed by author Peter Geoghegan, in his widespread and illuminating conversations with activists and supporters, 'propelled by social media, grassroots Yes groups, often with little or no connection to a central office, sprung up across the country'.[24] They were sometimes wary of what they saw as the controlling motives of the SNP leadership and its top-down approach, but, as my own experience of Yes meetings in Sligachan, Portree and other places on the Isle of Skye illustrates, SNP and non-SNP pro- independence activists could and did work together with good humour, tolerance and to good effect. More evident was the fact, as noted by Geoghegan, that the 'teams of well-paid, well-dressed communications professionals' of Better Together and the 'brutal efficiency' of their top-down managerialist mode of operation sharply contrasted with the more relaxed, informal and democratic style of the Yes movement as a whole.[25]

The Yes campaign experienced an increasingly strong, albeit very uneven and ultimately unsuccessful, social appeal. Despite Gordon Brown's late interventions and the 'Vow', the majority of those voters who left their choice very late opted for Yes. There is general agreement that Yes was most popular among those working-class people in large urban areas adversely affected by both long-term de-industrialization and globalization and the immediate impact of the coalition government's austerity measures. Most prominent among the big cities voting Yes were Glasgow, with 53.49 per cent, and Dundee, top of the list with 57.35 per cent. Both were traditional Labour strongholds, but the SNP had already become the dominant political force in Dundee.[26] More generally, 50.2 per cent of native-born Scottish residents voted Yes, as did two-thirds of the people in Scotland's most deprived neighbourhoods. Many of these were Catholics who cast off their traditional view that the SNP was the creature of Protestantism. Yes offered these predominantly working-class, and often left-leaning, people the hope of a brighter future, whereas a No vote signified support for a discredited and 'broken' Conservative and increasingly Labour past and present.[27]

The voting age for the referendum had been reduced to sixteen years, and many forward-looking young people supported the Yes campaign. The latter also derived much of its energy and strength from the fact that there developed a successful alliance between often younger left-wing, middle-class activists and their counterparts in the working class. Although women were active in the Yes movement – they were certainly prominent on Skye – in general, women were more reluctant to take a chance on independence than were men.[28] Finally, as Devine maintained, Yes was underpinned by *both* civic nationalism and 'a demand for radical change and social justice', by identity politics and radical ideology.[29] This crucial fact was grasped and fully expressed by both Salmond and Sturgeon during the referendum campaign and ever since. It has served the cause of independence extremely well to the present day.

Conversely, in many of the relatively prosperous areas of Scotland, with less unemployment and higher incomes and living standards, No prevailed. Edinburgh, with its large and prosperous middle class in the professions, in banking and in finance more generally, joined Dumfries and Galloway, the Borders and the Northern Isles as the strongest areas of pro-Union support. The Scottish Borders topped the No list with 67 per cent, followed by Orkney, Shetland, Dumfries and Galloway with 66 per cent, Edinburgh, 61 per cent, and the rich farming and gas-and-oil areas respectively of Perthshire and Aberdeenshire with 60 per cent. Many of these areas also contained large numbers of older voters and people born outside Scotland, but within the rest of the UK. Dumfries, Galloway and the Borders also had a well-established tradition of in-migration from south of the border and strong family-, kinship- and work-based ties with England. A sense of 'Britishness' was particularly marked in those areas of Scotland geographically either closest to or the furthest north of England. Fife (55 per cent), the Western Isles (53.42 per cent) and The Highlands (52.92 per cent) also voted No, albeit with lesser margins between No and Yes than in the strongest No areas. Many No voters were also probably influenced by the overwhelmingly No stance of the press and other parts of the media. Only in the third week of November 2014 would the first daily Scottish newspaper in favour of independence, the *National*, come into existence.[30]

As noted earlier, fears about jobs, livelihoods, pensions, the currency and the future proved to be the decisive factor in deciding the outcome of the referendum campaign. These fears were more marked among older than younger people and women than men. While the Yes movement paid some attention to economic and financial issues, it did so with insufficient clarity, precision, conviction and authority. As Geoghegan concluded, 'Nationalists failed to adequately address big-ticket economic questions. Most voters believed that their lives would not be better – and could be significantly

worse – in an independent Scotland'. Furthermore, even 'some 180,000 SNP voters said
No to independence'.[31] Yet the outcome had been far from a foregone conclusion,
especially as referendum day approached. Many No supporters doubtless shared
George Osborne's 'enormous sense of relief' that their side had won.[32]

The post-referendum period, November 2014–May 2015

Following the referendum, Yes supporters were predictably disappointed and some
doubtless feared the worst for their cause. Yet during the next few months a remarkable
and in many ways unexpected turnaround occurred in their fortunes. This saw the
extremely rapid fall of the Labour Party in Scotland and the remarkable and historic
gains made by the SNP at the general election of May 2015.

Immediately after the referendum, it became evident that deep and largely
unpredicted change was underway. More than 70,000 people joined pro-independence
parties, with the Greens and the Scottish Socialists, as well as the SNP, reporting
'unprecedented surges in membership'.[33] By December 2014 the SNP's membership
had quadrupled to over 100,000, mainly at Labour's expense. (Scottish Labour's
membership stood at around 13,000 in 2014.) By this time Labour's situation and
prospects in Scotland had become parlous. They would soon become catastrophic. Not
only had considerable numbers of its traditional supporters vote Yes in the referendum,
but late in October the party's leader, Johann Lamont, resigned because she maintained
that the UK Labour Party had haughtily treated the Scottish party as its 'branch office'.
There was also widespread bitterness and disillusionment among Scottish Labour's
core voters and many of its local activists around the fact that their party, including its
leader, Ed Miliband, had 'got into bed', in Better Together, with the hated Tories during
the referendum campaign. Miliband would also reject a 'formal pact' between Labour
and the SNP during the 2015 election campaign. To compound matters, Jim Murphy,
Scottish Labour's new leader, was a committed Blairite. He had supported the war in
Iraq, tuition fees and served as a Cabinet minister. His New Labour stance hardly
endeared him to 'old' Labour in Scotland. The polls recorded that a massive swing from
Labour to the SNP was taking place in Scotland and accurately predicted unprecedented
Labour losses and SNP gains in the forthcoming general election.[34]

In later November 2014, the *National*'s first editorial maintained that in post-
referendum Scotland, 'the status quo is no longer an option' and there existed 'an
unquenchable desire for greater devolution'. It was with this 'uppermost in mind' that
the newspaper had been launched. It would 'fly a vibrant flag for independence and the
right for Scots to govern themselves'. The new daily, furthermore, both saw itself as
being 'for all Scots, be they relatively new to these shores or those who have lived here
all their lives' and capable of persuading those who voted No to change their minds in
the future'. The *National*, for the most part, would loyally support the SNP and its
radical civic nationalism.[35]

The kind of radical Scottishness advocated by the *National* and the Yes movement
greatly expanded its appeal in the wake of the failed referendum. As indicated earlier, it
found its main institutional voice in the ascendant and increasingly hegemonic SNP.

As Nicola Sturgeon declared during the May 2015 general election campaign, the SNP set out to be the best representative of Scotland's nationalist and radical 'voice' in the country as a whole and in the parliaments at Holyrood and Westminster. In contrast, Sturgeon portrayed Scottish Labour as taking its constituents 'for granted for far too long', in entering into a 'toxic alliance' with the Tories in 2014 and in 'backing for more Tory-style cuts'.[36]

Sturgeon and the SNP saw the May election as revolving around Scotland's voice and 'standing up for Scotland', rather than around independence. Immediately after the election, the first minister declared that the 'tectonic plates in Scottish politics' had shifted 'decisively'. The SNP captured a truly outstanding 50 per cent of the vote and fifty-six out of Scotland's total of fifty-nine Westminster seats, while Scottish Labour dramatically collapsed from forty-one seats in 2010 to one seat in 2015. The Tories held on to their single seat. The election, Sturgeon continued, was 'an overwhelming vote for Scotland's voice to be heard and for an end to continued austerity'. The SNP, moreover, would 'do our best' to represent No as well as Yes voters and to 'demand that the powers Scotland was promised in the referendum are delivered in full'.[37]

To be sure, the Smith Commission, set up by David Cameron immediately following the No vote in the 2014 referendum, had fulfilled some of the promises of the 'Vow' – especially in relation to more devolved control over tax rates and bands, some welfare payments, air passenger duty and the crown Estate's assets – but it was a case of too little, too late. The Commission's package of measures fell considerably short of maximum devolution, or 'devo-max', under which Westminster would devolve all powers to Holyrood apart from matters concerning monetary policy, defence and foreign affairs.[38] Cameron had also lost the trust of many north of the border by resorting in his immediate post-referendum elation to what they saw as a petty and spiteful form of narrow English nationalism. The Prime Minister declared that, in compensation for the additional powers promised to Holyrood, English MPs would be afforded a veto over legislation applying only to England in the form of 'English votes for English laws' (EVEL).[39]

Faced by these inadequate and mean-spirited responses from Westminster, Sturgeon concluded both that the votes cast for the SNP in the election were about 'Scotland's "voice", rather than independence', and the immediate future task was to make sure that that voice be heard 'more loudly'. In the eyes of the first minister, Scotland and its expressed demands could no longer be 'ignored' and 'pushed aside' by 'Westminster governments'.[40]

Scottish self-determination and independence, 2015–2020

Radical Scottishness on the Isle of Skye

Between the May 2015 election and the outcome of the EU referendum, in June 2016, the spirit of radical Scottishness gained further momentum. In this section I will begin by illustrating this general development with reference to my own experience of politics on the Isle of Skye.

I had moved to Skye in August 2014 from a life mainly spent working and living in and around Manchester. From that date onwards until the time of writing the final part of this chapter, in 2021, I encountered widespread and persistent, albeit fluctuating, expressions of radical Scottishness while attending meetings and talking extensively to people mainly in favour of Scottish independence.

The vast constituency of Ross, Skye and Lochaber, the largest by geographical size in Britain, was created in 2005. Before that date Skye had been part of the Ross, Cromarty and Skye constituency, from 1983 to 1997, and of Ross, Skye and Inverness West from 1997 to 2005. Between 1983 and 2015 Skye was represented by Charles Kennedy, the progressive national leader of the Liberal Democrats from 1999 to 2006. Kennedy was a man of considerable learning, wit, warmth and modesty. He had gained immense popularity and affection in the constituency by his approachable and likable personality and by assiduously attending to the concerns of his widely scattered constituents. By 2015, illness, however, had taken a sad toll on Kennedy's ability successfully to carry out his political duties.

At the May 2015 landslide election for the SNP throughout Scotland, Ian Blackford, the SNP candidate for Ross, Skye and Lochaber, and a future leader of the SNP group at Westminster, indeed defeated Kennedy by the impressive margin of 5,000 plus votes and received a substantial 48 per cent of the votes cast. Blackford is an Edinburgh-born former banker and businessman, and a proud Hibernian (Hibs) football supporter. He had 'first joined the SNP as a teenager in the 1970s', although he had become 'a Labour member in 1982 for a couple of years'. Extremely hardworking, articulate and able, Blackford epitomized not only the soaring confidence and competence of the SNP in general, but the very positive belief in radical self-determination for Scotland that was sweeping the country and which led to the SNP's outstanding election victory in Scotland and Labour's fall. Blackford, furthermore, was one of the people who early in 2016 kindly responded to my request to voters in the Ross, Skye and Lochaber constituency to answer a questionnaire about Scotland's ongoing 'political revolution'. Let me explain.

On 6 January 2016 I sent a letter to the *West Highland Free Press*, a weekly newspaper mainly serving Skye, Wester Ross and the Outer Hebrides. The *Free Press* had been started in 1972 by Labour left-wingers Brian Wilson, Jim Innes, Jim Wilkie and Dave Scott. I explained in the letter that I was a retired history professor who was keen to know more about the views of people in the constituency who had voted in the 2005, 2010 and 2015 general elections, the 2014 referendum and who intended to vote in the forthcoming May 2016 elections to the Scottish parliament. I asked those interested to be prepared to complete a written questionnaire and take part in 'selected interviews'.

I received over 100 e-mail or telephone responses and engaged in innumerable conversations with interested people from across the political spectrum. I received thirteen fully completed six-page questionnaires, plus one completed by spoken rather than by written means. I also had informal interviews with three people. Of the total of fourteen questionnaires, seven were provided by women and seven by men. Thirteen came from voters living on Skye itself and one resided in another part of the constituency. The ages of these fourteen ranged from early-forties to mid-seventies, although the vast majority were in their fifties and sixties. Only one of the fourteen had been born and raised on Skye. Of the other thirteen, four had been born in England, one in India and eight in Scotland. All fourteen had spent over six years in Skye, Ross and Lochaber, although most of them had lived there for considerably longer and had spent most of their lives in Scotland. In terms of length of residence, the majority, therefore, could be considered locals, although it is very difficult to know whether they qualified as such in cultural and social terms in the eyes of the native-born of the constituency, especially those in the older and Gaelic-speaking communities.

The occupations of my respondents were mixed. Most, like many people in the Highlands, had performed or been able to 'turn their hands' to a number of what would generally be seen as working- and middle-class paid and unpaid jobs. These included receptionist, taxi driver, voluntary worker, sales manager, self-employed designer, business person, teacher, engineer, farmer, head gardener, crofter, author, computer programmer, provider of tourist and hospitality services and 'senior banker'. By 2016, however, the vast majority were either still in or had retired from middle-class occupations.[41]

Their political journeys and profiles ranged widely, from Conservatism, the Labour Party, the Liberal Democrats, the Greens and the SNP. Yet the responses of both those who completed the questionnaire in writing and those with whom I talked could not be considered as representative of the political views and voting patterns of voters as a whole in the constituency. This was because their numbers were too small and, as we will see below, they overwhelmingly did not articulate the views of No voters. Yet their responses were invaluable as illustrations of Yes and predominantly SNP viewpoints.

Of the fourteen who answered the questionnaire, none described themselves as either a No voter or a Conservative, although one had moved to the left in his early twenties partly as a reaction against the early influence of his Conservative father. This son's journey would take him from the Labour Party to the Scottish Greens, support for Yes in 2014 and a vote for the SNP in 2015. He had come to see the SNP as the only realistic option to 'push forward a progressive and green agenda' and promote 'fairness, equality and anti-nuclear weapons'. Another respondent, a woman in her sixties who had been born in England, and moved from London to Skye in the early 1970s, had voted for the first time in her life in 2005. Her vote had been for the Conservatives in order 'to get New Labour out'. I 'couldn't stand Tony Blair, Gordon Brown, Alastair Campbell, Peter Mandelson et al.,' she declared. This respondent soon became a strong and hardworking SNP activist and a Yes voter in order to 'get a better voice' for and 'greater democracy' for Scotland. Yet in 2021 she decided, along with some other prominent local SNP figures, to take the very difficult decision to leave the party.

Her departure constituted a protest against what she experienced as the SNP's increasing centralization and remoteness, its escalating internal machinations, divisions and conflicts, its unresponsiveness to the views of grassroots members and activists and its continuing procrastination and prevarication on the key issue of independence. All these locals who left the SNP decided to join the former SNP leader, Alex Salmond's newly formed Alba Party. The latter urged people to 'vote for your local pro-independence candidate' on the constituency ballot paper and for the Alba Party on the regional or 'list' ballot paper in order to return an independence 'supermajority' at Holyrood. Unlike SNP MSPs, Alba MSPs would commit themselves very actively to campaign for independence from the very outset of the new parliament and to exert intense extra-parliamentary, as well as parliamentary, pressure upon the Westminster government in order to 'accelerate independence'.[42]

Two respondents, both born in England, had moved from Labour to the SNP. One of these, a man and a Skye resident for seven years, had voted for Labour in the 2005 and 2010 elections. The other, a woman, resident on Skye for thirteen years, turned from Labour to the SNP at the 2010 election. Both of them had voted Yes in the 2014 referendum and warmly adopted the SNP in 2015 and 2016. The woman, who had 'always been anti-Tory and what you might call hard left', had 'marched with the anti-Nazi League and joined various protests and supported the Labour Party' from the 1970s onwards. 'Since living a while in Scotland', and 'seeing the way Labour used its power within Scotland', she had changed to the SNP as 'the party to represent my interests'. The key goal was to create 'a more equal and fair Scotland'. The man came to the realization that the SNP, in keeping with his own views, was 'more left of centre' than Labour, especially in terms of 'Trident renewal, social equality and foreign policy'.

A further three respondents, one woman and two men, expressed their long-term sympathies as lying with the Liberal Democrats and/or the Greens, although two of them turned to the SNP at the May 2015 election. One of them had taken exception to the Lib-Dems entering into coalition with the hated Tories, while the other saw the SNP, especially under Nicola Sturgeon, as the best way to achieve 'a fair and equal society'. 'Pure green policies' had been 'trumped by the more urgent need to achieve an independent Scotland'. All three respondents, like many other people I had contact with, had great respect for Charles Kennedy and were saddened by his worsening health and declining political powers. They wanted more devolution for Scotland and greater local-community empowerment. They all voted Yes in 2014. Two of them objected to the 'centralizing' actions of the SNP.

The other seven respondents had supported the SNP for most, and in some cases all, of their adult lives and without exception had voted Yes in 2014. Two, both men, were veteran activists and a third, a woman, had supported and campaigned for the SNP for the majority of her political life. The first veteran had spent sixty-nine of his seventy-four years in Scotland, had lived in the constituency for twenty-eight years and had been a member of the SNP since 1966. He had served as the election agent for the party in Perth and Kinross against the Conservative, Alec Douglas-Home, at the 1970 general election. Douglas-Home had served as prime minister between 1963 and 1964. This respondent had also been election agent for the SNP candidate in Orkney and Shetland in the 1994 election against Jo Grimond, the former Liberal Party leader. As in Perth and Kinross, the SNP came second in Orkney and Shetland. He had, furthermore, served two terms of office more recently as a Skye councillor on the Highland Council, based in Inverness. His abiding belief was that 'even if we were to be less well off we should be responsible for our own economy/decisions/the way we are governed, together with our own agreements/treaties/relationships with other countries'. He hoped to 'live long enough to see the final step to being a country again with a seat in the United Nations (UN) and taking our rightful place among all other nation states in the world'.

The second veteran SNP activist, and the most prominent SNP leader among my respondents, was Ian Blackford, himself. Born in Edinburgh in 1961, Blackford had moved from Lanarkshire to Skye in 2004. He maintained that the SNP would 'put first the interests of those living in Scotland' and establish a 'fairer and wealthier' independent country.

The third SNP veteran activist, a woman, had experienced a far more varied political career than the other two. In her sixties, this woman had been born and raised by Conservative-voting parents in Glasgow. Yet at the tender age of thirteen she had campaigned for an SNP candidate in Glasgow in a strong Labour constituency. This respondent had been a Skye resident for thirty-nine years and since 2003 had been a self-employed entrepreneur. Keen to 'green' the environment, she had voted for Charles Kennedy up to the 2005 election in the pragmatic belief that he was in the strongest position to influence the political agenda in the Highlands and at Westminster. Yet from 2005 onwards her loyalties lay with the SNP. She wrote that working and voting for the SNP was a 'no brainer', being the 'only way to achieve a yes vote for independence'. An 'avid reader', she had developed an early and keen interest in Scottish history and described herself as 'Scottish middle class – definitely not British'. This activist was one of those who left the SNP for Alba in 2021.

In addition to the above, there were four long-time SNPers who, at least in terms of their present activities, strictly speaking are better described as keen supporters rather than activists. The first, a man in his sixties, had lived much of his life as a banker in Edinburgh, but had longstanding familial ties with Skye. 'Since adulthood', he had believed that 'the people best capable to govern Scotland effectively are the residents living here' and that the SNP was the only party equipped fairly and efficiently to run the country. Another respondent in this category, a woman who had also moved from Edinburgh to Skye, agreed and added that it was 'time for change'. The third, a man born into a Glasgow family 'who were always talking about politics' and in which the children were 'always encouraged to make up our own minds', described himself as 'a lifelong Scottish Nationalist' and 'Scottish working class'. He had performed a variety of jobs including taxi driver, pub and restaurant manager and fishmonger. He strongly believed that the Scottish people were 'perfectly capable' and best equipped to 'run our own affairs'. He denounced the 'increasingly malign influence of Westminster' in Scotland's affairs, the 'Tory' policies of New Labour and Labour's 'sell-out' in 2014. 'Independence', he maintained, would 'open the door to a better, fairer Scotland' in which there would be much less inequality and far fewer food banks and 'people begging in the streets'. The fourth was a woman who had been born in Edinburgh in the 1950s, for 'many years' had grown up in Africa and volunteered in India and taught in Scotland. She had married a 'Highlander whose family were SNP supporters' and raised her daughter 'who now stands as a candidate for the SNP at the May 2016 election'. (The daughter was successful and is now a leading SNP figure at Holyrood.) In the view of this fourth supporter, the SNP was 'the best option at the moment to give Scotland a sense of identity'.

In conclusion, the written and spoken comments of virtually all those with whom I had contact, and certainly of all the respondents to the questionnaire, support the thesis of the development of a strong modern groundswell in favour of radical Scottishness. Their actions suggest that, despite their varied political characteristics and journeys and the triumph of the No side in 2014, radical Scottishness and its leading party-political expression, the SNP, quickly became ascendant thereafter.

From 2016 to 2020

Overview

The purpose of this section is to integrate and expand upon the material contained in earlier chapters in this study in order to chart the fortunes of Scottish self-determination, mainly in the form of independence, between 2016 and 2020.

I present five main arguments. First, from mid-2016 onwards, the SNP interpreted Scotland's 'voice', in the form of the call for greater democratic self-determination, as being far more in favour of complete independence from the UK rather than more devolved powers from Westminster. Second, the movement for Scottish independence did not enjoy linear growth and appeal between 2016 and 2019. Third, by the end of 2019 and throughout 2020, however, its fortunes had considerably improved. As reflected in the polls, by the end of 2020 a majority of those living in Scotland, including a significant number of No voters in 2014, now strongly supported independence. As in 2014, there was frustration and anger at being ruled by Tory governments they had not voted for and a Westminster establishment too often unsympathetic, neglectful and indeed hostile to their needs and wishes. This was seen particularly around the issue of Brexit. Above all, they wanted the democratic right fully to decide their own future. They expected the SNP, furthermore, both to achieve a majority at Holyrood as a result of the May 2021 Scottish elections and to move early in the life of the new parliament to a second independence referendum. Fourth, they were opposed by a Tory government and Labour and Liberal Democrat parties all implacably opposed to both the holding of a second referendum and the further fragmentation of the Union. All these anti-SNP organizations saw the 2014 independence referendum as a 'once-in-a-lifetime' event and the SNP as the chronic purveyor of political, social and cultural ideas based upon exaggerated grievances, sour grapes and largely unwanted and unproductive division and conflict. Fifth, as we will see in the final part of this chapter, something had to give to break this deadlock.

Chronology

As a result of the Scottish elections of May 2016, the SNP lost its overall majority at Holyrood, but only by two seats. It could also usually rely upon the votes of the pro-independence Scottish Greens to ensure a majority vote on key issues. A month after the elections, the June EU referendum produced a 62 per cent to 38 per cent vote for Remain in Scotland, as opposed to the 52 per cent to 48 per cent vote for Leave in the UK as a whole. As a party wholly committed to the EU, the SNP maintained that it was 'democratically unacceptable' for the country to be forced to exit the EU against its majority wish. For the SNP and many others in favour of Remain, this constituted yet one more, but extremely important, example of Scotland being forced, against its will, to bend to the wishes of a 'dictatorial' Westminster.

For Sturgeon, the outcome of the EU vote constituted the trigger, the key 'change in material circumstances', that would fully justify the calling of a second referendum on Scottish independence and persuade sufficient numbers of voters, including No voters from 2014, to opt for Yes. The referendum, furthermore, would probably come within two years in the event of a 'hard Brexit', according to Sturgeon. The first minister accordingly made immediate plans to push the cause of independence with renewed urgency and vigour.

For the four and a half years following the EU referendum, the issues of Brexit and Scottish independence became inextricably connected. Alongside austerity and, most recently, the coronavirus pandemic, they dominated the political scene in Scotland.

Declining support for the SNP and independence, 2016–2017

As observed in Chapter 1, between the EU referendum and the June 2017 general election, the SNP's predicted 'surge' for Indyref2 and independence in the face of continuing 'Tory austerity', and the prospect of a 'hard Brexit', did not materialize. While polling suggested that support for Scottish independence stood at around 46 per cent in August 2016, as compared with 45 per cent in 2014, by the beginning of 2017 it was declining, especially among women. Some argued that around 500,000 voters deserted the SNP between the 2015 and 2017 general elections. There was, furthermore, little enthusiasm for holding a second referendum.

To be sure, there was a resurgence of support for independence, to between 49 per cent and 51 per cent, by April 2017. This was largely in response to May's Lancaster House speech, her aggressive defence of the Union and attack on the 'obsessive', 'divisive' and 'mismanaging' SNP government and the triggering of Article 50 by the Westminster parliament. This resurgence, however, did not last long. By June 2017 support for Scottish independence had dipped to around 43 per cent. Many people in Scotland had become 'poll weary' after voting on several occasions since 2014 and did not welcome another referendum on Scottish independence in the immediate future.

This feeling was seized upon by Labour and the Liberal Democrats, but more so by Ruth Davidson and the Scottish Tories. All these parties defended the 'better together' aspects of the Union and launched a full-frontal attack on the SNP's 'unwanted' and 'divisive' call for another referendum. They also maintained that the SNP's 'obsession' with independence had led its government to pay sufficient attention to 'bread-and-butter issues' such as health, education and living standards.

These oppositional forces were successful in ensuring that the June 2017 general election mainly revolved around the independence issue and not around the SNP's preferred areas of the 'disasters' of austerity and Brexit. Davidson, in particular, became increasingly popular as her Scottish Conservatives increased their representation at Westminster from one to thirteen seats. Scottish Labour gained six seats to bring its total representation in the UK parliament to seven, while the Liberal Democrats moved from one to four Scottish seats. In contrast the SNP lost twenty-one seats, or over a third, of its, albeit remarkable, total of fifty-six seats won at the 2015 general election.

As also seen in Chapter 1, poll weariness, the setback at the election and concern about Scotland's relatively high budget deficit and its low growth rate led the SNP to adopt a markedly more cautious and defensive approach to the issue of Scottish independence. Even before the election result was known, the SNP's manifesto highlighted the party's and the government's progressive, anti-austerity credentials. This was done in an attempt to bring selected socio-economic matters to the forefront of voters' minds and to demonstrate that the SNP was more progressive than Corbyn's radicalized Labour Party. In contrast, the SNP listed another independence referendum as the last of its manifesto commitments. It declared that a vote would be held only at the end of the Brexit process, in 2019 or, more likely 2020, rather than, as previously stated, during 2018 and 2019 before the UK's scheduled departure from the EU on 29 March 2019.

Although understandable in this less auspicious political climate, the SNP's caution and procrastination on the independence issue certainly led to some disquiet and criticism within its ranks and the wider independence movement. In the wake of the election result, the SNP judiciously decided to undertake a year-long 'listening' exercise in order to recapture lost trust and support among the public and step up its attacks on 'Tory Brexit'.

By the end of 2017 these initiatives seemed to be working. In December the polls recorded that support for Scottish independence had increased to 47 per cent. Yet in overall terms there was little cause for renewed optimism. The polls taken since 2014 – almost ninety of them – conclusively showed that there had been little, if any, consistent and significant change in support for an independent Scotland. In addition, some now feared that independence was becoming become secondary to, and even obscured by, the increasingly all-consuming and protracted issue of Brexit.

Partial recovery, 2018–2019

As indicated in Chapter 2, as 2018 progressed there, however, were signs that the fortunes of both the SNP and independence were undergoing a partial recovery. A number of factors combined to underpin this improvement. Above all, there were the continuing and increasingly severe problems afflicting Theresa May's attempts to secure Brexit. These were reflected in the acute Tory divisions and resignations around the July Chequers agreement, the EU's abrupt rejection of May's plan at Salzburg in September and the increasingly desperate attempts and repeated failures of the government to gain parliamentary approval for its Brexit deal struck with the EU in November. Brexit, indeed, had become a 'horror show' and a 'shambles'. The SNP continued to claim, but this time with mounting intensity and expectancy, that the 'disaster' of Brexit would lead to a significant poll increase in support for independence in Remain Scotland.

The improved performance of the Scottish economy also helped matters. For the first time a majority of voters in Scotland expressed the belief that they would be better off, or at least not worse off, under independence. The report of the Sustainable Growth Commission in May 2018, a milestone in the economic history of devolved Scotland, also attempted to reassure the public that it had noting to fear and much to gain from the 'sensible', 'responsible' and 'prudent' management of the economy by a post-independence SNP government.

In what would become an increasingly familiar and loud refrain, the SNP, furthermore, accused the government at Westminster of brazen 'power grabs'. In the eyes of the SNP, these were seen, for example, in the government's attempted seizure of control over a number of devolved issues, such as fishing and farming, and its wish to sideline and silence Scottish MPs during parliamentary debates on issues of importance to Scotland. As also seen in Chapter 2, matters came to a head at Westminster in June 2018 when no Scottish MP was given time to speak to the crucially important issue of the withdrawal bill and devolution. The Scottish parliament had already rejected the withdrawal bill, but 'Scotland's voice', in the opinion of the SNP's leader in the House of Commons, Ian Blackford, had been 'scandalously silenced' on the issue at Westminster. Blackford and his SNP colleagues also believed that, in the wake of Brexit, Westminster would attempt to 'grab back' or reserve for its own deliberation and control an increasing number of devolved issues. Following heated exchanges, Blackford was ordered to leave the chamber. All his SNP colleagues followed him. Above all, the 'power grab' issue symbolized, and would continue to demonstrate, to a growing number of people in Scotland that the UK government had become even more undemocratic and dictatorial, that the Union, a supposed partnership of equals and mutual respect, increasingly was based upon 'fraud and myth' and that the Tories, in particular, no longer really believed in the devolved settlement in Scotland.

By May 2018, support for Scottish independence stood at 48 per cent and the SNP's membership had surged to well over 100,000. The party soon came to enjoy a massive lead in the polls and significantly captured the traditional Labour stronghold of Glasgow. For many who took part in the large and impressive pro-independence marches in Glasgow, Edinburgh and other parts in Scotland in the spring, summer and autumn, the key question now revolved around the timing rather than the prospect of Indyref2.

If we fast forward to the end of May 2019, the issue of Brexit remained of overriding importance, while the prospects for independence continued to be quite good. As we saw near the end of Chapter 2, Theresa May had resigned over Brexit and the Conservative Party was still hopelessly divided over Europe. It had also failed miserably at the local and European elections held in May, as did the fence-sitting Labour Party. In contrast, Farage's Brexit Party had triumphed at the European elections, while the unequivocally pro-Remain parties, the Liberal Democrats, the Greens, the Alliance Party and the SNP, had done well. The SNP, in fact, returned three of Scotland's six Members of the European Parliament (MEPs) in its best performance at a European election. The party's conference in late April had been a success and was followed by an 'All Under One Banner' pro-independence march of around 100,000 people in Glasgow in early May. Other successful marches would be held during the summer months. The polls, moreover, now indicated that support for Scottish independence, fuelled mainly, if somewhat tardily, by the seemingly endless and increasingly farcical and embarrassing Brexit saga, had reached 49 per cent. This was its highest percentage point in four years. Scotland had also become even stronger in its backing for Remain. Sturgeon lost no time in announcing her intention to hold Indyref2 in 2020.

As matters transpired, however, a further delay became inevitable. As seen in Chapter 3, this was because, like all four of the UK's governments, the Scottish government's attention from the later part of March 2020 onwards was almost entirely consumed by the fight against the global coronavirus pandemic.

The 2020 independence surge

At the same time, however, it was, ironically, during 2020 that the long-predicted surge in support for Scottish independence finally took place. In that year no fewer than seventeen consecutive polls demonstrated, beyond a shadow of doubt, that there now existed a clear majority in Scotland in favour of independence. As journalist Judith Duffy observed, a YouGov survey of January 2020 showed Yes to be in the lead, by 51 per cent to 49 per cent, for the first time since early 2015. This lead, furthermore, lasted throughout the entire year and reached a highpoint of between 56 per cent and 58 per cent in October.[43] Almost a third of No voters in 2014, moreover, had changed their minds and were now unsure or would vote Yes. Women were particularly prominent among those who had moved away from No. Devine thus noted that the 'gender gap' of 2014, whereby 'men were more likely than women to vote for independence', seemed to have 'mainly vanished' in 2020. And while the '"grey vote"' remained 'crucial to the Union cause' – 'in 2020 more than two-thirds of those aged 65 and over in Scotland opposed independence' – 'no less than 79% of those aged 16 to 24' – a significant number of whom would not have been eligible to vote in 2014 – 'supported Yes'. Time was thus 'now on the side of national self-determination', concluded Devine.[44]

There was a consensus among political commentators that the newfound majority support for independence was mainly triggered by the experience of Brexit. As we saw in the last chapter, Boris Johnson and his key advisers, Dominic Cummings and Lee Cain, pulled off a masterstroke by making the slogan 'Get Brexit Done' the centre-piece of their triumphant general election campaign of late 2019. This was followed at the end of January 2020 by the successful negotiation of the withdrawal deal. Almost a year later, on Christmas Eve 2020, the UK and the EU signed up to the future free-trade and no quotas deal. The UK parliament overwhelmingly voted, by 521 to 73, to accept the deal. The vote in favour included Starmer's increasingly pragmatic Labour Party. In Starmer's view, Johnson's 'thin' deal was better than no deal.[45] On 31 December 2020 the transition period formally ended, and the UK henceforth took on the mantle of being a 'sovereign global power', freed, at last, at least in the eyes of the Brexiters, from the 'shackles' of the EU behemoth.

Johnson's spectacular Brexit triumphs, so popular in 'Little England', nevertheless, cut very little ice in predominantly Remain Scotland. As noted in Chapter 3, at the December 2019 general election the SNP had performed extremely well, capturing another thirteen seats at Westminster in addition to its very respectable total of thirty-five. The SNP, furthermore, had fought the election on a clear commitment to hold another referendum on Scottish independence in 2020. Early in January 2020, and notwithstanding appalling weather, approximately 80,000 people turned out in Glasgow in support of independence. Further well-attended marches followed in other centres.

The party and the independence movement continued their anti-Brexit campaign throughout 2020, and in December the Scottish parliament voted ninety-two to thirty against Johnson's trade deal with the EU. This successful vote included Scottish Labour, the Greens and the Liberal Democrats, but, entirely predictably, not the Scottish Conservatives.

While the Stormont Assembly also opposed the trade deal, the Labour-dominated Welsh Senedd fell in line behind Keir Starmer's pro-deal stance. Sturgeon condemned the deal as 'disastrous', a 'democratic, economic and social calamity'. It would 'fuel her party's push for a second independence referendum in May's 2021 Holyrood elections'. 'Only independence' would 'protect Scotland's interests', according to the first minister. Sturgeon asked the EU to 'keep the lights on' because Scotland would be 'back soon'.[46]

The dominant issue of Brexit was accompanied by sharply contrasting popular verdicts on the leadership of Johnson and Sturgeon in relation to the pandemic. As outlined in Chapter 3, while Johnson's record on coronavirus from March 2020 to the beginning of 2021 was widely seen as incompetent, dithering, vacillating and confusing, as being consistently behind the curve, Sturgeon was perceived by large sections of the public, not only in Scotland, but also in the UK as a whole, as being far more competent, consistent, clear and decisive. For example, a study for BBC Scotland in November 2020 estimated that while almost three quarters of adults in Scotland believed that the Scottish government was handling the pandemic well, only 25 per cent of them thought the same of the UK government. Boris Johnson's performance in relation to the pandemic, furthermore, received only a 19 per cent approval rating, while Nicola Surgeon received 74 per cent.[47]

To be sure, Sturgeon's government was not immune from criticism. For example, early in the pandemic there occurred a very high and unacceptable number of deaths in care homes in Scotland. These arguably resulted more from the failings of private care-home owners rather than the actions of the government. The balance of available evidence, however, also lends itself to the conclusion that Sturgeon's government could and should have both adopted a tougher policy towards private care homes bringing in untested outside care staff, particularly from south of the border, and done far more to prevent the transfer of untested elderly patients from outside high-risk institutions, especially hospitals, to care homes. In April 2021 Jeane Freeman, the cabinet secretary for health and sport, admitted that the transfer policy had been 'mistaken'. The response of Nicola Sturgeon, however, was far more guarded. The first minister declared that her government had acted in a manner thought to be the 'best at the time', as it was 'based on the evidence we had', but admitted that the experience had taught the government the lesson of acting differently towards care homes as the pandemic developed.

Scottish Labour and other political opponents of the SNP maintained that the Scottish government's policy towards the protection of care-home residents during the early months of Covid-19 had 'catastrophically failed', while many locals endorsed the view of one Independent Skye councillor that the government had been 'negligent'. Whatever the truth of the matter, Sturgeon, however, was publicly perceived to be a far more effective, sincere and convincing communicator during the first year of the pandemic than the blustering, procrastinating and prevaricating Johnson.[48]

2021: overall strengths and successes

Johnson's and the Conservative Party's poll ratings continued to fall at the beginning of 2021, while those of Sturgeon and the SNP government for the most part remained high. As journalist David Connett wrote in the *Guardian* at the beginning of January 2021, the most recent poll evidence, albeit gathered before Johnson's successful trade deal with the EU, showed that, in the event of an immediate general election, Johnson would lose his own parliamentary seat of Uxbridge and South Ruislip, the Tories would forfeit eighty-one parliamentary seats overall and Labour would gain eighty-two. This would leave Labour with 37.7 per cent of the vote and the Tories with 35.6 per cent. This substantial swing would come about because people were 'deeply unhappy' with Johnson's handling of Brexit and the Covid-19 crisis, according to Connett. The competent and cautious, if somewhat uninspiring, Starmer, furthermore, had pulled back most of the 26-point lead the Tories had gained over Labour by late 2019, while the SNP was predicted to win fifty-seven out of Scotland's fifty-nine seats at Westminster in the event of an election.[49] An *Opinium* poll, of 2,003 people, for the *Observer* newspaper, taken at the end of the first week in January, furthermore, recorded that 43 per cent against 40 per cent of the respondents believed that Johnson should resign as leader of the country and that Labour now led the Tories by 1 percentage point, by 40 per cent to 39 per cent.[50] By the middle of January this lead stretched to 4 points as public confidence in Johnson's handling of the pandemic continued to fall and support for Starmer's competence continued to grow.[51]

There was also the widespread perception in Wales that, despite the very serious nature of the Covid situation in the principality, Labour's Mark Drakeford was handling the crisis far more calmly and effectively than Johnson. This was accompanied by a reported 'surge' in favour of Welsh independence, especially among younger people in Wales, during the latter part of 2020.[52] And, while a reported 47 per cent of people in Northern Ireland still wanted to remain in the UK, 42 per cent now supported a united Ireland.[53]

Alongside the issues of Brexit and Covid, Boris Johnson's attitudes and actions towards the SNP, devolution and Scotland itself, had a major and unintended positive impact upon support for Scottish independence. In the view of Devine, Johnson, a 'duplicitous buffoon', became the 'best recruiting sergeant ever' for independence and the SNP's 'most accomplished recruiter'. Even the new Tory leader in Scotland, Douglas Ross, recognized this fact and effectively counselled his leader in Westminster to keep his thoughts on Scotland largely to himself.[54]

From his election in July 2019 onwards, Johnson had hardly endeared himself to Scots with his Thatcherite advocacy of a highly centralized, 'dictatorial' and 'unitary' form of Unionism.[55] This was seen, for example, in September 2020 when the Tory government's proposal to create a single internal market in the UK in the post-Brexit period was interpreted by all the devolved administrations, despite Johnson's strong protestations to the contrary, as another attempted 'power grab' by Westminster. Under the Internal Market Bill the Westminster government would have the power to override the wishes of the devolved parliaments on important matters such as food and drink standards and pricing and spending rules. In the opinion of Sturgeon and the SNP as a whole, Johnson's proposal was not only in breach of international law in seeking to negate parts of his withdrawal agreement with the EU, but also constituted a fundamental attack upon the principle and practice of devolution itself. As such, it constituted 'an abomination' which would 'cripple devolution', according to the first minister.[56]

In November 2020 Johnson, furthermore, reportedly told a meeting of Conservatives that devolution had been 'a disaster north of the border' and that it was Tony Blair's 'biggest mistake'. In response to the predictable outrage caused by these claims, the Prime Minister characteristically effected a sharp U-turn by declaring that he had been misunderstood: it was not devolution itself, but devolution, as practised by the ruling SNP, that had been disastrous.[57] In both November 2020 and in early January 2021 Johnson repeated his view that the vote on Scottish independence was a once-in-a-lifetime event and would not be conducted again for '25 to 40' years, or 'until 2055'.[58]

Johnson's hostility to another Scottish referendum, moreover, was shared by Keir Starmer and the Labour Party. To be sure, Starmer did not agree either with Johnson's long time frame for the holding of Indyref2 or that the *status quo* in relation to the Union was satisfactory. Rather, Labour's leader proposed the establishment of a new commission to explore the question of further devolution within the UK, with Gordon Brown at the helm, and in the foreseeable future for priority to be afforded to policies designed to address the closely related economic and health crises. Given the 'precarious' times, Starmer saw a 'divisive' Indeyref2 as being of lesser importance than finding effective solutions to these crises and promoting national recovery. He also wrongly claimed, in view of the polling evidence in Scotland, that Scottish independence wasn't 'a priority on the doorsteps'.[59] The expression of this viewpoint, combined with his support for Johnson's post-Brexit trade deal with the EU, of course, did not endear Starmer and UK Labour to those in Scotland eager to grasp the prize of independence. The prospect of Gordon's Brown's key re-appearance on the devolution stage, furthermore, occasioned much anger in view of his central role in the No campaign of 2014, the largely unfulfilled promises of the 'Vow' and his hostility to and misrepresentation of 'the Nationalists'.

At the same time, however, the wisdom of committing to another referendum soon after the May 2021 elections was subject to growing debate and disagreement in Scotland itself, even among supporters of independence. In terms of the latter, Devine counselled patience and strategic thinking rather than 'knee-jerk emotional reactions'. He concluded that priority lay with the economy, health and national recovery and that, furthermore, it was not 'morally acceptable' for the Scottish government to push ahead with Indyref2 'in 2021 or 2022'. Some prominent figures in the independence movement, such as Kenny MacAskill, MP and Jim Sillars, the ex-SNP deputy leader, agreed that it would be better to adopt a gradualist approach and prioritise national recovery. Yet Sturgeon's deputy, John Swinney, countered by arguing that Indyref2 remained a top priority and that it was not incompatible with tackling the pandemic. Rather, independence would enable the Scottish people 'to choose how we rebuild as a country' from Covid, declared Swinney. Sturgeon fully endorsed this viewpoint.[60] As we will see below, these debates would become more frequent and intense as the May elections approached.

Finally, the changed economic situation also played a significant role in raising the level of support for independence. Unlike the case in 2014, 'Project Fear' – around threats to pensions, people's livelihoods, access to the NHS and the strong pound-sterling – carried much less popular weight in 2020. Although much remained to be done in terms of reaching general agreement within the independence movement around the direction, details and viability of economic policy in an independent

Scotland,[61] John Curtice and his team of researchers found that the economic case for independence was being viewed far more favourably by voters in Scotland in 2019 and 2020 than it had been previously.[62] The proven competence and efficiency of SNP governments had helped to bring about this important development, while Scotland's deficit could no longer realistically be isolated and highlighted for special condemnatory treatment in a Covid-ravaged UK economy in which spiralling deficits and debts had become the norm.

The UK economy as a whole, moreover, was in a far more parlous state and the advantages of remaining wedded to it far less apparent than in 2014. In opposition to the wish of the majority in Scotland, Brexit had become a fact of life. As seen in Chapter 3, the UK was experiencing its worst recession in 300 years and during 2020 GDP had fallen by almost 10 per cent. Asset-based inequality continued to rocket, while, as observed by the *Guardian*, government incompetence had resulted in 'one of the worst death tolls in Europe and the worst economic recession among large advanced economies'. Despite Sunak's economic support and rescue packages and the roll-out of the potentially game-changing anti-Covid vaccines, the chances of the UK economy recovering as fast as its major competitors were not good. Short-term financial gain still took prominence over long-term productive investment. In short, the perceived economic risks of independence were considerably lower than in 2014, while the advantages were much higher.[63]

From February to the May elections

The fortunes of the major parties: the SNP

The electoral fortunes of the SNP and independence continued to prosper beyond January 2021. By the end of that month, another poll, the twentieth in succession, showed a majority in favour of independence. Between 52 per cent and 57 per cent now wanted independence and a second referendum within the next five years; John Curtice, furthermore, predicted that the SNP was on course to achieve a landslide in the May Holyrood elections. This was followed in early February by the twenty-first poll to show a majority for independence.[64]

During February the SNP announced that it would soon set out details on the timing and potential question(s) for Indyref2, while Mike Russell, the cabinet secretary for the constitution, Europe and external affairs, presented the party's 'roadmap' to independence document to around 1,000 members attending the party's promised virtual National Assembly. The document reaffirmed that the SNP would seek a second referendum if it won a majority in the May elections. It would do so, moreover, by constitutional and legal means. A request would be made to Boris Johnson to grant the Scottish parliament a section 30 order in order to hold Indyref2. In the very likely event of a refusal by the Prime Minister, the Scottish government would present a legal challenge to establish if Holyrood itself could stage a referendum. The document did not speculate further in the event of the constitutional and judicial routes proving to be ineffective. The SNP leadership, however, was very keen to avoid any hint of their government's possible employment of extra-parliamentary, 'direct action' methods.

They did not want to provide ammunition to their opponents about a possible SNP resort to unconstitutionality and violence in order to achieve independence.

Significantly, however, the document did state that the proposed referendum would be held *after* the pandemic. This seemed to contradict Swinney's and Sturgeon's earlier statement, noted above, that an effective response to Covid-19 would be a key part of the programme of recovery in an independent Scotland and would not precede or have priority over it. Was the SNP leadership, as in 2017, 2018 and 2019–2020, beginning to procrastinate and possibly lose its nerve in the face of criticism and changing circumstances over the independence issue? Some raised the question whether the SNP government was more interested in retaining power than in taking the risk of holding Indyref2 in the near future and perhaps losing it.[65]

Scottish Labour

The fortunes of the SNP's political opponents continued to plummet. This was particularly the case in terms of Scottish Labour. In January 2021 Richard Leonard became the fifth Scottish Labour Party leader to depart since 2014 and the ninth in the past two decades. Leonard, the leader since 2017, explained his decision to resign in terms of the fact that 'speculation' about his own position was hindering Labour's attempt to get its message across to the electorate and his own ability to 'unite the party'.

In truth, the resignation was hardly a surprise. Scottish Labour continued to perform very badly at the polls, Leonard was not well known to the public and, as an ally of Corbyn, his position had come under probable threat once Starmer gained the leadership. Like Corbyn and John McDonnell, Leonard was not opposed to the principle of the people of Scotland having the democratic right, via the ballot box, to hold another independence referendum. But, as noted above, Starmer did not agree with this position. Starmer's view, moreover, was the dominant one within Scottish Labour and Leonard's position was effectively overruled.

As a result, Leonard's position as leader had become untenable. Scottish Labour remained, in essence, compelled to work within and accept the decisions of the highly centralized UK Labour Party, even as the realities of devolution and rising public sentiment in favour of Scottish independence demanded the need for more flexibility, sensitivity to the prevailing public mood and autonomy for the Scottish party. 'Bone-headed' commitment to the Union was bringing Scottish Labour few, if any rewards. Pollsters estimated that by 2020 'more than a third' of Labour voters in 2019 had come to support the SNP and independence'.[66]

The Scottish Conservatives

Meanwhile, the Scottish Conservatives were in disarray. Post-Brexit red tape, involving extra costs, checks and delays, provided to be an immediate disaster for Scottish fishers attempting to export their fresh seafood to Europe. Although the Westminster government saw these problems as teething ones and offered some financial compensation, representatives of the Scottish fishing industry were not convinced. They pointed out that sections of their industry were already suffering major financial losses and very real threats of closure. These were not the benefits of Brexit that many Scottish fishing communities had anticipated and been promised and their faith in the Tories sharply declined. This manifested itself in Tory leader Douglas Ross's constituency of Moray and elsewhere on the north-east coast of Scotland. An opinion poll for the *Scotsman* in January, showed a 5-point fall for the Tories in Scotland since December. The newspaper also reported that the Tories could lose fourteen of their thirty-one seats at Holyrood as a result of the May elections.[67]

Boris Johnson and his government responded by ramping up their essentially 'better together', pro-Union campaign. Johnson paid a visit to Scotland in late January to promote the virtues of the 'mighty union'. He also sought to hire more Union advisers for his government's Union Directorate, and claimed both that Scotland faced financial ruin in the event of independence and that the SNP government was incompetent and inefficient, as seen in its allegedly slow roll-out of the vaccine programme. By the end of February, however, there was precious little evidence that the pro-Union campaign was having the desired effect. For example, Oliver Lewis, the former head of research at the Vote Leave campaign under Cummings and a 'Boris loyalist' for over five years, lasted only two weeks as the newly appointed head of the Union Directorate. Lewis had decided to resign because his position reportedly had become 'untenable'. This led Kirsten Oswald, the SNP's deputy leader at Westminster, to declare that Johnson's 'taxpayer-funded anti-independence campaign' was 'completely falling apart'.[68]

Despite the fact that over 15 million people had received their first vaccination, the UK, furthermore, still had the dreadful records of having the highest number of Covid deaths in Europe and one of the worst for Covid deaths per capita in the world by mid-February. The polls also continued to point to a resounding SNP victory and majority in Holyrood as a result of the May elections.[69]

The SNP and the Independence movement: serious challenges and conflicts

Yet events were suddenly to take a turn for the worse for the SNP. In January and February, the party was rocked by serious and potentially highly damaging divisions and conflicts concerning the sacking of Joanna Cherry, QC, from the SNP's frontbench team at Westminster and former leader Alex Salmond's allegations against the Scottish government, the SNP and Nicola Sturgeon.

Cherry's sacking revolved around issues of transgender rights, feminism and charges of bullying. In February Salmond appeared before the cross-party parliamentary body investigating the Scottish government's botched inquiry into allegations of sexual misconduct made against him in 2018. In his submission to the government inquiry, Salmond claimed that senior government and SNP figures, including Peter Murrell, the SNP's chief executive officer and Sturgeon's husband, had made a 'deliberate, prolonged, malicious and concerted' effort to wreck his reputation, have him imprisoned and 'removed from public life' in Scotland. (In March 2020 a jury had found Salmond to be not guilty on twelve charges of sexual assault: another charge resulted in a 'not proven' verdict.) Salmond also claimed, in spoken and written evidence, that the first minister herself had breached the ministerial code of conduct in providing the parliamentary inquiry with false information concerning recollections of her meetings with him about the sexual harassment allegations.[70]

As noted above in relation to the resignation of SNP activists in Skye, other critics within the wider Yes movement charged that the SNP still did not have a viable plan for independence, especially around economic policy, that it was once again too slow to grasp the independence nettle and that it required more political competition from pro-independence bodies to sharpen up its performance.[71] An albeit short and selective report from the Centre for Economic Performance at the London School of Economics (LSE), furthermore, claimed that independence would leave Scotland considerably poorer in terms of trade and per capita income.[72]

Yet by the end of February none of these problems and criticisms had seemingly made a dent in the SNP's popularity among the public. A new grass-roots, mass membership organization of the Yes movement, Now Scotland, furthermore, met with immediate success in its attempts to 'unify and bring people together and get the positive message for independence across'. Now Scotland made it clear that it was not a new political party.[73]

March and April, however, were very troubled months for the SNP and the independence movement in general. On 23 March the parliamentary committee of inquiry published its conclusions that Sturgeon had indeed misled parliament about her meetings with Salmond, but that she had not done so 'knowingly'. The inquiry members voted five to four in favour of this decision, largely along partisan party-political lines. Sturgeon's reputation for honesty had thus been seriously questioned by the inquiry, rather than completely undermined. The Scottish Tories' motion of no confidence in Sturgeon, moreover, was heavily defeated in the Scottish parliament, by sixty-five to thirty-one votes. While accepting the inquiry's conclusions, the first minister continued forcefully to defend her reputation and her recollections of the meetings with Salmond. Sturgeon also criticized the 'partisan' nature and findings of the inquiry and the leaks of its findings to the press before their official publication. Sturgeon also strongly denied that there had been an SNP or government plot or conspiracy against Salmond and rebuked him for failing to express any public remorse for the plight of the women complainants.[74]

A day earlier, the extremely important independent report into Sturgeon's actions by Ireland's former director of public prosecutions, James Hamilton, QC, was published. Most significantly, the report found that although the first minister had provided an 'incomplete' account of her meetings with Salmond, she had *not* broken the ministerial code in any way. If Hamilton had reached a guilty verdict, Sturgeon almost certainly would have been obliged to resign and the future of the SNP and independence and the outcomes of the May elections thrown into considerable doubt and disarray.[75]

The SNP's resilience and triumph at the May elections

Having survived this serious crisis, Nicola Sturgeon emerged wiser and even more determined, as the most 'serious' and 'experienced' leader in Scotland, to continue to fight the good fight. The first minister saw the upcoming Holyrood elections as the 'most important in Scottish history'. In her eyes they constituted a truly historic or 'watershed' moment as 'we set about building a better Scotland and a better world'. Sturgeon believed that, as in the 1930s United States, the choice for voters was stark: fear and a return to a discredited past or, as in the case of president Franklin D. Roosevelt, 'courage, optimism and vision' for a new future. The first minister asked whether the voters wished to emerge from the present crisis and achieve recovery and regeneration by left-of-centre, radical and Scottish means, or did they want more of Boris Johnson and a 'return of raw Thatcherism'? In Sturgeon's eyes, the first choice involved Scottish independence, membership of the EU, more inclusivity, equality, fairness and moves towards a more prosperous and secure country, with a guaranteed minimum standard of comfort and security for all, in the form of a Citizen's Basic Income. The second involved a 'hard Brexit', a smaller state committed to austerity, welfare cuts and anti-social deregulation, hostility to immigrants and dictatorial and outmoded control by Westminster. For the first minister, the key question of the election revolved around freedom of choice and direction, especially the desired pathway out of the Covid- and related crises. Sturgeon asked the electorate, 'What kind of country do you want to build and where should the decisions about that recovery be made?'[76]

Unlike her main opponents – Douglas Ross and the Tories, Anas Sarwar and Labour and Willie Rennie and the Liberal Democrats – Sturgeon did not pose a binary divide between recovery and the constitutional question. Contrary to the shared emphasis in the election campaigns of these opponents, for the SNP it was not a case of either recovery or Scottish independence. Rather, for Sturgeon, the two issues were closely 'interlinked'. To be sure, the SNP's immediate post-election priority would be further successfully to tackle and suppress the virus. Beyond the immediate term the country, however, had to decide which kind of recovery, which pathway out of the crisis, it wanted. From the perspective of Sturgeon and the SNP, this necessarily involved resort to a second independence referendum in order to allow 'the people' to choose. This would take place during the first half of the new parliament. If successful, Indyref2 would empower the SNP and its allies to create an independent Scotland committed to a progressive, anti-Tory future. Thus, while the election revolved around the immediate priority of recovery, Scotland's right to choose the nature and direction of its future, by means of Indyref2, was also an integral part of the necessary election- and post-election national conversations. While the issue of independence remained a secondary and divisive one for the main opposition parties, committed as they were to 'Putting Recovery First' and 'Stopping the SNP and Indyref2', it remained a central and unifying force for the SNP.

Sturgeon further maintained that if the electorate returned either an SNP majority or a majority of SNP and other MSPs committed to independence, then Boris Johnson would, despite his protestations to the contrary, and despite Alba's serious doubts about Johnson's response, abide by the clear democratic will of Scotland's people and grant a Section 30 order. This would enable the Scottish government to hold an independence referendum. As noted earlier, Sturgeon was also determined to attain Indyref2 by purely constitutional and legal means, even if this meant that the achievement of independence might be slower than desired by members of Alba and likeminded others in the wider independence movement. Johnson was not to be afforded an excuse or opportunity to deny the holding of the referendum for the reason that the SNP and the government had acted unconstitutionality.[77]

A key question, of course, was whether the divisions and conflicts within the independence movement would adversely affect support for Sturgeon, the SNP and the Yes movement. During March and April, polling evidence suggested that a dip in support for all three was taking place. Yet by late April and early May, the evidence was far less clear cut. When considered as a whole, it seemed to suggest that the combined forces of the SNP and the ascendant Greens were on course to achieve a clear majority at Holyrood. It also suggested that, after its initial promise, the new Alba Party, founded at the end of March by retired TV presenter Laurie Flynn, and with Salmond as its leader, might win just one seat and that Labour, under the resourceful and confident Sarwar, was 'neck and neck' with the Tories in the constituencies but trailing them in the regional list. As observed by John Curtice and other experts, majority support for both the SNP and independence was on a 'knife-edge'. There was also a broad consensus that Sturgeon had easily performed best in the four televised leaders' debates.[78]

The results of the May elections demonstrated that Sturgeon and the SNP had very successfully met the serious challenges outlined above. The party won sixty-four seats, one more than in 2016. This was, by any standards, an excellent performance. Although the SNP had fallen one seat short of an outright majority of sixty-five, it had impressively won its fourth successive Scottish parliamentary election, following those in 2007, 2011 and 2016, and had gained its largest ever vote share. The voters had clearly been impressed by the SNP's record in government, its overall level of competence and, in particular, the stewardship of Sturgeon during the pandemic. The first minister had not only survived her recent trials, but had emerged from them stronger, more focussed and more determined than ever. Sturgeon stood head and shoulders above all the other party leaders in Scotland and, I would argue, in the UK as a whole. A formidable and courageous politician, Sturgeon relates easily to the daily concerns, hopes and aspirations of most citizens. Between them, moreover, the SNP and the Greens held seventy-two seats in the new parliament. The Greens, headed by the forward-looking and independence-supporting Lorna Slater and Patrick Harvie, had added two seats to the six they held in 2016. As a result, there emerged a clear majority at Holyrood – seventy-two in all – in favour of Indyref2 and independence.[79]

True to her pre-election promise, Nicola Sturgeon announced that her government would first attend to the diminishing pandemic and then move to address Indyref2 and the framing of a recovery and growth programme by a newly independent Scotland. As the first minister informed Boris Johnson just after the elections, a second independence referendum had become 'a matter of when, not if'.[80] Contrary to the belief of Alba and other independence critics of the SNP, Sturgeon thus immediately and clearly laid down the independence challenge to Johnson.

Alba, itself, had a very disappointing election. It failed to win a single seat, despite receiving more than 40,000 votes and recruiting over 5,000 members in its brief, six-week history. Some commentators, indeed, viewed Alex Salmond as being increasingly out of touch with the younger, greener and feminist activists attracted in large numbers to the independence cause. Many of these activists doubtless agreed with Sturgeon that

Salmond's 'seemingly unapologetic behaviour' towards his female staff complainants was totally unacceptable.[81]

The Conservatives under Douglas Ross managed to hold on to the thirty-one seats and the second place they had reached in 2016. Labour dropped two seats to a total of twenty-two and the Liberal Democrats fell by one to four seats.

Conclusion

This chapter has examined the fluctuating fortunes of the demand for radical self-determination for Scotland between the referendum of 2014 and the Scottish parliamentary elections of May 2021. It has shown that this demand did not necessarily amount to one for complete independence. Rather, as seen most prominently in 2014 and 2015, the SNP, the main representative of the self-determination movement, at times sought a stronger and louder voice for Scotland *within* the United Kingdom. Despite instances to the contrary, the period dominated by Brexit, however, saw demands for self-determination and Scottish independence become increasingly synonymous.

Between 2016 and 2019, support for independence fluctuated. Yet by the end of 2019, and throughout 2020, the polls suggested that a majority of people living in Scotland had come to support independence. Although the current situation suggests that support for Yes and No is split at 50 per cent to 50 per cent, the new SNP-dominated Scottish government has clearly revealed its intention to campaign for another independence referendum during the first half of the current parliament. Others, such as Labour's Gordon Brown and Keir Starmer, still hope to find a middle-way, in the form of a more devolved UK, to the current impasse between Unionism and national independence.[82] There is little immediate prospect, however, that Boris Johnson will accept either the SNP's demand that he abides by the democratic 'will of the people' in Scotland or Labour's plans for more devolution. Johnson's right-wing brand of 'muscular Unionism', furthermore, is fundamentally at odds with the 'radical Scottishness' of the SNP and the wider independence movement. We have thus reached an impasse or an interregnum, as described by Antonio Gramsci, in the profound present crisis of society in the UK.

I will conclude this chapter by offering three brief replies to the questions posed in the Introduction around the issues of Conservative hegemony, the SNP's and wider independence movement's challenge to it and the possible outcome of the present crisis, including the country's political future.

First, we have seen that while clearly dominant in England, Boris Johnson and his party undoubtedly face a strong challenge to their continued 'rule' in the UK as a whole. As matters currently stand, the main challenge undoubtedly comes from the popular, centre-left independence forces in Scotland. I have grouped these forces together under the general heading of 'radical Scottishness'.

Second, radical Scottishness should be seen as the leading force in a wider and growing left-of-centre, civic nationalist and in some instances social-democratic movement. This movement is evident in Wales, the island of Ireland and in the 'submerged' radical potential of England. As argued by historian David Edgerton, Scotland's radical experiment could possibly act as the progressive beacon of a 'new democratic settlement' throughout the British Isles and across the Irish Sea.[83] In this way, the further break-up of the UK would resolve the UK's present crisis in radical rather than conservative ways.

Third, at the same time, we, however, must observe that the overall balance of political, ideological, social, economic and cultural forces is currently far too precarious, and events far too unpredictable, for us to forecast the outcome of the present crisis with much, if any, degree of certainty. Sufficient time quite simply has not elapsed, and events are far too much in flux and contingent, to reveal whether Johnson's Conservatism or Sturgeon's left-of-centre nationalism will prevail. As argued by economist Larry Elliott, an independent Scotland, furthermore, would face serious economic difficulties in attempting to combine a high fiscal deficit with re-joining the EU and expanding the economy.[84] These crucial issues should be revisited once the future becomes clearer, if it does, beyond the outcomes of the probable Indyref2 of 2023 and the general election of 2024.

To the Present

Introduction

Previous chapters have examined the intensification of the crisis mainly from 2017 to May 2021. The purpose of this final chapter is to bring my narrative up to the summer of 2022. This has been a most dramatic time. Above all else, it has seen the resignation of Boris Johnson, albeit against his will and predictably 'unrepentant' and 'bullish' about his own and his government's record.[1] It has also seen what has rapidly become a bad-tempered fight between the two favourites to succeed Johnson, Liz Truss and Rishi Sunak. Whatever the outcome of the leadership contest, the future will almost certainly see both the demise of Johnson's eclecticism and pragmatism, especially on economic matters, and, as observed by the *Guardian*'s Martin Kettle, 'a massive lurch to the right'.[2] The present crisis will not end. In all probability it will get considerably worse in terms of the state of the economy, most people's living standards and industrial conflict.[3] The battle for Scottish independence will come to a head in 2023 and it is likely that progressive nationalist and left sentiment on the island of Ireland and in Wales will further increase. New fantastical and backward-looking 'solutions' to the crisis will probably arise, alongside existing 'morbid symptoms', while radicalism will compete with conservatism for future hegemony. In short, the combined crisis will continue, and the outcome of the current impasse or interregnum remains difficult to predict. The resignation of Johnson, however, provides a fitting point of closure for this study, or, as what one of my reviewers aptly termed, a 'capstone for the thesis of the book'.

Boris Johnson: from triumph to downfall

As we saw in Chapter 3, the revival of Boris Johnson's fortunes in the first half of 2021 culminated in the Conservative triumph at the May local elections and the spectacular by-election victory in the traditional Labour seat of Hartlepool in the same month. The successful and early roll-out of the vaccination programme against Covid-19 was probably the major factor in this triumph, although popular support for Brexit and Johnson's 'levelling up' policy, combined with the revival of the economy and improved projections for economic growth, were also contributory factors.

Six months later, Johnson's fluctuating fortunes had once again taken a serious turn for the worse. As noted in Chapter 3, even before the May elections a 'rat' or 'rats' had leaked allegations to the press about Johnson's improper funding for refurbishment of his Downing Street flat, his 'arrangement' with Sir James Dyson around tax avoidance and his distasteful and insensitive reported comments in late October 2020 about preferring to see bodies 'pile high in their thousands' rather than impose a third national lockdown in response to soaring cases of Covid-19.[4]

Further alarm bells rang for Johnson and the Conservatives at various points during the summer and autumn of 2021. For example, in June Matt Hancock resigned as health secretary after failing to observe social distancing rules.[5] In September there arose widespread opposition to the government's social-care policy. A cap on personal contributions to care was to be achieved by means of a rise in national insurance contributions. Critics, including Tories such as the former prime minister Sir John Major, maintained that this was a regressive policy in that it placed a disproportionate burden on younger and lower-income earners. It also broke Johnson's 2019 election pledge not to raise national insurance contributions. As Major concluded, funding for social care from general taxation would be a much fairer and progressive system.[6]

In October and November the government launched an underhand and discredited attack on the standards commissioner, Kathryn Stone, whose cross-party committee had found former minister and friend of Johnson, Owen Paterson, to have committed an 'egregious' breach of lobbying rules. Paterson had received payment from two companies when lobbying parliament on their behalf. Johnson strongly defended his old ally and friend, ordered a three-line whip on Conservative MPs to prevent Paterson being suspended from parliament for thirty days, as recommended by the committee, and attacked the commissioner and the system of investigation. (Paterson controversially claimed that it lacked a right of appeal.) The whip was successful in terms of the parliamentary vote going in favour of the government, but the whole affair reflected badly on the government. It led to widespread charges of government favouritism, cronyism, unfairness and a failure not to abide by tried and tested rules. During the ensuing furore, Paterson resigned as an MP rather than face suspension. At the same time, he continued to deny that he had done anything wrong. Johnson emerged from the affair with his reputation badly damaged within his own party and more widely. John Major described Johnson's behaviour as 'shameful and wrong' and 'politically corrupt'. The left-of-centre *Observer* agreed. It denounced the Prime Minister as a man 'utterly lacking in integrity' with 'no regard for standards in public life'.[7]

The Paterson affair was followed, in November, by the disappointing news that there was insufficient funding to meet the government's promise to build a complete and fully integrated high-speed railway line (HS2) between London and the north-west of England. The eastern leg of the line to Leeds would be scrapped, as would a full, high-speed link between Leeds and Manchester. These decisions met with dismay and angry protests, including those by 'red-wall' voters and MPs, that Johnson's promises to 'level up' and his support for the Northern Powerhouse project, were falling short.[8]

Between November 2021 and June 2022 numerous charges and proven instances of Johnson's and his government's difficulties, broken and unfulfilled promises, hypocrisy, mendacity, sleaze, cronyism, incompetence and lack of trust and legitimacy dominated UK politics. In November the government was shown to be scaling back social-care support for poorer households, while the economy was slowing down and living costs and taxes rising. Despite inflated government expectations and Johnson's largely upbeat predictions, the Climate Change Conference in Glasgow (COP 26) did not go far enough in its plans to reduce the adverse impact of climate change. Johnson continued to be vague and evasive about the source of funding for the refurbishment of his flat in Downing Street and in January was shown to have sought funding from outside Conservative sources. Notwithstanding home secretary Priti Patel's hard-line stance, more small and unsafe boats were crossing the Channel and more refugees experiencing heartbreak and tragedy. While the Prime Minister was widely perceived by right-wing, as well as centre and left media outlets, to have 'lost his grip', Labour's star under Starmer was rising. The patriotic and newly confident Labour leader intensified his efforts to appear, in contrast to Johnson, to be in touch with the public as a competent, ethical, honest, responsible and trusted prime minister in waiting. By mid-November Labour had edged ahead, by 1 point, in the polls for the first time since January 2021, while Starmer was now just 1 point behind Johnson in terms of the best prime-minister stakes.[9]

During December Johnson's fortunes declined even further. In the context of the sudden arrival and very rapid spread of a new variant of Covid, Omicron, ninety-nine Tory MPs, many of them describing themselves as libertarians, voted in parliament, albeit unsuccessfully, against Johnson's proposed Covid vaccine certificates. This was the biggest rebellion of his premiership.[10] By Christmas, there arose the possibility of a Covid 'firebreak' lockdown. In the event, this did not materialize despite the highly infectious nature and spread of the new, albeit less dangerous, variant.

There did, however, develop an even more widespread, profound and dangerous crisis of trust and confidence in the probity and fairness of Johnson and his colleagues around what would become the long-running and self-inflicted disaster of 'partygate'. This arose out of leaked revelations that parties, involving drinking and close social mixing, had been held in Downing Street and in other buildings in London housing prominent Tories, during periods of lockdown and other Covid-related restrictions. During these periods, of course, social mixing and access to leisure had been severely limited for the public and people had not been able to visit family or friends, or relatives suffering and sometimes dying from Covid in care homes and hospitals.

The first casualty of partygate was Allegra Stratton, the Prime Minister's former press secretary turned spokesperson for the COP 26 summit. In a video leaked to ITV, Stratton and her colleagues joked about what constituted a party with reference to the Christmas Party held in Downing Street in December 2020. At that time, all inside gatherings of two or more people were banned in London, as were work-based parties. A tearful Stratton apologised for her insensitive behaviour and resigned at the end of the first week in December. During the outrage that followed, a 'furious' Johnson also apologised – this time for the 'frivolous' behaviour of his staff – and promised a full investigation. Keir Starmer and many others in parliament and the country did not accept this. Starmer accused Johnson of 'taking the public for fools' after a week during which Downing Street refused to confirm what had taken place at the party. As Laura Kuenssberg, then the BBC's political editor, declared, the controversy and furore over parties during Covid restrictions was 'far from over'. There were claims of 'at least three other gatherings' and 'one other confirmed'. The opposition parties would not let go of the matter, while the Conservative Party was becoming 'more sour by the day'.[11] In another major blow to the government, the leading civil servant, Simon Case, also resigned over partygate just over a week later. Case, the cabinet secretary, had been appointed by Johnson to conduct the investigation into the Downing Street party. Yet it was now alleged that Case, himself, had organized a drinks party for up to twenty of his staff in his Whitehall offices in December 2020. Sue Gray, a veteran civil servant, replaced Case as head of the investigation.[12]

There was widely perceived to be one rule for prominent Tories and their friends and colleagues and another for the public at large. Although Johnson had denied for weeks that such parties had taken place, it became plain to growing numbers of the public that he was wrong and that he was either a fool or a knave. Memories of the Dominic Cummings affair, and his alleged breaking of the Covid rules in May 2020, flooded back into public consciousness.

By 11 December, in the wake of cronyism, sleaze and, increasingly, the lack of trust in the Prime Minister, Labour had gained a 9-point lead in the polls, according to the latest *Opinium* poll for the *Observer*. This was 1 point more than during the Cummings affair. Five days later the Tories disastrously lost a massive 23,000 majority in Owen Paterson's former rock-solid Tory seat, North Shropshire, in an almost unprecedented 34 per cent swing to the jubilant Liberal Democrats. The by-election result was widely interpreted as a damning judgement on the Prime Minister's leadership, competence and honesty.[13] The result in North Shropshire followed the Liberal Democrats' unexpected gain from the Conservatives in the Chesham and Amersham by-election in June 2021. During the third week of December, Lord David Frost, Johnson's very close Brexit ally and chief Brexit negotiator, resigned from the cabinet. Like many increasingly vociferous and rebellious others in the ranks of front-line Tories, Frost voiced his opposition to the 'Labour-like' 'tax and spend' aspects of Johnson's policies, his Covid restrictions and the stalemate around the Northern Ireland protocol.[14]

By this point in time, Johnson's poll ratings had fallen to their lowest level since he became prime minister. He was in serious danger of completely losing his control and authority within his party and public respect and trust. Many, including prominent Tories and parts of the Tory press, predicted that the increasingly rambling and incoherent Johnson would be very fortunate to remain as prime minister during 2022. This prediction would prove to be accurate. This time the Prime Minister's renowned, Houdini-like ability to escape from adversity and bounce back, usually more upbeat than ever, would not save him.[15]

As winter moved into spring, Johnson's plight became ever more desperate. In early February he was forced to accept the resignation of one of his most trusted and admired aides, Munira Mirza. Mirza had worked for Johnson for some fourteen years, most recently in the key role as director of the Number 10 policy unit. Mirza's resignation was based upon her rejection of Johnson's allegation that Starmer, as the director of public prosecutions (DPP), had failed to prosecute the paedophile Jimmy Savile.[16]

On 25 May, Sue Gray's important full report was published. It investigated fifteen party-gate events between May 2020 and April 2021. Gray found some of them to have been 'drunken, rowdy' and lasting until the early hours. The Metropolitan Police, furthermore, had issued 126 fines by the end of May. Johnson, however, refused to accept a charge of wrongdoing. This was despite the fact that the Prime Minister, Carrie Johnson and Rishi Sunak themselves had been fined by the police. Johnson did express regret and was 'deeply sorry' for the passage of events, but he consistently denied that he had knowingly broken the rules and sought to mislead parliament. His initial denial of the existence of parties and his claims that 'Covid rules were followed at all times' and 'I certainly broke no rules', gave way to the hardly credible claim that his involvement and presence were 'work-related' in order to 'boost morale'. Johnson declared that it 'never occurred to him' that the gatherings had broken the rules, but that, as strongly recommended by Gray, he would continue to do his utmost to improve leadership and managerial structures and processes in Downing Street and the Cabinet office. Johnson concluded that he would 'survive', 'fix it' and carry on with complete the good work his government was doing.[17]

The latter was reflected most clearly in Johnson's vociferous and unequivocal support for Ukraine and its opposition to the Russian invasion. The Prime Minister was at his best in condemning the brutality and unjustified nature of the invasion and the brave and heroic response of the Ukrainian people. His words and actions, such as the promise of military support in the form of missiles and vehicles and a surprise trip in April to meet the Ukrainian president, Volodymyr Zelenskiy, met with widespread national and international approval. One of the Prime Minister's hopes, of course, was that his support for Ukraine and his greatly enhanced international standing would divert the public's attention from partygate and convince his own MPs that it was not a good time to change their leader.[18]

As matters transpired, however, these hopes were not fulfilled. For example, in contrast to those held a year earlier, the May 2022 local elections were 'punishing' ones for the Conservatives. Senior figures in the Conservative Party and many Conservatives in the country blamed Johnson's leadership failings for the loss of 'swaths' of its southern heartlands to the Liberal Democrats and the 'flagship' London boroughs of Westminster and Wandsworth to Labour. As the *Guardian* observed, the Conservative Party lost 'about 350 council seats in England' and 'plunged to its worst position in Scotland for a decade'. The Liberal Democrats gained eight councils in England, while Labour did very well in London where it won or regained control of twenty-one of the thirty-two boroughs. Outside of the capital, the outcome for Labour in England, however, was 'mixed'. The party continued to do well in Wales, where it won the highest proportion of seats, and reasonably so in Scotland where it regained its position, at the expense of the Tories, as the second largest party at the local level.

The shared conclusion of the *Guardian* and leading psephologist, Sir John Curtice, was that, while Labour 'showed progress', it was, contrary to Keir Starmer's claim, not doing enough, especially to reconnect with its traditional voters in the North, to suggest that it either could or would convincingly win the next general election.[19] In Scotland as a whole, the SNP continued to be the dominant force in local government as it slightly increased its share of councillors. The party enjoyed its most spectacular and nail-biting victory on Glasgow city council where it beat Labour by just one seat.[20]

In Northern Ireland, predictions that Sinn Fein would win the May elections for the Stormont Assembly proved to be accurate. In a 'historic shift in the balance of power', Sinn Fein, under its leader, Michelle O'Neill, overtook, for the first time, the DUP as the largest single party in the devolved government, by twenty-seven to twenty-five seats. This development, combined with the Westminster government's continuing threat unilaterally to suspend parts of the Northern Ireland protocol – itself part of the legally binding Brexit deal between the UK and the EU – aroused more extensive fears that the Union, at least in its present 'muscular' form, would be further weakened. Much of the blame was directed at Boris Johnson. He was the obvious embodiment of authoritarian, centralized Unionism and the main UK architect of the 'oven ready' Brexit deal which he now sought to overturn in relation to the protocol. The wounded DUP threatened to stall power-sharing at Stormont in the event of the protocol not being changed to their liking.[21]

Matters came to a head for Johnson between June and early July. Two developments in June proved to be crucial. First, polls conducted at the end of May and the beginning of June showed that a majority of the public, around 56 per cent, believed that the Prime Minister had lied over partygate and that he could no longer be trusted to tell the truth and continue to command their respect. As such, he should no longer remain in office.[22]

Second, and even more dramatically, on 6 June Sir Graham Brady, the chair of the 1922 committee, publicly announced that more than the required fifty-four or 15 per cent of Conservative MPs had written letters to him to express no confidence in the Prime Minister. This outcome, as in the past, automatically triggers a vote of confidence on the part of the government's MPs in the sitting prime minister. The result, announced by Brady, on the evening of 6 June, showed that an unexpectedly large minority of Conservative MPs, 148 or 41-plus per cent, had no confidence in Johnson. The Prime Minister had formally won the contest, having received a total of 211 votes or 58-plus per cent. There was, however, a widespread consensus, in the media and among politicians, that Johnson had been badly 'wounded', that he had become a 'lame duck' prime minister (Nicola Sturgeon), that he was 'unfit for office' and completely 'out of touch' with public opinion (Keir Starmer), that his future was highly uncertain, and that he had very effectively lost the support of the large number of backbenchers who were not on the government's payroll. The support received by Johnson, furthermore, was well below that received by Theresa May, John Major and Margaret Thatcher in previously comparable votes. All three of these former prime ministers subsequently lost their premierships.

Most significantly perhaps, while the staunch Tory newspapers, the *Daily Mail* and the *Daily Express*, continued to support him, the equally pro-Johnson *Daily Telegraph*, the Prime Minister's political and philosophical media 'home', lost faith in its former champion. According to Ben Riley-Smith, the *Telegraph*'s political editor, Johnson had won a 'hollow' victory, his 'authority' had been 'crushed', the Tories 'torn apart'. The large number of Tory rebels were 'circling to finish him off as Prime Minister'. Johnson, himself, declared, in typically upbeat fashion, that he had won the vote and wanted to 'move on' and 'bash on'. But, in truth, his future and that of his government, indeed his party, was perilous. In sum, the Prime Minister's and the Tories' full 'legitimation crisis' was now upon them. Most commentators reiterated the view that Johnson would be out of office 'in a year'.[23]

As matters transpired, the denouement arrived far sooner. On 23 June, by-elections were held in Tiverton and Honiton in Devon and Wakefield in West Yorkshire. They both dealt hammer blows to the Conservative Party. In Tiverton and Honiton there was a 30 per cent swing to the Liberal Democrats. The latter overturned a huge Conservative majority of 24,000 plus to win by 6,144 votes. This was the largest by-election defeat in history in terms of the size of the majority overturned. As in their earlier spectacular triumphs in North Shropshire and Chesham and Amersham, the Liberal Democrats were absolutely delighted. The election was a damning judgement both on Johnson and the former Conservative MP for Tiverton and Honiton constituency, Neil Parish, who had been caught watching pornography on his mobile telephone while in the House of Commons. Parish had resigned. Ed Davey, the Liberal Democrats' leader, urged the Prime Minister also to 'do the right thing' and go.[24]

Before its capture in December 2019 by the Tories, Wakefield had been consistently Labour. The by-election took place because its Conservative MP, Imran Ahmad Khan, had been found guilty of the sexual assault of a fifteen-year-old boy and jailed in May. The by-election in this 'red wall' seat resulted in a Labour victory. Labour won comfortably by 4,925 votes and in so doing overturned the Tory majority of 3,358. Keir Starmer welcomed the 'great result' and congratulated the local party on being 'absolutely focused on the issues affecting working people'.[25]

While declaring that the two by-election results were 'not brilliant', Boris Johnson expressed his determination to 'keep going'. In contrast, many Tory MPs, fearful for their own seats, plotted their next move to get rid of him. In a major blow to the Prime Minister, Oliver Dowden resigned as the Conservative Party chair. Dowden shared Conservative supporters 'distress' and 'disappointment' at 'the latest in a run of very poor results', while former Conservative prime minister, Lord William Hague, openly feared that the next national poll could be a 'disaster' for his party.[26] Dowden's resignation followed that of Lord Geidt, Johnson's former ethics adviser. Geidt had resigned suddenly and without explanation in mid-June, although he was known to be unhappy with Johnson's handling of partygate and the possibility that the Prime Minister had misled parliament.[27] To compound matters, by the end of June the country was facing rising inflation, a looming cost of living crisis, a recession and the start of what was to be a wave of industrial conflict.[28]

As noted above, MPs Imran Khan and Neil Parish had been forced to step down as a result respectively of sexual assault and impropriety. These acts had become part of a pattern of improper and in some cases illegal sexual behaviour on the part of leading Conservative men. For example, in November 2017 Sir Michael Fallon had suddenly resigned as defence secretary. Fallon admitted that his past behaviour towards women had 'fallen short'. He had been accused of sexual harassment by a female reporter in addition to other allegations of sexual misconduct. The Fallon scandal constituted the 'final straw' for Prime Minister Theresa May. Yet, only a month later, May felt obliged to sack Damian Green, the first secretary of state and a longstanding friend and ally. Green had to depart because he had lied about the presence of pornographic images on his House of Commons computer in the past. He had also been under investigation for charges of sexual harassment against a female Tory activist. Both the Fallon and Green cases took place against the background of an increasing number of allegations of sexual assault and harassment by male and predominantly Conservative MPs at Westminster. In July 2020 the ex-Tory MP, Charles Elphicke, was found guilty on three counts of sexual assault against two women and jailed for two years. Finally, in May 2022, an unnamed Conservative MP was arrested on suspicion of rape and other sexual offences. The cases of Imran Khan and Neil Parish were thus part of an established and deplorable pattern of Conservative sleaze, sexual harassment and sexual abuse.[29]

It was within this appalling context that the Christopher Pincher affair took place. At the end of June, a drunken Pincher, the deputy chief whip, groped two men at a private members' club in London. The Prime Minister claimed that he had been unaware of any allegations against Pincher before he had promoted him to the post of chief whip in February. Yet Pincher's alleged multiple sexual transgressions were well known in and around Westminster. Johnson subsequently changed his story, from the claim that he did not know about any 'specific' allegations to an outright admission that he had been informed about Pincher's behaviour before the latter's promotion. Johnson ended up by issuing a humiliating apology: he had made a 'bad mistake'. An 'embarrassed' and remorseful Pincher resigned his government post.[30]

The Pincher scandal was thus the latest in a string of sleaze scandals directly involving prominent Conservatives and occurring on Johnson's watch.[31] Yet its importance as a trigger for Johnson's departure cannot be overstated. As journalist Jessica Murray declared, the Pincher affair and the discredited role of the Prime Minister in it, proved to be 'the straw that broke the camel's back for Boris-Johnson's scandal-ridden premiership'.[32] Johnson's many and repeated failures to 'come clean', his lies, equivocations, apologies and eventual truth-telling had once again been revealed as enduring and fundamental weaknesses in his character. The credibility of the government, moreover, was bare. It could no longer lead, command and enjoy the respect, trust and legitimacy of its own MPs and the wider public.

In the wake of the Pincher scandal, events moved very quickly. By 6 July the majority of Conservative MPs and the cabinet were in open revolt. Most prominently, Sajid Javid, the health secretary, and the chancellor, Rishi Sunak, had resigned along with more than fifty other ministers and aides. Javid regretted the fact that under Johnson's leadership the country had not been 'competent in acting in the national interest' and had not displayed the necessary 'humility, grip and new direction' demanded by the public and 'a large number of our colleagues'. Sunak declared that the government was not being conducted 'properly, competently and seriously' and that 'standards' needed to be restored. Rees-Mogg, Priti Patel, Liz Truss and Nadine Dorries were predictably among the few high-profile Tories who remained loyal to Johnson. In their eyes, Sunak, in particular, had acted 'treacherously' towards the Prime Minister. This would later be reflected in their support for Truss and opposition to Sunak as Johnson's successor.[33]

The next day, 7 July, Johnson bowed to the inevitable and resigned. As briefly noted in the Introduction, his resignation speech, however, was far from gracious, generous or apologetic. The Prime Minister offered no remorse, no apologies for government failures and unacceptable suffering and loss of lives (most notably at the height of the pandemic) and no thanks to his colleagues. Rather, he found the negative judgement passed on him by his parliamentary colleagues to be 'eccentric', as part of a 'powerful herd instinct' at Westminster, especially when Labour was 'only a handful' of points ahead, when 'we're delivering so much' and in view of his many achievements. He was 'immensely proud' of 'getting Brexit done', the UK's the early vaccine rollout and his championing of freedom in Ukraine. In truth, this was the speech of a man who was totally deceiving himself, who had lost touch with reality. Johnson finished his premiership as he had begun it, as the supreme egotist and narcissist, the 'Great I AM', of contemporary politics in the UK.[34]

The future

The material presented in this chapter compels me to revisit my two conclusions offered in Chapters 3 and 4 about possible ways out of the present crisis. First, in Chapter 3, I suggested that, as of May 2021, Boris Johnson's eclectic and pragmatic brand of Conservatism and hegemonic conservative common-sense constituted 'the most obvious and popular way out of UK capitalism's ongoing and most challenging combined crisis of modern times'. Second, in Chapter 4, I, however, qualified this first conclusion by arguing that the 'radical Scottishness' of the SNP and the wider movement for Scottish independence, provided a serious challenge to Conservative hegemony and a possible stimulus to the wider development of left-of-centre progressivism and civic nationalism throughout the UK. As a consequence, 'the further break-up of the UK' could possibly help to resolve the crisis 'in radical rather than conservative ways'. In conclusion, I wish to revise my first conclusion and confirm my second.

In my updated narrative in this chapter, from May 2021 to the summer of 2022, we have clearly seen that Boris Johnson's many failures and eventual resignation mean that my first conclusion is no longer valid. Johnson's fall, furthermore, must be viewed alongside the currently chaotic and profoundly divided state of the Conservative Party and the continuation, indeed worsening, of the wider societal crisis. The latter is manifesting itself most immediately in spiralling inflation and living costs, imminent recession, market turbulence and spreading industrial conflict.[35]

While the fortunes of the Conservative Party plummet, those of the Labour Party, moreover, continue to strengthen and suggest that it will become the foremost threat to the Conservatives, certainly in England and Wales, for the foreseeable future. At the time of Johnson's resignation, Labour enjoyed a poll lead of around 11 points, according to YouGov. For the remainder of July this trended at 7.3 per cent, but by the third week in August it had reached between 8 and 15 points. This was partly in response to internal Tory warfare and Starmer's commitment to an energy price freeze. There is currently general agreement that, as matters stand. Labour stands a very good chance of achieving a majority at the next general election.[36]

By way of qualification and possible correction, we must note that this positive situation for Labour, of course, may change as events unfold. It is also worth adding that while Starmer's very conscious attempts to move Labour to the centre ground of politics and avoid charges of controversy and extremism have made the party more respectable and, many would argue, more electable, questions and doubts still remain. For example, is Starmer going too far in forbidding his MPs to join picket lines and counselling against strong support for strikes? After all, we have to remember that this is a time of extreme financial difficulty for many workers and that the vast majority are voting for industrial action as a last, and often desperate, resort. This action, moreover, is widespread and cross-class in character. It involves middle-class barristers protesting against severe government cuts to legal aid budgets, as well as workers in the 'gig economy' and in more traditional forms of employment, for example, in transport and the public sector. The groups involved are characterized *both* by their diversity *and* a shared goal to rely upon themselves, upon trade-union and more informal means of collective self-help, to improve their lot. They are striking in the face of government and employer intransigence, massive bonuses for bosses, glaring and escalating inequality, raging inflation, the threat of recession and sharply falling real wages. There is no evidence, furthermore, that large sections of the public are unsympathetic to those taking industrial action. In the future, the Labour Party leadership may well regret its current failure more firmly to connect with its 'traditional' constituents and potentially new recruits within the working class and to increase its middle-class support, including those who are left of centre.[37]

Starmer's judgement and abilities as a leader, and potential future prime minister, may also be questioned. On the one hand, he has undoubtedly provided calm leadership, steadied the ship after the internal party turbulence of the Corbyn era and increased Labour's centrist and patriotic appeal. On the other hand, we may reasonably ask whether Starmer has the ability to think and act quickly on his feet, to be charismatic and successfully to offer the public and the electorate a popular, alternative modernizing vision of the UK in the manner of Tony Blair and Harold Wilson. After all, he is a somewhat pedestrian and awkward politician to whom spontaneity, creativity, vision, enthusiasm and the 'common touch' do not seem to come naturally.[38]

Starmer has also declared that Labour will not enter into alliances with other anti-Tory parties. This could prove to be a serious mistake, especially with regard to the Liberal Democrats. Having triumphed so spectacularly in recent by-elections, the progressive Liberal Democrats, under their strong and intelligent leader, Ed Davey, now constitute the main threat to the Tories in key 'blue wall' constituencies in the south of England. Yet, in rejecting a potential alliance with the Liberal Democrats, Starmer has forfeited a good opportunity to begin to build a potentially election-winning progressive alliance.[39]

Finally, while Starmer's Unionist opposition to the independence-seeking SNP is far more understandable, there is surely much scope for Starmer and Labour in Scotland, under Anas Sawar, to be more flexible on Scotland's democratic right to hold Indyref2 and the wider question of Unionism and Scottish independence. We have already seen that a significant number of members and supporters of Scottish Labour – some 40 per cent – support independence. Does Labour seriously want to risk their future support? In truth, unless the Labour Party dramatically restores much of its former strength in Scotland very quickly, and evidence drawn from the recent past and the present would suggest this is highly unlikely, its chance of winning the next general election is much reduced.

My argument that the movement for Scottish independence offers a potentially radical way out of the crisis, still holds for the post-May 2021 period. For example, the SNP has maintained its remarkable electoral forward march and continues to be the hegemonic force in Scotland. It has won four successive Scottish elections, in 2007,

2011, 2016 and 2021.[40] We saw in Chapter 4 that the SNP fought the May 2021 Scottish elections on the explicit promise that, if successful, it would commit to a second independence referendum during the first half of the new parliament. Nicola Sturgeon has since set Indyref2 for 19 October 2023 and is confident of success. The SNP has also made a submission to the Supreme Court to see if that referendum may be held even in the (very likely) absence of a Section 30 order from the Westminster government. The Scottish government, furthermore, is currently busy making plans and writing papers making the case for independence.[41]

To be sure, questions, difficulties and obstacles continue to exist. These range from the consequences of the likely event of a negative verdict from the Supreme Court, to the fact that support for independence in Scotland has fallen from a highpoint of 55 per cent on the eve of Christmas 2021 to around 50 per cent during 2022. The potentially problematic and major issues of Scotland's future currency and control over monetary policy, and its continued weaknesses in terms of marked inequalities in health, education, wealth and land ownership, still remain. Some important voices on the left of politics, moreover, continue to dismiss the SNP as a force for authentic social-democratic change.[42]

Yet Sturgeon and her party, alongside the wider independence movement, remain extremely popular and continue to offer their country an independent, fairer and more equal future. Sturgeon, herself, continues to be trusted by the electorate and is still widely supported for her perceived efficient and caring handling of the Covid crisis. In my view, the SNP leader has more than proven herself to be an extremely able, efficient, tough and determined leader who communicates extremely well with the public and is not prepared to countenance defeat at the hands of her opponents. The first minister arguably continues to stand head-and-shoulders above all the other main party leaders in the UK.[43]

Radicalism in Scotland, furthermore, continues to have the considerable potential, as argued in Chapter 4, to act as an inspiration to the further spread of left-of-centre sentiment and organization in Wales, Northern Ireland and the Republic of Ireland and to spark them into renewed and more extensive life in England. Many of those disillusioned by Labour's 'New Labour' turn will potentially become part of this wider and emboldened progressive left-of-centre movement. Significantly, the post-Corbyn Labour Party has already lost over 100,000 members, many of whom were attracted to Corbyn's socialism. In short, 'radical Scottishness' and its wider effects continue to offer a wider radical, as opposed to a conservative, way out of the crisis.

These combined developments – of Tory gloom, of Labour resurgence and optimism and continuing SNP strength and influence – raise the intriguing possibilities that the Conservatives will not only lose the 2024 general election, but also their intellectual leadership and legitimacy that have underpinned their long period of parliamentary domination and societal hegemony. In any event, the study of the future battle for hegemony and domination throughout the UK undoubtedly will produce many more Gramscian-type 'morbid symptoms', divisions and conflicts. Its study, with politics being central to its outcome, will form a potentially fascinating sequel to the present book.

Notes

Introduction

1 The idea of 'the end of history' has been most closely associated with the work of political scientist, Francis Fukuyama. See his 'The End of History?', *The National Interest*, 16 (1989), 3–18.

2 Martin Jacques, *When China Rules the World: The End of the Western World and the Birth of a New Global Order* (London; Penguin, 2012); Karl Marx and Friedrich Engels, *The Communist Manifesto* (London: Penguin, 1970), pp. 85–6. See also Gareth Stedman Jones, *Karl Marx: Greatness and Illusion* (London: Allen Lane, 2006), pp. 377–82.

3 Andrew Gamble, *The Spectre at the Feast: Capitalist Crisis and the Politics of Recession* (Basingstoke: Palgrave Macmillan, 2009), Introduction, ch. 1.

4 Adam Tooze, *Crashed: How a Decade of Financial Crises Changed the World* (London: Allen Lane, 2018).

5 For example, Brexit has not generally been studied in a fully integrated way, as a key aspect of the wider combined present crisis. For Brexit, see Anthony Seldon, with Raymond Newell, *May at 10* (London: Biteback Publishing, 2019); David Cameron, *For the Record* (London: William Collins, 2019); Tim Shipman, *All Out War: The Full Story of Brexit* (London: William Collins, 2017); idem, *Fall Out: A Year of Political Mayhem* (London: William Collins, 2017).

6 Robert Skidelsky, *Money and Government: A Challenge to Mainstream Economics* (London: Penguin, 2019), ch. 8; idem, 'Austerity Doesn't Work – Its Death Is Long Overdue', *Prospect Magazine*, 17 July 2017; Paul Krugman, 'The Austerity Delusion', *Guardian* ('The Long Read'), 29 April 2015.

7 'Definition of Permacrisis'. *Collins English Dictionary*. https://www.collinsdictionary. com/dictionary/english/permacrisis.

8 Quintin Hoare and Geoffrey Noel Smith (eds), *Selections from the Prison Notebooks of Antonio Gramsci* (London: Lawrence and Wishart, 1973), p. 276.

9 Fintan O'Toole, *Heroic Failure: Brexit and the Politics of Pain* (London: Head of Zeus, 2018). See also, Anthony Barnett, *The Lure of Greatness: England's Brexit and America's Trump* (London: Unbound, 2017).

10 Bob Jessop, *The State: Past Present Future* (Cambridge: Polity Press, 2018), p. 105.

11 Hoare and Smith, *Selections Prison Notebooks*, pp. 12–13, 55–6 (n5), 57–8, 275–6.

12 In this context see journalist and writer Paul Mason's fascinating and challenging thesis that 'capitalism has mustered a new social force that will be its gravedigger' – of global 'networked humanity' in revolt, of 'the working class "sublated"', Paul Mason, *PostCapitalism: A Guide to our Future* (London: Allen Lane, 2015), ch. 7, especially pp. 212–13.

13 Ben Wray, 'An Election at the Apex of the Crisis of the UK', *Commonspace*, 30 October 2019.

14 David Edgerton, 'Brexit Is a Necessary Crisis – It Reveals Britain's True Place in the World', *Guardian*, 9 October 2019; idem, *The Rise and Fall of the British Nation:*

A Twentieth-Century History (London: Penguin, 2019), pp. xxxi–ii, chs. 4, 5, 12; Will Hutton, 'How Could It Be that the Tories Have Turned Their Backs on the Best of British Industry?', *Observer*, 17 November 2019; Rajeev Syal, 'Rich Donors Hand Tories £5.7m Election Funding Boost', *Guardian*, 21 November 2019; Phillip Inman, 'CBI Member Survey Reveals Huge Support for Remaining in the EU', *Guardian*, 15 March 2016; Larry Elliott, 'CBI Chief Fires Parting Shot Over Slow Pace of Brexit Negotiations', *Guardian*, 28 October 2020; Eivind Friis Hamre and William Wright, 'Brexit and the City: The Impact So Far', *New Financial*, April 2021; Paul Wallace, 'The Humbling of the CBI', *Prospect Magazine*, 21 July 2021; Gerard Lyons, 'To Ensure that the City Continues to Flourish, We Need to Make the Most of Brexit', *Policy Exchange*, 25 February 2022.

15 *BBC News*, 'Politics', 'Boris Johnson Challenged Over Brexit Business Expletive', 26 June 2018, https://www.bbc.co.uk/news/uk-politics-44618154; Paul Wallace, 'The Humbling of the CBI', *Prospect Magazine*, 21 July 2021.

16 Hoare and Smith, *Prison Notebooks*, pp. 55–60, 181–2, 185, 206–8, 228–9, 238–9, 275–6.

17 Jurgen Habermas, *Legitimation Crisis* (Cambridge: Polity Press, 1988 [1973]), pp. 75–92, 95–7.

18 The following important publications appeared after I had finished writing the relevant parts of my book: Robert Ford, Tim Bale, Will Jennings, Paula Surridge, *The British General Election of 2019* (Cham, Switzerland: Palgrave Macmillan, 2021); Adam Tooze, *Shutdown: How Covid Shook the World's Economy* (London: Allen Lane, 2021); Hilary Cooper and Simon Szreter, *After the Virus: Lessons from the Past for a Better Future* (Cambridge: Cambridge University Press, 2021); David Spiegelhalter and Anthony Masters, *Covid By Numbers: Making Sense of the Pandemic with Data* (London: Penguin, 2021).

19 Gary Younge, 'Everyone Thought the Election was a Foregone Conclusion. They Had No Idea What Was Really Going On', *Guardian*, 17 June, 2017.

20 Owen Jones, 'This Defeat Is the End of the Brexit PM. Bring on the General Election', *Guardian*, 30 March 2019.

Chapter 1

1 *Guardian*, 20 April, 4, 5, 6, 8, 9, 15 May 2017; *The Times*, 19 April 2017.

2 Alex Nunns, *The Candidate: Jeremy Corbyn's Improbable Path to Power* (London: OR books, 2017), pp. 288–90.

3 *Guardian*, 22, 23, 26, 27 May 2017; Gary Younge, 'A Resurgent Corbyn Has Become Labour's Best Hope of Survival', *Guardian*, 22 May 2017; *National*, 23 May 2017.

4 John Harris, 'Corbyn Has Shown There's a New Way of Doing Politics. Straight Talking Is Back', *Guardian*, 3 June 2017; May Bulman, 'Conservatives to Fall 18 Seats Short of Majority, Latest YouGov Model suggests', *Independent*, 3 June 2017; *Guardian*, 'Election 2017', 10 June 2017; Richard Seymour, *Corbyn: The Strange Rebirth of Radical Politics* (London: Verso, 2017), p. 232.

5 *Scottish Daily Mail*, 10 June 2017.

6 https://www.bbc.co.uk/news/election/2017/results; Kevin Rawlinson and Peter Walker, 'Lib Dems' Night of Mixed Fortunes as Clegg Loses Seat but Cable Returns', *Guardian*, 9 June 2017.

7 *Scottish Daily Mail*, 10 June 2017; *BBC News*, 'Election 2017', https://www.bbc.co.uk/news/election/2017/results/Scotland.

8   For these newspapers, see the following sources: *BBC News*, 'Scotland's Papers: Tories
     "Turn on May" and Indyref Election Impact', https://www.bbc.co.uk/news/uk-
     scotland-4023824; Graham Ruddick, '"Tories Turn on Theresa": Papers across the
     Spectrum on May's Future', *Guardian*, 10 June 2017; James Walsh and Guardian
     Readers, 'Readers on General Election Fallout: "May Won't Survive"', *Guardian*,
     10, 17 June 2017.
9   *Scottish Daily Mail*, 10 June 2017.
10   *Scottish Daily Mail*, 10 June 2017; *Guardian*, 10, 17 June 2017; *National*, 9, 10 June
     2017.
11   Gary Younge, 'Everyone Thought the Election was a Foregone Conclusion. They Had
     No Idea What Was Really Going On', *Guardian*, 17 June 2017.
12   This section is heavily indebted to Tim Shipman's excellent exposure of the Prime
     Minister's failings and weakness. See *Fall Out: A Year of Political Mayhem* (London:
     William Collins, 2017), chs. 15, 17, 18, 20, 21. See also Jessica Elgot, 'Notable by Their
     Absence: May and Corbyn Haunt TV Leaders' Debate', *Guardian*, 19 May 2017; John
     Crace, 'The Mays Produce Pure TV Valium', *Guardian*, 10 May 2017; idem, *I Maybot:
     The Rise and Fall* (London: Guardian Faber Publishing, 2017).
13   *Guardian*, 31 May 2017.
14   Heather Stewart and Peter Walker, 'Greek-Style Collapse Cited as May Talks Tough on
     Pay Cap', *Guardian*, 6 July 2017; *BBC News*, 'Election 2017 Conservative Manifesto
     Summary: Key Points At-a-glance', https://www.bbc.co.uk/news/
     election-2017-39960311; Allister Heath, 'The Tories' Historic Triumph will be
     Bittersweet for Economic Liberals', *Daily Telegraph*, 11 May 2017.
15   Heather Stewart, Rowena Mason, 'May Manifesto Rejects Legacy of Cameron Era',
     Guardian, 19 May 2017.
16   Shipman, *Fall Out*, pp. 227–8, 291–2, 335; *BBC News*, Election 2017.
17   Shipman, *Fall Out*, p. 279.
18   Shipman, *Fall Out*, pp. 286–91; *BBC News*, 'Election 2017'; Phillip Inman, 'Social Care
     Tory Plans Are a Tax on Dementia, Critics Say', *Guardian*, 19 May 2017. The Scottish
     Tories decided against introducing the means-tested winter fuel payment. See Michael
     Settle, 'Scottish Tories Rule Out Winter Cash Raid', *Herald*, 19 May 2017.
19   Shipman, *Fall Out*, pp. 291, 295, 315; Stewart, Mason, 'May Manifesto'.
20   Shipman, *Fall Out*, pp. 278, 300–1, 304–5.
21   Shipman, *Fall Out*, pp. 278, 306; *Guardian*, leader, 'Not So Strong and Stable After All.
     May Pulls the Emergency Cord', 23 May 2017.
22   Polly Toynbee, 'After May's U-Turn She Can't Accuse Anyone of Weakness', *Guardian*,
     23 May 2017; Anushka Asthana and Jessica Elgot, 'May's Manifesto Meltdown: U-Turn
     on "Dementia Tax" Leaves PM on Back Foot', *Guardian*, 23 May 2017; Shipman, *Fall
     Out*, pp. 301, 309–10.
23   *Guardian*, leader, 'Not So Strong'.
24   Alan Travis, 'Poll May Wins Hearts of Working Class', *Guardian*, 16 May 2017; Michael
     Savage, 'Trust in Theresa May Raises Tory Hopes in Labour's Northern Heartlands',
     Observer, 7 May 2017; Matthew Goodwin, 'Chequers Has Made a Labour Win Possible',
     Daily Telegraph, 30 July 2018.
25   *Guardian*, Election 2017, 10 June 2017; Nunns, *Candidate*, pp. 377–8.
26   Travis, 'Poll May Wins Hearts of Working Class'; idem, 'Guardian/ICM Poll. Labour
     Has Lost Its Traditional Lead in the Heartlands', *Guardian*, 10 May 2017.
27   Owen Jones, 'My Message to the Labour Right – There's No Going Back', *Guardian*,
     6 July 2017.

28 Nunns, *Candidate*, pp. 377–8; Andrew Hindmoor, 'Why the Left's Hellish Vision Is So Ruinous', *Observer*, 11 March 2018.

29 *Observer*, Election 2017 (Robert Ford), 11 June 2017; *Guardian*, leader, 'The Tories Run on Fear and Do Not Deserve Our Vote. Labour Does because It Offers Hope', 3 June 2017.

30 Nunns, *Candidate*, ch. 15; Toby Helm, 'Ditch Jeremy Corbyn Before It's Too Late, Sadiq Khan Tells Labour', *Guardian*, 21 August 2016; Rowena Mason, 'Labour on Edge of a Split that Would Finish Party, Says Smith', *Guardian*, 4 August 2016.

31 Rowena Mason, 'Labour Leadership: Jeremy Corbyn Elected with Huge Mandate', *Guardian*, 12 September 2015; Nunns, *Candidate*, pp. 253–63.

32 *BBC News*, Politics, 24 September 2016, https://www.bbc.co.uk/news/uk-pols37461219; George Eaton, 'How Jeremy Corbyn Won the Labour Leadership Election', *New Statesman*, 24 September 2016; Heather Stewart and Rowena Mason, 'Labour Leadership: Jeremy Corbyn Wins Convincing Victory Over Owen Smith', *Guardian*, 24 September 2016; John O'Farrell, *Things Can Only Get Worse? Twenty Confusing Years in the Life of a Labour Supporter* (London: Doubleday, 2017); Nunns, *Candidate*, pp. 280–5.

33 Seymour, *Corbyn*, pp. 191–5; Jeremy Corbyn, 'We Can't Leave the Negotiations with Europe to the Tories', *Guardian*, 8 July 2016; Andrew Gamble, 'The Resistible Rise of Theresa May', in Mark Perryman, *The Corbyn Effect* (London: Lawrence and Wishart, 2017); Rafael Behr, 'Corbyn's Cosy Brexit Pitch Is a Gamble, but He's Beating May', *Guardian*, 27 June 2016; Corbyn interview with Jeremy Paxman, *Channel Four*, 29 May 2017; Keir Starmer, 'Theresa May's Brexit Plan has Potentially Disastrous Gaps in It', *Guardian*, 18 January 2017; Anushka Asthana, 'Labour Tells Its MPs to Cancel Leave and Prepare for Three-line Whip', *Guardian*, 6 February 2017; Heather Stewart and Anushka Asthana, 'Lib. Dem. Leader Accuses Labour's Corbyn of Giving Up Over Brexit', *Guardian*, 19 January 2017.

34 Ewen MacAskill, 'Jeremy Corbyn's Team Target Labour Membership of 1 Million', *Guardian*, 27 September 2016; Rowena Mason, 'Jeremy Corbyn's Labour Conference Speech – the Key Points Analysed', *Guardian*, 28 September 2016; Nunns, *Candidate*, pp. 277–85; Monica Poletti, Tim Bale, Paul Webb, 'Explaining the Pro-Corbyn Surge in Labour's Membership', LSE Research Online, *LSE European Politics and Policy (EUROPP) Blog*, 25 November 2016.

35 Shipman, *Fall Out*, pp. 194, 198, 202; Polly Toynbee, 'Corbyn Is Rushing to Embrace Labour's Annihilation', *Guardian*, 19 April 2017; Martin Kettle, 'A Warning to Corbyn: The Centre Ground Hasn't Disappeared, It Is Being Reshaped', *Guardian*, 30 September 2016.

36 For these by-elections see *Guardian*, 24, 25 February 2017; *Observer*, 26 February 2017. See Nunns, *Candidate*, p. 296 for Owen Jones.

37 For the local elections see *Guardian*, 4, 5, 6, 8, 9 May 2017, especially Jonathan Freedland, 'No More Excuses: Corbyn Is to Blame for this Meltdown', *Guardian*, 6 May 2017.

38 Nunns, *Candidate*, pp. 355–62.

39 *Guardian*, 10 May, 3 June 2017. But for notable *Guardian* exceptions see George Monbiot, 'If There Was a Time to Vote Labour, It Is Now', 26 April 2017; Gary Younge, 'Everyone Thought the Election Was a Foregone Conclusion'; and Owen Jones, 'My Message to the Labour Right'. Both Monbiot and Owen Jones reaffirmed their support for Corbyn after losing faith in his leadership in the wake of the defeat in Copeland. See Nunns, *Candidate*, p. 296. Although Polly Toynbee, another prominent *Guardian*

columnist, continued to be critical of Corbyn, she was full of praise for Labour's anti-austerity manifesto and the promise it offered the country in the future. See Toynbee, 'Britain Could Be So Much Better – This Leak Proves It', *Guardian*, 12 May 2017.

40 *Guardian*, 26, 27 May, 3 June 2017; Nunns, p. 376; Shipman, *Fall Out*, ch. 19; Seymour, *Corbyn*, pp. 218–22.

41 Nunns, *Candidate*, pp. 298–300, 346, 376–7; Ewen MacAskill and Dan Roberts, '"What a Guy" – Corbyn Looks to Sanders to Help Swing Support', *Guardian*, Election 2017, 10 May 2017.

42 *Guardian,* 3 June 2017; Nunns, *Candidate*, p. 314.

43 Nunns, *Candidate*, p. 314; Mason. 'Corbyn's Labour Conference Speech'; *New Statesman*, 28 September 2017 for Corbyn's full conference speech.

44 Heather Stewart, 'Tories Redeploy the "Bombshell" Against Labour Tax Plans', *Guardian*, 4 May 2017; Shipman, *Fall Out*, pp. 273–7; Larry Elliott, 'Ten Years after Blair, the Old Problems Remain', *Guardian*, 15 May 2017; Rowena Mason and Anushka Asthana, 'Corbyn Pins Election Hopes on Housing Reform Pledges', *Guardian*, 9 May 2017; Ewen MacAskill and Toby Helm, 'Labour Pledge to Outlaw Zero-Hours Contracts', *Observer*, 30 April 2017.

45 Heather Stewart, 'Moment of Truth. Labour's Fraught Path to MPs' Crucial Brexit Vote', *Guardian*, 19 September 2018.

46 Alan Travis, 'Uncertainty Over Brexit Prompts Fall in Immigration', *Guardian*, 26 May 2017; Rowena Mason and Jessica Elgot, 'Labour "in Agreement" Brexit Will End Free EU Movement', *Guardian*, Election 2017, 26 April 2017.

47 For Labour's policies and its manifesto see Nunns, *Candidate*, pp. 299–300, 304–6, 313–14; Seymour, *Corbyn*, pp. 223–7, 249–50; Shipman, *Fall Out*, ch. 7; *BBC News*, Election 2017, 'Labour Manifesto At-a-glance: Summary of Key Points', 16 May 2017, https://www.bbc.co.uk/news/election-2017-39933116; *Daily Telegraph*, leader, 'A Blueprint for a Socialist Britain', 11 May 2017; *Guardian*, front page, 'Election 2017' and leader, 12 May 2017.

48 For the history of the SNP and Scottish nationalism, see Ben Jackson, *The Case for Scottish Independence: A History of Nationalist Political Thought in Modern Scotland* (Cambridge; Cambridge University Press, 2020); T.M. Devine, *Independence or Union: Scotland's Past and Scotland's Present* (London: Allen Lane, 2016); Ewen A. Cameron, *Impaled upon a Thistle: Scotland since 1880* (Edinburgh: Edinburgh University Press, 2011); Gerry Hassan and Simon Barrow (eds), *A Nation Changed? The SNP and Scotland Ten Years On* (Edinburgh: Luath Press, 2017); Ewan Gibbs and Rory Scothorne, '"Origins of the Present Crisis?" The Emergence of "Left-Wing" Scottish Nationalism', in Evan Smith and Matthew Worley (eds), *Waiting for the Revolution: The British Far Left from 1956* (Manchester: Manchester University Press, 2017); Thomas A. Stewart, 'The Labour Party and the Rise of Scottish Nationalism in Dundee since the 1990s', paper presented to the 'Labour ad Nationalism' conference, UK Society for the Study of Labour History, University of Huddersfield, May 2018.

49 Gerry Hassan and Eric Shaw, *The Strange Death of Labour in Scotland* (Edinburgh, Edinburgh University Press, 2012); Devine, *Independence or Union*, pp. 147–50, 155–66, 211–12, 221–31; Cameron, *Impaled*, chs. 11, 12, 13, 14; Ewan Gibbs, *Coal Country: The Meaning and Memory of Deindustrialization in Postwar Scotland* (University of London Press, 2021); Jim Phillips, Valerie Wright and Jim Tomlinson, *De-Industrialisation and the Moral Economy in Scotland since 1955* (Edinburgh: Edinburgh University Press, 2021); Andrew Perchard, 'A Little Local Difficulty? Deindustrialization and Glocalization

in a Scottish Town' and Jim Phillips, 'The Moral Economy of Deindustrialization in Post-1945 Scotland', in Steven High, Lachlan MacKinnon, Andrew Perchard (eds), *The Deindustrialized World: Confronting Ruination in Post-Industrial Places* (Vancouver, University of British Columbia Press, 2017).

50 *Sunday Herald*, EU Crisis Special Edition, 26 June 2016; *National*, 24, 25 June 2016; *Herald*, 25 June 2016.

51 McAlpine reported on the research in his talk at the Aros Centre, Portree, Isle of Skye, 23 September 2017. See also *National*, 24 October 2017; Lisa O'Carroll, 'What's the Point?' Why the Worn-Down Residents of Easterhouse May Not Vote', *Guardian*, 6 June 2017.

52 Alan Travis, 'SNP General Election Manifesto: Key Points and Analysis', *Guardian*, 30 May 2017.

53 Severin Carrell, 'Scottish Tories Back in Contention Twenty Years on from New Labour', *Guardian*, 24 April 2017; Ruth Wishart, 'Ruth Davidson Dealt a Telling Blow in Scotland –She May Have Saved May Too', *Guardian*, 9 June 2017; *BBC News*, 'General Election 2017: SNP Loses a Third of Seats Amid Tory Surge', 9 June 2017, https://www. bbc.co.uk/news/uk-scotland-scotland-politics-40192707; *National*, 29 May 2017. Davidson, however, would subsequently declare that she was not interested in becoming a future prime minister. See *The Sunday Times*, 16 September 2018.

54 Kevin McKenna, 'Day of Reckoning Looms for a Scottish Labour that Turned Its Back on Its Roots', *National*, 10 May 2017; *National*, 12 May, 7 June 2017.

55 Shipman, *Fall Out*, p. 391; *National*, 12 May 2017 (Salmond), 22, 29 May 2017; https:// twitter.com/alexsalmond/stats/862653727659917312.

56 Michael Fry, 'Despite the SNP's Blind Spots, They Are the Best Hope for Our Economy', *National*, 6 June 2017; Gordon MacIntyre-Kemp, 'The Economy Is the Key to Winning Independence', *National*, 16 June 2017.

57 *Guardian*, leader, 'The Guardian View on the SNP Manifesto: A Step Back for Sturgeon', 30 May 2017; SNP, 'Manifesto 2017', https://www.snp. org/manifesto; *BBC News*, Election 2017, 'SNP Manifesto Summary: Key Points At-a-glance', 30 May 2017; 'Re-elect Ian Blackford as MP for Ross, Skye and Lochaber', Election Communication (SNP, nd); 'Proud of What We've Achieved', (SNP, nd); *National* (George Kerevan), 29 May 2017.

58 Alan Travis, 'SNP General Election Manifesto': Key Points and Analysis', *Guardian*, 30 May 2017.

59 Travis, 'SNP General Election Manifesto'.

60 See, for example, 'Elect Peter O'Donnghaile for Ross, Skye and Lochaber Constituency', Election Communication (Scottish Labour, nd); 'Your Choice in This Election Is Clear', (Scottish Liberal Democrats, nd). *BBC News*, Election 2017, https://www.bbc.co.uk/ news/politics/constituencies/S 14000055; Highland Council, 'UK Parliamentary General Election Results 2015', https://www.highland.gov.uk/info/799/elections_ and-voting/605uk-parliamentary-general-election/6; *BBC News*, Election 2017, Sarah Smith, 'Is Scotland on the Cusp of a Tory Resurgence?', 2 June 2017, https://www.bbc. co.uk/news/election-2017-40105177.

61 *Guardian*, leader, 'Scottish Defiance Can Puncture Theresa May's Complacency', 6 June 2017.

62 For example, some SNP members and many YES supporters on the Isle of Skye were disappointed to learn of the SNP's long delay for a second referendum. This viewpoint was strongly expressed in response to a lecture 'The Election: An Overview', given by the author to the Skye SNP branch on 12 June 2017.

63 *The Times*, 28 June 2017.

64 *The Times* (Hamish Macdonnell), 7 June 2017.

65 *The Times*, 3 July 2017; *Guardian*, 8 July 2017.

66 Shipman, *Fall Out*, pp. 458–64; *Guardian*, 8, 10 July 2017.

67 Shipman, *Fall Out*, pp. 431–44, 466–72, 476–80.

68 Shipman, *Fall Out*, pp. 458–61, 482–501; Jason Groves, 'We Can't Be Shackled to EU Rules after Brexit, May Warns Cabinet', *Daily Mail*, 20 December 2017.

69 *Guardian*, 8, 10 July 2017.

70 Jon Henley, 'Theresa May's Florence Speech: Key Points', *Guardian*, 22 September 2017; Shipman, *Fall Out*, pp. 499–501; *BBC News*, 'A Quick Guide: What Is the Brexit Transition Phase?', 1 February 2018, https://www.bbc.co.uk/news/uk-politics-42906950; Alex Barker and Martin Arnold, 'What Difference Will the Brexit Transition Make?', *Financial Times*, 19 March 2018; Rob Merrick, 'Dozens of EU Directives Could Come into Force during the Brexit Transition without the UK Having Say on Them, Says Leaked Report', *Independent*, 6 February 2018.

71 See, for example, Nick Timothy, 'No Deal Is Better than Partition or Vassalage', *Daily Telegraph*, 18 October 2018.

72 Henley, 'May's Florence Speech'.

73 Shipman, *Fall Out*, pp. 472–4.

74 Shipman, *Fall Out*, p. 503; *Daily Telegraph*, 5 October 2017.

75 *Daily Telegraph*, 5 October 2017; Shipman, *Fall Out*, pp. 503–9; Andrew Sparrow and Kevin Rawlinson, '"Conservative Conference 2017: May Interrupted by Man Trying to Give Her P45" – As It Happened', *Guardian*, 4 October 2017.

76 Shipman, *Fall Out*, pp. 508–9, 513–16; *European Council*, 19–20 October 2017, https://www.consilium.europa.eu/en/meetings/european-council/2017/10/19-20.

77 *Guardian*, editorial, 'Britain and Europe', 18 October 2017.

78 *Observer*, editorial, 'The Observer View on Brexit Developments', 9 December 2017.

79 Chris Morris, 'Brexit Deal: Theresa May's Agreement with Brussels', *BBC News Politics*, 8 December 2017, https://www.bbc.co.uk/news/uk-politics-42280487.

80 Lisa O'Carroll, 'Brexit and the Irish Border Question Explained', *Guardian*, 19 September 2018; Jennifer Rankin, 'EU Pressing Ahead to Plan for No-Deal Eventuality', *Guardian*, 1 November 2018.

81 Daniel Boffey, Lisa O'Carroll, Heather Stewart, '"It's a British Mess". The Border Problem that Won't Go Away', *Guardian*, 5 November 2018.

82 Fintan O'Toole, 'The Hard-Won Kinship between Britain and Ireland Is Threatened by Brexit Idiocy', *Observer*, 26 November 2017; Martin Kettle, 'Brexit Looks Likelier than Ever to Tear the UK Apart', *Guardian*, 11 October 2018; Michael Fry, 'Brexit Is English Rebellion Wrapped in a Union Flag', *National*, 27 November 2018.

83 Lisa O'Carroll, 'Sinn Fein: Referendum Demand if No Deal Reached', *Guardian*, 16 October 2018.

84 *Daily Mail*, 14 December 2017; *Sun*, 17 December 2017; *Observer*, editorial, 'For All May's Talk of Meritocracy, She Does Nothing but Reinforce Privilege over Opportunity', 3 December 2017.

85 Heather Stewart, 'Damian Green Sacked as First Secretary of State after Porn Allegations', *Guardian*, 21 December 2017; Rajeev Syal and Anushka Asthana, 'Priti Patel Forced to Resign over Unofficial Meetings with Israelis', *Guardian*, 8 November 2017. For May as an 'inflexible' and 'awkward' 'plodder', but also a 'gritty' 'stayer', see Anne McElvoy, 'Even with Her Closest Allies Gone, May Hangs on as Normal Rules Fall Away', *Observer*, 24 December 2017.

86	*Daily Mail*, 30 December 2017. While regarding May as 'not the perfect politician', the Tory-supporting *Sun* joined the *Mail* in seeing the 'determined', 'courageous' and 'quietly dignified' prime minister – defiant in the face of all the criticism and 'the brickbats thrown at her' and keen 'to get on with the task' – as 'the best person to lead Brexit', *Sun*, 17 December 2017.

87	Liam Thorp and Amy Coles, 'Jeremy Corbyn Given Rock Star Reception as He Declares Merseyside "Music Capital of UK"', *Liverpool Echo*, 20 May 2017; Nadia Khomami and Hannah Ellis-Peterson, 'Jeremy Corbyn Calls for Unity in Glastonbury Speech', *Guardian*, 24 June 2017.

88	*Guardian*, editorial, 'The Guardian's View on Corbyn's Speech: His Best Yet', 27 September 2017; Anushka Asthana, Jessica Elgot, Rowena Mason, 'Jeremy Corbyn: Neoliberalism Is Broken and We Are Now the Centre Ground', *Guardian*, 27 September 2017; Jessica Elgot, Anushka Asthana, Ewen MacAskill, 'Corbyn Avoids Single Market Row as Motion Fails to Make the Cut', *Guardian*, 25 September 2017; *BBC News*, Politics, https://www.bbc.co.uk/news/live/uk-politics-41385169, 25 September 2017.

89	Tim Sculthorpe, 'One More Time! Labour Leader Played into a Booze-fuelled Karaoke Party with His Own "Oh Jeremy Corbyn" Anthem at the End of his Conference in Brighton', *Daily Mail Online*, https://www.dailymail.co.uk/news/article-4924908/Final-night-Labour-s-conference-Brighton.html, 27 September 2017.

90	'Guardian's View on Corbyn's Speech'; *Sun*, 27 September 2017; *BBC News*, Politics, 25 September 2017.

91	Nick Cohen, 'Labour Conference? More Like the Cult of Saint Jeremy', *Observer*, 1 October 2017.

92	*Guardian*, editorial, 'The Guardian View on the Austerity Budgets: End the Social and Economic Failure', 16 November, 2017; Aditya Chakrabortty, 'Hammond's "Make-or-Break Budget" Wasn't Bold – Just More of the Same', *Guardian*, 22 November 2017; Larry Elliott, 'After Seven Years of Pain, The Austerity Experiment is Over', *Guardian*, 9 June 2017; Letter to the *Guardian* from Joseph Stiglitz, Ha-Joon Chang and 111 Others, 'The Chancellor Must End Austerity Now – It Is Punishing an Entire Generation', *Guardian*, 19 November 2017.

93	Aditya Chakrabortty, 'Austerity, Not Brexit, Has Doomed the Tory Party', *Guardian*, 14 November 2017.

94	*Guardian*, editorial, 'The Guardian View on Budget 2017: A Missed Opportunity', 22 November 2017.

95	Heather Stewart and Larry Elliott, 'Hammond Masks Gloomy Outlook with Stamp Duty Cut', *Guardian*, 22 November 2017; 'Guardian View on Budget'; Josie Cox, 'Budget 2017 Reactions: How City Investors, Economists and Other Experts Have Responded', *Independent*, 22 November 2017; *BBC News*, Business, 'Budget 2017 Reaction and Updates', 22 November 2017, https://www.bbc.co.uk/news/live/business-42026814. *Channel Four News*, 22, 23 November 2017.

96	Cox, 'Budget 2017'; Philip Inman, 'UK Faces Two Decades of No Earnings Growth and More Austerity, Says IFS', *Guardian*, 23 November 2017.

97	*Daily Telegraph*, opinion, 22 November 2017; *BBC News*, 'The Papers', 23 November 2017, https://www.bbc.co.uk/news/blogs-the-papers-42090204.

98	Chakrabortty, 'Hammond's "Make-or-Break Budget"'.

99	'Jeremy Corbyn's Autumn Budget 2017 Response in Full', *New Statesman*, 22 November 2017; Stewart and Elliott, 'Hammond Masks Gloomy Outlook'.

100 *Guardian*, editorial, 'The Guardian View of Labour and Soft Brexit: So Far, So Good', 26 August 2017; Keir Starmer, 'No "Constructive Ambiguity", Labour Will Avoid Brexit Cliff Edge for UK Economy', *Guardian*, 26 August 2017; Shipman, *Fall Out*, pp. 488–9.

101 *Observer*, 27 August 2017; *Guardian*, 28 August 2017; Amelia Hill, '"Hostile Environment": The Hardline Home Office Policy Tearing Families Apart', *Guardian*, 28 November 2017.

102 Emma Bean, 'Keir Starmer: Labour Has Six Tests for Brexit – If They're Not Met We Won't Back the Final Deal in Parliament', *Labour List*, 27 March 2017; Heather Stewart, 'Brexit: Labour Threatens to Defeat Theresa May over "Great Repeal Bill"', *Guardian*, 13 July 2017; Elgot, Asthana, MacAskill, 'Corbyn Avoids Single Market Row'.

103 Zoe Williams, 'Labour Can't Afford to Get Emotional over Brexit', *Guardian*, 25 September 2017; *Guardian*, editorial, 'The Left's Politics Are Being Changed in Interesting Ways', 25 September 2017; Patrick Wintour and Rowena Mason, 'Labour Voters Could Abandon Party over Brexit Stance, Poll Finds', *Guardian*, 27 December 2017; *Guardian*, editorial, 'On Brexit and Most Other Issues, Britain Is a Place of Two Tribes', 4 January 2018.

104 Heather Stewart, 'Keir Starmer Clashed with Corbyn on Brexit "to Brink of Resignation"', *Guardian*, 18 September 2018; Anushka Asthana and Libby Brooks, 'Labour Would Pay for Single Market and Customs Benefits, Says Starmer', *Guardian*, 11 December 2017; Toby Helm, 'Corbyn Convenes Labour "Away Day" to Discuss Shift on Brexit Policy', *Observer*, 28 January 2018; Andrew Sparrow, 'Corbyn Brexit Speech to Put May on Spot', *Guardian*, 26 February 2018; *Channel Four News*, 26 February 2018.

105 *Observer*, 14 January 2018; *Guardian*, 15 January 2018.

106 Ewen MacAskill, '"Labour Is Coming Back in Scotland" – Party Predicts Revival as Corbyn Takes Tour North', *Guardian*, 23 August 2017.

107 Mhairi Black, 'Changing the Branch Manager Won't Improve Labour's Fortunes', *National*, 2 September 2017.

108 *Herald*, 30 August 2017; Kathleen Nutt, 'Labour Factions Emerge in Battle to Replace Kezia', *National*, 1 September 2017.

109 Libby Brooks, 'Rivals Battle for Labour Leadership in Scotland amid Revival of Youth Vote', *Guardian*, 28 October 2017; *Commonspace*, 20 November 2017; '"Wee Ginger Dug" (Paul Kavanagh), A New Leader, but Same Old Problem for Labour', *National*, 6 September 2017.

110 *The Times*, 28 June 2017.

111 Black, 'Changing the Branch Manager'.

112 Fry, 'Brexit Is English Rebellion'; Nicola Sturgeon, 'Britain Deserves a Better Brexit than the One May Is Offering', *Guardian*, 22 November 2018; Henry McLeish, 'The EU Is Where Our Interests Lie. The Long Term Future of the UK Is Now in the Hands of the Labour Party and Corbyn Must Seize the Opportunity', *National*, 23 November 2018.

113 Andrew Learmonth, '"I Want Us to Shape the Future", Says Sturgeon in £45m Plan', *National*, 1 September 2017; 'A Nation with Ambition: The Government's Programme for Scotland 2017–2018', 5 September 2017, https://www.gov.scot/publications/ nation-ambition-governments-programme-Scotland-2017-18/; Programme for Government – Gov.Scot, https://www.gov.scot/programme-for-govt/; Andrew Learmonth, 'FM's "Fresh, Bold, and Controversial" Plan for Scotland', and James Dornan, 'A Package to Tackle Poverty and Inequality', *National*, 6 September 2017; Lesley Riddoch, 'Scotland Sets Forth on a Progressive Course to Tackle the Big Issues', *National*, 7 September 2017; 'Programme for Government: Four-Page Special', *National*, 6 September 2017.

114 The front-page headline in the *National* for 13 September 2017 ran: 'The 111 Power Grabs: After 20 Years of Devolution Westminster Bids to Take Back Control'. See also the articles by Andrew Learmonth ('Holyrood "At Risk of Death by 111 Power Grabs"') and Michael Russell ('Twenty Years on, Founding Principles of Our Parliament Are Facing Grave Threat') in the same 13 September issue of the *National*; Liam Furby, 'EU Withdrawal Bill. What Happens Now?, 12 September 2017, https:// www.snp. org/eu-withdrawal-repeal-bill-what-happens-now/.

115 Andrew Learmonth, 'Sturgeon: Morally Bankrupt Tories Have Lost Plot', *National*, 7 September 2017.

116 Kevin McKenna, '47% Yes? Independence Is Now Ours for the Taking', *National*, 6 December 2017; *Commonspace*, 18 September 2017; *Guardian*, 5 December 2017.

117 Kevin McKenna, 'SNP Must Not Listen to the Media Pundits. What's the Point of Being a Party Just Like All the Others?', *National*, 11 October 2017.

118 Martin Kettle, '"Invincible No More", Sturgeon Will Have to Go Back to Basics', *Guardian*, 10 October 2017; Libby Brooks, 'Signs of Burn Out at SNP Conference: "I'm Not Quite Sure What We're For Now"', *Guardian*, 9 October 2017.

119 Severin Carrell, 'Sturgeon Proposes Cheap, State-owned Energy for Scotland', *Guardian*, 10 October 2017; idem, 'SNP Dampens Hopes for Public Sector Pay Increase in Scotland', *Guardian*, 9 October 2017; *BBC*, Parliament-SNP Conference, 2017, https://www.bbc.co.uk/programmes/b098pkxp; Kettle, '"Invincible no More"'.

120 Andrew Learmonth, 'Unemployment Down by 12,000 as Labour Market Grows', *National*, 17 August 2017; idem, '"I Want Us to Shape the Future"'; Simon Johnson, 'SNP Minister Claims that 0.1pc Growth is "Good News"', *Daily Telegraph*, 5 October 2017; *The Times*, 3 July 2017; *National*, 5 October 2017; *Guardian*, editorial, 9 October 2017; George Kerevan, 'Here's How £1bn Barnett Boost Can be Put to Best Use for Scots Budget', *National*, 10 December 2018.

121 Kevin McKenna, 'Will No-one Bridge the Chasm between Rich and Poor?', *Observer*, 3 September 2017; idem, 'Devolution Was Set Up to Fail, but Twenty Years on We Are Still Better for It', *National*, 13 September 2017; McAlpine's talk at the Aros Centre, Portree, 23 September 2017; *National* (McAlpine), 24 October 2017; *Commonspace* (McAlpine), 22 November 2018.

122 Severin Carrell, 'Forget about Independence for Now, SNP Tells Sturgeon', *Guardian*, 7, 9 October 2017; *National*, 18 November 2017; *BBC News at Ten*, 8 October 2017; *Channel Four News*, Jon Snow interviews Nicola Sturgeon, 9 October 2017.

123 McLeish, 'The EU Is Where Our Interests Lie'; *Commonspace*, 21 November 2018 (Wray), 22 November 2018 (McAlpine); *National*, 24 October 2017; McAlpine, Aros Centre, 23 September 2017; idem, 'A Scotland Withdrawal Bill, and Other Indy Tasks at Hand', *Commonspace*, 6 December 2018.

124 Kathleen Nutt, 'Pressure Mounts on Corbyn over Brexit', *National*, 29 January 2018; Sean Bell, 'Explainer: Breaking Down the Scottish Government's Brexit Impact Study', *Commonspace*, 15 January 2018; Alyn Smith, 'The SNP Is Fighting to Stop Brexit – But in a Way that Protects Scotland's Interests', *National*, 11 January 2018; *Commonspace*, 31 January, 21 February 2018.

Chapter 2

1   Jacquelin Magnay, 'Tory MPs Mutiny as Defiant May Enters "Death Spiral"', *Australian*, 24 May 2019.

2   *Daily Telegraph*, 'Theresa May's Resignation Speech in Full: P.M. Tearful as She Declares She Will Quit on June 7', 24 May 2019; *Guardian*, 'Prime Minister Theresa May's Resignation Speech in Full – Video', 24 May 2019.

3   Sean Clarke, Pablo Gutierrez, Frank Hulley-Jones, 'European Election Latest Results 2019: Across the UK', *Guardian*, 27 May 2019; Andrew Learmonth, 'Labour and Tories Humiliated in European Vote', *National*, 27 May 2019.

4   Gursimran Hans, 'Brexit WARNING: Boris Johnson Says Tories Face "EXTINCTION" if EU Exit is Delayed Further', *Daily Express*, 5 June 2019; Matthew d'Ancona, 'If I Were Jeremy Corbyn I'd Be Praying for a Boris Victory', *Guardian*, 20 May 2019.

5   Bob Jessop, 'The Organic Crisis of the British State: Putting Brexit in Its Place', *Globalizations*, 14, 1 (2017), 133–41. See also, Frederico Fabbrini (ed.), *The Law and the Politics of Brexit* (Oxford, Oxford University Press, 2017).

6   Edgerton, *Rise and Fall British Nation*, pp. 389–94.

7   Neville Kirk, *Labour and the Politics of Empire: Britain and Australia 1900 to the Present* (Manchester: Manchester University Press, 2011), pp. 151–2.

8   Edgerton, *Rise and Fall British Nation*, pp. 266–74, 277–8.

9   Toby Helm, 'British Euroscepticism: A Brief History', *Observer*, 7 February 2016; Michael Portillo, 'The Trouble with the Tories', *Channel Five*, 1, 8 August 2019; Nicholas Crowson, 'How Europe became the Tories' Eternal Battleground', *Observer*, 9 December 2018; Denis MacShane, *Brexit: How Britain Will Leave Europe* (London: I.B. Taurus, 2015).

10 Crowson, 'How Europe Became'; Paul Routledge and Simon Hoggart, 'Major Hits Out at Cabinet', *Guardian*, 25 July 1993.

11 Mary C. Murphy and Jonathan Evershed, 'The DUP and the European Union: From Contestation to Conformance and Back Again. . .', *Irish Political Studies*, 35, 3 (2020), 378–98.

12 Alan Sked, 'I Founded UKIP. It's a National Joke Now and Should Disappear', *Guardian*, 22 January 2018; 'Farage: The Man Who Made Brexit', *Channel Four*, 29 January 2020; Robert Ford and Matthew Goodwin, *Revolt on the Right: Explaining Support for the Radical Right in Britain* (London: Routledge, 2014).

13 Cameron, *For the Record*, pp. 64–5, chs. 45–7. See also Shipman, *All Out War*, pp. 7–8, chs. 25, 26, Conclusion.

14 Edgerton, *Rise and Fall British Nation*, p. 271.

15 Edgerton, *Rise and Fall British Nation*, p. 271; Helm, 'British Euroscepticism'.

16 Neil Kinnock, 'Why I Changed My Mind about Britain in Europe', *Prospect Magazine*, 6 April 2018.

17 Devine, *Independence or Union*, p. 192; Jackson, *Case for Scottish Independence*, pp. 149–54.

18 *Mirror*, 24 June 2016; *Guardian*, 25 June 2016; *BBC News*, 'EU Referendum Results', https://www.bbc.co.uk/news/politics/eu-referendum/results; Gaby Hinsliff, 'Grey Power and the New Battle of Britain', *Guardian*, 5 May 2017; MacShane, *Brexit*, vii, xxii.

19 *YouGov*, 'How Britain Voted', 27 June 2016; *Guardian*, 25 June 2016.

20 Owen Jones, 'We're Sold a Lie about Brexit and Class: Don't Fall for It', *Guardian*, 7 April 2017; Matthew J. Goodwin and Oliver Heath, 'The 2016 Referendum, Brexit and the Left Behind: An Aggregate-level Analysis of the Result', *Political Quarterly*, 87, 3 (2016), 323–32; idem, 'Brexit Vote Explained: Poverty, Low Skills and Lack of Opportunities', *Joseph Rowntree Foundation*, 31 August 2016; Julian Coman, 'A Party in Crisis: Can Labour Reconnect with Its Heartlands?', *Observer*, 12 February 2017.

21 Goodwin and Heath, '2016 Referendum'; Roger Eatwell and Matthew Goodwin, *National Populism: The Revolt against Liberal Democracy* (London: Pelican, 2018); Harold D. Clarke, Matthew Goodwin and Paul Whiteley, *Why Britain Voted to Leave the European Union* (Cambridge: Cambridge University Press, 2017).

22 Gary Younge, 'How Did We End Up Here?', *Guardian*, 30 June 2016; Michael Crick, *One Party after Another: The Disruptive Life of Nigel Farage* (London: Simon and Schuster, 2022); Aditya Chakrabortty, ' Migration has Benefitted the UK. It's Time to Bust the Myths', *Guardian*, 17 May 2018; Alan Travis, 'The Newcomer Paradox: Leave Was Strongest in Places without Migrants', *Guardian*, 30 June 2016; Jonathan Wadsworth, Swati Dhingra, Gianmarco Ottaviano, John van Reenen, *Brexit and the Impact of Immigration on the UK* (London: LSE, Centre for Economic Performance, 2016); Migration Advisory Committee, *EEA Migration in the UK: Final Report*, September 2018.

23 O'Toole, *Heroic Failure*, xvi–xvii, ch. 1, 182–201; *Guardian*, 28, 30 June 2016.

24 See the references in note 18; Larry Elliott, Severin Carrell, Heather Stewart, 'McCluskey Sparks Labour Backlash over Tough Line on Free Movement', *Guardian*, 13 November 2019.

25 Phillip Inman, 'CBI Member Survey Reveals Huge Support for Remaining in EU', *Guardian*, 15 March 2016; Larry Elliott, 'CBI Chief Fires Parting Shot over Slow Pace of Brexit Negotiations', *Guardian*, 28 October 2020; Hamre and Wright, 'Brexit and the City', *New Financial*, April 2021.

26 *YouGov*, 'How Britain Voted', 27 June 2016; *Guardian*, 25 June 2016; *The Times*, 26 June 2016; *National*, 29 June 2016.

27 See, for example, *Daily Telegraph*, 31 January 2018.

28 *BBC One*, Panorama, 'Britain's Brexit Crisis', 9 pm, 18 July 2019 (Nick Robinson).

29 See *Guardian* editorial, 'Theresa May Must Find the Nerve to Show Her Hand on Trade after Brexit', 7 February 2018.

30 *Guardian*, 27 January 2018; Andrew Rawnsley, 'How and Why Britain Might Be Asked to Vote Once More on Brexit', *Observer*, 14 January 2018.

31 For a liberal, consensual approach to political leadership see the insightful essay by the chief political correspondent of the Australian Broadcasting Corporation (ABC), Laura Tingle, *Follow the Leader: Democracy and the Rise of the Strongman Quarterly Essay* (Carlton, Vic., Australia, Schwartz, 2018).

32 Matthew d'Ancona, 'This Debacle Cannot Go On. May Must Stand Down' *Guardian*, 5 February 2018.

33 Polly Toynbee, 'May Can't Win: The Brexit Factions Will always Be at War', *Guardian*, 29 January 2018.

34 Rafael Behr, 'Brexit Ultras versus Tory Realists. That's the Real Battle', *Guardian*, 6 February 2018; *National*, 6 February 2018; Jonathan Freedland, 'Brexit Reveals Our Political System Is Failing. The 48% Must Have a Voice', *Guardian*, 10 February 2018.

35 Alan Tovey, 'UK Economy Growing at Worst Rate since the Financial Crisis', *Daily Telegraph*, 18 June 2018; Jack Maidment, 'Government Minister Suggests Brexit Could Be Reversed if Gloomy Economic Forecasts Are Anywhere Near Right', *Daily Telegraph*, 31 January 2018; Larry Elliott, 'UK Economy Suffers Weakest Growth in Five Years', *Guardian*, 28 April 2018.

36 Jessica Elgot, Heather Stewart, Peter Walker, 'Revealed: The £80bn Cost of hard Brexit', *Guardian*, 8 February 2018; David Conn, 'What Has the EU Done for Us? We Still Don't Have an Answer!', *Guardian*, 10 July 2019.

37 Richard Partington, 'UK Economy: Hiring on Hold, Output Down, Pessimism Up', *Guardian*, 12 June 2018; *Guardian*, editorial, 'What the Chancellor Calls an Optimistic Vision Is Merely Economic Myopia', 14 March 2018.

38 Larry Elliott and Julia Kollewe, 'Economy Bounces Back as Services Perform Well and Hot Weather Lifts Spending', *Guardian*, 5 July 2018.

39 Ruth Davidson, 'Dear Tories, I'm Afraid the Crash Generation Doesn't Trust Us', *Guardian*, 19 May 2018; Peter Walker, 'Authoritarian Attitudes Make Tory Members "A Breed Apart"', *Guardian*, 4 January 2018; Ian Jack, 'Like Banksy's Artwork, the Union Is Eating Itself in Public', *Guardian*, 13 October 2018; Jonathan Freedland, 'Labour's Fudge over Brexit Once Worked. But It Can't Go On', *Guardian*, 5 May 2018; Phillip Inman, 'Labour Is Dreaming if It Believes UK Wants Socialism', *Observer*, 18 February 2018.

40 *Guardian*, editorial, 'The Guardian View on the EU Draft Withdrawal Agreement: Exposing Theresa May's Leadership Void', 28 February 2018; *Guardian*, editorial, 'This Desperate Failure of Leadership from Mrs May Cannot Go on Much Longer', 1 March 2018.

41 *Gov.UK*, 'PM Speech on Our Future Economic Partnership with the European Union', https://www.gov.uk/government/speeches/pm-speech-on-our-future-economic-partnership-with-the-european-union, 2 March 2018.

42 *Observer*, editorial, 'The Observer View on Theresa May's Brexit Speech', 4 March 2018.

43 Alex Barker and Martin Arnold, 'What Difference Will the Brexit Transition Make?', *Financial Times*, 19 March 2018.

44 Daniel Boffey, Anushka Asthana, Lisa O'Carroll, 'Theresa May under Fire over Brexit Transition Deal', *Guardian*, 19 March 2018; Sean Bell, 'Scottish Fishing Industry Victim of "Massive Sellout" by the Tories, Says Nicola Sturgeon', *Commonspace*, 19 March 2018; Dan Roberts, 'We Were Hijacked, Lied To. That's the Anger on the Coast', *Guardian*, 24 March 2018.

45 Barker and Arnold, 'What Difference'.

46 Boffey, Asthana, O'Carroll, 'Theresa May'.

47 Boffey, Asthana, O'Carroll, 'Theresa May'.

48 Labour Party, *Theresa May's Failed Brexit Plan*, 17 September 2018, https://labour.org.uk/.../2018.

49 Jonathan Freedland, 'Labour's Fudge over Brexit Once Worked. But It Can't Go On', *Guardian*, 5 May 2018; John Harris, 'Where's Jeremy Corbyn? Lost in a Vision of Labour's Past', *Guardian*, 25 June 2018.

50 Matthew d'Ancona, 'Tories Must Resist Declaring Peak Corbyn', *Guardian*, 7 May, 2018; *Guardian*, editorial, 'No Late Changes, But These Results Have Big Lessons and Implications', 5 May 2018.

51 For Labour and anti-Semitism see *Guardian*, 26, 27, 28, 31 March, 2, 5, 6, 24, 27 April, 4, 8 August 2018; *BBC News at Ten*, 26 March 2018; *Channel Four News*, 2 April 2018; *National*, 2, 3, 26 April 2018; *Observer*, 1 April 2018.

52 Amelia Gentleman, 'Home Office Pauses "Hostile Environment" Policies after Windrush Fury', *Guardian*, 12 July 2018; *Daily Telegraph*, editorial, 'Home Secretary Needs to Rectify the Shambles', 30 April 2018; Sonia Sodha, 'May Is Already Creating the Next Generation of Windrushers', *Guardian*, 3 May 2018; Ian Drury and John Stevens, 'Rudd Is Forced to Quit', *Daily Mail*, 30 April 2018; Hugh Muir, 'The Windrush Scandal Is Institutional Racism, Pure and Simple', *Guardian*, 30 April 2018.

53 See the editorials in the *Guardian*, 8 August 2018 and the *Daily Telegraph*, 9 August 2018; Andrew Sparrow, 'New Tory Chair Appears to Renege on Promise of

Islamophobia Inquiry', *Guardian*, 5 August 2019; Owen Jones, 'Where Is the Outrage about the Tory Party's Islamophobia?', *Guardian*, 10 July 2019; Nazia Parveen, 'Boris Johnson's Remarks "Led to Surge in anti-Muslim Attacks"', *Guardian*, 2 September 2019.

54 Aditya Chakrabortty, 'Migration Has Benefitted the UK. It's Time to Bust the Myths', *Guardian*, 17 May 2018.

55 Kathleen Nutt, 'Sturgeon Slams "Echoes of Nigel Farage" in Corbyn Speech', *National*, 10 March 2018.

56 Alasdair Clark, 'Refugee Rights Campaigners Welcome Labour's Break from Its "Blairite Record" on Hostile Environment', *Commonspace*, 17 May 2018.

57 Kathleen Nutt, 'Scottish Independence Given Boost by Views on the Economy', *National*, 10 January 2018; *National*, Newsdesk, 'Scottish Economy Growth Rate has Overtaken the UK', 1 May 2019; Michael Fry, 'Good Social Policies Need a Thriving Economy to Take Root', *National*, 3 April 2018.

58 Nan Spowart, 'FM: Indy must be an Option amid Brexit "horror show"', *National*, 8 January 2018; Nutt, 'First Minister Refuses to Rule Out 2018 Indyref2'.

59 *Commonspace*, 1 February 2018; Gregor Young, 'MSPs to Back New Tax System Ahead of Holyrood Vote', *National*, 20 February 2018; Andrew Learmonth, 'Budget Set for Green Light after Tax Plans Are Backed', *National*, 21 February 2018.

60 Philip Sim, 'What's in the SNP's Growth Commission Report?', BBC News, https://www.bbc.co.uk/news/uk-scotland-scotland-pols-44237956, 25 May 2018; Richard Murphy, 'The Scottish Growth Commission Gets Its Economics Very Badly Wrong', *Tax Research UK*, 25 May 2018; Andrew Sparrow, 'SNP Economic Plan for Independence Means "Decade of Austerity", Says Scottish Labour', *Guardian*, 25 May 2018; Andrew Wilson, 'We Owe It to the Next Generation to Examine Whether There Is a Better Future', *National*, 26 May 2018; Hugh Macdonald, 'Sturgeon Praises New Economic Prospectus as "Foundation" of the Independence Case', *National*, 26 May 2018; George Kerevan, 'Report Fails to Make Indy Case to a Section of Voters Critical to Success', *National*, 28 May 2018; Michael Fry, 'Wilson Delivers the Most Impressive Economic Paper since Devolution', *National*, 26 May 2018; Severin Carrell, 'SNP "Needs Austerity after Independence"', *Guardian*, 26 May 2018.

61 George Kerevan, 'Independence Won't Be Won with Rhetoric but through Concrete Actions', *National*, 12 August 2019.

62 Gordon Macintyre-Kemp, 'UK Government Is Starting to Dismantle Devolution', *National*, 14 June 2018; Andrew Learmonth, 'Chaos in the Commons as SNP Walk Out of PMQs', *National*, 14 June 2018; Ian Blackford, 'We Will Not Simply Sit By while Scotland's Voice Is Scandalously Silenced', *National*, 14 June 2018.

63 Tom Devine, 'Brexit Bill Blunder Will Increase Impetus for Independence', *National*, 14 June 2018; Andrew Learmonth, 'Poll Shows Indy Majority within "Touching Distance"', *National*, 8 June 2018.

64 Learmonth, 'Poll Shows'.

65 Carolyn Leckie, 'Why Now Is the Perfect Moment to Call Indyref2', *National*, 16 April 2018.

66 Andrew Wilson, 'We Need to Put the Question When the Scottish People Are Ready to Answer', *National*, 31 January 2019; Andrew Learmonth, 'Call for Calm in SNP's Debate on Indyref2 Timing', *National*, 13 April 2018.

67 See Robin McAlpine's opinion pieces in *Commonspace*, 4 September 2017, 11, 18 January 2018.

68 Kevin McKenna, 'As Westminster Dithers, Scottish Nationalists Are Salivating over Spoils of Brexit', *Observer*, 18 February 2018.

69 Heather Stewart and Pippa Crerar, 'Javid Joins Brexiters to Derail May on Customs', *Guardian*, 3 May 2018; *Guardian*, editorial, 'Cabinet Divisions over a Customs Union Are a Proxy for Deeper Tory Divisions', 3 May 2018; Gordon Rayner, 'Boris: May Must Show More Guts on Brexit', *Daily Telegraph*, 8 June 2018.

70 *BBC News*, 'At-a-Glance: The New UK Brexit Plan Agreed at Chequers', 7 July 2018, https://www.bbc.co.uk/news/uk-politics-44749993; idem, 'Brexit: David Davis's Resignation Letter and May's Reply in Full', 9 July 2018, https://www.bbc.co.uk/news/uk-politics-44761416.

71 *BBC News*, 'At-a Glance'; Alex Hunt and Brian Wheeler, 'Brexit: All You Need to Know about the UK Leaving the EU', *BBC News*, 27 September 2018, https://www.bbc.co.uk/news/uk-politcs-32810887; *Observer*, editorial, 'The Observer View on How Theresa May's Fragile Deal Would be a Disaster for Britain', 8 July 2018.

72 *BBC News*, '"Brexit": Davis's Resignation Letter'.

73 Andrew Rawnsley, 'Theresa May's Grand Plan Has Left Her Stranded in No Women's Land', *Observer*, 15 July 2018; O'Toole, *Heroic Failure*, pp. 58–63, 82–94, 133–51, 164–74; James Bickerton, '"Flawed" Chequers Plan Attacked by Boris Johnson and David Davis in Joint Brexit Assault', *Daily Express*, 18 October 2018; *Guardian*, editorial, 'A Battle over Brexit Was Always Inevitable for the Tories. Now It Has Arrived', 10 July 2018; *BBC News*, 'Boris Johnson's Resignation Letter and May's Reply in Full', 9 July 2018, https://www.bbc.co.uk/news/uk-pols-44772804; *Channel Four News*, 9 July 2018; Boris Johnson, 'Victory for Brussels is Inevitable. In Adopting Chequers We Have Gone into Battle Waving the White Flag', *Daily Telegraph*, 3 September 2018; idem, 'This Is the Plan to Take Back Control of our Democracy and Deliver What People Voted For', *Daily Telegraph*, 28 September 2018; Gordon Rayner, 'I Will Vote Down May's Brexit Plan, Warns Mogg', *Daily Telegraph*, 9 July; idem, 'The Brexit Dream Is Dying', *Daily Telegraph*, 10 July 2018; *Daily Telegraph*, editorial, 'Divorced , but Still Living in the Annexe', 9 July 2018; Gaby Hinsliff, 'Stand By for a Brexit Revolt in the Tory Shires', *Guardian*, 11 July 2018; Gordon Rayner, Christopher Hope, Steven Swinford, 'Chequers Deal Is Dead, Say Rebels', *Daily Telegraph*, 17 July 2018.

74 Michael Portillo, 'The Trouble with the Tories', *Channel Five*, 1, 8 August 2019; Fintan O'Toole, 'It Was Never about Europe. Brexit Is a Very British Neurosis', *Guardian*, 18 January 2019.

75 David Lidington, 'Our Brexit Solution Will Enable Us to Take Back Control', *Observer*, 8 July 2018; Dan Sabbagh, Patrick Wintour, 'PM Claims Brexit on "Smooth and Orderly" Course as More Tories Quit', *Guardian*, 11 July 2018.

76 Ben Bradley, 'Why I Voted to Depose My Party Leader', *Daily Telegraph*, 13 December 2018.

77 Toby Helm, 'Mandelson Joins Brexiters with Attack on May's EU "Humiliation"', *Observer*, 15 July 2018; Peter Mandelson, 'Half In and Half Out, Chequers Plan Offers Worst of Both Worlds', *Observer*, 15 July 2018.

78 Edward Malnick and Anna Mikhailova, 'Disastrous Brexit Deal Will Cost Tories Power, Warn MPs', *Sunday Telegraph*, 8 July 2018; *Sunday Telegraph*, editorial, 'The Weekend that Brexit Dream Dies', 8 July 2018; Bickerton, '"Flawed" Chequers Plan', *Express*, 18 October 2018; *Guardian*, 'Battle over Brexit', 10 July 2018; *Observer*, editorial and Will Hutton, 8 July 2018.

79 Peter Walker, 'Tories "Too Weak and Too Divided" to Protect UK over Brexit, Says Corbyn', *Guardian*, 17 October 2018; Matthew Goodwin, 'Chequers Has Made a Labour Win Possible', *Daily Telegraph*, 30 July 2018.

80 Kathleen Nutt, 'Sturgeon Warns Tory Disarray Increases the Possibility of UK Leaving the EU without a Deal', *National*, 11 July 2018; Larry Elliott, 'Pound Slides as No-Deal Brexit Fears Prompt Global Sell off', *Guardian*, 9 August 2018.

81 Tom Newton Dunn, 'Trump Rips into PM on Brexit Plan', *Sun* (Scottish edition), 13 July 2018; Jessica Elgot and Peter Walker, 'I Didn't Criticise PM. That Is Fake News, Says Trump', *Guardian*, 14 July 2018.

82 Dan Sabbagh, Heather Stewart, 'May's Brexit Surrender Infuriates Remainers', *Guardian*, 17 July 2018; Pippa Crerar, 'Relief for May as She Sees Off Tory Rebels', *Guardian*, 18 July 2018.

83 Charles Grant, 'Europe's Reply to May's Plan Could Cost Her More Ministers', *Guardian*, 11 July 2018; Daniel Boffey, 'We'd Need to See a Major Shift in UK Politics, EU Officials say', *Guardian*, 23 July 2018; Tom Embury-Dennis, 'Brexit: Michel Barnier "Strongly Opposes" May's Chequers Proposals, Warning Offer Would Be End of EU', *Independent*, 2 September 2018; Greg Heffer, 'Michel Barnier Trashes Theresa May's Chequers Plan for Brexit as "End for EU"', *Sky News*, 2 September 2018.

84 *BBC News*, 'Theresa May Says It's Chequers or No Deal' 17 September 2018, https://www.bbc.co.uk/news/uk-politics-4559083, *Channel Four News*, 17 September 2018; *Guardian*, editorial, 'The Guardian View on Mrs. May's Chequers Plan: Dead in Salzburg', 20 September 2018; See also the *Telegraph*'s front page and editorial comment, 21 September 2018, for the 'insulting' behaviour of the EU and May's defiant response; Dan Sabbagh and Daniel Boffey, '"I Have Treated the EU with Respect. The UK Expects the Same", Theresa May', *Guardian*, 22 September 2018; *Observer*, editorial, 'PM Has Only Herself to Blame for EU Slapdown', 23 September 2018.

85 Johnson, 'This Is the Plan to Take Back Control', *Daily Telegraph*, 28 September 2018; James Bickerton, '"Flawed" Chequers Plan ATTACKED by Boris Johnson and David Davis in Joint Brexit Assault', *Daily Express*, 18 October 2018.

86 *Channel Four News*, 4, 24, 25 September 2018, 8 January 2019; *Guardian*, editorial, 'Corbyn's Party Must Root Out Antisemitism and Fight for Palestinian Rights', 6 September 2018; Heather Stewart, 'Starmer: People's Vote on Deal Could Include Option to Cancel Brexit', *Guardian*, 25 September 2018; Martin Kettle, 'Can Labour Solve the Brexit Question? Now It's Imaginable', *Guardian*, 27 September 2018; *Guardian*, editorial, 'Corbyn Catches the Zeitgeist at a Crucial Moment for His Party', 27 September 2018; Dan Sabbagh, 'Get a Good Brexit Deal or Face Labour Veto, Corbyn Tells May', *Guardian*, 27 September 2018; Matthew Taylor, 'Speech's Key Themes: Eyes Fixed on Electorate as Leader Sets Out his Stall', *Guardian*, 27 September 2018; Pippa Crerar and Jessica Elgot, 'Corbyn Pledges Radical Plan to End "Greed-is-Good" Capitalism', 26 September 2018; Jeremy Corbyn, 'Labour Could Do a Better Brexit Deal. Give Us the Chance', *Guardian*, 6 December 2018.

87 Kevin McKenna, 'Like Chris McEleny, My Support for Independence Is Now a "Philosophy"', *National*, 17 October 2018; Kenny MacAskill, 'Want Independence? Help Save England from Brexit', *National*, 24 October 2018; Tom Gordon, 'Grassroots Push for New Campaign on Independence', *Herald*, 16 October 2018; Severin Carrell and Dan Sabbagh, 'SNP Party "Could Ruin May's Plans and Win Softer Brexit', *Guardian*, 9 October 2018; *National*, 10 October (Sturgeon's conference speech); Andrew Learmonth, 'Sturgeon Tells SNP Indy Is on the Way', *National*, 10 October 2018.

88 *Channel Four News*, 3 October 2018; *Guardian*, 4 October, for front-page pictures of May dancing; Dan Sabbagh and Pippa Crerar, 'May Appeals to "Decent Patriots" in

Effort to Halt Johnson Leadership Bid', *Guardian*, 3 October 2018; Steven Swinford, 'We're a Decent, Moderate and Patriotic Party, Declares May', *Daily Telegraph*, 3 October 2018; Heather Stewart, 'Back Me on Brexit and I Will End Decade of Austerity, Pledges May', *Guardian*, 4 October 2018; Theresa May, 'Labour Voters Should Look Again at My Tory Party, Here for the Many', *Observer*, 7 October 2018.

89   Andrew Rawnsley, 'Let's Dance as if It's the 1970s All Over Again'. Who Will Have a Hit with This?', *Observer*, 7 October 2018; Toby Helm, 'Voters Strongly Back "Trustworthy" May as Johnson's Leadership Campaign Falls Flat', *Observer*, 7 October 2018; Simon Johnson, 'Mundell Says Attention-Seeker Johnson Is Costing Conservatives Scottish Votes', *Daily Telegraph*, 3 October 2018.

90   Pippa Crerar, Heather Stewart, Dan Sabbagh, 'May Fights to Assert Authority as Tory Brexit Divisions Erupt', *Guardian*, 1 October 2018; Pippa Crerar, 'Corbyn Accuses Hammond of Breaking May's Promise over End to Austerity', *Guardian*, 30 October 2018; *Guardian*, editorial, 'Austerity Has Not Ended. It Has Only Eased Because It Is Self-defeating', 30 October 2018; Michael Fry, 'Austerity Is Not Over. It Won't Be Until Our Mediocre Politicians Start to Dream Big', *National*, 30 October 2018; Heather Stewart, Larry Elliott, 'Delivered: A Budget of Tax Cuts and Spending to Shore up May', *Guardian*, 30 October 2018; Robert Skidelsky, 'Ten Years on, We Need to Get Ready for Another Crash', *Guardian*, 12 September 2018; William Keegan, 'It's Not Too Early to Tell that Brexit Would Be a Disaster', *Observer*, 9 September 2018.

91   Heather Stewart, 'Blow for May as Another Johnson Quits over Brexit', *Guardian*, 10 November 2018; Daniel Capurro, 'No Ordinary Jo Steps Out of the Shadow of big Brother', *Daily Telegraph*, 10 November 2018; Boris Johnson, 'My Brother is Right – This Is the Biggest Statecraft Failure since Suez', *Daily Telegraph*, 12 November 2018; Steven Swinford, 'Boris: Cabinet Must Stage a Mutiny', *Daily Telegraph*, 12 November 2018.

92   Jessica Elgot, '"EU Willing to Extend Brexit Transition", Says Irish Foreign Minister', *Guardian*, 17 October 2018.

93   *Daily Telegraph*, editorial, 'Finishing Line in Sight', 14 November 2018; Gordon Rayner, 'Burdened and Beleaguered but the Lady's Still Not for Turning', *Daily Telegraph*, 16 November 2018; Emily Jones, 'The Negotiations', in Frederico Fabbrini (ed.), *The Law and the Politics of Brexit*, vol. II, *The Withdrawal Agreement* (Oxford, Oxford University Press, 2020).

94   Daniel Boffey and Jennifer Rankin, 'The Details: Citizens' Rights, the Divorce Bill and Trade', *Guardian*, 26 November 2018; Dan Sabbagh, Daniel Boffey, Pippa Crerar, 'May Battles on all Fronts to Save Her Brexit Deal', *Guardian*, 23 November 2018; Daniel Boffey and Jennifer Rankin, 'Political Declaration. What Is Resolved and What Is in the Long Grass', *Guardian*, 23 November 2018; Kathleen Nutt, 'Mundell Accused of U-Turn on Fishing Resignation Pledge', *National*, 23 November 2018.

95   Dan Sabbagh and Daniel Boffey, 'Tories Fear May Will Agree Indefinite Customs Union to Solve Irish Border Question', *Guardian*, 12 October 2018; 'Fintan O'Toole, 'A "Precious Union"? The Brexiters Really Don't Care', *Guardian*, 11 October 2018; Dan Sabbagh, 'May Survives Stormy Cabinet Meeting as Brexit Fears Intensify', *Guardian*, 24 October 2018; Katy Balls, 'Dominic Raab's Resignation Could Spell the End for May's Brexit Plan', *Guardian*, 15 November 2018; Steven Swinford, 'May Faces "Moment of Truth" on Brexit Deal', Daily Telegraph, 14 November 2018; Steven Swinford, 'DUP Accuses PM of Backstop Betrayal and Warns of Consequences', *Daily Telegraph*, 10 November 2018; Heather Stewart and Daniel Boffey, 'May Brexit Plan: A Split Cabinet, A Split Party and A Split Nation', *Guardian*, 15 November 2018;

Daily Telegraph, 14, 15, 16 November 2018 for Rees-Mogg and Boris Johnson; John Redwood, 'This Deal Is Even Worse for Us than Staying in the EU', *Guardian*, 16 November 2018; *Guardian*, 16, 20 November 2018 for Morgan and Gove; Rory Carroll, Michael Savage, Toby Helm, 'Britain on Verge of Historic Blunder, Warns Johnson in Bid to Woo DUP', *Guardian*, 25 November 2018.

96 *Daily Telegraph*, editorial, 'Mrs May Must Rescue Brexit – and Herself', 16 November 2018.

97 *Guardian*, editorial, 'The Signing of This Deal Is a Sobering Moment, but the Brexiters Charge On', 26 November 2018.

98 Mattha Busby, 'People's Vote March: "700,000" Rally for New Brexit Referendum – As It Happened', *Guardian*, 20 October 2018.

99 Andrew Sparrow, 'Corbyn Says Deal Is "26 Pages of Waffle" and "Blindfold Brexit" We All Feared', *Guardian*, 22 November 2018; *Channel Four News*, 15, 22 November 2018; *ITV News at Ten and STV, Scotland Tonight*, 22 November 2018; Dan Sabbagh, 'Labour: PM to Be Pressed on Fallback If Deal Fails', *Guardian*, 16 November 2018.

100 *STV, Scotland Tonight*, 20 November 2018; Kathleen Nutt, 'SNP and Labour to Reject Plan', *National*, 21 November 2018; idem, 'Mundell Accused of U-Turn on Fishing Resignation Pledge', *National*, 23 November 2018; idem, 'Sturgeon Insists Scotland Receive Equal Treatment', *National*, 15 November 2018; Andrew Learmonth, 'Blackford Accuses May of Misleading MPs on Brexit Deal', *National*, 6 December 2018; Michael Fry, 'Brexit Is English Rebellion Wrapped in a Union Flag'; Robin McAlpine, 'We're Letting History Pass Independence By – the Movement Should Be Angry', *Commonspace*, 22 November 2018; Patrick Harvie, 'The Time Has Come for Our First Minister to Act on Indy', *National*, 16 November 2018; Andrew Learmonth, 'Sturgeon Urged to Call Indyref2 as Tories Implode', *National*, 16 November 2018; David Jamieson, 'Analysis: Whose Brexit Is This and What Does It Mean for Scottish Independence?', *Commonspace*, 20 November 2018.

101 Tony Blair, 'It's Elementary, the Only Way Out Is a Referendum', *Daily Telegraph*, 16 November 2018.

102 Heather Stewart, Dan Sabbagh, Daniel Boffey, 'PM Fails to Rule Out Resigning If Tory MPs Block Her Deal', *Guardian*, 24 November 2018.

103 Toby Helm, 'Labour Gains Three-point Lead as May's Brexit Plan Hits Buffers', *Observer*, 18 November 2018.

104 *Channel Four News*, 27, 28 November 2018; *ITV News at* Ten, 27 November 2018.

105 Helm, 'Labour Gains Three-point Lead'.

106 Heather Stewart, Jessica Elgot, Rajeev Syal, 'May Staggers on after Three Brexit Defeats in a Single Day', *Guardian*, 5 December 2018.

107 Gordon Rayner, 'The Day May Lost Control', *Daily Telegraph*, 5 December 2018; *Channel Four News*, 7 December 2018.

108 Toby Helm, 'No Hope of Success and No Plan B, but May Still Won't Blink', *Observer*, 9 December 2018; *Channel Four News*, 10, 11, 12, 13, 17, 18 December 2018; Kate Lyons, '"Her Goose Is Cooked": Newspapers Ask How Long Theresa May Can Last', *Guardian*, 13 December 2018; *Daily Telegraph*, editorials, 11, 12 December 2018; *Daily Express*, *Daily Mail*, 11 December 2018 for support for May; *BBC News Special on Brexit*, 12 December 2018; Jon Henley, 'What Is Going On in Brexit – and What Might Happen Next?', *Guardian*, 11 January, 2019; *Guardian*, front page and editorial, 'May's Brexit Deal Did Not Survive Contact with the Commons. What Will?', 16 January 2019; *Daily Mirror*, *Daily Telegraph*, *Daily Express*, *Daily Mail*, 16 January 2019 on May's defeat in parliament; Heather Stewart, Jessica Elgot, Lisa O'Carroll, 'PM's Brexit

Plan B to Renegotiate Backstop', *Guardian*, 21 January 2019; Matthew Weaver and Daniel Boffey, 'EU Dismisses Tory Compromise Plan as Unworkable', *Guardian*, 29 January 2019; Steven Swinford, 'Tears of Rage, "Appalling Disloyalty" and Kamikaze Remainers: Inside the Remarkable Brexit Cabinet Meeting', *Daily Telegraph*, 26 February 2019; David Wooding, 'Brexit Party Boost. More than 100,000 Members have Joined Nigel Farage's New Brexit Party', *Sun*, 17 February 2019.

109 Jonathan Freedland, 'The Question for Labour: Why Are You Sticking with Corbyn?', *Guardian*, 26 October 2019; *Observer*, editorial, 'Brexit. Chaos Reigns. The Only Viable Option Left Is a Second Vote', 16 December 2018; Owen Jones, 'Why Isn't Labour Surging?', *Guardian*, 30 November 2018.

110 Freedland, 'The Question for Labour'; Rob Edwards, 'Poll Study Shows Surge for Remain', *Sunday National*, 17 February 2019 (for Curtice); Andrew Rawnsley, 'Only When MPS Stare into the Abyss will They Agree to a People's Vote', *Observer*, 21 October 2018; *Channel Four*, 'Brexit: What the Nation Really Thinks', 5 November, 8–9 pm, 2018. I am grateful to Mark Aherne, a Coffey supporter, for the then MP's poll, n.kirk@mmu.ac.uk, e-mail correspondence, 3 January 2019.

111 Heather Stewart, 'Corbyn Confirms Brexit Would Go Ahead If Labour Were to Win Snap Election', *Guardian*, 22 December 2018; William Keegan, 'Labour's Leader only Listens to the Leavers. Why?', *Observer*, 13 January 2019; Jessica Elgot and Rajeev Syal, 'Leader of Unite Warns Labour Against Backing "People's Vote"', *Guardian*, 6 December 2018; Heather Stewart, Peter Walker, Rajeev Syal, 'Corbyn Could Face String of Resignations If He Backs "People's Vote"', *Guardian*, 17 January 2019.

112 *Guardian*, editorial, 'The Guardian View on the Labour Split: A Mistake but Also a Warning', 19 February 2019; Polly Toynbee, 'I Backed the SDP. But This Labour Schism Makes No Sense at All', *Guardian*, 19 February 2019.

113 Kathleen Nutt, 'Sturgeon Calls on Corbyn to Go for a No Confidence Motion', *National*, 11 December 2018; idem, 'May Met with Calls to Quit as MPS Demand Brexit Deal Vote', *National*, 13 December 2018; *BBC News*, Politics, 'Theresa May Sets January Date for MPs' Brexit Vote', 17 December 2018.

114 Kathleen Nutt, 'First Minister to Reveal Indyref2 Plan "Soon"', *National*, 8 January 2019; David Jamieson, 'Analysis: the Independence Movement's Diverging Strategies', *Commonspace*, 21 January 2019.

115 Kathleen Nutt, 'Organisation Sets Out to Make a New Case for Independence', *National*, 4 February 2019.

116 Severin Carrell, 'Nicola Sturgeon: Salmond Charges Won't Affect Scottish Independence Drive', *Guardian*, 27 January 2019.

117 Heather Stewart, 'MPs Ignore May's Pleas and Defeat Her Brexit Deal By 149 Votes', *Guardian*, 12 March 2019. See also the *Daily Telegraph*, 13 and 14 March, 2019, for references to May's 'loss of control' and her 'betrayal of Brexit' (Farage).

118 For Brexit developments between March and early April, see Polly Toynbee, 'John Bercow's Ruling Has Breathed New Life into the People's Vote', *Guardian*, 19 March 2019; Harry Yorke, James Crisp, Jack Maidment, Steven Swinford, 'May Accused of Going "On Bended Knee" to EU as She Warns MPs the UK Has "Had Enough" of Brexit Indecision', *Daily Telegraph*, 20 March 2019; Steven Swinford, Christopher Hope, Jack Maidment, 'Exclusive: Theresa May Told by Chairman of 1922 Committee that Tory MPs Want Her to Quit over Brexit' *Daily Telegraph*, 21 March 2019; Jessica Elgot and Peter Walker, 'May Urged to Go as She Hints at Pulling Third Vote on Brexit Deal', *Guardian*, 23 March 2019; Frances Perranolin and Andrew Sparrow, Brexit Live, 'DUP Accuses May of Being "Far Too Willing to Capitulate" to EU – Live

News', *Guardian*, 23 March 2019; Toby Helm and Michael Savage, 'One Million Join March against Brexit as Tories Plan to Oust May', *Observer*, 24 March 2019; Thomas Colson and Adam Bienkov, 'What Will Happen Now with Brexit after the Third Rejection of the British Parliament to the Agreement between the EU and Theresa May?', *Business Insider*, 29 March 2019; Andrew Sparrow, Politics Live, 'All Eight Indicative Vote Options Defeated by MPs', *Guardian*, 28 March 2019; Heather Stewart, Jessica Elgot, Rowena Mason, 'May Calls for Cabinet Showdown as MPs Reject All Brexit Options', *Guardian*, 2 April 2019; Jessica Elgot, 'Bill to Prevent No-Deal Brexit Passes Commons by One Vote', *Guardian*, 4 April 2019.

119 Peter Walker, 'May to Ask for Short Brexit Extension and Reaches Out to Labour', *Guardian*, 3 April 2019; Daniel Boffey and Rowena Mason, 'Theresa May Agrees to October Brexit as Donald Tusk Warns UK "Don't Waste this Time"', *Guardian*, 11 April 2019; Peter Walker and Heather Stewart, 'May and Corbyn Blame Each Other as Brexit Talks Collapse', *Guardian*, 18 May 2019.

120 Heather Stewart, Rowena Mason, Peter Walker, 'May's Final Effort to Win Backing Falls Flat as MPs Reject "New Deal"', *Guardian*, 22 May 2019; Kate Lyons, '"End of the Road": What the Papers Say as Pressure Builds on Theresa May', *Guardian*, 23 May 2019; Heather Stewart, 'Theresa May Announces Her Resignation', *Guardian*, 24 May 2019; Kathleen Nutt, 'Few Tears Shed in Scotland as Theresa May Quits as Prime Minister', *National*, 25 May 2019; Graham Russell, '"Broken by Brexit": What the Papers Say about May's Farewell Speech', *Guardian*, 25 May 2019.

121 *Guardian*, editorial, 'The Guardian View on Theresa May's Farewell Speech: She Threw Away Her Shot', 17 July 2019; Gary Younge, 'Farewell Then, Theresa. Your Best was Never Good Enough', *Guardian*, 19 July 2019.

122 Tingle, *Follow Leader*, p. 9. For Seldon and Newell, May made 'unforced errors . . . through ignorance, intransigence and ineptitude', *May at 10*, xxi.

123 *Guardian*, editorial, 'The Guardian View on May and Brexit: A Prime Minister Gone Rogue', *Guardian*, 21 March 2019; Jason Cowley, 'May Was a 1950s Conservative: Resolute but Charmless, and Will Be Remembered for Failure', *New Statesman*, 31 May–6 June 2019, p. 7; Nick Miller, 'May Blames MPs for Stalemate', *Sydney Morning Herald*, 22 March 2019; Greg Sheridan, 'Sad End for a Prime Minister Who Promised So Much But Delivered Nothing', *Weekend Australian*, 25–26 May 2019.

124 *Channel Four News*, 14 January 2019; Jon Henley, 'A Shambles on which the Sun Never Sets: How the World Sees Brexit', *Guardian*, 6 April 2019; *Special Broadcasting Service* (SBS) World News, 13, 31 March 2019; Peter Hartcher, 'Lessons for All from Brexit Crisis', *Sydney Morning Herald*, 9 April 2019.

125 Heather Stewart and Patrick Wintour, 'Tories Lose Over 1,300 Seats in Local Elections as Major Parties Suffer', *Guardian*, 4 May 2019; John Curtice, 'The Tories Are Feeling the Heat as the Voters Desert Them for the Brexit Party', *Daily Telegraph*, 18 April 2019.

126 *International Express*, editorial, 'Stalwart Ann Signing Up to Brexit Party Is Mighty Wake-up Call for Tories', 1 May 2019; Toby Helm and Michael Savage, 'Poll Surge for Farage Sparks Panic among Tories and Labour', *Observer*, 12 May 2019.

127 Sean Clarke, Pablo Gutierrez, Frank Hulley-Jones, 'European Election Latest Results 2019: Across the UK', *Guardian*, 27 May 2019; Andrew Learmonth, 'Labour and Tories Humiliated in European Vote', *National*, 27 May 2019; Michael Savage, 'Tories in for a Brexit Party Trouncing, while Remainers Abandon Labour', *Observer*, 19 May 2019; *BBC News*, 'Northern Ireland Politics European Elections: Long, Dodds and Anderson Elected', 27 May 2019, https://www.bbc.co.uk/news/uk-northern-ireland-politics-48370936; *BBC News*, 'EU Elections 2019: SNP to Have Three MEPs as

Labour Vote Collapses', 27 May 2019, https://www.bbc.co.uk/news/uk-scotland-484174424; Michael Savage, 'Brexit Party Tops Westminster Election Poll for First Time', *Observer*, 2 June 2019.

128 Rowena Mason, 'Boris Johnson: UK Will Leave EU in October, Deal or no Deal', *Guardian*, 25 May 2019; *BBC TV*, 'Our Next Prime Minister', BBC One, 8 pm, 18 June 2019.

129 *Full Fact*, 13 July 2018, https://fullfact.org/europe; Larry Elliott, 'Corbyn Is Right. Labour Needs Both Leavers and Remainers', *Guardian*, 6 June 2019; Polly Toynbee, 'Labour Is on the Brink in Peterborough: This Byelection Is a Battle over Its Future', *Guardian*, 6 June 2019.

130 Toby Helm, 'Labour Must Back Second Brexit Vote or Lose Next Election', Tom Watson Warns', *Observer*, 26 May 2019; Paul Mason, 'Labour Has No Choice but to Back Remain Loud and Clear', *Guardian*, 19 June 2019; John Gray, 'Sleepwalking into the Fire', *New Statesman*, 31 May–6 June 2019, pp. 31–3; Jessica Elgot and Rowena Mason, 'Corbyn Pledges Labour Will Back Referendum on Any Brexit Deal', *Guardian*, 30 May 2019; Jessica Elgot and Heather Stewart, 'Corbyn Rebuffs Calls to Win Back Voters with Move towards Remain', *Guardian*, 20 June 2019; *BBC News*, Politics, 'Peterborough By-election: Labour Beats Brexit Party to Hold Seat', 7 June, https://www.bbc.co.uk/news/uk-politics-48532869; *BBC News*, Scotland Politics, 'Scottish Labour Backs Brexit Referendum Policy', 8 June 2019, https://www.bbc.co.uk/news/uk-scotland-politics-48558355; Rob Ford on Twitter, 'Remain Voters Outnumber Leave Voters among the 2017 Labour Vote in Almost Every Labour Leave Seat', https://twitter.com/robfordmancs/status/1114065322120744961.

131 *BBC News*, Philip Sim, 'What Does the SNP's Currency Vote Mean?', 28 April 2019; Andrew Wilson and John Curtice, 'Scottish Currency', *YouTube*, 28 April 2019; Robin McAlpine, 'Conference Voted to Kill Sterlingisation and There Is No Place Left for the "Six Tests", *Commonspace*, 2 May 2019; *UK Pol*, *Political Speech Archive*, 'Nicola Sturgeon – 2019 Speech at SNP Conference', 30 April 2019; *National*, News Desk, 'Huge Turnout for Glasgow's All Under One Banner Independence March', 4 May 2019; Elisabeth O'Leary, 'Brexit Drives Support for Scottish Independence to 49%: You Gov', *Reuters*, 27 April 2019.

132 Kevin McKenna, 'Nicola Sturgeon's Strike for Independence Should Not Let the SNP Off the Hook', *Observer*, 28 April 2019; Michael Fry, 'SNP Need to Let Markets Work. That's How We'll Up Our Productivity', *National*, 30 April 2019. John Harris, 'My England Is in a Mess. Scotland's Case for Splitting Away Is Stronger than Ever', *Guardian*, 29 April 2019.

133 Kathleen Nutt, 'Nicola Sturgeon Renews Indyref2 Call as Theresa May Quits', *National*, 25 May 2019.

134 Owen Jones, 'This Defeat Is the End of the Brexit PM. Bring on the General Election', *Guardian*, 30 March 2019.

Chapter 3

1 Alasdair Sandford, 'The Road to Brexit: What Happened in Boris Johnson's First Six Months as UK Prime Minister', *Euronews*, 24 January 2020, https://www.euronews.com/2020/01/24/the-road-to-brexit-what-happened-in-boris-johnson-s-first-six-months-as-uk-prime-minister; Lisa O'Carroll, 'Events Dear Boy: Timeline of Boris Johnson's Busy 18 Months', *Guardian*, 29 April 2020.

2   Richard Partington, 'UK Government Borrowing Hits Highest December Level on
    Record', *Guardian*, 22 January 2021; Larry Elliott, 'Bobby Kennedy Was Right: GDP Is
    a Poor Measure of a Nation's Real Health', *Guardian*, 18 January 2021; Polly Toynbee,
    'There's Too Much Optimism about Post-pandemic Britain', *Guardian*, 23 March 2021;
    James Foley, 'Prince Charming: Ridicule Is Nothing to Be Scared Of. . .', *Commonspace*,
    Source Direct, 24 March 2021.

3   *BBC News*, Politics, 'Boris Johnson Wins Race to Be Tory Leader and Prime Minister',
    23 July 2019, https://www.bbc.co.uk/news/uk-politics-49084605.

4   Boris Johnson, *The Churchill Factor: How One Man Made History* (London: Hodder
    and Stoughton, 2014); idem, 'The Churchill Factor', *YouTube Politics and Prose*,
    22 November 2014; idem, 'Third Margaret Thatcher Lecture', Centre for Policy Studies,
    28 November 2013.

5   Heather Stewart and Peter Walker, 'Britain Shuts Down', *Guardian*, 21 March 2020;
    'Johnson, 'Third Thatcher Lecture'; Stephen Buranyi, 'The Fixation on Freedom that
    Could Seriously Harm Our Health', *Guardian*, 19 January 2921. The notion of the
    'Free-born Englishman' (sic) ironically is most closely associated in academic circles
    with the work of the Marxist historian, Christopher Hill, and the tradition of popular
    radicalism, including radical patriotism, in English history. See, for example, Hill, *The
    World Turned Upside Down: Radical Ideas During the English Revolution* (London:
    Penguin, 1991); Raphael Samuel (ed.), *Patriotism: The Making and Unmaking of British
    National Identity* (London: Routledge, 1989).

6   Sandford, 'Road to Brexit'.

7   Jessica Elgot and Peter Walker, 'Jo Johnson Quits as MP and Minister, Citing "National
    Interest"', *Guardian*, 5 September 2019; Toby Helm, Michael Savage, Andrew Rawnsley,
    Daniel Boffey, 'Amber Rudd Quits Cabinet and Attacks PM for "Political Vandalism"',
    Observer, 8 September 2019; Alasdair Sandford, 'Brexit Timeline: Boris Johnson's
    Month of Turmoil in September', *Euronews*, 30 September 2019, https://www.
    euronews.com/2019/09/30/Brexit-timeline.

8   Sandford, 'Brexit Timeline'; Owen Bowcott, Ben Quinn, Severin Carrell, 'Johnson's
    Suspension of Parliament Unlawful, Supreme Court Rules', *Guardian*, 24 September 2019.

9   Kate Proctor and Peter Walker, 'Boris Johnson: I'd Rather Be Dead in a Ditch than
    Agree Brexit Extension', *Guardian*, 5 September 2019.

10 Politics Home Staff, 'Boris Johnson's Speech to the 2019 Conservative Party
    Conference', https://www.politicshome.com/news/article, 2 October 2019.

11 Chris Morris, 'Brexit Deal: Where Have the UK and EU Compromised?', *BBC News*,
    17 October 2019; Heather Stewart, Jennifer Rankin, Lisa O'Carroll, 'Johnson Accused
    of Misleading Public over Brexit Deal after Northern Ireland Remarks', *Guardian*,
    8 November 2019; David Phinnemore, 'The DUP Hates the Protocol, but It Is Here
    to Stay', *Guardian*, 5 February 2021.

12 Heather Stewart and Daniel Boffey, 'MPs Reject Boris Johnson's Attempt to Fast-track
    Brexit Deal', *Guardian*, 22 October 2019.

13 Heather Stewart and Daniel Boffey, 'Johnson Tells MPs: Back My December 12
    Election Bid', *Guardian*, 25 October 2019.

14 Andrew Learmonth, 'Sturgeon Sets Out Terms for "Alliance" to Keep Tories Out',
    National, 26 November 2019.

15 *Guardian*, editorial, 'The Guardian View on a Liberal Democrat Revoke: A Promise
    that Won't Be Redeemed', 16 September 2019; Peter Walker, Simon Murphy, Libby
    Brooks, 'Jo Swinson Quits as Liberal Democrat Leader after Losing Her Own Seat',
    Guardian, 13 December 2019.

16 Peter Mandelson, 'Labour Shouldn't Fall Out Over Brexit. It Ought to Focus on What Happens Next', *Guardian*, 3 December 2020.

17 Frances Perraudin, 'Independent ex-MPs Who Left Labour and Tories Fail to Win', *Guardian*, 13 December 2019; *BBC News*, 'Politics', 'General Election 2019: Anna Soubry Disbands Independent Group for Change', 19 December 2019, https://www.bbc.co.uk/news/uk-politics-50858811.

18 *ITV*, 'Johnson versus Corbyn; The ITV Debate', 19 November 2019; *BBC News*, 'Election 2019', 'General Election 2019: Boris Johnson and Jeremy Corbyn Clash over Brexit', 6 December 2019.

19 *BBC News*, 'Politics', 'Corbyn Wants an Election Despite Warning from Tony Blair', 2 September 2019, https://www.bbc.co.uk/news/uk-politics- 49552403.

20 *BBC News*, 'Politics', 'UK Set for 12 December General Election', 29 October 2019, https://www.bbc.co.uk/news/uk-politics-50229318; *Guardian*, editorial, 'Voters Must Seize a Fleeting Chance to Stop Boris Johnson in His Tracks', 11 December 2019.

21 Heather Stewart, 'Watson Quits as Deputy as Corbyn Strengthens Grip', *Guardian*, 7 November 2019.

22 *BBC News*, 'Election 2019', 'Labour Party Manifesto 2019: 12 Key Policies Explained', 21 November, 2019, https://www.bbc.co.uk/news/election-2019-50501411; Gary Younge, 'After a Decade of Decay, Only Labour Offers a Hopeful Future', *Guardian*, 22 November 2019; Heather Stewart, 'Corbyn Unveils Labour's Most Radical Manifest for Decades', *Guardian*, 22 November 2019; Rowena Mason, 'Labour to Unveil Compromise Position on Immigration', *Guardian*, 17 November 2019; Owen Jones, 'Labour Needs Its Leave Voters – or a Johnson Era Beckons', *Guardian*, 28 November 2019.

23 *BBC News*, 'Election 2019', 'Labour Party Manifesto'; *Daily Telegraph*, editorial, 'Seven Days to Stop Jeremy Corbyn', 5 December 2019; *Daily Telegraph*, editorial, 'Johnson Is Winning the Brexit Argument', 10 December 2019; Rowena Mason, 'Thornberry Vows to Stand and Hits Out at Labour's "Catastrophic Folly', *Guardian*, 19 December 2019; Emily Thornberry, 'Labour Gifted Johnson this Election. It Can't Happen Again', *Guardian*, 19 December 2019; Heather Stewart, 'Brexit Row Tore at the Heart of Corbyn's Campaign', *Guardian*, 22 January 2020; Rajeev Syal, Rowena Mason, Heather Stewart, 'A "Nightmare Campaign" and a Leader Hard to Sell', *Guardian*, 18 December 2019.

24 Dan Sabbagh, 'Labour Is Gaining Share, but It May Not Be Enough', *Guardian*, 9 December 2019; Robert Booth and Rajeev Syal, 'Labour Ahead with BAME Electorate as Parties Tailor Manifestos to Win Votes', *Guardian*, 5 December 2019; Michael Savage, 'Conservatives Open Up 19-point Gap with 47% Share of the Vote', *Observer*, 24 November 2019.

25 *BBC News*, 'Election 2019: Results', https://www.bbc.co.uk/news/election/2019; Daniel Wainwright, 'General Election 2019: How Labour's "Red Wall Turned Blue"', https://www.bbc.co.uk/news/election-50771014, 13 December 2019; *Lord Ashcroft Polls*, 'How Britain Voted and Why: My 2019 General Election Post-vote Poll', 12 December 2019; Rosa Prince, 'How Boris Sacrificed the Remain South East to Breach the Red Wall', *Daily Telegraph*, 13 December 2019; John Harris and John Domokos, 'Working-class Voters Desert Labour as "Red Wall" Crumbles', *Guardian*, 13 December 2019; Dan Sabbagh, 'Voting Analysis: Britain Divided by Age and Class', *Guardian*, 14 December 2019.

26 *BBC News*, 'Election 2019; Results', https://www.bbc.co.uk/news/election/2019/results/ Wales; Darren Loucaides, 'The Brexit Party Folded, But Make No Mistake: Farage Won

It for Johnson', *Guardian*, 13 December, 2019; David Maddox, 'Nigel Farage Plans to Watch Boris Johnson "Every Step of the Way" in Next Brexit Stage', *Sunday Express*, 2 February 2020; Daniel Trilling, 'This Election May Be the End of Farage, But Not of Faragism', *Guardian*, 15 November 2019.

27 See, for example, John Crace, 'Boris the Narcissist', *Guardian*, 24 June 2020. Sylvie Bermann, the French ambassador to the UK from 2014 to 2017, described Johnson as intelligent and charming, but also as a power-driven 'unrepentant and inveterate liar'. See Patrick Wintour, '"Inveterate Liar": How Top Envoy Saw the PM', *Guardian*, 25 February 2021.

28 Katrina Navikas, *Loyalism and Radicalism in Lancashire 1798–1815* (Oxford: Oxford University Press, 2009); Patrick Joyce, *Work, Society and Politics: The Culture of the Factory in Later Victorian England* (Brighton; Harvester Press, 1980); Deborah Mattinson, 'Red Wall Still Backs Johnson (For Now)', *Observer*, 6 September 2020; Edward Docx, 'In the Court of the Clown King', *Guardian*, 18 March 2021; Payne, *Broken Heartlands*, pp. 3, 18, 29, 57–83, 59–61, 380–7, 391–2.

29 For Conservatism's long opposition to the 'alien other', Kirk, *Labour and the Politics of Empire*, Part III, 'The Politics of Loyalism'.

30 Tim Adams, 'A Year after Johnson's Swaggering Greenwich Speech, 100,000 Dead', *Observer*, 31 January 2021; Peter Walker and Kate Proctor, 'Johnson Promises "Dawn of a New Era" but Celebrations Will Be Muted', *Guardian*, 31 January 2020; Heather Stewart, Daniel Boffey, Rowena Mason, 'Clashes Loom as Johnson and Barnier Stand Firm on Trade Talk Ambitions', *Guardian*, 4 February 2020.

31 Peter Walker, 'Tories Restore Party Whip to 10 MPs Who Sought to Block No-deal Brexit', *Guardian*, 29 October 2019.

32 Rowena Mason and Peter Walker, 'Jeremy Corbyn "Very Sad" at Election Defeat but Feels Proud of Manifesto', *Guardian*, 13 December 2019; Kate Proctor, 'Corbyn Tells Angry MPs It Was All about Brexit', *Guardian*, 18 December 2019; Andy Beckett, 'The Heartlands May Be Gone for Ever. Labour Needs New Ones', *Guardian*, 11 January 2020; Margaret Hodge, 'The Party's Survival Depends on More than Discarding Corbyn', *Observer*, 2 February 2020; Martin Farrer, 'Jeremy Corbyn's Interview with Andrew Neil – What the Papers Say', *Guardian*, 27 November 2019; *Guardian*, editorial, 'The *Guardian* View on Antisemitism and Labour: A Shadow over the Body of Politics', 26 November 2019. See the *Observer*, 5, 26 January 2020 for a useful guide to the main contenders for the Labour leadership.

33 Stewart, Boffey, Mason, 'Clashes Loom'; Daniel Boffey, 'Barnier Rejects Call for Canada-style Deal with EU', *Guardian*, 19 February 2020; Daniel Boffey, 'Britain Being Forced to "Bend to EU Norms" Claims Brexit Envoy', *Guardian*, 20 May 2020; Daniel Boffey and Lisa O'Carroll, 'Brexit Talks: UK Must Be More Realistic, Says Berlin's EU Envoy', *Guardian*, 5 June 2020.

34 Fintan O'Toole, 'Independence Day Will Expose Brexit as a Ruse to Free an Imaginary Nation', *Observer*, 26 January 2020.

35 Larry Elliott, 'Taking Back Control Is Not the Same as Pulling up the Drawbridge', *Guardian*, 19 February 2020; Richard Partington, 'UK Faces Weakest Growth Outside Recession since Second World War', *Guardian*, 27 December 2019.

36 Larry Elliott and Heather Stewart, 'Tories Splash the Cash, but Will It Hit the Right Targets?', *Guardian*, 12 March 2020; Richard Partington, 'Public Spending "Heading to 40% of GDP under Johnson"', *Guardian*, 24 February 2020; Richard Partington and Mark Sweeney, 'Bank Makes Emergency Cut to 0.25%', *Guardian*, 12 March 2020; Larry Elliott, 'Spending Bonanza to Underscore the End of Austerity', *Guardian*,

12 March 2020; Rowena Mason, 'It Looks Like a Victory for Cummings', *Guardian*, 12 March 2020.

37 Rowena Mason, Heather Stewart, Peter Walker, 'Sajid Javid Resigns as Chancellor in Boris Johnson Reshuffle', *Guardian*, 13 February 2020; Elliott and Stewart, 'Tories Splash the Cash'; Kate Proctor, 'Theresa May Leads Warnings about Long-term Impacts of Abandoning fiscal Discipline', *Guardian*, 12 March 2020; Larry Elliott, 'Spending for Growth: Sunak's Bid to Bury Austerity', *Guardian*, 'Budget 2020', 12 March 2020; Will Hutton, 'This Tory Budget Is Keynes Reborn', *Observer*, 15 March 2020; Phillip Inman, 'We Could All End Up Paying Dear for Sunak's Largesse', *Observer*, 15 March 2020.

38 Andrew Learmonth, 'Majority of Voters Believe FM has Indyref2 Mandate', *National*, 5 February 2020.

39 Martin Hannan, 'Shock Opinion Polls in Ireland's Election', *National*, 5 February 2020; Rory Carroll, 'Irish General Election: Who Won and What Happens Now?', *Guardian*, 10 February 2020; idem, 'Sinn Fein Leader Declares Election Victory and Calls for Talks on Coalition', *Guardian*, 11 February 2020; Fintan O'Toole, 'Ireland's Shock Poll Result Was a Vote Against the Success of Globalisation', *Observer*, 16 February 2020.

40 For the classic account see Tom Nairn, *The Break-up of Britain: Crisis and Neo-Nationalism* (Champaign, Illinois: Common Ground Publishing, 2015). See also Martin Kettle, 'The Success of Sinn Fein Surely Brings the UK's Breakup Nearer', *Guardian*, 13 February 2020; Julian Coman, 'Is a Quiet Revolution Edging Wales Down the Road to Independence?', *Observer*, 25 April 2021; John Harris, 'As the UK Comes Apart, Its Flag Is Suddenly Everywhere', *Guardian*, 22 March 2021; Gavin Esler, *How Britain Ends* (London: Head of Zeus, 2021); Ailsa Henderson and Richard Wyn Jones, *Englishness: The Political Force Transforming Britain* (Oxford: Oxford University Press, 2021).

41 Simon Jenkins, 'Priti Patel Is Out of Her Depth. And that Is Johnson's Fault', *Guardian*, 25 February 2020; Aaron Walawalkar, 'Home Office Chief Sir Philip Rutnam Quits over Priti Patel "Bullying"', *Guardian*, 29 February 2020.

42 Sarah Boseley, 'WHO Declares Pandemic and Slams "Alarming Levels of Inaction" in Curbing Virus', *Guardian*, 12 March 2020; *Guardian*, editorial, 'As New Coronavirus Spreads in China We Should Be Alert Not Afraid', 22 January 2020.

43 Lily Kuo, 'Trump Sparks Anger by Calling Coronavirus the "Chinese Virus"', *Guardian*, 17 March 2020.

44 Archie Bland, 'Is Britain Really a Nation of Libertarians?', *Guardian*, 24 September 2020; Michele Gelfand, 'How Our "Loose" Rule-breaking Culture Helped to Spread Covid', *Guardian*, 2 February 2021 'Haroon Siddique, 'Poll Finds New Sense of Unity since Covid', *Guardian*, 1 March 2021; Jon Lawrence, *Me, Me, Me? The Search for Community in post-War England* (Oxford: Oxford University Press, 2019), Introduction.

45 Boseley, 'WHO Declares Pandemic'.

46 James Foley, 'The UK Passed a Grim Milestone Yesterday' *Commonweal*, *Source Direct*, 27 January 2021; Lucy Campbell, 'Multiple Failures: How the Government Fell Short – Again and Again', *Guardian*, 15 January 2021; *Guardian*, editorial, 'Boris Johnson Shows No Interest in Learning from His Lethal Blunders', 28 January 2021; Devi Sridhar, 'Five Fatal Errors that Led to the UK's 100,000 Covid Deaths', *Guardian*, 28 January 2021; John Crace, 'As the Death Toll Rises, PM Remains More Interested in Cheap Political Point-Scoring', *Guardian*, 14 January, 2021.

47 Marina Hyde, '"Turn the Tide in 12 Weeks"? It's Another Line for the Side of a Bus', *Guardian*, 21 March 2020; Eleanor Ainge Roy, 'New Zealand and Australia Close

Borders to Foreigners Amid Coronavirus Crisis', *Guardian*, 19 March 2020; David
Conn, Felicity Lawrence, Paul Lewis, Severin Carrell, David Pegg, Harry Davies, Rob
Evans, 'The Inside Story of the Covid-19 Crisis in the UK', *Guardian*, 30 April 2020;
David Conn, '"I Thought It Was Appalling that the Atletico Fans Were Allowed to
Come"', *Guardian*, 23 March 2020.

48 Heather Stewart and Ian Sample, 'Coronavirus: Enforcing UK Lockdown One Week
Earlier "Could Have Saved 20,000 Lives"', *Guardian*, 11 June 2020.

49 Neil Ferguson, '"One Year Ago, I First Realised How Serious It Was. Then It Got
Worse. . .", *Observer*, 14 March 2021; Phillip Inman, 'UK Slump "to Exceed Other Rich
Countries"', *Guardian*, 11 June 2020.

50 *Gov.UK. HM Treasury*, 'Summary of Existing Support', 8 January 2021; Larry Elliott
and Jessica Elgot, 'Sunak Extends the Safety Net', *Guardian*, 3 March 2021.

51 Heather Stewart and Larry Elliott, 'First Churchill, Now Roosevelt: Johnson Promises
"UK New Deal"', *Guardian*, 30 June 2020.

52 Larry Elliott, 'Forty Years on, Johnson Has Gone Even Further than Benn on State Aid',
Guardian, 14 September 2020.

53 Jessica Elgot and Heather Stewart, 'Upbeat Johnson Claims UK Can "Repel" the Virus
as It Is "The Greatest Place on Earth"', *Guardian*, 7 October 2020.

54 John Harris, 'It's Boris Johnson's Path or Rishi Sunak's Way': The Tories Can't Have
Both', *Guardian*, 25 October 2021.

55 Johnson failed to meet representatives of *Covid-19. Bereaved Families for Justice UK*
on a reported six occasions. Robert Booth, 'Experts and Bereaved Hit Out at PM's
Virus Claims', *Guardian*, 28 January 2021; Nesrine Malik, 'Our Leaders Are Due a
Reckoning over the UK's Covid Tragedy', *Guardian*, 1 February 2021; *Observer*,
editorial, 'Care Home Death Toll Is an Indictment of Our Society', 3 May 2020.

56 Lucy Campbell, 'Multiple Failures: How the Government Fell Short – Again and Again',
Guardian, 15 January 2021; Allyson Pollock, 'Why England's Contact Tracing Is in
Chaos', *Guardian*, 31 July 2020; *Channel Four News*, 10 September 2020; *BBC News*,
UK, 'Coronavirus: Concerns over Boris Johnson's "Moonshot" Testing Plans',
10 September 2020, https://www.bbc.co.uk/news/uk-54097050; Damir Sencar, '
Report Finds that UK Test and Trace Never Met 24 Hour COVID Deadlines', *Open
Access Government*, 10 March 2021, www.openaccessgovernment.org/uk-test-and-
trace-2/105878; Rajeev Syal, 'Test and Trace: "No Evidence It Contributed to Infections
Fall', *Guardian*, 10 March 2021; Heather Graham, 'Johnson defends Test and Trace App
after Spending £37 Billion', *National*, 11 March 2021; *Guardian*, editorial, 'Britain Has
Paid a Terrible Price for the Failure of Test and Trace', 11 March 2021.

57 Sarah Boseley, 'UK Virus Experts Criticize Award of Testing Contracts to Private
Firms', *Guardian*, 4 August 2020; Jonathan Freedland, 'Dodgy Deals, Millions Wasted:
This Is a Government of Sleaze', *Guardian*, 8 August 2020; Jon Stone, 'Government
Goes to Court to Defend Contract Handed to Company with Links to Dominic
Cummings', *Independent*, 13 February 2021; *Sky News*, 'Matt Hancock Urged to Deal
with Government "Cronyism" after It Lost High Court Ruling', 21 February 2021.

58 See the articles by Peter Bone, 'I Am a Committed Leaver but This Is a Moral Issue,
Not Political. He Must Go', and Toby Helm, 'Voters Want Adviser Sacked as Approval
of Johnson Plunges', *Observer*, 31 May 2020.

59 Rowena Mason, 'PM's Lockdown Release Leaves Britain Confused and Divided',
Guardian, 11 May 2020.

60 See the *Observer*'s editorials for 7 and 14 June 2020, 'The Government's Response to
Covid-19 Has Been Dire. A Public Inquiry Is Needed Now' and 'As Britain Flounders,

Europe Charts Its Recovery'; Toby Helm, 'Three Months On...How Has Lockdown Changed Britain?', *Observer*, 21 June 2020.

61 Robert Booth and Pamela Duncan, 'UK Virus Death Toll Reaches 50,000', *Guardian*, 3 June 2020.

62 Andrew Rawnsley, 'Even Tories Increasingly Fear They Have Inflicted the Worst of All Worlds on Britain', *Observer*, 14 June 2020; Heather Stewart and Rajeev Syal, 'Chaos at No 10 Sparks Disquiet on Tory Backbenches', *Guardian*, 20 June 2020.

63 Andrew Rawnsley, 'The Coronavirus Crisis Won't Give Boris Johnson an Alibi for a Calamitous Brexit', *Observer*, 7 June 2020; *Guardian*, editorial, 'A Dangerous Void Looms in Britain's Future Relations with the European Union', 11 June 2020.

64 Toby Helm, 'Starmer Overtakes Johnson as Preferred Choice for Prime Minister According to Latest Opinium Poll for the Observer', *Observer*, 27 June 2020; Toby Helm, Mark Townsend, Julian Coman, Robin McKie, 'Revolt over Easing of Lockdown Spreads as Poll Slump Hits PM', *Observer*, 17 May 2020.

65 Rajeev Syal, 'Starmer Allies Hope Emphatic Win Will Allow Labour to Rebuild in His Image', *Guardian*, 4 April 2020; Toby Helm, 'How "Tenacious, Diligent" Starmer Won Over a Shell-shocked Party', *Observer*, 5 April 2020; Toby Helm, '100 Days on, Keir Starmer's Quiet Revolution Takes Hold', *Observer*, 12 July 2020; Peter Walker, 'Starmer Says Labour Must Work with Business to Create a Fairer Society', *Guardian*, 19 February 2021.

66 Rowena Mason, 'Starmer Warns PM: Get a Grip or Risk Second Wave of Coronavirus', *Guardian*, 3 June 2020; Michael Savage, 'Labour Takes Poll Lead as Parties See Major Switch in Fortunes', *Guardian*, 26 September 2020; Toby Helm, 'Johnson Faces Revolt on Covid Diktats as Poll Figures Slump', *Observer*, 27 September 2020; Sir Keir Starmer, 'We Need a PM with a Plan. We Are Not Asking for Miracles', *Daily Telegraph*, 9 October 2020.

67 Polly Toynbee, 'Keir Starmer Has to Defeat the Tories on Patriotism', *Guardian*, 22 September 2020.

68 Jessica Elgot, 'Labour Plunged into Crisis after Corbyn Suspended', *Guardian*, 30 October 2020; Rajeev Syal, Peter Walker, Dan Sabbagh, 'Corbyn-supporting MPs Discussed Quitting Labour', Ian Lavery Says', *Guardian*, 31 October 2020.

69 Martin Kettle, 'No 10 Is Back to Its Old Tricks: Diversion and Scapegoating', *Guardian*, 2 July 2020; Marina Hyde, 'Blame the Care Homes', *Guardian*, 8 July 2020.

70 *Scottish Government*, 'COVID-19: Scotland's Strategic Framework Update', February 2021.

71 *Office for National Statistics*, 'Coronavirus (COVID-19) in 10 Charts', 24 September 2020.

72 *Guardian*, editorial, 'The Public's Caution Makes a Lot More Sense than the Government's Recklessness', 4 July 2020; Jessica Elgot, Heather Stewart, Simon Murphy, 'A Hell of a Year. Tories Reassess Their "Leader for the Good Times"', *Guardian*, 23 July 2020; Larry Elliott and Heather Stewart, 'Mass Unemployment Fears Despite Sunak's "Plan for Jobs"', *Guardian*, 9 July 2020; *Guardian*, editorial, 'The Chancellor's U-Turn Is Bad for Him. But It's Good for the Country', 10 October 2020; *BBC News*, Business, 'Budget 2021: Rishi Sunak to Extend Furlough Scheme until September', 3 March 2021, https://www.bbc.co.uk/news/business-56259094.

73 Stewart and Elliott, 'First Churchill, Now Roosevelt', *Guardian*, 30 June 2020.

74 *Telegraph*, Comment, 'A Remarkable First Year in Office for the PM', 24 July 2020. See also Larry Elliott, 'Why Are Voters Not Turning to Labour as the Economy Stalls?', *Guardian*, 7 August 2020.

75 Martyn Brown, 'Boris Johnson's Unforgettable First Year at Number 10-from Brexit to Intensive Care', *Daily Express*, 18 July 2020.

76 Martin Fletcher, 'Boris Johnson's First Year as PM: Incompetence and Maliciousness', *New Statesman*, 20 July 2020.

77 Fleet Street Fox Columnist, 'After Boris Johnson's First Year in Office, It's Clear the Doomsters and Gloomsters Got It Wrong', *Mirror*, 24 July 2020.

78 Toby Helm, 'Johnson Faces Tory Wrath as Party Slumps in Shock Poll', *Observer*, 30 August 2020.

79 Heather Stewart, Kate Proctor, Sally Weale, 'Government Forced into Humiliating Exams U-Turn', *Guardian*, 18 August 2020; *Daily Telegraph*, editorial, 'This Testing Fiasco Dents Public Confidence', 6 October 2020; Michael Savage, 'Conservatives Turn on Boris Johnson over Handling of UK Covid Crisis', *Observer*, 4 October 2020; *ITV*, 'News at Ten', 28 September 2020; *Guardian*, editorial, 'When Things Go Wrong, this Government Relies on Blame, Fear and Prejudice', 21 August 2020.

80 Toby Helm, 'Johnson at Bay, Starmer on the Rise . . . and Sunak Waiting in the Wings', *Observer*, 6 September 2020; *Telegraph*, 'Testing Fiasco', 6 October 2020; Savage, 'Conservatives Turn on Boris Johnson', *Observer*, 4 October 2020.

81 *BBC News*, UK, 'Covid: UK at a "Critical Point" in Pandemic, Top Scientists to Warn', 21 September 2020, https://www.bbc.co.uk/news/uk-54229845; *Daily Telegraph*, editorial, 'Rethink Covid Rules before It's Too Late', 8 October 2020; Heather Stewart, Josh Halliday, Helen Pidd, 'Starmer Heaps Pressure on PM with Call for National Lockdown', *Guardian*, 14 October 2020; Robin McKie, 'Our Incompetent Leaders Played Down the Virus to Protect the Economy', *Observer*, 1 November 2020.

82 Jack Hardy, 'New Lockdown Now to Save Christmas, Says Sage Adviser', *Daily Telegraph*, 9 October 2020; Christopher Hope, 'Red Wall Backlash over Tighter Restrictions', *Daily Telegraph*, 9 October 2020; *Daily Telegraph*, editorial, 'Is the NHS Ready for a Second Wave?', 9 October 2020; *Guardian*, editorial, 'Failure to Control the Second Wave Is Deepening the North–South Divide', 9 October 2020; Peter Walker, Ian Semple, Heather Stewart, 'New Covid-19 Rules Don't Go Far Enough, Say Experts', *Guardian*, 9 October 2020.

83 Elgot and Stewart, 'Upbeat Johnson Claims UK Can "Repel" the Virus'.

84 Peter Walker, 'Papers Turn on Johnson over Covid Measures', *Guardian*, 9 October 2020; *Daily Telegraph*, editorials, 'Jam Tomorrow Won't Solve Problems Today', 7 October 2020, 'Rethink Covid Rules before It's Too Late', 8 October 2020; *Daily Telegraph*, editorial, 'A Year In and the End Is Still Unclear', 23 March 2021; Sarah Knapton, 'Unscrutinised Data is Being Used to Justify Draconian Measures', *Daily Telegraph*, 9 October 2020; Richard Littlejohn, 'Time to Abandon the Air Raid Shelter, Sound the All Clear . . . and Win this War', *Daily Mail*, 23 March 2021.

85 *Daily Express*, editorial, 'Let's Back Boris and His Vision for Brexit Britain', 7 October 2020.

86 *BBC News*, Scotland, 'Covid: Scotland to Enter New 5-level Alert System', 23 October 2020, https://www.bbc.co.uk/news, uk-scotland-54661494; *BBC News*, UK, 'Covid-19: PM Announces Four-week England Lockdown', 31 October 2020, https://www.bbc.co.uk/news/uk-54763956.

87 Ferguson, 'One Year Ago'.

88 *BBC News*, Health, 'England Covid Tier Rules: What Are the Rules?', 14 December 2020, https://www.bbc.co.uk/news/health-545119652020; *BBC News*, 31 December 2020; *Channel Four News*, 17 December 2020; *ITV News*, 19 December 2020; Peter Walker, Natalie Grover, Daniel Boffey, 'Impose National Lockdown or Risk "Human

Disaster", Scientists Tell PM', *Guardian*, 22 December 2020; Jessica Elgot and Peter Walker, 'Tough New Curbs "For Months" as 1 in 50 Now Have Virus', *Guardian*, 6 January 2021; Caelainn Barr, Nicola Davis, Pamela Duncan, 'Worst Day Yet for Covid Deaths in Britain as Toll Passes 100,000', *Guardian*, 14 January 2021.

89 Jessica Elgot and Peter Walker, 'PM Imposes New Lockdown and Warns Worst Yet to Come', *Guardian*, 5 January 2021; *BBC News*, UK, 'Covid: England's Third National Lockdown Legally Comes into Force', 6 January 2021, https://www.bbc.co.uk/ news/uk-55554550; Niamh McIntyre, Pamela Duncan, Caelainn Barr, 'January's Daily UK Death Toll Averages More than 1,000 Figures Show', *Guardian*, 30 January 2021.

90 Ferguson, 'One Year Ago'; Spiegelhalter and Masters, *Covid by Numbers*.

91 Ian Bremner, 'The Best Global Responses to the COVID-19 Pandemic – 1 Year Later', *Time*, 23 February 2021; Emma Graham-Harrison and Helen Davidson, 'Tale of Two Islands: How Taiwan Triumphed as Britain Floundered', *Guardian*, 24 March 2021; Linda Geddes, 'Covid: Could Britain Have Been More Like New Zealand?', *Guardian*, 5 February 2021. For commitments to neoliberalism, the running down of the public health and wider public infrastructure and their deleterious effects upon the battle against Covid-19, see Cooper and Szreter, *After the* Virus, and Adam Tooze, *Shutdown*.

92 Robert Booth, 'Delaying England's Winter Lockdown "Caused up to 27,000 Covid Deaths"', *Guardian*, 18 March 2021; *Guardian*, editorial, 'Easing Restrictions over Christmas Risks a Dangerous Third Wave', 16 December 2020; Andrew Rawnsley, 'With His Sudden U-turn over Christmas, Boris Johnson Caps a Year of Debacles', *Observer*, 20 December 2020.

93 Gabriel Scally, 'Government Decisions Have Paved the Way to This Crisis', *Guardian*, 12 January 2021.

94 Roger Booth and Ian Sample, '"We Need to Know". Pressure on No 10 to Trigger Covid Inquiry', *Guardian*, 17 March 2021.

95 Richard Partington, 'UK Economy Hit by Record Slump in 2020 but Double-dip Recession Avoided', *Guardian*, 12 February 2021; 'Heather Stewart and Larry Elliott, 'Spend Now, Pay Later: Sunak Flags Major Tax Rises as Covid Bill Soars', *Guardian*, 4 March 2021; Larry Elliott, 'Government Borrowing Hits Peacetime Record of £303bn', *Guardian*, 24 April 2021.

96 Richard Partington, 'UK Economy Rallies as Firms Get Ready for Summer Spending', *Guardian*, 25 March 2021; idem, 'A Year of Covid Crisis: A Glimmer of Economic Hope at the End of the Tunnel', *Guardian*, 31 March 2021; idem, 'Economy Set to Grow at Fastest Rate since 1941', *Guardian*, 26 April 2021.

97 Larry Elliott and Heather Stewart, 'Biggest UK Slump in 300 Years', *Guardian*, 26 November 2020; Kenan Malik, 'Age-old Notions of the Noble Savage Haunt Views of Working-class Life', *Observer*, 24 January 2021; Polly Toynbee, 'There's Too Much Airy Optimism about Post-Covid Britain. Prepare for Brutal Cuts', *Guardian*, 23 March 2021; *Observer*, editorial, 'Joe Biden Is Proving to Be an Unlikely Revolutionary', 11 April 2021'; *Guardian*, 'Opinion' section, 4 March 2021 for views on the budget; Salma Shah, 'The Tories Still Need to Reconcile Their 'Red-Wall' and True Blue Supporters', *Guardian*, 5 October 2021.

98 *BBC News*, Chris Morris, 'Brexit: Why Is the Internal Market Bill Controversial?', 8 December 2020, https://www.bbc.co.uk/news/54088596.

99 Lisa O'Carroll and Daniel Boffey, 'The Brexit Deal: Here's What's in It', *Guardian*, 26 December 2020; Toby Helm, 'Fishing Industry Chiefs Cry "Betrayal" as MPs Fear Rush to Ratify Deal', *Observer*, 27 December 2020.

100 *Guardian*, editorial, 'The *Guardian* View of Brexit: A Tragic National Error', 28 December 2020; *Observer*, editorial, 'A Deal that Makes Us Poorer, Reduces Global Influence and Imperils the Nation's Integrity', 27 December 2020.

101 *Scottish Daily Mail*, 26 December 2020; *Scottish Daily Express*, 26 December 2020; Charles Moore, 'Johnson Succeeded Where Others Failed because He Accepted the Logic of Brexit', *Daily Telegraph*, 26 December 2020.

102 Alasdair Sandford, 'Brexit Trade Deal: Nine Claims by Boris Johnson or His Ministers that Are Untrue', *Euronews*, 6 January 2021; 'Future of UK Finance: City of London Faces Uncertainty under EU–UK Trade Deal', *YouTube – Euronews*, 1 January 2021; Hamre and Wright, 'Brexit and the City', *New Financial*, April 2021.

103 *Observer*, editorial, 'Spin Can't Hide the Grim Effect of Brexit on British Trade', 14 March 2021; Caitlin Hutchinson, 'Londonderry: Police Attacked and Children as Young as 12 Involved in Disturbances in Northern Ireland', *Herald*, 5 April 2021; *Guardian*, editorial, 'Boris Johnson's Duty in Northern Ireland Is to Respect Treaties', 18 March 2021; Rory Carroll, 'Clashes Reflect Young Loyalists' Fear of Being Marginalised over Brexit "Concessions"', *Guardian*, 6 April 2021.

104 *BBC News*, Health, The Visual and Data Journalism Team, 'Covid Vaccine: How Many People in the UK Have Been Vaccinated So Far?' 2 April 2021, https://www.bbc.co.uk/news/health-55274833.

105 Richard Partington, 'Economy Set to Grow at Fastest Rate since 1941', *Guardian*, 26 April 2021.

106 Keir Starmer, '"We Must Be Bold and End the Idea that Inequality Is Inevitable … Let's Get Britain Working Again"', *Observer*, 4 April 2021; Josh Halliday, 'Hartlepool Byelection Poll Sounds Alarm Bells for Labour', *Guardian*, 7 April 2021.

107 Martin Kettle, 'Starmer Has a Second Shot at Making a Good First Impression', *Guardian*, 1 April 2021.

108 See the *Scottish Daily Express*, the *Daily Mail* and the *Daily Telegraph*, 27 January 2021.

109 Katy Balls, '"Feathers Have Been Ruffled"; Life after Cummings at No. 10', *Spectator*, 22 January 2021; *Observer*, editorial, 'The Observer View on Emerging from Covid Lockdown', 28 March 2021.

110 Peter Walker and Aubrey Allegretti, 'Cummings Hits Back with Astonishing Attack on PM', *Guardian*, 24 April 2021.

111 Aubrey Allegretti, Jessica Elgot and Rajeev Syal, 'PM's Fury as Watchdog Launches Inquiry into "Cash for Curtains"', *Guardian*, 29 April 2021.

112 Peter Walker, 'Post-Cummings Quiet Life Goes to Pot as "No 10 Sources" Leak and Brief', *Guardian*, 23 April 2021.

113 *ITV News*, 'Peston's Politics', Robert Peston, 'Boris Johnson "Did Make Bodies Piled High in Their Thousands" Comment', 26 April, 2021; Jessica Elgot and Robert Booth, 'Pressure Mounts on Johnson Over Alleged "Let the Bodies Pile High" Remarks', *Guardian*, 26 April 2021; Gordon Rayner, '"Let the Bodies Pile High". What Really Happened on Night Boris Johnson was Accused of Outburst', *Daily Telegraph*, 27 April 2021.

114 Aubrey Allegretti, '"Chatty Rat": How the Blame Game Unfolded', *Guardian*, 26 April 2021; Ian Sample, 'Virus Fallout: What the Cummings Row Is About', *Guardian*, 27 April 2021.

115 Robert Booth, 'Outrage as No 10 Rules Out Urgent Inquiry into Pandemic Mistakes', *Guardian*, 26 April 2021; Jessica Elgot and Robert Booth, 'Pressure on Johnson after Claim of Slur on Covid Dead', *Guardian*, 27 April 2021.

116 Kalyeena Makortoff, '"Timeline of a Scandal; How Cameron Lobbied for Finance Firm', *Guardian*, 24 April 2021.

117 Rajeev Syal, 'Greensill had no Contract for His Downing Street Role, MPs Are Told', *Guardian*, 27 April 2021.

118 Seth Thevoz, 'David Cameron Then and Now: How the Ex-PM Changed his Tune on Lobbying', *Open Democracy UK: News*, 12 April 2021.

119 Josh Halliday, Helen Pidd, Steven Morris, 'Local Elections: Poll Lead Falls, but Tories Insist Voters Not Concerned By Sleaze', *Guardian*, 27 April 2021; Toby Helm, Robyn Vinter, Michael Savage, 'Tory Poll Lead Slashed as Key Elections Loom Across Britain', *Observer*, 2 May 2021; Toby Helm and Robyn Vinter, 'Labour Hopes Tory Sleaze Will Lift Its 'Red Wall' Vote. In Dudley, They're Not So Sure', *Observer*, 2 May 2021.

120 See the *Guardian*, 8 May 2021, for the following: Heather Stewart and Peter Walker, 'Labour in Turmoil after Tories Inflict Huge Defeats'; Heather Stewart, 'How Did a Tory Triumph in Another Former Red Wall Seat? It Was Jabs, Jobs and Hope'; Aditya Chakrabortty, 'The Answer to Labour's Losses Won't Be Found in Focus Groups'; Robert Ford, 'Labour Has Tried to Move On from Brexit . . . But English Voters Just Won't Let Them', *Observer*, 9 May 2021.

121 Richard Partington, 'UK Set for Strongest Growth since Wartime, Says Bank', *Guardian*, 7 May 2021.

122 Jonathan Freedland, 'The Charge Sheet that Should Have Felled Johnson Years Ago', *Guardian*, 1 May 2021; *Channel Four News*, 27 May 2021. Habermas, *Legitimation Crisis*, pp. 46–8, 68–75.

123 For examples, see Aditya Chakrabortty, 'Anyone Who Trusts Johnson to "Level Up" the UK is Deluded', *Guardian*, 14 October 2021.

Chapter 4

1 Devine, *Independence or Union*, pp. 232, 237–41; *BBC1 Scotland*, 'Yes/No Inside the Indyref', episode 2, 'From the Date to the Debates', 29 August 2019, episode 3, 'Down to the Wire', 5 September 2019; Peter Geoghegan, *The People's Referendum: Why Scotland Will Never Be the Same Again* (Edinburgh: Luath Press, 2015), p. 140.

2 Cameron, *For the Record*, pp. 315–19, 552–7; Geoghegan, *People's Referendum,* p. 55.

3 Devine, *Independence or Union*, p. 241.

4 Jim Gallagher, 'Making the Case for Union: Exactly Why Are We Better Together?', ch. 6 in Aileen McHarg, Tom Mullen, Alan Page, Neil Walker, *The Scottish Independence Referendum: Constitutional and Political Implications* (Oxford: Oxford University Press, 2016); John Lloyd, *Should Auld Acquaintance Be Forgot: The Great Mistake of Scottish Independence* (Cambridge, Polity Press, 2020). See the excellent reviews of Lloyd's book by Tom Devine (*Herald*, 28 March 2020) and Jim Phillips (*Scottish Labour History*, 55, 2020), 262–7. See also *Better Together Ephemera* (PB9.215.25), *Conservative Friends of the Union* (PB9.215.29/3), *Scotland Says Naw* (PB9.215.30/9), *Conservative Party* (PB9.215.29/4), *Scottish Labour Party Ephemera* (PB9.215. 29/5) in the *2014 Scottish Independence Referendum Collection* (SIRC), National Library of Scotland (NLS), Edinburgh.

5 Cameron, *For the Record*, p. 550; HM Treasury, 'Why Scotland Is Better Off as Part of the UK', 19 June 2014, www.gov.uk/news; *BBC1*, 'From Date to Debates'.

6 Gallagher, 'Making the Case', pp. 143–4; HM Treasury, 'Why Scotland Is Better Off'; *Conservative Friends of the Union*; Devine, *Independence or Union*, p. 239.

7   Gallagher, 'Making the Case', pp. 144–6.
8   Lord Ashcroft, 'How Scotland Voted and Why', *Lord Ashcroft Polls*, 19 September 2014; *Conservative Friends of the Union*; *Scottish Labour Party Ephemera*.
9   Gallagher, 'Making the Case', p. 136; HM Treasury, 'Why Scotland Is Better Off'.
10 *Better Together News*, 'Let's Stay United – Fergie', 18 September 2014 (PB9.215.25, 2) SIRC.
11 Ashcroft, 'How Scotland Voted'. For the continuing and overriding importance of the idea of democratic self-determination see, for example, the Letters page (Roger Read, Val Machin, Alastair McLeish), *Guardian*, 12 February 2021.
12 Ashcroft, 'How Scotland Voted'.
13 Devine, *Independence or Union*, p. 207; Colin Kidd and Malcolm Petrie, 'The Independence Referendum in Historical and Political Context', ch. 2 in McHarg, Mullen, Page, Walker, *Scottish Independence Referendum* (p. 45).
14 Geoghegan, *People's Referendum*, p. 131; Gordon Brown, 'The Britain of Emma Raducanu Shows Why Nationalists Are Losing the Argument', *New Statesman*, 16 September 2021; Rory Scothorne, 'Why Gordon Brown's "New Britain" Doesn't Feel Like a Home for Scotland', *New Statesman*, 21 September 2021; Gerry Hassan, 'The Myth of Brown's Britain', *Sunday National*, 3 October 2021.
15 Geoghegan, *People's Referendum*, p. 166; *BBC*, 'From Date to Debates'.
16 Cameron, *For the Record*, pp. 303–4, 313, 315, 318, 549, 556.
17 See, for example, Gordon Brown, 'Boris Johnson Blames Devolution, But in Truth He's Long Been Hostile to Scotland', *Guardian*, 20 November 2020.
18 Devine, *Independence or Union*, pp. 184, 251–3.
19 Geoghegan, *People's Referendum*, pp. 140, 165. For the most recent, left-wing and pro-independence critique of the SNP government, see Neil Davidson, James Foley, and Ben Wray, *Scotland After Britain* (London: Verso, 2022).
20 *Scottish Government Ephemera* (PB9.215.28/10); *Scottish National Party* (PB9.215.29/6), SIRC.
21 *Women for Independence* (PB9.215.31/6), SIRC.
22 *Labour for Independence* (PB9.215. 30/13), SIRC.
23 Devine, *Independence or Union*, pp. 242–4.
24 Geoghegan, *People's Referendum*, p. 148.
25 Geoghegan, *People's Referendum*, pp. 142, 147.
26 Devine, *Independence or Union*, pp. 247–8; Thomas, A.W. Stewart, 'The Labour Party and the Rise of Scottish Nationalism in Dundee since the 1990s', paper presented to the 'Labour and Nationalism' conference of the UK Society for the Study of labour History, University of Huddersfield, May 2018. I am grateful to the author for sending me a copy of his paper.
27 Gallagher, 'Making the Case', pp. 146–7; Geoghegan, *People's Referendum*, pp. 13, 20, 34, 53–4, 156–8; 165–6; Stewart, 'Labour Party in Dundee'; Devine, *Independence or Union*, pp. 225, 248–51.
28 Devine, *Independence or Union*, pp. 249–51.
29 Devine, *Independence or Union*, p. 250.
30 Devine, *Independence or Union*, pp. 247–53; Geoghegan, *People's Referendum*, p. 55, 79–80, 138–9, 150–4.
31 Geoghegan, *People's Referendum*, pp. 163, 165; Devine, *Independence or Union*, p. 147.
32 *BBC1 Scotland*, 'Yes/No Inside the Indyref'.
33 Geoghegan, *People's Referendum*, p. 10; Devine, *Independence or Union*, p. 257.

34 Devine, *Independence or Union*, 240, 257, 261–2; Fiona Simpkins, 'The Conflicting Loyalties of the Scottish Labour Party', in Emmanuelle Avril and Yann Beliard (eds), *Labour United and Divided from the 1830s to the Present* (Manchester: Manchester University Press, 2018), pp. 238–9, 249.

35 The *National* started publication on 24 November 2014. It's first editorial was entitled 'Welcome to the Daily Newspaper that Supports Independence'.

36 Nicola Sturgeon, '"The Tectonic Plates in Scottish Politics Have Shifted Decisively"', *National*, 9 May 2015.

37 Sturgeon, 'Tectonic Plates'; idem, 'We, the Scottish People, Cannot Now Be Ignored', *Guardian*, 9 May 2015; Tom Clark, 'How a Historic Tide of Political Change Swept Away All Before It'; *Guardian*, 'Election 2015 Results', 9 May 2015; Marina Hyde, 'A Lesson from the World of Showbiz: When You're Hot, You're Hot', *Guardian*, 29 April 2015; *Guardian*, editorial, 'A Divided Country Has Spoken. David Cameron Must Raise His Game This Time around', 9 May 2015.

38 Devine, *Independence or Union*, pp. 258–9; Geoghegan, *People's Referendum*, pp. 169–70.

39 Devine, *Independence or Union*, pp. 256–7. In retrospect Cameron wished that he had left the 'longstanding' issue of 'English Votes for English Laws' until the Conservatives' September party conference. As he wrote in *For the Record* (p. 555), 'Friday, 19 September 2014 was a day for magnanimity, nothing more'.

40 Sturgeon, 'We the Scottish People'; 'Cameron in Vow to Bring in Agreed Devolution to Nation "As Fast as I Can"', *National*, 9 May 2015.

41 I am extremely grateful to them all for their interesting and illuminating responses. For further information please contact the author at n.kirk@mmu.ac.uk.

42 See the various 'Electoral Communications from the ALBA Party' in the run-up to the May election. See Severin Carrell, 'Resistance to Referendum "Will Crumble" If Scots Back It – Salmond', *Guardian*, 7 April 2021.

43 Judith Duffy, 'The End of the Union Is Nigh – Killed by Johnson and Covid', *Sunday National*, 27 December 2020.

44 Tom Devine, 'Reflections on 2020', Part One: 'Pandemic and Brexit', *Sunday National*, 27 December 2020. See also Judith Duffy, 'Record Level of Scots Believe Yes Would Win in Referendum', *Sunday National*, 11 October 2020; Eve Livingston, 'Young Scots Rally to Independence – But Doubts Linger over Scale of Shift in Opinion', *Observer*, 18 October 2020; *ITV*, 'News at Ten' and *STV*, 'Scotland Tonight', 14 October 2020.

45 *Guardian*, editorial, 'This Deeply Flawed, Unscrutinised Deal Is a Bad Start to a New Era', 31 December 2020.

46 Gerry Hassan, 'Taking Back Control: The Rise of People Power in Scotland', *Sunday National*, 12 January 2020; Nan Spowart, 'Thousands Descend on Inverness for Highlands and Islands Indy March', 26 January 2020; Devine, 'Pandemic and Brexit'; Andrew Learmonth, 'Sir John Curtice's Social Attitudes Survey Reveals Huge Shift in Indy Support', *National*, 3 November 2020; Gerry Hassan, 'Independence: The New Normal', *Sunday National*, 18 October 2020; Laura Webster, 'Nicola Sturgeon: Scotland Will Be Back Soon, Europe', *National*, 1 January 2021; Severin Carrell and Rory Carrell, 'Holyrood and Stormont Reject "Disastrous" Brexit Trade Deal', *Guardian*, 30 December 2020.

47 Gary Flockhart, 'BBC Poll Suggests Nicola Sturgeon's Government Has Handled Covid-19 Pandemic Better than Boris Johnson', *Scotsman*, 19 November 2020.

48 Peter Davidson, 'Nicola Sturgeon Responds after Jeane Freeman Admits Covid "Mistake" in Transferring Patients to Care Homes', *Daily Record*, 9 April 2021; Conor

Hatchett, 'SNP "Catastrophically Failed" Residents as Care Home Death Figures Published', *The Scotsman*, 19 April 2021; Adam Gordon, 'Government "Negligent" on Care Homes', *West Highland Free Press*, 23 April 2021; Simon Murphy, '"Cummings Should Have Quit", Says Scottish Tory Leader', *Guardian*, 26 October 2020; *Guardian*, editorial, 'Once Again, the Prime Minister Is Fatally Behind the Coronavirus Curve', 5 January 2021; James Foley, 'Lockdown Return Highlights Deeper Failings', *Commonweal, Source Direct*, 5 January 2021; John Harris, 'The Covid Crisis Is Hastening the Breakup of the UK', *Guardian*, 24 August 2020.

49 David Connett, 'Boris Johnson Would Lose Majority and Seat in Election Tomorrow – Poll', *Guardian*, 2 January 2021.

50 Michael Savage, 'Boris Johnson Should Resign as Prime Minister, 45% of People Tell Survey', *Observer*, 10 January 2021.

51 Conrad Duncan, 'Labour Opens Up a 4-point Lead over Tories as Approval of Boris Johnson's Covid Response Plunges', *Independent*, 17 January 2021; Andrew Rawnsley, 'Why Senior Labour Figures Think Their Party Needs to Start Upping Its Game', *Observer*, 17 January 2021.

52 *Channel Four News*, 25 September 2020.

53 Damien Gayle, 'UK at Risk of Becoming Failed State, Says Gordon Brown', *Guardian*, 25 January 2021.

54 Devine, 'Looking Ahead to 2021', Part Two, 'Trump and Independence', *Sunday National*, 3 January 2021; Duffy, 'Johnson Has Been the "Best Recruiting Sergeant Ever" for Independence', *Sunday National*, 22 November 2020.

55 Michael Keating, *State and Nation in the United Kingdom: The Fractured Union* (Oxford: Oxford University Press, 2021).

56 Kathleen Nutt, 'Independence Is Our Only Protection', *National*, 10 September 2020.

57 *Guardian*, editorial, 'Covid, Brexit and Boris Johnson Leave the UK's Fate on the Edge', 30 December 2020; Kathleen Nutt, 'New Plan B Backed by Cherry Set for Conference', *Sunday National*, 8 November 2020; Xander Richards, 'Boris Johnson Slammed for Claim Devolution Is "Disaster North of Border"', *National*, 16 November 2020; Andrew Learmonth, 'Boris Johnson "Caught Red-handed" in Contempt for Scottish People', *National*, 18 November 2020; Angus Cochrane, 'Boris Johnson: I'm Not to Blame for Surge in Support for Scottish Independence', *National*, 4 October 2020.

58 Kathleen Nutt, 'New Plan B'; idem, '"Obscene" Veto on Scottish Independence Vote Will See Tories "Swept Away"', *National*, 4 January 2021.

59 Andrew Learmonth, 'Keir Starmer Claims PM Saying Yes to Indyref2 Would Be "Irresponsible"', *National*, 22 December 2020; Lesley Riddoch, 'Why Keir Starmer's Dismissal of Independence Referendum Was a Poor Show', *Scotsman*, 11 January 2021.

60 Devine, 'Looking Ahead to 2021'; John McLelllan, 'The Case for Postponing Indyref Vote Is Getting Stronger', *Scotsman*, 9 January 2021; James Foley, 'One More Time', *Source Direct*, 11 January 2021; Kirsteen Paterson, 'Nicola Sturgeon Pledges to Deliver Indyref2 Amid Demands for Vote Call-off', *National*, 6 January 2021; Mark McLaughlin, 'Independence Is Essential to Recovery Insists John Swinney', *The Times*, 11 January 2021.

61 For a succinct account of the potential economic strengths and problems facing an independent Scotland see Larry Elliott, 'Sturgeon Can Promise to Spend Big Knowing It Is Still the Treasury Footing the Bill', *Guardian*, 3 May 2021; Gerry Hassan, 'Independence: A Story about All of Us', *Sunday National*, 6 December 2020; Lloyd, *Should Auld Acquaintance*.

62 Hassan, 'Independence'; Andrew Learmonth, 'Sir John Curtice's Social Attitudes Survey Reveals Huge Shift in Indy Support', *National*, 3 November 2020.

63 Learmonth, 'Sir John Curtice'; Larry Elliott, 'Double-dip Will Be the Likely Outcome of the Great Hibernation', *Guardian*, 9 January 2021; *Guardian*, editorial, 'It Is the Real Economy, Mr Sunak, that Needs Rescuing Not the City', 12 January 2021; Richard Partington, 'UK Economy Hit by the Biggest Annual Decline in 300 Years', *Guardian*, 13 February 2021.

64 *Sunday National*, editorial, 'Blueprint for an Independent Nation Becoming Crucial', 17 January 2021; idem, 'An independence Referendum Is a Right – and a Necessity', 24 January 2021; idem, 'Indyref2 Campaign Has Started, It's Time to Get to Work', 14 February 2021.

65 *Sunday National*, editorials, 17, 24 January, 14 February 2021; *BBC News*, 'Scotland Politics', 24 January 2021; Libby Brooks, 'Sturgeon to Seek Independence Vote if SNP Wins Majority in May', *Guardian*, 25 January 2021; Judith Duffy, 'Countdown for Bill to Pave Way for Indy Referendum', *Sunday National*, 14 February 2021. *Commonweal* was prominent among those pro-independence organizations raising doubts upon the SNP leadership's actual commitment to Indyref2. See, for example, the two pieces by James Foley, 'One More Time', and 'Johnson's Jaunt: Kamikaze Unionism?', in *Source Direct*, 11 January 2021 and 28 January 2021.

66 Judith Duffy, 'Scottish Labour Ditch Plans to Discuss Support for Second Independence Referendum', *National*, 12 January 2020; Gerry Hassan, 'The Problem Is Scottish Labour, Not the Leader', *Sunday National*, 17 January 2021; Simpkins, 'The Conflicting Loyalties of the Scottish Labour Party', p. 239; James Foley, 'Slabbed through the Heart', *Commonweal*, *Source Direct*, 15 January 2021; Ben Wray, 'Slabification is the Disease which No Leader Has a Cure for', *Commonweal*, *Source Direct*, 3 September 2020; Laura Webster, 'Richard Leonard Quits as Scottish Labour Leader after 3 Years in Role', *National*, 14 January 2021; Severin Carrell, 'Scottish Labour Leader Richard Leonard Steps Down', *Guardian*, 14 January 2021.

67 Peter Walker, Severin Carrell, 'Post-Brexit Red Tape Is New Threat to Fishing Industry, Tory MPs Say', *Guardian*, 15 January 2021.

68 Peter Walker and Heather Stewart, 'Oliver Lewis Quits as Head of No 10's Union Unit after Two Weeks', *Guardian*, 19 February 2021.

69 Martin Kettle, 'Johnson's Bid to Save the Union', *Guardian*, 26 January 2021; Kathleen Nutt, 'Gimmicks and Symbolism Won't Be Enough to Save the Union, Former First Minister Tells Bungling Boris', *Sunday National*, 31 January 2021; *Sunday National*, editorial, 'Indyref2 Campaign'; Duffy, 'Countdown for Bill'; *Statista*, Coronavirus (Covid-19) Deaths Worldwide per One Million Population as of February 16, 2021, https://www.statista.com/statistics/1104709/coronavirus-deaths-worldwide-per-million-inhabitants/; *STV*, 'Scotland Tonight', 8 February 2021.

70 See the *Sunday National*, 7 February 2021 for divisions within the SNP, especially the 'Special Report' by Kirsteen Paterson and Judith Duffy; Severin Carrell, 'What Exactly Is the Alex Salmond Controversy All About?', *Guardian*, 11 January 2021; Libby Brooks and Severin Carrell, 'Joanna Cherry Sacking Brings Trans Rights Row Off Twitter and into the Light', *Guardian*, 5 February 2021; *ITV*, 'Scotland Tonight', 8 February 2021; *Guardian*, editorial, 'The Salmond v Sturgeon War Is about More than Just a Power Struggle', 26 February 2021; Andrew Learmonth, 'Alex Salmond Claims Senior SNP Staff Plotted to Have Him Imprisoned', *National*, 22 February 2021.

71 James Foley, 'Scotland-Now?', *Commonspace, Source Direct*, 3 February 2021.

72 Neil Pooran, 'Independence Would Hit Scottish Economy Harder than Brexit, *Scotsman*, 3 February 2021.

73 Judith Duffy, 'More than 1k Join Now Scotland', *Sunday National*, 7 February 2021.

74 See Dani Garavelli, 'Sturgeon Still Faces Questions – But This Marks a Fresh Start', *Guardian*, 24 March 2021; Severin Carrell, 'Sturgeon Cleared of Breaching Code over Alex Salmond Inquiry', *Guardian*, 23 March 2021; Richard Mason, 'MSPs Vote Against Motion of No Confidence in Nicola Sturgeon', *National*, 23 March 2021.

75 Severin Carrell and Libby Brooks, 'Nicola Sturgeon Accused of Misleading Parliament over Alex Salmond', *Guardian*, 23 March 2021; Simon Johnson, 'Nicola Sturgeon Misled Parliament, Holyrood Inquiry Concludes', *Daily Telegraph*, 23 March 2021; Libby Brooks, 'What Did Report that Cleared Sturgeon of Misleading Scottish Parliament Say?', *Guardian*, 22 March 2021.

76 Nicola Sturgeon, 'UK Government Should Not Overturn a Free and Fair Election', *Observer*, 25 April 2021.

77 Libby Brooks, '"I Feel Stronger". Sturgeon Looks Beyond Covid-19 and Salmond', *Guardian*, 12 April 2021; Neal Ascherson, 'Is Time Running Out for the Union as the Case Grows for a New Independence Vote?', *Observer*, 18 April 2021; See Nicola Sturgeon, 'It is Essential We Take the Right Path', *National*, 4 April 2021; Libby Brooks, 'Scotland at the Crossroads', 2 May 2021; Nicola Sturgeon, 'UK Government Should Not Overturn a Free and Fair Election', *Observer*, 25 April 2021; idem, 'Fear Risks Holding Us Back ... Vision Can Drive Us Forward', *National*, 2 May 2021; Severin Carrell, 'Resistance to Referendum "Will Crumble" If Scots Back It – Salmond', *Guardian*, 7 April 2021; Libby Brooks and Jessica Elgot, 'PM Will Allow Second Referendum if SNP Wins, Says Sturgeon', *Guardian*, 11 April 2021.

78 John Curtice on *BBC Scotland*, 'The Campaign', 3 May 2021; Kathleen Nutt, 'Johnson Says Only Tories Can Stop SNP as He Attacks Labour', *National*, 15 March 2021; David Clegg, 'For Alex Salmond and His New Alba Party, the Prospects Are Not Looking Good', *Guardian*, 3 April 2021; Judith Duffy, 'Salmond: Yes Campaign Has Been 'Reborn' after Launch of Alba Party', *Sunday National*, 4 April 2021; Richard Mason and Angus Cochrane, 'Poll Predicts Tories Will Be Biggest Losers as Holyrood Gets 29-seat Yes Majority', *National*, 5 April 2021; Laura Webster, 'Scottish Election: SNP on Track to Win Majority in Latest Ipsos MORI Poll', *National*, 7 April 2021; Brooks, 'Scotland at Crossroads'; James Foley, 'A Yes Slump?', *Source Direct*, 30 April 2021; Andy Gregory, 'Nicola Sturgeon Claims She Alone Offers "Serious Leadership" as Poll Says SNP on Course for Holyrood Majority', *Independent*, 2 May 2021; Caitlin Hutchison, 'Scottish Election 2021: Who Do You Think Won the BBC Leaders' Debate?', *Herald*, 4 May 2021; Jody Harrison, 'Scottish Election: Final Opinion Polls Suggest SNP on Course for a Majority', *Herald*, 5 May 2021. See also the *National*, 6 May 2021, especially the articles by Kathleen Nutt ('FM Vows to Let Scotland Choose after Covid Crisis'), Nicola Sturgeon ('A Vote for the SNP is a Vote for the Chance to Decide Scotland's Future as an Independent Country') and Gregor Young ('Hopes of an SNP Majority Rest with Nine Key Seats').

79 Kathleen Nutt, 'Sturgeon Tells PM: Scotland Has Voted for Indyref2'; Judith Duffy, 'The Story of the Green Campaign', *Sunday National*, 9 May 2021.

80 Libby Brooks, '"When, Not If": Sturgeon's Challenge to Johnson on Fresh Independence Vote', *Guardian*, 10 May 2021; Kirsteen Paterson, Kathleen Nutt, Abbi Garton, 'The Inside Story of the SNP Campaign', *Sunday National*, 9 May 2021.

81 Libby Brooks, 'Rejection of Salmond Reinforces Diversity Shift', *Guardian*, 10 May 2021; Martin Hannan, 'What Went Wrong with Alex Salmond's Alba Campaign, and What Comes Next?', *National*, 8 May 2021.

82 Gordon Brown, 'Many Scots Want a Better Union, Rather than Independence', *Guardian*, 10 May 2021.

83 David Edgerton and Kirsty Hughes, 'Brexit, Ideology and the Decline of the British State', Scottish Centre on European Relations, Podcast, 14 April 2021. For the situation in Wales, where between 25 per cent and 30 per cent are predicted to vote yes in a referendum on Welsh independence, see Richard Wyn Jones, 'Is Wales Following Scotland in a Bid for Independence?', *Guardian*, 26 April 2022. In Northern Ireland Sinn Fein is 'in pole position' to overtake the DUP and become 'the largest single party in the devolved government'. See Lisa O'Carroll, 'Could a Sinn Fein Win Be a Tipping Point for Northern Ireland?', *Guardian*, 26 April 2022.

84 Elliott, 'Sturgeon Can Promise to Spend Big'; Libby Brooks, 'Scotland's Finance Chief Says Soaring Deficit Is No Barrier to Independence', *Guardian*, 19 August 2021; Gerry Hassan, 'Kenmure Street Is Wake-up Call to Plan How We Will Win Indyref', *National*, 16 May 2021.

Chapter 5

1   See Heather Stewart, 'Boris Johnson's Resignation Speech: What He Said and What He Meant', *Guardian*, 7 July 2022'; Martin Farrer, '"PM's Long Goodbye": What the Papers Said about Boris Johnson's Sort-of Resignation', *Guardian*, 8 July 2022.

2   Martin Kettle, 'A Post-Johnson Era Is Emerging: It Looks Like a Big Lurch to the Right', *Guardian*, 11 August 2022; Peter Walker, 'Lurch to the Right: Tory Stance May Be Out of Step with Many Voters', *Guardian*, 1 August 2022.

3   Larry Elliott, Phillip Inman, Heather Stewart, 'Bank Raises Rates and Warns of 13% Inflation', *Guardian*, 5 August 2022; Nick Cohen, '"All In It Together"? Even that Pretence has Gone – Sacrifice Is Now for the Workers', *Observer*, 3 July 2022; Polly Toynbee, 'Would-be Tory Leaders Won't Face Up to the Dire State of the NHS', *Guardian*, 26 July 2022.

4   See Chapter 3 above, p. 126.

5   Josh Halliday, 'Scandal and After Scandal: Timeline of Tory Sleaze under Boris Johnson', *Guardian*, 1 July 2022.

6   John Besley, 'Why Is There Criticism of the Prime Minister's Social Care Reform Plan?', *Evening Standard*, 6 September 2021.

7   Aubrey Allegretti, 'MP Owen Paterson Faces Suspension for Breaking Lobbying Rules', *Guardian*, 26 October 2021. For Major and the *Observer*, see *Observer*, editorial, 'The *Observer* View on No 10's Handling of the Owen Paterson Affair', 7 November 2021.

8   The Editorial Board, 'Boris Johnson's Broken Promises to Northern England', *The Financial Times*, 21 November 2021.

9   *BBC News*, Science and Environment, 'What Was Agreed at the Glasgow Climate Conference?', 15 November 2021, https://www.bbc.co.uk/news/science-environment-56901261; *Guardian*, editorial, 'The Verdict on the Prime Minister Will Be Shaped by the Economy Too', 13 November 2021; Michael Savage, 'Labour Records First Poll Lead over Tories since January', *Guardian*, 13 November 2021; Toby Helm and Michael Savage, 'Has Boris Crashed the Tory Car?', *Observer*, 21 November 2021; Aubrey Allegretti, Rowena Mason, Joanna Partridge, 'Johnson Is "Losing the Confidence" of Tory Party', *Guardian*, 23 November 2021.

10 Dominic Penna and Lucy Fisher, 'Boris Johnson Suffers Huge Rebellion as Almost 100 Tory MPs Vote Against Covid Passports', *Daily Telegraph*, 14 December 2021;

Allison Pearson, 'Jab Passports Are a Chilling Betrayal of Tory Values', *Daily Telegraph*, 15 December 2021.

11 *BBC News*, 'Politics', 'Allegra Stratton Resigns over No 10 Christmas Party Video' and Laura Kuenssberg, 'Far from Over', 8 December 2021, https://www.bbc.co.uk/news/uk-politics-59584736.

12 *BBC News*, 'Politics', 'Top Civil Servant Simon Case Quits No 10 Party Probe Amid Rule Breach Claims', 18 December 2021, https://www.bbc.co.uk/news/uk-politics-59701369.

13 Toby Helm, 'Labour Races to Nine-point Lead in Polls in Wake of Sleaze Controversies at No 10', *Guardian*, 11 December 2021. Madeline Grant, 'Conservative Grassroots Will Never Forgive Boris', *Daily Telegraph*, 15 December 2021; Jedidajah Otte, '"Self-inflicted Wounds": Press Verdict on Tories' North Shropshire Loss', *Guardian*, 17 December 2021.

14 Heather Stewart, '"It's Like the Wizard of Oz" – Frost's Exit Reveals PM as Isolated and Exposed', *Guardian*, 20 December 2021.

15 Martin Kettle, 'No Amount of "Reboots" Can Hide the Truth: Johnson Is Finished', *Guardian*, 9 February 2022; Eleni Courea, 'Johnson Is Hanging by a Thread', *New York Times*, 1 February 2022.

16 Heather Stewart and Peter Walker, 'Munira Mirza: Boris Johnson's "Powerful Nonsense Detector"', *Guardian*, 3 February 2022.

17 Ashley Cowburn, 'Boris Johnson Sang "I Will Survive" to New No 10 Communications Chief', *Independent*, 7 February 2022; Jill Lawless, 'Boris Johnson Says Sorry after Report Slams Lockdown Parties', *ABC News*, 31 January 2022; *YouTube*, 'Partygate: Boris Johnson's Repeated Denials and Excuses', 12 April 2022; Peter Walker, 'Sue Gray Report: Full Breakdown of Findings about No 10 Parties', *Guardian*, 25 May 2022.

18 Rowena Mason and Heather Stewart, 'Crisis Helping PM to Leave Partygate Woes Behind', *Guardian*, 19 March 2022; Robert Ford, 'Going, Going – But Still Not a Goner', *Observer*, 17 April 2022.

19 Rowena Mason, Heather Stewart, Aubrey Allegretti, 'Johnson Blamed for Tory Election Woes', *Guardian*, 7 May 2022; *UK Parliament: House of Commons Library*, 'Local Elections 2022: Results and Analysis', 13 May 2022, https://commonslibrary.plmt.uk/research-briefings/cbp-9545; *Institute for Government*, 'Did Labour Win Back Lost Ground in Scotland and Wales?, https://www.institutefor government.org.uk/publication/elections-2022/labour-scotland-wales; *BBC Radio Four*, 'World at One', 6 May 2022 (for John Curtice).

20 See the *National*'s sixteen-page coverage of the elections, 7 May 2022.

21 Lisa O'Carroll, 'Stormont Elections: Could a Sinn Fein Win Be a Tipping Point for Northern Ireland?', *Guardian*, 26 April 2022; Rory Carroll, Lisa O'Carroll, Toby Helm, 'Seismic Sinn Victory Fuels Debate on Future of the Union', *Observer*, 8 May 2022; Lisa O'Carroll and Rory Carroll, 'DUP Says It Is Ready to Stall Power Sharing if Protocol Not Altered', *Guardian*, 9 May 2022; Fintan O'Toole, 'A United Ireland Isn't Coming Soon, but It's Certainly Closer', *Guardian*, Journal, 9 May 2022; Leo Varadkar, 'We Agreed the Protocol in Good Faith. That Is Now in Tatters', *Guardian*, 20 May 2022; Michael Savage, 'Germany and Ireland Denounce PM's Bid to Ditch Northern Ireland Protocol', *Observer*, 3 July 2022.

22 Toby Helm, Michael Savage, Phillip Inman, 'Johnson Is Trashing Tory Identity, Party Grandees Warn', *Observer*, 29 May 2022; Toby Helm, 'Boris Johnson Prays His Number Hasn't Come Up as Tory Grassroots Anger Grows', *Observer*, 5 June 2022.

23 *Channel Four News, News at Ten and Scotland Tonight*, 6 June 2022; *National*, 7 June 2022 (Nicola Sturgeon on Johnson). For a good survey of newspaper reactions, see Martin Farrer, '"Out in a Year": What the Papers Say about Tory Vote on Boris Johnson', *Guardian*, 7 June 2022.

24 Peter Walker, 'Tories Lose Two Key Byelections on Same Night in Wakefield and Tiverton and Honiton', *Guardian*, 24 June 2022.

25 Ben Riley-Smith, 'Tory Rebels Plot Next Move to Oust Boris Johnson', *Daily Telegraph*, 24 June 2022; Tom Airey and Julia Bryson, 'Wakefield By-Election: Labour Win a Great Result, Says Keir Starmer', *BBC News*, 'Leeds and West Yorkshire', 24 June 2022, https://www.bbc.co.uk/uk-england-leeds-61896693.

26 Peter Walker, 'Oliver Dowden Resigns as Conservative Party Chair after Byelection losses', *Guardian*, 24 June 2022; Jack Maidment, Dominic Penna, Nick Gutteridge, Will Bolton, Josh White, 'Defiant Boris Johnson Vows to Fight On after By-elections as Lord Hague Warns of "Disaster"', *Daily Telegraph*, 24 June 2022.

27 Heather Stewart, Aubrey Allegretti, Rowena Mason, 'Boris Johnson's Ethics Adviser Lord Geidt Resigns after Partygate Grilling', *Guardian*, 15 June 2022.

28 Peter Walker, 'Is a Summer of Discontent Looming?', *Guardian*, 21 June 2022.

29 Halliday, 'Scandal after Scandal'; Jamie Doward, 'Revealed: Why Michael Fallon Was Forced to Quit as Defence Secretary', *Observer*, 4 November 2017; *BBC News*, 'Politics', 'Damian Green Sacked after "Misleading Statement" on Porn Claims', 21 December 2017, https://www.bbc.co.uk/news/uk-politics-42434802.

30 Rowena Mason, 'Chris Pincher: A Timeline of Allegations and Investigations', *Guardian*, 4 July 2022; *Firstpost*, 'World', 'Explained: The Chris Pincher Scandal that Rocked UK Politics and Put Boris Johnson's Future in Trouble', 6 July 2022, 10876001.html.

31 Megan Specia, 'The Pincher Scandal Is Only the Latest in a Long Line of Controversies for Johnson', *New York Times*, 7 July 2022.

32 Jessica Murray, '"No Credibility": Pincher's Electors on Disgraced MP', *Guardian*, 26 July 2022.

33 Heather Stewart, Rowena Mason, Jessica Elgot, 'PM on the Brink after Javid and Sunak Quit', 6 July 2022; Dan Sabbagh, '"I Believe Standards Are Worth Fighting For', *Guardian,* 6 July 2022.

34 Stewart, 'Johnson's Resignation Speech'; Farrer, '"PM's Long Good Bye": What the Papers Said'; Heather Stewart and Jessica Elgot, '"It's (Almost) Over', *Guardian*, 8 July 2022; Jason Groves, 'The Long Goodbye', *Scottish Daily Mail*, 8 July; *Scottish Sun*, editorial, 'Humiliating Exit for Boris', 8 July 2022.

35 See Zoe Williams' excellent interview with Mick Lynch, the impressive leader of the National Union of Rail, Maritime and Transport Workers (RMT), 'A Lot of People Tell Me I'm Doing Good', *Guardian*, 'G2', 23 August 2022; Donald Macintyre, 'Why Britain Is Going on Strike', *Observer*, Focus, 28 August 2022.

36 Henry Zeffman, 'Labour Takes Biggest Lead in Ten Years as Cost of Living Crisis Bites', *The Times*, 20 August 2022; Toby Helm, 'Labour Surges amid Tory Fears over Truss's Tax Cut Plans', *Observer*, 21 August 2022; *Guardian*, editorial, 'Sir Keir Starmer's Energy Bills Freeze Is Smart Politics in a Cost of Living Crisis', 16 August 2022.

37 *Guardian*, editorial, 'Starmer Has Strengthened His Team. But He Must Keep the Party's Left on Board', 1 December 2021; Andy Beckett, 'Starmer Must Double Down on This as Tory "Chaos", 70s-Style', *Guardian*, 23 April 2022; Jessica Elgot, 'Back to the Red Wall. Leader Takes to Factory Floor to Win Over Voters', *Guardian*, 16 February 2022.

38 Andrew Rawnsley, 'Keir Starmer Should Learn from How Wilson and Blair Led Labour to Success', *Observer*, 5 December 2021.

39 John Harris, 'The Tories Are Teetering. An Alliance Could Overthrow Them', *Guardian*, 27 June 2022.

40 Kathleen Nutt, 'Support for Independence "Soars" to 55 Per Cent, New Poll Finds', *National*, 1 December 2021; Martin Kettle, 'Sturgeon Is Being Forced to Play the Long Game', *Guardian*, 2 December 2021; Laura Webster, 'Scottish Independence Support on the Rise amid Boris Johnson Chaos, Pollster Finds', *National*, 21 January 2022; Andrew Rawnsley, 'Scotland's Future Won't Be Settled until There Is a Second Referendum', *Observer*, 3 July 2022.

41 Severin Carrell, 'Sturgeon in Bid for New Referendum in Late 2023', *Guardian*, 29 June 2022; Simon Johnson, 'Sturgeon to "Forge Ahead" with Indyref2', *Daily Telegraph*, 15 June 2022; Alyn Smith, 'Why the New Indy Paper Is a Breath of Fresh Air', *National*, 15 June 2022.

42 *Channel Four News*, 28 June 2022; Robbie Mochrie, 'It All Being about the Scottish Economy, Isn't Stupid', *National*, 7 May 2022; Angus Cochrane, 'Scottish Independence: Yes and No Sides "Neck and Neck", Poll Finds', *National*, 30 June 2022; Davidson, Foley, and Wray, *Scotland after Britain*.

43 For Nicola Sturgeon see the Interview with Libby Brooks, 'Onwards and Upwards', *Guardian*, Saturday, 13 August 2022; Craig Meighan, 'Scotland about to "Call a Day" on UK, Insists Sturgeon', *Sunday National*, 14 August 2022.

Bibliography

Primary sources

Archives

Material consulted in SIRC: Better Together ephemera; Better Together News; Conservative Friends of the Union; Conservative Party ephemera; Labour for Independence ephemera; Radical Independence Conference ephemera; Scotland Says Naw ephemera; Scottish Government ephemera; Scottish Labour Party ephemera; Scottish National Party ephemera; Women for Independence.

National Library of Scotland, Edinburgh, UK, The 2014 *Scottish Independence Referendum Collection* (SIRC).

Neville Kirk's Oral History Project, Questionnaires on *The Contemporary Political Revolution in Scotland*, 2016, Skye and Lochalsh Archive Centre, Portree, Isle of Skye.

Newspapers and journals (printed and online)

Australian
Bella Caledonia
Business Insider
Commonspace
Commonweal
Daily Express
Daily Mail
Daily Mail Online
Daily Mirror
Daily Record
Daily Telegraph
Euronews
Evening Standard
Financial Times
Full Fact
Guardian
Herald
Independent
International Express
Labour List
Liverpool Echo
National
National Interest
New Financial

New Statesman
New York Times
Observer
Open Access Government
Open Democracy UK
Policy Exchange
Prospect Magazine
Quarterly Essay
Reuters
Scotsman
Scottish Daily Express
Scottish Daily Mail
Scottish Sun
Source Direct
Spectator
Sun
Sunday Express
Sunday Herald
Sunday National
Sunday Telegraph
Sunday Times
Sydney Morning Herald
Tax Research
The Sunday Times
The Times
Time
UK Pol: Political Speech Archive
Weekend Australian
West Highland Free Press

Other online and media sources

ABC News
Alba Party, 'Electoral Communications' (for the May 2021 Scottish elections)
BBC News
BBC News, 'Business', 'Budget 2017 Reaction and Updates', 22 November 2017, https://www.bbc.co.uk/news/live/business-42026814
BBC News, 'Election 2017', https://www.bbc.co.uk/news/politics/constituencies/S 14000055
BBC News, 'Election 2017', https://www.bbc.co.uk/news/election-2017-40105177
BBC News, 'General Election 2017: SNP Loses a Third of Seats amid Tory Surge', 9 June 2017, https://www.bbc.co.uk/news/uk-scotland-scotland-politics-40192707
BBC News, 'Election 2017', https://www.bbc.co.uk/news/election/2017/results/Scotland
BBC News, 'Conservative Manifesto: Theresa May Targets Mainstream Britain', https://www.bbc.co.uk/news/election-2017-39956541
BBC News, 'Election 2017 Conservative Manifesto Summary: Key Points At-a-glance', https://www.bbc.co.uk/news/election-2017-39960311
BBC News, Election 2017, 'Labour Manifesto At-a-glance: Summary of Key Points', https://www.bbc.co.uk/news/election-2017-39933116

BBC News, Election 2017, 'SNP Manifesto Summary: Key Points At-a-glance', 30 May 2017

BBC News, 'Elections', https://www.bbc.co.uk/news/election/2017/results

BBC News, 'EU Referendum Results', www.bbc.co.uk/news/poltics/eu-referendum/results

BBC News, 'Politics', 25 September 2017, https://www.bbc.co.uk/news/live/uk-politics-41385169

BBC News, 'Scotland's Papers: Tories "Turn on May" and Indyref Election Impact', June 2017, https://www.bbc.co.uk/news/uk-scotland-4023824

BBC News, 'The Papers', 23 November 2017, https://www.bbc.co.uk/news/blogs-the-papers-42090204

BBC News, 'Politics', 'Damian Green Sacked after "Misleading Statement" on Porn Claims', 21 December 2017, https://bbc.co.uk/news/uk-politics-42434802

BBC News, 'A Quick Guide: What Is the Brexit Transition Phase?', 1 February 2018, https://www.bbc.co.uk/news/uk-politics-42906950

BBC News, 'Politics', 'Boris Johnson Challenged Over Brexit Business Expletive', 26 June 2018, https://www.bbc.co.uk/news/uk-politcs-44618154

BBC News, 'At-a-Glance: The New UK Brexit Plan agreed at Chequers', 7 July 2018, https://www.bbc.co.uk/news/uk-politics-44749993

BBC News, 'Brexit: David Davis's Resignation Letter and May's Reply in Full', 9 July 2018, htttps://www.bbc.co.uk/news/uk-politics-44761416

BBC News, 'Boris Johnson's Resignation Letter and May's Reply in Full', 9 July 2018, https://www.bbc.co.uk/news/uk-pols-44772804

BBC News, 'Theresa May Says Its Chequers or No Deal' 17 September 2018, https://www.bbc.co.uk/news/uk-politics-4559083

BBC News, 'Politics', 'Brexit: Dominic Raab and Esther McVey among Ministers to Quit over EU Effect', 15 November 2018, https://bbc.co.uk./news/ek-politics-46219495

BBC News Special on Brexit, 12 December 2018

BBC News, 'Politics', 'Theresa May Sets January Date for MPs' Brexit Vote', 17 December 2018

BBC News, 'Northern Ireland Politics European Elections: Long, Dodds and Anderson Elected', 27 May 2019, https://www.bbc.co.uk/news/uk-northern-ireland-politics-48370936

BBC News, 'EU Elections 2019: SNP to Have Three MEPs as Labour Vote collapses', 27 May 2019, https://www.bbc.co.uk/news/uk-scotland-484174424

BBC News, 'European Election 2019: UK Results in Maps and Charts', 27 May 2019, https://www.bbc.co.uk/news/uk-politics-48403131

BBC News, 'Politics', 'Peterborough By-election: Labour Beats Brexit Party to Hold Seat', 7 June 2019, https://www.bbc.co.uk/news/uk-politics-48532869

BBC News, 'Scotland Politics', 'Scottish Labour Backs Brexit Referendum Policy', 8 June 2019, https://www.bbc.co.uk/news/uk-scotland-politics-48558355

BBC News, 'Politics', 'Boris Johnson Wins Race to Be Tory Leader and Prime Minister', 23 July 2019, https://bbc.co.uk/news/uk-politics-49084605

BBC News, 'Politics', 'Corbyn Wants an Election despite Warning from Tony Blair', 2 September 2019, https://bbc.co.uk/news/uk-politics- 49552403

BBC News, 'Politics', 'UK Set for 12 December General Election', 29 October 2019, https://bbc.co.uk/news/uk-politics -50229318

BBC News, 'Election 2019', 'Labour Party Manifesto 2019: 12 Key Policies Explained', 21 November 2019, https://bbc.co.uk/news/election-2019-50501411

BBC News, 'Election 2019', 'General Election 2019: Boris Johnson and Jeremy Corbyn Clash over Brexit', 6 December 2019

BBC News, 'Election 2019: Results', https://bbc.co.uk/news/election/2019

BBC News, Election 2019, 'Election Results 2019: Analysis in Maps and Charts',
    13 December 2019, https://bbc.co.uk/news/election-2019-50770798

BBC News, 'Election 2019; Results', https://bbc.co.uk/news/election/2019/results/Wales

BBC News, 'Politics', 'General Election 2019: Anna Soubry Disbands Independent Group
    for Change', 19 December 2019, https://bbc.co.uk/news/uk-politics-50858811.

BBC News, UK, 'Coronavirus: Concerns over Boris Johnson's "Moonshot" Testing Plans',
    10 September 2020, https://bbc.co.uk/news/uk-54097050

BBC News, UK, 'Covid: UK at a Critical Point" in Pandemic, Top Scientists to Warn',
    21 September 2020, https://bbc.co.uk/news/uk-54229845

BBC News, Scotland, 'Covid: Scotland to Enter New 5-level Alert System', 23 October 2020,
    https://bbc.co.uk/news, uk-scotland-54661494

BBC News, UK, 'Covid-19: PM Announces Four-week England Lockdown', 31 October
    2020, https://bbc.co.uk/news/uk-54763956

BBC News, 'Health', 'England Covid Tier Rules: What Are the Rules?', 14 December 2020,
    https://bbc.co.uk/news/health -545119652020

BBC News, UK, 'Covid: England's Third National Lockdown Legally Comes into Force',
    6 January 2021, https://bbc.co.uk/news/uk-55554550

BBC News, 'Politics', 'Allegra Stratton Resigns over No 10 Christmas Party Video',
    8 December 2021, https://bbc.co.uk/news/uk-politics-59584736

BBC News, 'Scotland Politics', 24 January 2021

BBC News, 'Business', 'Budget 2021: Rishi Sunak to Extend Furlough Scheme until
    September', 3 March 2021, https://bbc.co.uk/news/business-56259094

BBC News, 'Health, The Visual and Data Journalism Team', 'Covid Vaccine: How Many
    People in the UK Have Been Vaccinated So Far?' 2 April 2021, https://bbc.co.uk/news/
    health-55274833

BBC News, 'Politics', 'Top Civil Servant Simon Case Quits No 10 Probe amid Rule Breach
    Claims', 18 December 2021, https://bbc.c.uk/news/uk-politics-59701369

BBC One, Panorama, 'Britain's Brexit Crisis', 18 July 2019 (Nick Robinson)

BBC One, 'Our Next Prime Minister', 18 June 2019

BBC, Parliament–SNP Conference, 2017, https://www.bbc.co.uk/programmes/b098pkxp

BBC Radio Four, 'World at One'

BBC Scotland

BBC1 Scotland, 'Yes/No Inside the Indyref', episode 2, 'From the Date to the Debates',
    29 August 2019, episode 3, 'Down to the Wire', 5 September 2019

Channel Five, Michael Portillo, 'The Trouble with the Tories', 1, 8 August 2019

Channel Four, 'Farage: The Man Who Made Brexit', 29 January 2020

Channel Four News

European Council, 19–20 October 2017, https://www.consilium.europa.eu/en/meetings/
    european-council/2017/10/19-20

Euronews

Firstpost

Gov.UK, 'PM Speech on Our Future Economic Partnership with the European Union',
    2 March 2018, https://www.gov.uk/government/speeches/pm-speech-on-our-future-
    economic-partnership-with-the-european-union

HM Treasury, 'Why Scotland Is Better Off as Part of the UK', 19 June 2014, www.gov.uk/
    news

Highland Council, 'UK Parliamentary General Election Results 2015', https://www.highland.
    gov.uk/info/799/elections_ and-voting/605uk-parliamentary-general-election/6

Institute for Government, 'Did Labour Win Back Lost Ground in Scotland and Wales?', www.instituteforgovernment.org.uk/publication/elections-2022/labour-scotland-wales

ITV, 'Johnson versus Corbyn; The ITV Debate', 19 November 2019

ITV, News at Ten

ITV, Peston

Joseph Rowntree Foundation

Labour Party, Theresa May's Failed Brexit Plan, 17 September 2018, https://labour.org. uk/.../2018

LSE European Politics and Policy Blog

Office for National Statistics, 'Coronavirus (COVID- 19) in 10 Charts', 24 September 2020.

Politics Home, 'Boris Johnson's Speech to the 2019 Conservative Party Conference, 2 October 2019, www.politicshome.com/news/article

Scottish Government, 'A Nation with Ambition: The Government's Programme for Scotland 2017–2018', 5 September 2017, https://www.gov.scot/publications/nation-ambition-governments-programme-Scotland-2017-18/

Scottish Government, 'COVID-19: Scotland's Strategic Framework Update', February 2021

Scottish Labour Party, election communications, 2017

Scottish Liberal Democrats, election communications, 2017

Scottish National Party, 'Manifesto 2017', https://www.snp. org/manifesto

Scottish National Party, election communications, 2017

STV, 'Scotland Tonight'

Sky News

Source Direct

Special Broadcasting Service (SBS), Australia, World News

Statista

STV, Scotland Tonight

Twitter, Ford, Rob, 'Remain Voters Outnumber Leave Voters among the 2017 Labour Vote in Almost every Labour Leave Seat', https://twitter.com/robfordmancs/status/1114065322120744961

UK Parliament: House of Commons Library, 'Local Elections 2022: Results and Analysis', 13 May 2022, www.commonslibrary.plmt.uk/research-briefing/cbp-9545

YouGov, 'How Britain Voted', 27 June 2016

YouTube, Johnson, Boris, 'The Churchill Factor', *YouTube Politics and Prose*, 22 November 2014

YouTube, Wilson, Andrew, Curtice, John, 'Scottish Currency', *YouTube*, 28 April 2019

Secondary sources

Books, chapters in books, pamphlets, articles, papers

Airey, Tom, and Bryson, Julia, 'Wakefield By-Election: Labour Win a Great Result, says Keir Starmer', *BBC News*, 'Leeds and West Yorkshire', 24 June 2022, https://bbc.co.uk/England-leeds-61896693.

Barnett, Anthony, *The Lure of Greatness: England's Brexit and America's Trump* (London: Unbound, 2017).

Brown, Gordon, 'The Britain of Emma Raducanu Shows Why Nationalists Are Losing the Argument', *New Statesman*, 16 September 2021.

Bulman, May, 'Conservatives to Fall 18 Seats Short of Majority, Latest YouGov Model suggests', *Independent*, 3 June 2017.

Cameron, David, *For the Record* (London: William Collins, 2019).

Cameron, Ewen A., *Impaled upon a Thistle: Scotland since 1880* (Edinburgh: Edinburgh University Press, 2011).

Clarke, Harold D., Goodwin, Matthew, and Whiteley, Paul, *Why Britain Voted to Leave the European Union* (Cambridge, Cambridge University Press, 2017).

Cooper, Hilary and Szreter, Simon, *After the Virus: Lessons from the Past for a Better Future* (Cambridge: Cambridge University Press, 2021).

Crace, John, *I Maybot: The Rise and Fall* (London: Guardian Faber Publishing, 2017).

Crick, Michael, *One Party after Another: The Disruptive Life of Nigel Farage* (London: Simon and Schuster, 2022).

Curtice, John, 'The Campaign', *BBC Scotland*, 3 May 2021.

Davidson, Neil, Foley, James, and Wray, Ben, *Scotland After Britain: The Two Souls of Scottish Independence* (London: Verso, 2022).

Devine, T.M., *Independence or Union: Scotland's Past and Scotland's Present* (London: Allen Lane, 2016).

Eatwell, Roger, and Goodwin, Matthew, *National Populism: The Revolt against Liberal Democracy* (London: Pelican, 2018).

Edgerton, David, *The Rise and Fall of the British Nation: A Twentieth-Century History* (London: Penguin, 2019).

Edgerton, David, and Hughes, Kirsty, 'Brexit, Ideology and the Decline of the British State', Scottish Centre on European Relations, Podcast, 14 April 2021.

Elkins, Caroline, *Legacy of Violence: A History of the British Empire* (London: Bodley Head, 2022).

Esler, Gavin, *How Britain Ends* (London: Head of Zeus, 2021).

Fabbrini, Frederico (ed.), *The Law and the Politics of Brexit* (Oxford: Oxford University Press, 2017).

Ferguson, Sir Alex, 'Let's Stay United – Fergie', *Better Together News*, 18 September 2014 (SIRC).

Ford, Robert, and Goodwin, Matthew, *Revolt on the Right: Explaining Support for the Radical Right in Britain* (London: Routledge, 2014).

Ford, Robert, Bale, Tim, Jennings, Will, and Surridge, Paula, *The British General Election of 2019* (Cham, Switzerland: Palgrave Macmillan, 2021).

Fukuyama, Francis, 'The End of History?', *The National Interest*, 16 (1989), 3–18.

'Future of UK Finance: City of London Faces Uncertainty under EU-UK Trade Deal', *YouTube–Euronews*, 1 January 2021.

Gallagher, Jim, 'Making the Case for Union: Exactly Why Are We Better Together?', in McHarg, Aileen, Mullen, Tom, Page, Alan, Walker, Neil, *The Scottish Independence Referendum: Constitutional and Political Implications* (Oxford: Oxford University Press, 2016).

Gamble, Andrew, *The Spectre at the Feast: Capitalist Crisis and the Politics of Recession* (Basingstoke: Palgrave Macmillan, 2009).

Gamble, Andrew, 'The Resistible Rise of Theresa May', in Mark Perryman, *The Corbyn Effect* (London: Lawrence and Wishart, 2017).

Geoghegan, Peter, *The People's Referendum: Why Scotland Will Never Be the Same Again* (Edinburgh: Luath Press, 2015).

Gibbs, Ewan, *Coal Country: The Meaning and Memory of Deindustrialization in Postwar Scotland* (London: University of London Press, 2021).

Gibbs, Ewan, and Scothorne, Rory, '"Origins of the Present Crisis?" The Emergence of "Left-Wing" Scottish Nationalism', in Smith, Evan, and Worley, Matthew (eds), *Waiting for the Revolution: The British Far Left from 1956* (Manchester: Manchester University Press, 2017).

Goodwin, Matthew J., and Heath, Oliver, 'The 2016 Referendum, Brexit and the Left Behind: An Aggregate-level Analysis of the Result', *Political Quarterly*, 87, 3 (2016), 323–32.

Goodwin, Matthew J., and Heath, Oliver, 'Brexit Vote Explained: Poverty, Low Skills and Lack of Opportunities', *Joseph Rowntree Foundation*, 31 August 2016.

Habermas, Jurgen, *Legitimation Crisis* (Cambridge: Polity Press, 1988 [1973]).

Hamre, Eivind, Friis and Wright, William, 'Brexit and the City: The Impact So Far', *New Financial*, April 2021.

Hassan, Gerry, and Barrow, Simon (eds.), *A Nation Changed? The SNP and Scotland Ten Years On* (Edinburgh: Luath Press, 2017).

Hassan, Gerry, and Shaw, Eric, *The Strange Death of Labour in Scotland* (Edinburgh: Edinburgh University Press, 2012).

Henderson, Ailsa, and Wyn Jones, Richard, *Englishness: The Political Force Transforming Britain* (Oxford: Oxford University Press, 2021).

Hill, Christopher, *The World Turned Upside Down: Radical Ideas During the English Revolution* (London: Penguin, 1991).

Hoare, Quentin and Nowell Smith, Geoffrey (eds), *Selections from the Prison Notebooks of Antonio Gramsci* (London: Lawrence and Wishart, 1973).

Hunt, Alex Hunt, and Wheeler, Brian, 'Brexit: All You Need to Know about the UK Leaving the EU', *BBC News*, 27 September 2018, htttps://www.bbc.co.uk/news/uk-politcs-32810887.

Jackson, Ben, *The Case for Scottish Independence: A History of Nationalist Political Thought in Modern Scotland* (Cambridge: Cambridge University Press, 2020).

Jacques, Martin, *When China Rules the World: The End of the Western World and the Birth of a New Global Order* (London: Penguin, 2012).

Jessop, Bob, 'The Organic Crisis of the British State: Putting Brexit in its Place', *Globalizations*, 14, 1 (2017), 133–41.

Jessop, Bob, *The State: Past Present Future* (Cambridge: Polity Press, 2018).

Johnson, Boris, *The Churchill Factor: How One Man Made History* (London: Hodder and Stoughton, 2014).

Johnson, Boris, 'Third Margaret Thatcher Lecture', Centre for Policy Studies, 28 November 2013.

Jones, Emily, 'The Negotiations', in Fabbrini, Frederico (ed.), *The Law and the Politics of Brexit*, vol. 2, *The Withdrawal Agreement* (Oxford: Oxford University Press, 2020).

Jones, Gareth Stedman, *Karl Marx: Greatness and Illusion* (London: Allen Lane, 2006).

Joyce, Patrick, *Work, Society and Politics: The Culture of the Factory in Later Victorian England* (Brighton: Harvester, 1980).

Keating, Michael, *State and Nation in the United Kingdom: the Fractured Union* (Oxford: Oxford University Press, 2021).

Kidd, Colin, and Petrie, Malcolm, 'The Independence Referendum in Historical and Political Context', in McHarg, Mullen, Page, Walker, *Scottish Independence Referendum*.

Kirk, Neville, *Labour and the Politics of Empire: Britain and Australia 1900 to the Present* (Manchester: Manchester University Press, 2011, 2014).

Kirk, Neville, 'The Election: An Overview', paper given by the author to the Skye SNP branch, 12 June 2017.

Lawrence, Jon, *Me Me Me? The Search for Community in post-War England* (Oxford: Oxford University Press, 2019).

Lloyd, John, *Should Auld Acquaintance Be Forgot: The Great Mistake of Scottish Independence* (Cambridge, Polity Press, 2020).

Lord Ashcroft Polls, 'How Scotland Voted and Why', 19 September 2014.

Lord Ashcroft Polls, 'How Britain Voted and Why: May 2019 General Election Post-vote Poll', 12 December 2019.

Lyons, Gerard, 'To Ensure that the City Continues to Flourish, We Need to Make the Most of Brexit', *Policy Exchange*, 25 February 2022.

MacShane, Denis, *Brexit: How Britain Will Leave Europe* (London: I.B. Taurus, 2015).

Marx, Karl and Engels, Friedrich, *The Communist Manifesto* (London: Penguin, 1970).

Mason, Paul, *PostCapitalism: A Guide to our Future* (London: Allen Lane, 2015).

Mattinson, Deborah, *Beyond the Red Wall: Why Labour Lost, How the Conservatives Won and What Will Happen Next?* (London, Biteback, 2020).

McHarg, Aileen, Mullen, Tom, Page, Alan, and Walker, Neil, *The Scottish Independence Referendum: Constitutional and Political Implications* (Oxford; Oxford University Press, 2016).

Migration Advisory Committee, *EEA Migration in the UK: Final Report* (London, September 2018).

Morris, Chris, 'Brexit Deal: Theresa May's Agreement with Brussels', *BBC News Politics*, 8 December 2017, htttps://www.bbc.co.uk/news/uk-politics-42280487.

Morris, Chris, 'Brexit Deal: Where Have the UK and EU Compromised?', *BBC News*, 17 October 2019.

Morris, Chris, 'Brexit: Why Is the Internal Market Bill Controversial?', *BBC News*, December 2020, https://bbc.c.uk/news/54088596.

Murphy, Mary C., and Evershed, Jonathan, 'The DUP and the European Union: From Contestation to Conformance and Back Again. . ', *Irish Political Studies*, 35, 3 (2020), 378–98.

Murphy, Richard, 'The Scottish Growth Commission Gets Its Economics Very Badly Wrong', *Tax Research UK*, 25 May 2018.

Nairn, Tom, *The Break-up of Britain: Crisis and Neo-Nationalism* (Champaign, Illinois: Common Ground Publishing, 2015).

Navikas, Katrina, *Loyalism and Radicalism in Lancashire 1798–1815* (Oxford: Oxford University Press, 2009).

Nunns, Alex, *The Candidate: Jeremy Corbyn's Improbable Path to Power* (London: OR Books, 2018).

O'Farrell, *Things Can Only Get Worse? Twenty Confusing Years in the Life of a Labour Supporter* (London: Doubleday, 2017).

O'Toole, Fintan, *Heroic Failure: Brexit and the Politics of Pain* (London: Head of Zeus, 2018).

Payne, Sebastian, *Broken Heartlands: A Journey through Labour's Lost England* (London: Macmillan, 2021).

Perchard, Andrew, 'A Little Local Difficulty? Deindustrialization and Glocalization in a Scottish Town', in High, Steven, MacKinnon, Lachlan, and Perchard, Andrew (eds), *The Deindustrialized World: Confronting Ruination in Post-Industrial Places* (Vancouver: University of British Columbia Press, 2017).

Perryman, Mark (ed.), *The Corbyn Effect* (London: Lawrence and Wishart, 2017).

Phillips, Jim, 'The Moral Economy of Deindustrialization in Post-1945 Scotland', in High, MacKinnon and Perchard (eds), *Deindustrialized World*.

Phillips, Jim, Wright, Valerie, and Tomlinson, Jim, *De-Industrialisation and the Moral Economy in Scotland since 1955* (Edinburgh: Edinburgh University Press, 2021).

Politics Home Staff, 'Boris Johnson's Speech to the 2019 Conservative Party Conference', 2 October 2019.

Samuel, Raphael (ed.), *Patriotism: The Making and Unmaking of British National Identity*, 3 vols. (London: Routledge, 1989).

Sandford, Alasdair, 'Brexit Timeline: Boris Johnson's Month of Turmoil in September', *Euronews*, 30 September 2019.

Sandford, Alasdair, 'The Road to Brexit: What Happened in Boris Johnson's First Six Months as UK Prime Minister', *Euronews*, 24 January 2020.

Sandford, Alasdair, 'Brexit Trade Deal: Nine Claims by Boris Johnson or His Ministers that Are Untrue', *Euronews*, 6 January 2021.

Scothorne, Rory, 'Why Gordon Brown's "New Britain" Doesn't Feel Like a Home for Scotland', *New Statesman*, 21 September 2921.

Scottish Labour, 'Elect Peter O'Donnghaile for Ross, Skye and Lochaber Constituency', Election Communication (May–June 2017).

Scottish Liberal Democrats, 'Your Choice in this Election is Clear' (May–June 2017).

Seldon, Anthony, with Newell, Raymond, Seldon, *May at 10* (London: Biteback Publishing, 2019).

Sencar, Damir, 'Report Finds that UK Test and Trace Never Met 24 Hour COVID Deadlines', *Open Access Government*, 10 March 2021, www.openaccessgovernment.org/uk-test-and-trace-2/105878.

Seymour, Richard, *Corbyn: The Strange Rebirth of Radical Politics* (London: Verso, 2017).

Shipman, Tim, *Fall Out: A Year of Political Mayhem* (London: William Collins, 2017).

Shipman, Tim, *All Out War: The Full Story of Brexit* (London: William Collins, 2017).

Sim, Philip, 'What's in the SNP's Growth Commission Report?', BBC News, https://www.bbc.co.uk/news/uk-scotland-scotland-pols-44237956, 25 May 2018.

Sim, Philip, 'What Does the SNP's Currency Vote Mean?, *BBC News*, 28 April 2019.

Simpkins, Fiona, 'The Conflicting Loyalties of the Scottish Labour Party', in Avril, Emmanuelle, and Beliard, Yann (eds), *Labour United and Divided from the 1830s to the Present* (Manchester: Manchester University Press, 2018).

Skidelsky, Robert, 'Austerity Doesn't Work – Its Death Is Long Overdue', *Prospect Magazine*, 17 July 2017.

Skidelsky, Robert, *Money and Government: A Challenge to Mainstream Economics* (London: Penguin, 2019).

Smith, Sarah, 'Is Scotland on the Cusp of a Tory Resurgence?', *BBC News*, Election 2017, 2 June 2017, https://www.bbc.co.uk/news/election-2017-40105177.

Spiegelhalter, David, and Masters, Anthony, *Covid By Numbers: Making Sense of the Pandemic with Data* (London: Penguin, 2021).

Stewart, Thomas A.W. 'The Labour Party and the Rise of Scottish Nationalism in Dundee since the 1990s', paper presented to the 'Labour and Nationalism' conference of the UK Society for the Study of Labour History, University of Huddersfield, May 2018.

Thevoz, Seth, 'David Cameron Then and Now: How the Ex-PM Changed his Tune on Lobbying', *Open Democracy UK: News*, 12 April 2021.

Tingle, Laura, *Follow the Leader: Democracy and the Rise of the Strongman*, Quarterly Essay (Carlton, Vic, Australia: Schwartz Books, 2018).

Tooze, Adam, *Crashed: How a Decade of Financial Crises changed the World* (London: Allen Lane, 2018).

Tooze, Adam, *Shutdown: How Covid Shook the World's Economy* (London: Allen Lane, 2021).

Wadsworth, Jonathan, Dhingra, Swati, Ottaviano, Gianmarco, and van Reenen, John, *Brexit and the Impact of Immigration on the UK* (London: LSE Centre for Economic Performance, 2016).

Wainwright, Daniel, 'General Election 2019: How Labour's "Red Wall Turned Blue", https://www.bbc.co.uk/news/election-50771014, 13 December 2019.

Wallace, 'The Humbling of the CBI', *Prospect Magazine*, 21 July 2021.

Wray, Ben, 'An Election at the Apex of the Crisis of the UK', *Commonspace*, 30 October 2019.

Index

A

Abbott, Diane 17
Alba Party 141, 143, 156, 157
Allen, Heidi 79, 80
Alliance Party of Northern Ireland 85, 147
Anti-Federalist League (now UKIP) 52
Arnold, Martin 62, 63
Article 50 15, 23, 30, 54, 98, 145
    extension of 79, 81
Ashcroft, Michael, Lord 101, 133, 134
Asthana, Anushka 63
austerity 3, 75, 104, 121
Australia 106, 108
    Covid cases and deaths in 119

B

backstop *see* Northern Ireland Protocol
Baker, Steve 57, 69, 117
Baldwin, Stanley 102
Bale, Tim 24
Bank of England 104, 128
Barker, Alex 62, 63
Barnier, Michel 35, 59, 63, 71–72
BBC 125, 126
BBC Scotland 149
Belfast (Good Friday) Agreement (1998)
    37, 56, 72
Benn, Hilary 22, 94
Benn, Tony 53, 109
Benn Bill 94–95
Bercow, John 67, 81, 82
Berger, Luciana 80
Biden, Joe, President 121
Black, Mhairi 44
Blackford, Ian 67, 78, 80, 88, 140, 142–143,
    147
Blair, Tony 16, 22, 53, 58, 78, 99, 134, 151, 170
Boffey, Daniel 63, 122
Bolsonaro, Jair 106
Bradley, Ben 70
Brady, Sir Graham 49, 59, 77, 83, 166

Brazil, Covid deaths in 119
Bremner, Stewart 136
Brexit 3, 6–7, 8, 9, 10, 17, 50, 54–57, 146,
    148, 149
    campaign for a second referendum 58
    Chequers agreement 57, 68–74
    divisions in the Conservative Party
        over 78
    Johnson and 102–103
    and the Labour Party 23, 27
    Leave voters 54–55
    May's Lancaster House speech 19
    May's negotiations 78–79
    negotiations 35, 37, 48, 112
    Remain voters 55–56
    results of referendum 52, 53
    Scottish vote for 12
    SNP's manifesto on 31
    trade deal with the EU 121–124
    transition period 62
    withdrawal bill 82
Brexit Party 50, 79, 85, 88, 101
Britain
    in the nineteenth century 51. *see also*
        United Kingdom
Brodkin, Simon 36
Brown, Gordon 53, 132, 134, 135, 136, 151,
    158
Brown, Keith 46
Brown, Martyn 115
Brown, Nick 113
Brownlow, David, Lord 126
Burnham, Andy 23, 116
by-elections
    Chesham and Amersham 164
    Copeland, Cumbria 24
    Hartlepool 127–128, 161
    North Shropshire 164
    Stoke-on-Trent Central 24
    Tiverton and Honiton 166, 167
    Wakefield 166, 167

C
Cable, Vince 15
Cain, Lee 91, 125, 148
Cameron, David 2, 8, 18, 20, 34, 53, 127, 132, 133, 134, 139
Campbell, Alastair 22, 86
Campbell, Lucy 110
Canada, free-trade agreement 62, 72
capitalism 1, 94
Case, Simon 164
Centre for Economic Performance, London School of Economics (LSE) 155
Chakrabortty, Aditya 41
Channel Four News 78, 125
Cherry, Joanna 154
China 106
    Covid cases and deaths in 119
Churchill, Winston 93, 102
CJEU *see* European Union (EU), Court of Justice
Clarke, Kenneth 94
class domination 4
Clegg, Nick 2, 15, 58, 132
Climate Change Conference in Glasgow (COP 26) 163
Coffey, Ann 80
Cohen, Nick 40
Common Agricultural Policy 61
Common Fisheries Policy 61, 62, 122
Common Market 53
Commonspace 6, 65
Commonweal 29, 67
Communist Party of Great Britain (CPGB) 53
Confederation of British Industry (CBI) 6, 56
Connett, David 150
Conservative Party 7, 10, 12, 13, 14, 18–21, 56, 105
    2017 election 19, 20–21
    2019 European elections 50, 85
    2020 virtual conference 116–117
    2021 poll ratings 149
    2022 local elections 165
    divisions in 78, 169
    hard Brexiteers in 58
    illegal sexual behaviour in 167–168
    Islamophobia within the 64

opposition to devolution in Scotland and Wales 134
contingent factors 17
Cooper, Yvette 23, 82
Copeland, Cumbria 24
Corbyn, Jeremy 8, 21, 33, 36, 38, 39–40, 41, 42, 43, 48, 50, 53, 71, 77, 83, 91
    and the 2017 general election 13, 14, 15, 16–17, 22–28
    and the 2019 general election 98–100
    on antisemitism in the Labour Party 113
    condemnation of terrorism 25
    conference speech 73
    and the European Parliament elections 87
    foreign policy 25
    opposition to cheap immigrant labour 65
    poll ratings in 2019 79
    resignation as Labour Party leader 103
    'socialism for the twenty-first century' 5
    support for Remain 54
    visit to Grenfell Tower 34
cost-of-living crisis 3
Covid-19 10, 91, 105–112
    anti-Covid vaccine policy 124
    Bereaved Families for Justice group 127
    care-home policy 110
    Coronavirus Job Retention Scheme (CJRS) 109
    deaths in private care homes during 149
    economic and social shocks 120–121
    furlough scheme 109, 120
    'herd immunity' notion 108
    national lockdowns 108–109, 117–119
    Omicron variant 163
    test, trace and isolate system 110, 111
    and the UK government 107–108, 119–128
    vaccination programmes 92, 124, 161
Crace, John 18, 102
Crashed: How a Decade of Financial Crises Changed the World (Tooze) 2
Crick, Michael 78
Crosby, Lynton 18, 20
Crowson, Nicholas 52
Cummings, Dominic 55, 91, 104, 105, 111, 115, 125, 126, 148, 164

Curtice, John 79, 87, 152, 157, 165
customs bill 71
customs union 42, 43, 58, 75, 96

D
Dacre, Paul 40
Daily Express 70, 115, 117, 166
Daily Mail 16–17, 38, 39, 40, 41, 83, 117,
    125, 126, 166
Daily Mirror 16, 41
Daily Record 16
Daily Telegraph 16, 36, 41, 70, 72, 77, 78,
    83, 115, 116, 117, 122, 166
d'Ancona, Matthew 59
Darling, Alistair 132, 133, 134
Darlington 102
Davey, Ed 167, 170
Davidson, Ruth 14, 16, 30, 32, 34, 43, 65,
    145
Davis, David 34, 57, 59, 63, 69, 73
De Gaulle, Charles 51
dementia tax 20–21
Democratic Unionist Party (DUP) 14, 15,
    35, 38, 52, 69, 78, 83, 97, 104, 165,
    166
    and the backstop 77
    opposition to May's deal 82
Devine, Tom 66, 67, 135, 136, 137, 148,
    150, 151
Diffley, Mark 80
Dilnot Report 19
Dodds, Nigel 77, 104
Dorries, Nadine 168
Douglas-Home, Alec 142
Dowden, Oliver 167
Drakeford, Mark 117, 118, 150
Duffy, Judith 148
Dugdale, Kezia 16, 30, 33, 43, 44
Dumfries 137
Duncan Smith, Iain 52, 63, 69
Dyson, Sir James 126, 162

E
Early Parliamentary General Election Bill
    97, 99
economic growth
    in 2018 59
    in 2021 124
Edgerton, David 6, 51, 159

Edinburgh 137
Electoral Commission 126
Elliott, Larry 104, 109, 159
Elphicke, Charles 167–168
Empire Windrush (SS) 64
Equality and Human Rights Commission
    (EHRC) 113
ERG (European Research Group) 57, 69,
    78
EU referendum *see* Brexit
European Charter of Fundamental Rights
    42
European Commission (EC) 60
European Council 62
European Economic Area (EEA) 34, 59
European Economic Community (EEC)
    50, 51
European Exchange Rate Mechanism
    (EERM) 52
European Parliament elections 50, 84–85,
    88, 147
European Research Group (ERG) 57, 69,
    78
European Union (EU) 50
    attitudes of the Brexit right in England
        towards 4
    Court of Justice 19, 35, 37, 61, 68
    customs arrangement between the UK
        and 69
    single market 43
    summit in Salzburg, Austria 72
    trading relationship between the UK
        and 103
    Withdrawal Agreement/Bill 45, 122,
        147
Euroscepticism 52
Evans, David 113
Evening Standard 18
Ewing, Winifred 28

F
Fallon, Sir Michael 39, 58, 167
Farage, Nigel 9, 50, 52, 55, 63, 79, 86, 88, 91,
    101
Farron, Tim 15
Ferguson, Neil 108, 118, 119
Ferguson, Sir Alex 133
Field, Frank 71
Fife 137

financial crash, 2007–2008 2, 3
financial services 56, 61, 76, 123
fishing rights 76, 78
Fixed-Term Parliaments Act 97
Fletcher, Martin 115
Flynn, Laurie 157
Foot, Michael 53
force, in class domination 4
Ford, Robert 87
For the Record (Cameron) 132
Foster, Arlene 77, 97
Freedland, Jonathan 59, 79
Freeman, Jeane 136, 149
free school meals 20, 112
Frost, David, Lord 122, 164
Fry, Michael 45, 66, 78

G
Gaitskell, Hugh 53
Gallagher, Jim 133, 134
Galloway 137
Gamble, Andrew 2
Gapes, Mike 80
Gauke, David 94
Geidt, Christopher, Lord 167
general elections
    2015 11, 140
    2017 8, 13, 14–17, 33–39, 145
    2019 97, 148
Geoghegan, Peter 136, 137
Glastonbury festival 39
Goldsmith, Sir James 52
Good Friday (Belfast) Agreement (1998)
    37, 56, 72
Gove, Michael 53, 58, 70, 76, 111, 123–124
Gramsci, Antonio 4, 5, 7, 158
Gray, Sue 164
Green, Damian 39, 58, 167
Green Party 15, 85, 138, 157
Greensill, Alex 127
Greensill Capital 127
Grenfell Tower fire 33–34
Grimond, Jo 142
The Guardian 27, 33, 37, 41, 42, 58, 63, 77,
    100, 104, 107, 114, 122, 125, 126,
    150, 152, 161
    on the 2017 election 17
    on Brexit 38
    on David Cameron 127

depiction of Boris Johnson 102
on division in Conservative Party over
    Brexit 70
on Jeremy Corbyn 25, 40, 79
on the May 2022 local elections 165
on a second Scottish referendum 46
on the SNP 32
on Theresa May 13, 16, 18, 21, 59, 60,
    78, 81, 84

H
Habermas, Jürgen 7, 128
Hague, William, Lord 52, 167
Hamilton, James 155
Hammond, Philip 18, 19, 36, 40, 41, 46, 58,
    60, 75, 94, 121
Hammond, Stephen 38
Hancock, Matt 108, 110–111, 162
Harding, Baroness 'Dido' 110
Hartlepool 127–128
Harvie, Patrick 67, 157
Heath, Edward 'Ted' 51
hegemony 4, 7
Herald 16, 31
Her Majesty's Revenue and Customs
    (HMRC) 71
Heseltine, Michael 52
Highlands 137
high-speed railway line (HS2) 162
Hill, Fiona 15, 18, 20
Hodge, Margaret 64
Hoey, Kate 71
Hopkins, Kelvin 71
Howard, Michael 52, 53
Howe, Geoffrey 52
Hunt, Jeremy 19, 91
Hutton, Will 6
Hyndburn 102

I
immigration 27, 42, 46, 55
Independent Group for Change (Change
    UK) 80, 98
India, Covid deaths in 119
Indyref2 3, 9, 30, 31–32, 47, 67, 74, 78, 88,
    131, 145, 147, 151, 152, 156, 157,
    170, 171
Innes, Jim 140
Institute for Fiscal Studies (IFS) 41

Internal Market Bill 96, 122, 150
International Holocaust Remembrance
    Alliance (IHRA) 73, 113
Irish border 35, 37, 68
Irish Sea, border in the 63, 96, 128
The Irish Times 38
Isle of Skye, Radical Scottishness on
    139–144
Israel 64

J
Javid, Sajid 104, 105, 168
Jessop, Bob 4, 50
Johnson, Boris 3, 5–6, 12, 19, 34, 35, 50, 53,
    57, 58, 68, 69, 75, 77, 82, 85–86, 88,
    89, 152, 158
    2019–2021 9–10, 91–129
    July 2019 to March 2020 92–103
    March 2020 to May 2021 103–105
    2021 poll ratings 149
    allegations against 162
    alternative to the Chequers plan 72
    attitudes towards the SNP, devolution
        and Scotland 150, 151
    behaviour and character of 129
    'better together,' pro-Union campaign
        154
    Brexit and 36, 55, 148
    as Conservative Party leader 91
    and Covid-19 92, 106, 149
    funding of refurbishment of Downing
        Street apartment 126
    and Indyref2 156
    and partygate 164–165
    personal and political assumptions
        92–94
    proroguing of parliament 95
    racism debates and 64
    resignation of 161, 168–169
    setbacks, defeats and triumphs 94–96
    speech at the Royal Naval College,
        Greenwich 103
    triumph to downfall 128–129, 161–169
    withdrawal agreement with the EU
        96–97
Johnson, Carrie (Symonds) 126, 165
Johnson, Joseph 75, 95
Johnson, Paul 41
Jones, Owen 9, 24, 54, 88

K
Kane, Rosie 136
Kennedy, Charles 140, 142, 143
Kerevan, George 31, 32, 66
Kettle, Martin 46, 114, 125, 161
Keynesianism 3
Khan, Imran Ahmad 167, 168
Kinnock, Neil 53
Kuenssberg, Laura 163

L
Labour for Independence 136
Labour Party 5, 7, 8, 12, 13, 14, 16, 58,
    98–100, 169
    2016 leadership contest 23
    2017 conference 39
    2017 general election 22–28, 39–44,
        101
    in 2020 103, 112
    antisemitism in 64, 73, 103, 113–114
    Brexit and 54, 56, 63–64, 86, 88
    and the Chequers plan 71, 73
    divisions and conflicts over Europe
        53
    European Parliament elections 85
    local elections 165
    Momentum 24, 25
    poll lead at time of Johnson's
        resignation 169
    in Scotland 29
Lamont, Johann 132, 138
Lansman, Jon 24
Lawson, Nigel 52
Leadsom, Andrea 79, 83
Leckie, Carolyn 67, 136
Lee, Philip 95
Legitimation Crisis (Habermas) 7
Leonard, Richard 44, 48, 87, 153
Leslie, Chris 42, 73, 80
Letwin, Oliver 82
Lewis, Oliver 154
Liberal Democrats 12, 14–15, 29, 77, 140,
    145, 164, 167, 170
    2019 European elections 85, 98
    in 2020 103
    as advocates of EU membership 54
Lidington, David 67, 70
Lilley, Peter 52
Loach, Ken 25

local elections 85
   2017 24
   2019 147
   2022 165

M
Maastricht Treaty 51
McAlpine, Robin 29, 47, 67
MacAskill, Kenny 151
McCluskey, Len 56, 80
MacDonald, Margo 28
McDonnell, John 17, 41, 42, 73
Mackay, Derek 46, 65
McKenna, Kevin 46, 47, 67–68, 87
McLeish, Henry 47
Macmillan, Harold 51
McVey, Esther 77
Magnay, Jacquelin 49
Mail on Sunday 21
Major, John 34, 51, 52, 134, 162, 166
Makortoff, Kalyeena 127
Mandelson, Peter 22, 70
Mann, John 71
Marx, Karl 1
Mattinson, Deborah 102
May, Philip 36
May, Theresa 3, 7, 8, 9, 13, 14, 15–16,
   19–21, 28, 33–36, 38–39, 40, 48, 55,
   88, 91, 104, 123, 126, 166
   2017 general election 18, 19–20, 25
   January–September 2018 57–74
   October–November 2018 74–78
   October 2018 to March 2019 74–81
   March to June 2019 81–83
   assessment of 83–84
   Brexit negotiations 56–57, 96, 146
   and the Fallon scandal 167
   as home secretary 64
   Lancaster House speech 145
   Mansion House speech 60–63
   resignation of 49–50, 83, 147
   and a second Scottish independence
     referendum 31
Merkel, Angela 72
Metropolitan Police 164
Mexico, Covid deaths in 119
Milburn, Alan 38
Miliband, Ed 14, 22, 35, 40, 53, 132, 134, 138
Mirror 115, 125

Mirza, Munira 164
Moore, Charles 122
Morgan, Nicky 76
Mortimer, Jill 128
Mundell, David 44, 78
Murdoch, Rupert 16
Murphy, Jim 44, 138
Murphy, Karie 25
Murphy, Richard 66
Murray, Jessica 168
Murrell, Peter 154

N
National 17, 78, 137, 138
National Health Service (NHS) 20, 121,
   132, 151
national living wage 19
Neil, Andrew 21, 25
New Labour 3, 134
New Statesman 115
New Zealand 106, 108
   Covid cases and deaths in 119
Northern Ireland 35, 37, 52, 75, 96, 150
   2019 general election 101
   December 2020 election 104
   2022 local elections 165–166
   access to the single market post-Brexit
     77
   European Parliament election 85
   hostility to Brexit in 105
   Remain voters 56
   technology to prevent hard border in
     72, 76
   UK's relationship with 123
Northern Ireland Assembly 96–97
Northern Ireland Protocol 37–38, 59, 61,
   62, 63, 68, 69, 72, 75, 76, 77, 78, 79,
   96, 122, 166
North Shropshire 164
Norway 34
Now Scotland 155
Nunns, Alex 13, 22, 26
Nuttall, Paul 15

O
Observer 40, 43, 58, 62, 70, 112, 122, 125,
   150, 162
   Opinium poll 164
   public support for Labour and Tories 78

O'Carroll, Lisa 38, 63, 122
Office for Budget Responsibility (OBR) 104, 120
Office for National Statistics (ONS) 59, 114
O'Neill, Michelle 165
One-Nation Conservatism 10, 103, 117
'Operation Moonshot' 110
Osborne, George 2, 18, 40, 104, 133, 138
Oswald, Kirsten 154
O'Toole, Fintan 4, 38

P
Palestine 64
Parish, Neil 167, 168
'partygate' 163, 164–165
Patel, Priti 39, 58, 105, 163, 168
Paterson, Owen 162, 164
Paxman, Jeremy 18, 25
People's Vote (campaign) 98
permacrisis 4
Peston, Robert 126
Pincher, Christopher 168
Plaid Cymru 15, 85, 101
Poletti, Monica 24
politics 7
    and outcomes of crises 2
Portillo, Michael 52, 70
Prenton Park 13, 39
private care homes, deaths during the
    Covid-19 pandemic in 149
Progress Scotland 80
'Project Fear' 136, 151
Public Accounts Committee 111
public sector pay cap 19

R
Raab, Dominic 77
racism 64
Radical Scottishness 134–135, 139–144, 158, 171
Rashford, Marcus 112
Rawnsley, Andrew 58
Reagan, Ronald 2
Redwood, John 77
Rees-Mogg, Jacob 57, 58, 63, 69, 73, 77, 82, 168
Referendum Party (RP) 52
Rennie, Willie 30, 156

Resolution Foundation (RF) 41
Riley-Smith, Ben 166
Rise of the Meritocracy, The (Young) 36
Robertson, Angus 14, 31, 80
Roosevelt, Franklin D. 156
Ross, Cromarty and Skye 140
Ross, Douglas 150, 154, 156, 158
Ross, Skye and Inverness West 140
Ross, Skye and Lochaber 140
Rudd, Amber 34, 64, 95
Russell, Michael/Mike 45, 152
Rutnam, Sir Philip 105
Ryan, Joan 80

S
Sabbagh, Dan 100
SAGE 108, 116, 118
Salmond, Alex 14, 28, 30, 31, 32, 54, 80, 125, 132, 133, 134, 137, 154, 157, 158
    Alba Party 141
    independence referendum campaign 135
Sanders, Bernie 25
Sarwar, Anas 156, 157, 170
Savile, Jimmy 164
Scally, Gabriel 120
Scientific, Advisory Group for
    Emergencies (SAGE) 108, 116, 118
Scotland 11–12, 37, 66–67, 131–159
    2014 independence referendum 3
    November 2014–May 2015 138–139
    2015–2010 139–143
    2016–2017 145–146
    2016–2020 144–149
    May 2016 Scottish Parliament election 144
    2017 general election 16, 22
    2018, economic growth in 65
    2018–2019 146–147
    2020 independence surge 148–149
    in 2021 149–152
    from February 2021 to the May
        elections 152–158
    access to the single market post-Brexit 77
    Brexit in 56, 105, 144
    Common Fisheries Policy 62
    devolution in 134
    economic growth 46

European Parliament elections in 85
independence movement in 3, 46, 125
Johnson's unpopularity in 88
radical Scottishness 134–135, 171
second referendum for independence.
   see Indyref2
Scotsman 17, 154
Scott, Dave 140
Scottish Borders 137
Scottish Conservatives 29–30, 32, 153–154
Scottish Daily Express 17, 122
Scottish Daily Mail 15–16, 122
Scottish Greens 144
Scottish independence referendum, 2014
   28, 131–134
   'Better Together' campaign 132, 134
   No votes 137
   referendum campaign 131–132
   voting age for 137
   Yes campaign 134–138
Scottish Labour Party 30, 43, 87, 132, 139,
   145, 149, 153
   Labour for Independence 136
   leadership crisis 44
Scottish Liberal Democrats 30
Scottish Nationalists 12
Scottish National Party (SNP) 7, 14, 16, 17,
   28–33, 43, 54, 56, 77, 88, 97, 98, 118,
   131, 132, 134, 135, 141, 142–143,
   170–171
   November 2014–May 2015 138
   2015 general election 139
   2016–2017, decline of support for the
     SNP and independence 145–146
   2016 Scottish elections 144
   2017 general election 44–48
   2019 general election 101, 148
   February to the May elections 2021
     152–153
   2021 poll ratings 149–150
   2021 Scottish parliamentary elections
     155–158
   and Brexit 63
   and the Chequers plan 71
   commitments to Remain and Scottish
     independence 80
   conferences 46, 74, 87
   domination in Scotland 8–9, 11, 165

   and the Independence movement
     154–155
   local elections 85
   Programme for Government 45, 47
   and a second Scottish independence
     referendum 3, 31–32
   'Stronger for Scotland' manifesto 31
   views of immigration 65
Scottish Socialist Party (SSP) 67, 138
Scottish Tories *see* Scottish Conservatives
Scottish Trades Union Congress (STUC) 48
Scottish Unionist Party 29
Section 30 order 152, 156, 171
Serco 110
sexual harassment 39, 155, 167
Shapps, Grant 34
Shipman, Tim 21, 33, 34
Shuker, Gavin 80
Sillars, Jim 28, 54, 151
Sinclair, Paul 16
Single European Act 52
single market 42
Sinn Féin 15, 38, 104, 165–166
Sked, Alan 52
Skripal, Sergei 73
Skripal, Yulia 73
Slater, Lorna 157
Smith, Angela 80
Smith, John 53
Smith, Owen 22, 23
Smith Commission 139
social care 19, 20, 162
socialism 5, 94
Social Mobility Commission 38
Soubry, Anna 79, 80
South Korea 106
   Covid cases and deaths in 119
*The Spectre at the Feast: Capitalist Crisis
   and the Politics of Recession*
   (Gamble) 2
Spowart, Nan 65
Sridhar, Devi 108
Starmer, Keir 5, 12, 40, 42–43, 73, 86, 92,
   112–114, 115, 118, 124, 126, 148,
   149, 150, 158, 163, 164, 165, 169
   as leader of the Labour Party 170
   and a second Scottish referendum 151,
     153
   and the Wakefield by-election 167

state pension 20
Stewart, Heather 27, 81, 104
Stoke-on-Trent 24, 102
Stone, Kathryn 162
Stormont Assembly 103, 149
Stratton, Allegra 125, 163
Straw, Jack 22
strikes, support for 169–170
Stringer, Graham 71
Sturgeon, Nicola 10, 17, 30, 31, 33, 46, 47,
    54, 67, 71, 81, 87, 98, 125, 135, 137,
    142, 153, 154, 155–156
  and the 2015 general election 139
  and the 2017 election 32, 44
  2018 conference 74
  2021 poll ratings 149
  Brexit and 77
  on Corbyn's opposition to cheap
    immigrant labour 65
  and Covid lockdowns in 116, 118
  and Indyref2 80, 88, 144–145, 171
  leadership during the pandemic 149
  and the SNP Programme for
    Government 45
Sun 16, 17, 40, 41, 117
Sunak, Rishi 3, 103–104, 115, 127, 152, 161,
    165, 168
  2020 mini-budget 114
  2021 budget 109, 121
  eating out scheme 116
  rescue packages 120
Sustainable Growth Commission 66, 87,
    146
Swinney, John 151, 153
Swinson, Jo 98
Symonds, Carrie (Johnson) 126
systemic crisis, economic factors and 2

T
Taiwan, Covid cases and deaths in 119
teachers, pay rise 19
Thatcher, Margaret 2, 51, 52, 70, 93,
    100–101, 134, 166
Thornberry, Emily 86
The Times 16, 33
Timothy, Nick 15, 18, 19–20
Tingle, Laura 84
Tiverton and Honiton 166–167
Tooze, Adam 2

Tory Party *see* Conservative Party
Toynbee, Polly 59, 86
trade-union movement 56
Traditionalism 51
Travis, Alan 21
Treaty of Rome 51
Trump, Donald 17, 71, 106
Truss, Liz 3, 161, 168
Tusk, Donald 62, 72, 81

U
Ukraine, Russian invasion of 3, 165
Umunna, Chuka 42, 73, 80
unemployment 120–121
Unison (trade union) 23
Unite (trade union) 23, 56
United Kingdom (UK)
  Covid deaths in 119
  crises in 1–2
  customs arrangement between the EU
    and 69
  and Europe 50–54
  exports, to the EU and Northern
    Ireland 123
  recession in 152
  trading relationship between the EU
    and 103
United Kingdom Independence Party
    (UKIP) 15, 21, 52–53, 55, 101
United States, Covid deaths in 119

V
Vallance, Sir Patrick 112

W
Wakefield 166, 167
Wakefield, Mary 111
Wales 105
  2019 general election 101
  handling of the Covid crisis in 150
Watson, Tom 86, 99
Webb, Paul 24
Welsh Senedd 149
  vote against Johnson's withdrawal
    agreement 103
Western Isles 137
West Highland Free Press 140
Whitty, Chris 116, 118
Widdecombe, Ann 85

Wilkie, Jim 140
Williamson, Gavin 116
Wilson, Andrew 66, 67, 87
Wilson, Brian 134, 140
Wilson, Harold 51, 53, 170
Windrush Scandal 64
Wollaston, Sarah 16, 79, 80
Women for Independence 135–136
World Health Organization (WHO) 105, 106
Wray, Ben 6
Wuhan, China 105

Y
YouGov polls
    2017 general election 14, 33
    Conservative Party and Labour Party, 2022 169
    support for Scottish independence 87, 148
Young, Michael 36
Younge, Gary 9, 17, 26

Z
Zelenskiy, Volodymyr 165